Digital SLR Photography

ALL-IN-ONE

3rd Edition

by Robert Correll

for
dummies®
A Wiley Brand

Digital SLR Photography All-in-One For Dummies®, 3rd Edition

Published by: **John Wiley & Sons, Inc.**, 111 River Street, Hoboken, NJ 07030-5774, www.wiley.com

Copyright © 2017 by John Wiley & Sons, Inc., Hoboken, New Jersey

Published simultaneously in Canada

For general information on our other products and services, please contact our Customer Care Department within the U.S. at 877-762-2974, outside the U.S. at 317-572-3993, or fax 317-572-4002. For technical support, please visit https://hub.wiley.com/community/support/dummies.

Wiley publishes in a variety of print and electronic formats and by print-on-demand. Some material included with standard print versions of this book may not be included in e-books or in print-on-demand. If this book refers to media such as a CD or DVD that is not included in the version you purchased, you may download this material at http://booksupport.wiley.com. For more information about Wiley products, visit www.wiley.com.

Library of Congress Control Number: 2016959062

ISBN 978-1-119-29139-8 (pbk); ISBN 978-1-119-29140-4 (ebk); ISBN 978-1-119-29141-1 (ebk)

Manufactured in the United States of America

10 9 8 7 6 5 4 3 2 1

Table of Contents

Introduction

The real question today is, given the plethora of digital devices that take photos, why bother with digital SLRs? Seriously. Smartphones, tablets from Apple, Microsoft, Samsung, Amazon, and others, compact digital cameras, and even toys offer you a wealth of options. And you know what? They aren't necessarily bad ones. I understand how convenient it is to take a quick snapshot with a small, portable device. They are pretty easy to use and take decent photos.

However (you knew that was coming) digital SLRs (and by extension, dSLTs and the dSLR-sized mirrorless cameras) take fantastic photos. Pound for pound, if you're interested in photography, you will find no better device. You really can't beat the combination of power, flexibility, growth potential, and "accessorize-ability" of a dSLR.

Their greatest strength is a long history of using interchangeable lenses. You can mount different lenses on the same camera body, each one with unique strengths. That enables you to take pictures ranging from close-ups of jewelry, to wide-angle landscapes, to portraits of your friends and family, to super telephoto shots of the moon. And everything in between! I find this versatility breathtaking. Even if you stick to a single zoom lens, you will have more power in that one lens to take quality photos than any smartphone or tablet ever had.

The greatest weakness of the digital SLR is probably the fact that they intimidate people. If that's you, don't be. Given the technological world that we live in, if you can operate your smartphone, the GPS system on your car, and probably your refrigerator, you can become a successful photographer using a digital SLR.

The sky is the limit. Over the course of this book I hope to show you how to take advantage of the incredible strengths and versatility of digital SLRs, and become closely familiar with their lenses, the flash, software, and other accessories. My sincere hope is to help you become the photographer you want to be, and along the way, get the most out of your time and money.

About This Book

Digital SLR Photography All-in-One For Dummies, 3rd Edition, is for anyone who's interested in enjoying photography using a dSLR camera. My goal is to demystify and un-convolute the technical aspects and illustrate the artistic elements of dSLR photography.

You don't need to have a dSLR to enjoy this book; maybe it's on your wish list. If you do have a dSLR, you can immediately apply the knowledge you glean from these pages. You also don't need a brand new dSLR. I still use a Nikon D200, which was released in 2005, and a Canon D3200, which came out in 2012. Cameras change from year to year. I've tried to include a wide variety of cameras from different manufacturers, so you're bound to find the information you need no matter what camera you're using.

How This Book Is Organized

This book is split into six minibooks. Each minibook has its own broad focus, ranging from what you need to get started, to giving practical advice designed to help you photograph certain subjects. Within each minibook, you find the chapters that flesh things out. Some have more than others. That's okay. It just depends on the subject.

Here's a quick summary of each minibook.

Book 1: Pursuing Digital SLR Photography

I start out with a book that has everything you need to get started. I talk about dSLRs and how they work, what makes them tick, what the buttons do, how to handle and clean them, introduce you to lenses, show you how to work the menu, and how to set up the camera to start taking photos.

Book 2: Looking Through Lenses

This book goes into great detail about the different types of lenses you can use with a dSLR. You read about standard zoom lenses, explore how to photograph wide-angle scenes, get creative with macro and telephoto lenses, and explore unique lenses like tilt-shift and pinhole lenses. Along the way, I pass along tips and tricks for using each lens type and suggest what each is best for.

Book 3: Taking Creative Control

If you want to exercise more creative control over the photos your camera takes, then this book is for you. You see how exposure works, how to control it, and learn about the aperture (which affects depth of field), shutter speed (which controls motion blur), and ISO (which increases your camera's sensitivity to light). You also read about filters.

Book 4: Lighting the Scene

I start this minibook with a chapter on natural light. You see the difference between taking photos in the morning, late in the day, or at night. After that, I cover flash photography. If you take photos indoors or in poor light, knowing even a little about your camera's flash will help you take much better photos. In the last two chapters, you learn how to use your camera's built-in flash, see whether getting an external flash is right for you, and explore a ton of cool flash and lighting accessories and techniques.

Book 5: Managing and Processing Your Shots

This book is mostly about software. I explain how to manage your photos, how to quickly spruce them up, how to dig deeper into photo editing, and even how to express your artistry. You also see how to shoot and process panoramas and high dynamic range (HDR) photos.

Book 6: Showcasing Different Scenes

The last book has five chapters that focus on specific subjects. I've chosen some of my favorite photos to share and give you insight into how I took them.

Icons Used in This Book

Helpful icons are scattered throughout the book. They appear beside information I want you to pay particular attention to (or to avoid if you see fit). Each icon has a unique meaning:

The Warning icon highlights lurking danger. Pay attention and proceed with caution. Your equipment or photos or safety might be at stake.

REMEMBER

The Remember icon marks an interesting fact that you should tuck away in your brain to remember and use later. They're often facts. (With some wiggle room thrown in for good measure.)

TIP

The Tip icon points out helpful information that might save you time. It's something you might want to try or do. I love tips. If I could, I would make every paragraph a tip.

TECHNICAL STUFF

When you see this icon, you know that technical information lurks nearby. If that's not your cuppa tea, skip it.

Where to Go from Here

First, have a look at the table of contents. Next, jump to somewhere in the book that looks interesting or has information you want to know right now. Then go out and take some pictures. Rinse and repeat.

Do you want to start with lenses? Turn to Book 2 first. You don't even need to read the chapters within a minibook in order. If you want to immediately jump to the chapter on shutter speed, by all means do.

If you're new to photography, though, I *do suggest* starting at the beginning and reading the first minibook in order. When you've finished that, you should be able to turn to any place in the book and not get totally lost.

Lastly, when you have a minute, go to `dummies.com` to find the cheat sheet with this book. It's full of information you might find valuable.

The more photos you take with your dSLR, the more you learn about it and how to take great photos. So go out and start shooting!

1

Pursuing Digital SLR Photography

Contents at a Glance

IN THIS CHAPTER

» **Learning about digital SLRs**

» **Defining different dSLR types**

» **Understanding camera specifications**

» **Seeing what's new in the world of dSLRs**

» **Buying a dSLR and accessories**

Chapter **1**

Embracing Digital SLRs

What's so special about dSLRs? The short answer is: Lots! Digital SLRs are tremendous cameras. They take great photos, are versatile, friendly to new and casual users, serious enough for more advanced and professional photographers, and have the potential to accompany you through a lifetime of photography.

People sometimes think digital SLRs are complex, expensive, professional cameras that are hard to master. You don't have to feel intimidated. Learning to use them isn't hard. You don't have to start out with the model that has the most buttons and advanced features. You can find the right camera for you, no matter what your skill or interest level. Once you do, you'll be able to learn and grow at your own pace. The sky is the limit!

Introducing the Digital SLR

The *digital SLR* (also known as dSLR or DSLR) is the modern, digital descendant of the 35mm film-based camera called the SLR. Both types of camera are shown in Figure 1-1. In many ways, the relatively new Nikon dSLR on the left is a direct technological descendant of the much older Nikon FE2 film SLR on the right.

SLR stands for *single lens reflex,* and it identifies a class of camera with two unique characteristics: They have something called a reflex mirror, which enables the camera to use a single lens. Here are some details:

>> **Reflex mirror:** SLR cameras use a hinged *reflex* mirror (reflex means that it moves) to, when lowered, reflect light that enters the camera through the lens and bounce it around inside the camera body for various purposes. When you press the shutter button, the mirror moves up and out of the way, allowing light to expose the film or be collected by the image sensor when the shutter opens.

>> **Single lens:** SLR cameras can therefore use a single lens for all viewing, focusing, and metering. While that does not sound earth-shattering to us today, there was a time when photographers had to resort to using additional lenses or other mechanical devices (such as a framing rectangle on top of the camera) to view the scene and focus. Through-the-lens viewing, composing, metering, and focusing means that what you see is what you're going to get when you take the photo.

FIGURE 1-1: Digital SLRs (left) have come a long way from its predecessor (right).

SLRs and dSLRs also feature an interchangeable lens design. Although this isn't a unique property, it's often thought of as a defining characteristic. Lenses attach to the camera body and can be removed, making it possible to use different lenses with different qualities for different purposes.

Naming and Classifying Digital SLRs

This section shares and explains the information you need to decode the names and understand the basic characteristics of different types of digital SLRs available today. For example, you should be able to grasp the essential characteristics of the *Nikon D3300 24.2MP DX-format (APS-C) dSLR with 18-55mm lens* and how the *Sony A99 24.3MP full-frame A-mount dSLT with electronic viewfinder* differs from it just by reading the names.

There's obviously a lot going on with those two names. I've overloaded them with extra details to show you how much information can be embedded within camera names and listings. The rest of this section will help you identify the make and model, sensor size, pixel count, lens mount, mirror and viewfinder, and kit lens details of each camera.

Make and model

Let's start with the basic name of the camera. Each camera manufacturer has a method to its naming madness.

>> **Nikon** starts its dSLRs with the letter *D* (think *digital*), followed by a number. In general, the smaller the number, the more advanced and expensive the camera. For example, the D5 is currently Nikon's premier professional camera. The D3300, on the other hand, is an entry-level consumer camera.

>> **Canon** uses the acronym *EOS* (electro-optical system) and then a specific model number to identify its digital SLRs. For example, the Canon EOS 80D is a mid-range model. Canon uses the term *Rebel* to identify its consumer dSLRs. The Rebels sport one of two model numbers, depending on the market they are sold in. For example, the EOS Rebel T6i is also known as the 750D. You may see it written as the EOS Rebel T6i/750D.

>> **Sony** dSLRs and SLTs are identified by the letter A, followed by a two- or three-digit model number, such as the A99 or older A300. When you pronounce the name, you can say A as you would any other A, or you can say Alpha. New Sony models are all SLTs, which have translucent mirrors that do not need to move out of the way when you take a picture. The A77 II is a dSLT, although you may see it listed as an Interchangeable Lens Digital Camera (ILDC).

   Sony calls its digital Single Lens Translucent cameras SLTs. They are, in essence, dSLRs with the moving reflex mirror replaced by a translucent mirror that doesn't move. The more general acronym is dSLT. For more information on how dSLTs differ from dSLRs, jump ahead to the upcoming section, "Mirror and viewfinder type."

- » **Pentax** dSLRs use the letter *K* followed by an identifying number, such as the K-70 and K-3 II.

- » **Olympus** has phased out its digital SLRs in favor of the popular OM-D mirrorless "Micro Four Thirds" line (named *Micro* because they do not have the same mirror and optical viewfinder as standard Four Thirds system cameras). OM-D (I keep wanting to write "OM-G!") cameras have interchangeable lenses and most of the same features as dSLRs. Although I don't cover mirrorless cameras in depth in this book, they look, feel, and act like dSLRs in most ways. The main differences that you will notice are that they are smaller and thinner than most dSLRs. Like dSLTs, whose mirrors don't move, cameras like the OM-D E-M10 do not "clunk" when you take a photo. There is no mirror to move. Older Olympus dSLRs are designated by the letter *E* followed by a number, such as the E-5.

Sensor size

Digital SLR sensors vary in size. Aside from the differences in cost and the technical merits of using a smaller or larger sensor, sensor size has a profound impact on how photos look. In effect, smaller image sensors make it look like you've zoomed in compared to a camera with a larger sensor. The amount is expressed as a multiplier, and is called *crop factor.* I have more information on crop factor in the section "Delving into Camera Specifications," later in the chapter.

Here are the most popular sensor sizes and their crop factors:

- » **Full-frame:** dSLRs whose image sensors are the same size as a 35mm frame of film are called *full-frame* dSLRs. This is the gold standard of professional dSLR quality. The aspect ratio of these sensors, and hence the photos you take with them, is the same as 35mm film: 3:2. Full-frame cameras have a crop factor of 1.0x. Nikon full-frame cameras are labeled *FX*.

- » **Cropped-frame:** dSLRs whose sensors are smaller than a 35mm frame of film are called *cropped-frame*, cropped, or cropped-body dSLRs. There are several types of cropped-frame sensors:

  - ● **APS-C:** This is the standard sensor size for most consumer and mid-range digital SLRs. It's smaller than a 35mm frame of film, but far larger than a compact digital camera sensor. APS-C sensors have a crop factor that ranges from 1.5x (most APS-C cameras) to 1.6x (Canon). Nikon labels its APS-C cameras *DX*.

    TECHNICAL STUFF

    APS-C stands for *Advanced Photo System, Classic*. APS was a film format created in the mid-1990s. It had three print formats: C (classic print), H (wide print), and P (panoramic print). You chose the format you wanted using a switch on the camera. When developed, the print would come back cropped according to the setting you used. APS film cartridges were smaller and easier to load into cameras than 35mm film. APS cameras and film were quickly overshadowed by the introduction of affordable digital cameras and are not used anymore. Digital APS-C image sensors match the rough dimensions of APS film when shot in the classic format, hence the -C designation.

- **Four Thirds and Micro Four Thirds:** These sensors are much smaller than APS-C sensors and have a 4:3 aspect ratio. Four Thirds/Micro Four Thirds sensors have a crop factor from 1.8x to 2.0x.

- **APS-H:** This category is not very prevalent today. It's a "tweener" size. APS-H sensors are smaller than full-frame but larger than APS-C sensors. They have a crop factor of approximately 1.3x.

Figure 1-2 shows an APS-C cropped-frame Nikon dSLR sitting next to a full-frame Pentax camera. Both mirrors are raised, enabling you to see the relative size of the image sensors inside them. The difference in price? About $1,700, including the lenses.

FIGURE 1-2:
Comparing APS-C to full-frame.

Pixel count

You will often see a camera's pixel count — how many pixels make up each photo — listed as part of the name. Digital camera pixel counts are expressed as *megapixels (MP)*, or millions of pixels. Today, even new consumer-level dSLRs have 18MP or more. More advanced cameras have pixel counts ranging from 24MP to 36MP, topping out at an astounding 50MP, which rivals some medium-format cameras (the ones that cost $15,000 to $45,000).

The total number of megapixels affects your photos' pixel dimensions and file size, as shown in Figure 1-3. The photo's type, size, and dimension are just below the Image Quality line in this figure.

TIP

All other aspects being equal, the camera with more pixels will probably serve you better in the long run. While I hate to buy into the premise that more is always better, having greater resolution means that you can crop your photos and have more left over. Having more pixels can also help you fight the urge to upgrade your camera prematurely. Camera technology doesn't stand still, and you should enjoy the one you have for as long as you can.

Lens mount

Lenses attach to the body of the camera using a *lens mount*. Figure 1–4 shows a close–up of the mount on a Sony dSLR. It's pretty large, and has to be made of metal to stand up to the stresses of mounting different sized lenses. Here is a quick summary of the lens mounts that the top manufacturers use:

» **Nikon** uses the F-mount, which is standard on both its cropped (*DX format*) and full-frame (*FX format*) dSLRs. Nikon also uses the DX classification to identify lenses that are optimized to work on cropped-frame, DX-format camera bodies. Lenses without the DX identifier are compatible with DX and FX-format camera bodies. As a bonus, Nikon's FX-format camera bodies can use DX-format lenses in a special "DX crop" mode. This mode uses the area in the center of the image sensor and results in a smaller, cropped photo.

» **Canon** dSLRs use the EF lens mount on all its cropped and full-frame cameras. Canon uses the EF-S lens designation to identify lenses that are only compatible with cropped-frame Canon cameras. All Canon dSLRs can mount EF lenses. Only cropped-frame dSLRs can mount EF-S lenses.

» **Sony** uses the Alpha mount or A-mount (refer to Figure 1-4). Of note, DT lenses are compatible with cropped and full-frame bodies, but images are recorded cropped on the latter. Sony E-mount cameras such as the A7R and A6300 have dSLR-sized sensors without the mirror or optical viewfinder. A-mount SLR lenses can attach to E-mount cameras with a special adapter.

» **Pentax** dSLRs use the K-mount. There are several K-mount sub-types that feature different contacts and autofocus drive capabilities. In addition, adapters are available to mount old screw mount Pentax lenses to K-mount cameras.

» **Olympus** dSLRs use the Four Thirds mount while its newer mirrorless interchangeable lens cameras use the Micro Four Thirds mount. Note that you can attach Four Thirds lenses to a Micro Four Thirds body with the proper adapter, but not vice versa.

REMEMBER

When buying lenses, confirm that they are compatible with your camera body.

FIGURE 1-4: The lens mount determines what lenses are compatible with your camera.

Mirror and viewfinder type

Digital SLRs have a reflex mirror that sits in front of the closed shutter and covered image sensor. Its purpose is to reflect light that comes into the camera through the lens up and into the viewfinder (among other things). This is how you view the scene, and how the camera meters the light and focuses. When you press the shutter button, the mirror moves (this is what *reflex* means) quickly up and out of the way, allowing light to expose the sensor. When the exposure is over, it moves back into the down position.

Digital SLTs (single-lens translucent) cameras do not have a moveable mirror. They have a semi-transparent, or translucent, mirror that stays put when you take the photo. The mirror allows some light to shine through it and onto the image sensor while bouncing the rest up into the camera's viewfinder (or into another sensor that drives the electronic viewfinder). For most purposes, dSLTs look and function just like dSLRs.

Typical dSLR viewfinders are *optical.* You look through a prism that directs light from the reflex mirror to your eye. They work whether the camera is on or off.

Some cameras (especially dSLTs and mirrorless cameras) now use electronic viewfinders to display information. Sony's electronic viewfinders, for example, are small, high-resolution *organic light-emitting diode (OLED)* monitors. This type of viewfinder combines the functionality of a standard viewfinder with the LCD monitor on the back of the camera. Because you're looking at a monitor, anything that can be displayed on the back of your camera can also be shown to you in the viewfinder. You can compose and frame the scene normally, view photos during playback, see the camera's shooting display, and use the menu system — all without taking your eye away from the viewfinder. Truly awesome.

Figure 1-5 shows the electronic viewfinder of another Sony camera. This particular model extends outward from the body of the camera a bit. Optical viewfinders don't need as much space, and will appear flush with the body even on small cameras.

FIGURE 1-5: Whether optical or electrical, the viewfinder enables you to see through the lens.

Lenses

You can buy most dSLRs bundled with something called a *kit lens*. While they are not typically top-of-the-line lenses, kit lenses are decent and have enough versatility for most amateur photographers. Kits are designed to get you started with a good lens without breaking the bank.

Currently, many consumer kit lenses are standard 18-55mm zoom lenses. Depending on the camera, you may have the option of choosing different kit lenses. Very often, these alternate lenses are a step up in quality and price, and have different focal length ranges.

Turn to Book 1, Chapter 3 to learn more about lenses. You can also turn to Book 2, which covers a number of different lens types in depth.

Wrapping it up

Returning to the two cameras I mentioned in the introduction to this section, you should now understand that the Nikon D3300 is an F-mount, cropped-body dSLR from Nikon with an APS-C sized sensor. It is compatible with Nikon DX and FX-format lenses and captures photos that are 24.2 megapixels in size. It comes with an 18-55mm kit lens. The Sony A99 is full-frame A-mount dSLT. The photos it captures are 24.3 megapixels in size. It features a fixed translucent mirror along with an electronic viewfinder. The A99 is not generally sold as a kit so no lens information is listed.

Pricing Digital SLRs

Camera manufacturers design and create dSLRs for different audiences. This enables them to meet the needs of a wide range of people and sell more cameras. It gives you the freedom to choose a camera with the features, capabilities, and price that you want.

The following sections organize these market segments into three broad categories, each featuring cameras designed and priced to appeal to that audience. If you shop around, you'll see that Canon and Nikon have more than one dSLR in each category and are constantly updating their lineup. Not all camera manufacturers compete so heavily across the board.

Consumer dSLRs

Consumer dSLRs are great cameras for the average person. They range from entry-level models priced under $750 (see Figure 1-6) to more advanced consumer-level models that cost near $1,000. At this level, cameras are often sold as kits. This means that a basic zoom lens is sold with the camera body. The lens increases the overall cost slightly compared to buying the body only, but most consumers like the convenience of having everything they need to get started in one box. At this level, all dSLRs are made from polycarbonate and their image sensors are cropped-frame.

Compared to more expensive cameras, consumer dSLRs are less expensive, smaller, lighter, more convenient, and less intimidating. They have a plethora of automatic modes and are easy to use. They use different image sensors, processors, and other technologies than more expensive dLSRs, which limits their performance somewhat, but makes them affordable.

FIGURE 1-6:
The Nikon D3200
is a good example
of an entry-level
consumer dSLR.

At the more expensive end of the consumer level category, people want more features and a bit more performance out of their dSLR. These cameras tend to have higher maximum ISO speeds, better, articulated monitors, faster frame rates, and more options compared to entry-level models. They are also often slightly larger.

REMEMBER

All dSLRs can take fantastic photos. Don't let the *consumer or entry-level* distinction make you think they are toys. They're not. These cameras just aren't designed to perform in *all* situations or to be as customizable as more expensive cameras.

Mid-range models

Mid-range dSLRs are priced roughly between $1,000 and $1,500. They include a mix of enthusiast and pro-level features. This makes them a great choice for photographers who want a serious upgrade from a consumer-level camera and an inexpensive back-up option for professionals.

Mid-range dSLRs often have faster maximum shutter speeds than the less-expensive models, faster flash sync speeds, faster frame rates, better viewfinders, depending on the manufacturer, slightly larger LCD monitors with greater pixel counts, more professional setup options, a better autofocus system with more autofocus points, more custom shooting modes, more precise metering, better battery life, and a top LCD panel to display shooting information.

While this level of camera is considered light by professional standards, they're larger and heavier than consumer dSLRs. Magnesium alloy is often used to strengthen the camera body. Figure 1-7 shows the Canon EOS 80D.

FIGURE 1-7:
Mid-range
cameras add
even more power
and features.

Professional cameras

Professional dSLRs are designed to excel in a professional setting. They have all the bells, whistles, features, and performance pro photographers need. These cameras are large and rugged. They weigh more, are made from magnesium alloy, and have more features than consumer or mid-range models. They also shoot faster, focus better, and provide more reliable metering. You'll find flagship (the best model a company sells) cropped-frame and full-frame (see Figure 1-8) dSLRs at this level.

FIGURE 1-8:
The full-frame
Pentax K-1 is the
flagship of the
Pentax dSLR line.

Professional dSLRs that range from $1,500 to $2,500 have performance and form factor compromises that keep them relatively affordable. Ultra-high-end professional dSLRs run between $2,500 and $7,000. For example, the Canon EOS-1D X

Mark II body lists for approximately $6,000 and the Nikon D5 body lists for almost $6,500. These cameras represent the pinnacle of a company's dSLR lineup. They have the best sensors, image processors, autofocus and metering systems, best ISO performance, and have a whole host of other premier features. Simply put, they are the best cameras you can buy in the 35mm equivalent digital SLR format.

Delving into Camera Specifications

Camera *specifications* (informally called specs) are details that describe a camera's features and capabilities. Companies put this information on their websites and in the camera manual. Specifications can be technical, but this isn't rocket science. Knowing a few basics will help you understand what each camera is capable of, and you'll be able to compare models against each other.

TIP

Sometimes every camera has the same capability. In those cases, that specification is useless as a discriminator. File format is a good example. All dSLRs today save photos in two formats: Raw and JPEG. It wouldn't make any sense for you to go up to a salesperson and ask her to show you only the dSLRs that support Raw or JPEGs. They all do.

Basic information

I've already covered specifications like the camera name, pixel count, sensor size, and so forth, so I won't duplicate that here. If you need to review, flip back to the "Naming and Classifying Digital SLRs" section, earlier in this chapter.

Crop factor

When you look at camera listings and specifications you will quickly run across the term *crop factor*. As described earlier, crop factor is related to sensor size. Here's why it's important: Identical 50mm lenses will produce different photos when mounted on full-frame cameras versus cropped dSLRs. Why? Because the larger image sensor on the full-frame camera captures more of the scene than the smaller sensor on the cropped-frame camera. The smaller sensor captures a "cropped" area by comparison. By how much? By the amount of the crop factor. Figure 1-9 shows how much less a cropped-frame image sensor captures than a full-frame dSLR. It's important to note that this does not make cropped-frame cameras worthless. Quite the contrary. In fact, having larger pixel counts than ever before has enabled newer cropped-frame dSLRs to compete more effectively. They are able to capture much more detail than they used to.

TECHNICAL STUFF

Knowing the crop factor gives you the ability to compare lenses mounted on cameras that have different sensor sizes and the photos they capture. Multiply the focal length of the lens by the camera's crop factor to get the *35mm equivalent focal length.* You're able to compare mangos to mangos using 35mm equivalent focal lengths.

FIGURE 1-9: Smaller image sensors crop the scene by the amount of the crop factor.

ISO

ISO, also called *ISO speed* or *ISO sensitivity,* is a measure of the image sensor's sensitivity to light. The camera specification will list an ISO range. This range will begin at 50 or 100 and increase to something like 12800 or 16000, sometimes vastly more. See Book 3, Chapter 4 for more information on ISO. I am setting the ISO speed in Figure 1-10 to 3200, well below the maximum of 16000.

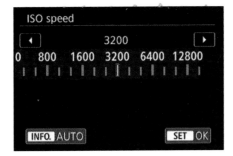

FIGURE 1-10: Setting the ISO.

REMEMBER

Higher ISOs improve your ability to shoot in low light and let you choose faster shutter speeds when capturing action. The downside to higher ISO is increased noise, especially in consumer cameras.

Shutter speeds

There are three shutter speeds that are listed in a camera's specifications: the fastest, slowest, and the flash sync speed (the fastest shutter speed you can use and still fire the built-in flash). The fastest shutter speeds in use today range from 1/4000 second for consumer dSLRs to 1/6000 or 1/8000 second for more advanced models (see Figure 1-11). The slowest shutter speed you can typically set is 30 seconds.

FIGURE 1-11: This camera has a maximum shutter speed of 1/8000 second.

Consumer dSLRs have sync speeds from 1/160 to 1/200 second while more expensive models are a bit faster (1/250 second). Faster shutter speeds are possible with an external flash and a feature called *high-speed sync*. I talk more about that in Book 4, Chapter 3.

Autofocus system

The autofocus system is another area where you can compare cameras. Each camera has a number of *autofocus (AF)* points and AF area selection modes. Cameras use AF points to automatically focus on subjects. Having several points spread over a large area gives you a greater chance of having an AF point where you need it. AF area selection modes enable you to choose how the camera decides which points to use. You can have the camera decide, or choose to manually select an individual point for greater precision. You can also choose a group of points, often called a Zone, to lock onto and track action, as shown in Figure 1-12.

Here are a few examples: The entry-level Canon T6 has 9 AF points located in the central region of the viewfinder. The similarly priced Nikon D3300 has 11 AF points, which cover the same basic area. More expensive cameras will have more AF points and a larger number of selection options. The Canon 80D and Nikon D7200, for example, have 45 and 51 AF points respectively, spread over a wide area.

OTHER SPECS

There are a number of other camera specifications that are not listed here because, frankly, they are either the same for most cameras or irrelevant to most photographers. This includes color spaces, release modes, file formats, white balance, and so forth. They may be interesting, but not the best way to decide what camera to buy. Generally speaking, you've decided on a camera before the point where things like metering technology make a difference.

FIGURE 1-12:
This camera has four AF point selection modes.

Movies

All current dSLRs shoot movies (Figure 1-13 shows this in action). Full HD video is the standard format. Most cameras also have an HD option, which is smaller than Full HD. Support for older VGA is diminishing. 4K video is emerging. Here are their sizes:

>> Full HD movies (including Sony AVCHD) are 1920 x 1080 pixels.

>> Sony cameras have a special intermediate HD movie mode recorded at 1440 x 1080 pixels but played back at 1920 x 1080 pixels. These movies use the MP4 format.

>> HD movies are 1280 x 720 pixels.

>> Standard definition (SD) movies are 640 x 480 pixels.

>> There are currently two types of 4K movies. Nikon dSLRs and Sony mirrorless camera movies are 3840 x 2160 pixels in size. Canon 4K movies are 4096 x 2160 pixels. Nikon and Sony set the size of their 4K movies according to the UHD alliance standard, which is twice the width and twice the height of Full HD. Canon uses the size established by the Digital Cinema Initiatives venture, which is twice the width and height of 2K video.

When you look at your camera's movie specs, look for how much control you have over movie settings, especially exposure and shutter speed, as well as different movie sizes, compression settings, formats, and frame rates.

Shooting modes and scenes

Digital SLRs have a handful of "classic" shooting modes (sometimes called *exposure modes*). They include programmed autoexposure, aperture-priority, shutter-priority, manual (you might see these four called PASM modes), and Bulb. Bulb mode may not be on the mode dial. When it isn't, it should be accessible as a function of shutter speed. Cameras like the Pentax K-3 II have new, ingenious modes like sensitivity priority automatic exposure, where you set the ISO like you would aperture or shutter speed, and shutter- and aperture-priority automatic exposure (think manual mode with Auto ISO).

Most cameras have several scene modes that help you take photos of specific subjects. You select the subject or shooting conditions, and the camera sets itself up to capture them most effectively. Standard scenes include Portrait (see Figure 1-14), Landscape, Action, and Close-up. Additional scenes vary from camera to camera and often include Night Portrait, Child, Candlelight, Sunset, Pet, Surf & Snow, Fireworks, and Food.

Many cameras have even more user-friendly modes designed to automate the camera and make shooting easier. Examples modes include Scene Intelligent Auto, Superior Auto, Sweep Panorama, various automatic HDR (High Dynamic Range) modes, time-lapse, multiple exposures, and more.

When comparing cameras, carefully investigate the automatic shooting modes and scenes they offer.

TIP

FIGURE 1-14:
This camera has several scene modes right on the dial.

In-camera processing

Most dSLRs allow you to process JPEGs and Raw files in-camera (the Raw file is converted and saved as a JPEG). You may be able to resize photos, crop them (see Figure 1-15), modify the exposure, white balance, color profile, and perform many other retouching tasks. Being able to touch up photos in the camera takes the pressure off of having to use a computer and complicated software to accomplish these tasks. I think they are incredibly useful features for most photographers to have.

FIGURE 1-15:
Look for in-camera processing features like cropping.

Filters and other creative effects

Look for fun filters and other special effects to add pizazz to your photos. They help you express your creativity without having to mess around with a computer. Each manufacturer has its own names. Canon calls them Creative Filters; Nikon has Filter Effects; Sony uses the term Picture Effects; and Pentax lists its effects as Digital Filters. Some specific examples include Toy Camera (always a fun filter to use), Miniature, High-Key, Retro, Replace Color, Monochrome, Pop Color, Posterization, Soft Focus, and many HDR effects. I'm applying a creative Art Bold effect to a photo in Figure 1-16.

FIGURE 1-16:
Creative effects and filters help make photography more fun for everyone.

Media

Digital cameras store photos and movies on memory cards. Be sure to look at your camera's specifications before buying new memory cards to confirm compatibility. For specialty cards such as FlashAir, check that company's website for compatible cameras. Here are the card types, then:

>> **SD cards** are the most prevalent type of memory card. They're reasonably small and thin. There are several types of SD cards (SD, SDHC, and SDXC), speed classes, and bus interfaces, each with different capabilities.

Eye-Fi SD cards enable your camera to wirelessly transfer photos and movies to a phone, computer, tablet, or other mobile device. You must install additional software or apps for everything to work.

Flucard is a card unique to Pentax cameras. Similar to Eye-Fi, these SD cards offer wireless connectivity between your camera and smartphone or computer. Unlike Eye-Fi, however, you can use your smartphone to control the camera during remote Live View shooting with a Flucard and the proper app installed.

If you prefer to look at other options, there are a handful of other Wi-Fi SD cards available. Toshiba FlashAir and Transcend Wi-Fi are two examples.

>> **CF (Compact Flash) cards** are an older memory card design, larger than SD cards. Despite this, they perform well and are often used in high-end cameras.

CFast cards, also known as CompactFast, are a newer, high-performance CF card variant with much faster read and write speeds. They are meant to support 4K video recording.

>> **Memory Stick** cards were created by Sony, and are used in its cameras. There are different versions of Memory Stick media. Variants currently in use are Memory Stick PRO-HG Duo HX, Memory Stick PRO Duo, and Memory Stick PRO-HG Duo.

>> **XQD** cards are another high-performance card used in newer Nikon cameras. They are intended to support high-speed still photo and 4K video recording.

Viewfinder specs

Take a look at two specifications relating to viewfinders:

>> **Frame coverage:** This specification, given as a percentage, identifies how much of the scene the viewfinder sees compared to the image sensor. Oddly enough, most dSLR viewfinders don't show you everything. This can be a problem when you're trying to frame a scene precisely, and why more expensive professional cameras feature 100 percent (see Figure 1-17) or near-total coverage.

FIGURE 1-17:
This camera has a nice, large viewfinder with 100 percent coverage.

Now, despite the fact that it can be a nuisance, don't obsess over having less than 100 percent coverage. You can still frame great shots. With experience, you'll be able to account for the differences between your viewfinder and image sensor and frame your shots accordingly. For example, I have learned to place people's heads a bit closer to the top edge of the viewfinder than appears necessary on many of my dSLRs. You can also crop photos in-camera or use software to achieve the perfect composition.

>> **Magnification:** Most digital SLRs shrink the scene slightly in the viewfinder compared to what you see with your unaided eye. Expressed as a multiplier, anything under 1.0x means the view is reduced. If it's over 1.0x, the view is magnified. Most cameras have magnification factors between .70x and .95x, with an exceptional few at or over 1.0x.

Image stabilization

Image stabilization is important when shutter speeds are slow and you are supporting the camera by hand. Camera movement robs you of a sharp photo. All new digital SLRs from the major manufacturers steady the image using one of two different approaches:

>> **Lens:** The image is stabilized in the lens, not in the camera body. Current lens-based stabilization systems are named differently, depending on the brand of camera. Canon calls its approach Image Stabilization (IS). Nikon uses the term Vibration Reduction (VR; see Figure 1-18). In both cases, the lens has a floating optical element that, when turned on, is gyroscopically stabilized. Subject to some limits, the IS/VR unit in the lens moves in opposition to camera movement. This keeps the image focused on the image sensor rather than jumping around.

FIGURE 1-18:
Nikon's lens-based image stabilization technology is called VR.

The advantage to lens-based stability systems is that everything benefits from stabilization: the autofocus system, the image sensor, the metering sensor, and what you see through the viewfinder or on the back monitor.

The main downside to lens-based image stabilization is that not all lenses have the feature. In addition, you have to keep buying new lenses to benefit from improvements and updates to the technology.

>> **Sensor:** This type of image stabilization occurs in the camera body. The camera adjusts the position of the image sensor in opposition to camera movement, thereby enabling you to capture a clear photo. Sony calls its technology SteadyShot (see Figure 1-19) while Pentax refers to its system as Sensor-shift Shake Reduction. Olympus features 3- or 5-Axis In-Body Image Stabilization; newer Sony's a7-series full-frame mirrorless models are equipped with 5-axis image stabilization as well.

FIGURE 1-19:
This camera
features
in-body image
stabilization,
complete with an
on/off switch.

The main advantage to body-based stability systems is that the sensor, and therefore the image, is stabilized no matter what lens is attached to the camera. The most expensive long-range super-telephoto lens in the world and the cheapest plastic lens will both benefit from in-camera stabilization. As you upgrade camera bodies, you get the latest and greatest implementation of image stabilization for all your older lenses.

Following Recent dSLR Developments

Digital SLRs continue to evolve. That is truly fantastic news, because photographers benefit from new capabilities and technology. Here are some recent dSLR developments and trends:

>> **Wi-Fi/NFC:** After lagging behind for many years, built-in Wi-Fi/NFC (near-field communication) features are becoming more prevalent in new dSLRs. You can connect your camera to a smartphone (see Figure 1-20), tablet, computer, printer, network computer, or the Internet to view, print, or transfer photos. You can often control the camera remotely using the same connection and the proper app.

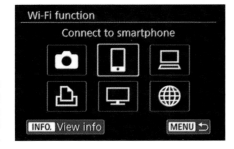

FIGURE 1-20:
Increased Wi-Fi
support is a
positive dSLR
development.

>> **Touchscreens:** Taking a cue from the popularity of smartphones and tablets, some new digital SLRs feature touchscreen monitors. You can drag, swipe, and tap through menus, photos (see Figure 1-21), and even use the touchscreen to focus and snap the shutter.

FIGURE 1-21:
Selecting a photo to view from the index view.

>> **In-camera processing:** Look for cameras to have even more processing options and filters.

>> **Higher ISO speeds:** Maximum ISO speeds continue to rise. Entry-level consumer cameras now have maximum ISOs in the range of 12800, while more advanced dSLRs can have astronomically high ISOs. Higher ISO speeds make shooting inside and in other low-light conditions easier. They also enable you to use less-capable lenses with smaller maximum apertures in a wider variety of conditions.

>> **Higher pixel counts:** Pixel counts also continue to rise. New consumer-level dSLRs have more pixels than professional models from years past. This means that you can take photos and make poster-sized prints without losing quality. You can also crop photos more without losing too much resolution.

>> **Expanded shooting modes:** Today's dSLRs offer more creative shooting modes and scenes than ever before.

>> **4K Video:** Today, all new dSLRs shoot Full HD movies, and the new trend is 4K video, which quadruples the resolution of Full HD (or 2K video, depending on the camera you're using).

>> **Articulated monitors:** More cameras feature articulated monitors that swing out from the back of the camera. This feature gives you greater flexibility in how you hold and position the camera. See Figure 1-22.

FIGURE 1-22:
Pull the monitor
out from the back
of the camera
and position it.

Shopping for a dSLR

Shopping for a dSLR doesn't have to be stressful. In fact, it can be downright fun. I offer you this general guide as someone who has "been there and done that" many times over the last several years. Be honest with yourself about your budget, what you want out of a camera, and the type of photos you want to take. Brush up on the dSLR categories and general specifications so that information about different features and capabilities is fresh in your mind before shopping.

Understanding the system

When you buy a digital SLR, you're buying into a system from a specific manufacturer, such as Canon, Nikon, Pentax, or Sony. You can't mix and match lenses (other than third-party lenses that are compatible with your system), camera bodies, flash units, or other accessories produced by different camera manufacturers. If you have already heavily invested in a specific brand, you'll have a harder time switching and gearing up with your new camera.

Going shopping

To shop for a digital SLR, follow these simple steps:

1. **Set a budget.**

   There's no sense in looking at a $3,400 camera if you can't afford it. Seriously, you will read accounts and people will tell you how much better that $3,400 camera is than the $800 model you're looking at until you're sick of it. Though they may be right in terms of some capabilities and technical details, their advice is entirely irrelevant to you and your decision. Your budget depends on you and is probably based largely on factors unrelated to photography.

   Therefore, set an initial budget. It will save you time and frustration. Your budget will help you identify the cameras you should look at in the next step.

Look for a sweet spot where your needs meet the price you can afford and the performance you want. Don't forget to factor in lenses, bags, tripods, filters, flashes, extra batteries, and remote shutter releases. Those things all add up. If money is no object, look instead at the dSLR categories I listed earlier and decide what level of camera you want to buy. This will narrow your search to more manageable proportions.

REMEMBER

Because of the pace of dSLR development, camera bodies are viable for a limited number of years. Quality lenses make a much better long-term investment. Think about that when setting your budget.

2. **Check out cameras that are in your price range.**

If you can, go to a store where you can handle cameras in your price range. Check out two or three models. Pick them up and hold them in your hand. Assess how they feel and whether they seem comfortable, too light, or too heavy. See if you can easily take the lens off and put it back on. Does one lens feel better or worse than another? Open the battery compartment. Take a look at where the memory card is stored. Press buttons. Go through the menus to see how they are set up and see if you find anything you dislike about them. Do they make sense to you or will you find them a constant source of irritation? Look through the viewfinder to see how the view is. Test out live view. Take a few photos, if possible, and look at them on the monitor.

REMEMBER

Conducting a hands-on test is the single greatest way to find out whether you like a camera or not — even if you've used cameras from that manufacturer before.

If you can't get to a store to handle cameras, the next best thing is to go online and look at the cameras in your price range, read reviews, look at manuals, and watch videos. See what other people think, and get second and third opinions. You may be able to rent the camera you are interested in and give it a practical road test. That's money well spent.

3. **Make a decision.**

Based on what you learned from the prior step, weed out cameras that aren't what you want. Review features and specifications to compare models and break ties.

REMEMBER

Specifications are relative. Technologies and performance characteristics change over time.

Finally, decide on which camera to buy. It's been my experience that getting the least expensive camera that you like and saving money for accessories and lens purchases is a solid approach. If there is a clear winner and it costs more than others, however, don't hesitate to buy it. You can always pick up more lenses later.

REMEMBER

This decision doesn't commit you for life (keep your receipt, though, in case you change your mind). Learn from this purchase and it will help you with the next one.

Investing in accessories

One of the great things about digital SLRs is the tremendous number of different types of accessories designed to help you out. While a camera and lens are all you really need, over time you'll discover things that you want to add, change, improve, or fix. I've put together a little list of accessories for you to think about:

>> **Lenses:** Of course lenses are the number one dSLR accessory. They come in all sizes and price points. Aside from the camera body, lenses are the most important component of digital SLR photography. They help determine the type and quality of shots you can take with your camera. Book 1, Chapter 3 has more information about lenses, as does Book 2.

>> **Filters and filter accessories:** Filters enable you to deal with challenging lighting conditions and create artistic effects. They screw on the front of your lens and affect the light coming into your camera (as opposed to being a software effect). Read about them in Book 3, Chapter 5.

>> **Focus-alignment tools:** These tools enable you to check whether your lenses are focusing properly or not.

>> **Built-in flash accessories:** These accessories modify the built-in flash. Some block the light, which is useful if you want to use your built-in flash as a wireless trigger but don't want its light contributing to the scene. Others soften and diffuse it.

>> **External flashes and accessories:** External flash units can be costly, but they add quite a bit of flexibility to your photography. Light stands, umbrellas, flash brackets, and other accessories assist you. See Book 4, Chapter 3 for more information about using an external flash and accessories.

>> **External microphone:** If you shoot video and your camera supports an external microphone, attach it to the accessory shoe and plug the cable into the camera, as shown in Figure 1-23. It's possible to record professional-quality stereo audio with very little effort this way.

>> **Backgrounds:** Paper or fabric backgrounds are important if you want to shoot portraits in a studio setting.

>> **Straps:** Secure your camera around your neck or to your wrist with a cool strap.

FIGURE 1-23:
Attach an external microphone for superior audio quality.

>> **Tripods and other supports:** Use a support to stabilize the camera when you can. Tripods, monopods, and other unique supports like the Gorrilapod (by Joby) are all very useful.

>> **GPS gear:** If your camera doesn't have built-in *GPS* (Global Positioning System) and you want to add location information to your photos, you can add GPS with an external unit. It can imprint your photos with the latitude and longitude where you took the photos. The information is stored the same way the camera model and exposure settings are stored. You can also geotag your images with information collected from your smartphone.

>> **White balance cards:** If the camera has a hard time getting the correct *white balance* (in general, photos should not have an overly blue or yellow color cast to them), pick up a white balance card. Mostly gray, they serve as a reference that enables you to calculate the correct color temperature of the scene. WhiBal is a good one. You can also use a white board or piece of paper as an economical alternative.

>> **Cases:** You can go crazy with cases: large ones, small ones, tiny ones, and everything in between. Standard cases have a handle and a shoulder strap. Sling bags go over your shoulder and are easy to walk around with; you can get into them quickly. Backpack cases are best for hiking.

>> **Protective covers:** You can buy silicon armor to keep your camera a bit safer than normal. See Book 1, Chapter 2.

>> **Underwater gear:** When you're shooting underwater, having the correct gear for you and your camera is an absolute necessity.

>> **Vests and other clothing:** Buying specialized photography clothing gives you additional pockets to stuff lenses and other accessories instead of constantly having to dig through your camera bag. Plus you'll look stylish and cool.

TIP

>> **LCD accessories:** *LCD hoods* are a great idea if you shoot movies. They keep light from shining on the monitor on the back of your camera, which makes it easier to see what's on the screen. *LCD loupes,* on the other hand, turn your monitor into something like a viewfinder. These are awesome and can be used when shooting movies or still photos in live view. You can also buy screen protectors that shield your LCD from scratches, just like on your smartphone.

>> **Eyecups:** You can buy larger eyecups for the viewfinder. They make viewing more comfortable, especially if you wear glasses.

>> **Viewfinder diopters:** If you can't adjust the viewfinder enough to correct for your vision, you may need to buy a *viewfinder diopter* that has a larger adjustment built in. See Book 1, Chapter 2 for more information.

>> **Power adapters:** If you are shooting inside and don't want your camera constantly running out of power, buy a compatible power adapter and never change another battery.

>> **Remotes:** Remotes are wonderful accessories for tripod-mounted cameras because you don't have to push the shutter button to take the photo. This reduces photographer-induced camera shake. You can also lock them to take Bulb exposures. Figure 1-24 shows a Canon wireless remote.

FIGURE 1-24:
Remotes are totally worth it; wireless remotes even more.

I don't have the space to list every type of dSLR accessory. Use this list as a start and keep looking!

Embracing dSLRs

Ultimately, only you can decide if a dSLR is the right camera for you. Every system, every camera, and every technology has tradeoffs. Digital SLRs aren't as small as compact or mirrorless cameras, as cool as tablets, as handy as your smartphone, or as simple to use as a paper weight. However, they have a lot going for them.

>> **They take great photos.** The dSLR is a fantastic tool that can help you take great still and moving pictures. That's what this is all about. In addition, they are flexible enough to perform well in a wide variety of situations and lighting. Whether you use your dSLR professionally or as a family camera, you will appreciate the quality of the photos, especially compared to those you can take with most smartphones and tablets. You're right in the action in Figure 1-25. As fun as other devices are, this shot would have been impossible for me to take with a smartphone, tablet, or a less capable camera.

FIGURE 1-25: The proof is in the pudding — photography worth pursuing.

>> **You can change lenses.** Tailor your camera to take the photos you want. Shoot close-ups, sweeping landscapes, macros, ultra-wide-angle shots, telephoto action, intimate portraits, family gatherings, slow waterfalls, and everything in between. Invest in superior quality lenses to make photos look even better. Figure 1-26 illustrates the point perfectly. While the compact Canon

camera is adequate, it will never have a lens other than the one it was built with. The Nikon dSLR, on the other hand, is sporting an outlandish 300mm telephoto lens. It can be swapped for something completely different in about 5 seconds.

FIGURE 1-26:
The ability to change lenses is a strength of the dSLR over a compact camera.

>> **Focusing is a strength.** Digital SLRs have world-class autofocusing technology and features. This is an important point. If you've tried to capture action or focus on a specific point using a smartphone or tablet, you know how frustrating it can be. Digital SLR autofocus technologies work with precision and flexibility to enable you to reliably focus on what you want, when you want.

>> **The viewfinders are awesome.** The worst dSLR viewfinder is larger, clearer, brighter, and better (see Figure 1-27) than any viewfinder you'll find on a compact or super-zoom camera, assuming it even has one. Many don't, which makes you rely exclusively on the LCD monitor on the back. Under many conditions, LCD monitors are okay. However, they don't work well in bright light. In addition, smartphones and tablets seem to suffer from display-lag at the worst time when taking photos. Digital SLR viewfinders outperform LCD monitors on most devices. And if you want to use the monitor on the back of the camera, you can.

>> **They have flash.** Most dSLRs have a built-in (see Figure 1-28) flash that is capable of lighting your scenes and subjects. All dSLRs have a hot shoe on top of their viewfinder, which enables you to mount an external flash (and other accessories) that you can rotate, swivel, and bounce. Try that with your iPad.

>> **There are plenty of price points.** Digital SLRs are not the most expensive camera option. While some are extremely pricey, many consumer models cost less than most tablets.

FIGURE 1-27: Digital SLR viewfinders just work; rabbit not included.

FIGURE 1-28: Pop up the flash for extra light.

» **You can make money with them.** Become a semi-pro or professional photographer with your dSLR. Start a studio. Become a wedding photographer. Make money selling news photos, sports photos, nature photos, the stars, advertising photos, stock photos, or artistic prints.

» **You're in control, but you don't have to be.** Digital SLRs enable you to control the camera as much or as little as you want. If you're new to photography, you can pick up an entry-level consumer model and start taking photos *right away*. If you're a professional, you have access to cameras with tremendous features and power you need to succeed.

In the final analysis, my advice is this: Don't spend years messing around with point-and-shoot cameras, smartphones, or tablets struggling to take better photos. If you're interested in photography, pick up a dSLR or dSLT and start taking gorgeous pictures and movies that you'll treasure for a lifetime today.

Chapter **2**

Handling, Cleaning, and Protecting Your Camera

G ood woodworkers know how to handle and care for tools like saws, hammers, screwdrivers, and lathes. Good photographers should know how to handle and care for their tools too. This practical chapter emphasizes working with your digital SLR, batteries, memory cards, developing cleaning techniques, protecting your camera, and more. These are important skills to master. With a little bit of practice, you'll quickly become proficient at them — and your photography will only get better.

Anatomy of a dSLR

I think one of the most effective ways to learn photography is to become more knowledgeable about your camera. Knowing what and where the controls are enables you to use them without having to stop and think about it all the time. When that happens, you'll find that you're focused on *photography,* not operating a sophisticated gadget. That's the good news. The even better news is that it's not really hard (like most things, effort is the greatest hurdle to get over).

Different cameras have different controls, but dSLR design is pretty standardized. The figures in this section show a mix of recent and older dSLRs.

Front and center

Figure 2-1 shows the front of a Canon T6i with the lens attached. The most obvious feature in this view is the lens, which secures to the camera body using the lens mount. Aside from the lens, the front of most cameras may have several other features. Examples include the lens release button (most often on the left as you look directly at the front of the camera; Pentax cameras are on the right), focus and flash controls, a depth-of-field preview button, remote sensors, self-timer lamps, AF illuminators, and possibly a microphone or two.

Red-eye reduction/
Self-timer lamp   Microphones

Remote sensor   Lens release button

FIGURE 2-1: Camera fronts do not typically have many controls.

Around back

Your office and the camera command center are around back. You'll do most of your work here: view and compose the scene, focus, adjust settings, review photos, and take photos. Learn the names and functions of all the buttons, knobs, levers, and screens. That will enable you to work them without hesitation.

Figure 2-2 shows the back of the Canon EOS Rebel T6i. Aside from the plethora of buttons, two other important features are the LCD monitor and viewfinder.

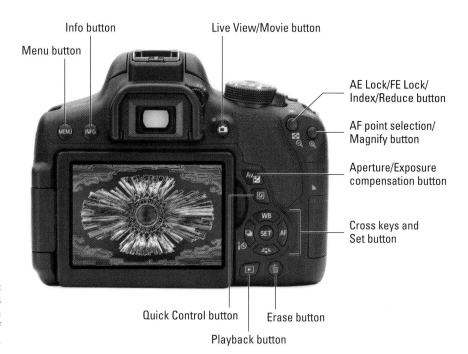

Info button

Menu button

Live View/Movie button

AE Lock/FE Lock/
Index/Reduce button

AF point selection/
Magnify button

Aperture/Exposure
compensation button

Cross keys and
Set button

FIGURE 2-2:
The back of this
camera has a
wide variety of
buttons.

Quick Control button

Erase button

Playback button

You'll use the monitor to display camera settings, shooting functions, and the menu; to play back photos and movies; and to frame and focus when shooting in Live View mode (a special viewing mode that displays the scene on the monitor instead of through the viewfinder). Your camera's LCD monitor is so important that you can't operate a modern dSLR without it. Protect it and keep it clean.

Many dSLRs and dSLTs come with articulated monitors. Although the style may vary, they all swing or move up and out from the back of the camera so you can position them. They can be faced inward to protect the monitor.

The primary purpose of the viewfinder is to show you the scene, but it also displays lots of helpful information relating to the shooting mode, exposure details, and the focus and metering modes you're in.

The other features on the back of the camera are normally organized into functional areas related to focus, exposure, or playback. Many times, buttons can have more than one purpose, depending on the mode your camera is in.

REMEMBER

Read your camera's manual if you need help finding a control or button. You might have to spend some extra time, like I did, to get past the confusing parts. You don't have to "get it" all at once.

Top and bottom

Figure 2-3 shows the top of the Canon T6i. At minimum, the top will have a power switch, a dial or button to set the shooting mode, and the shutter button. Some cameras have more than one large dial on the top of the camera (the Pentax K-1 has three!). You may also see one or more shooting function buttons that let you set the ISO speed and enter exposure correction. More expensive cameras have a top LCD panel. The pop-up flash (if applicable; many full-frame models and the odd cropped-frame model do not have a built-in flash) and accessory shoe (also called the *hot shoe*, which is used to mount accessories and an external flash to the camera) are located here.

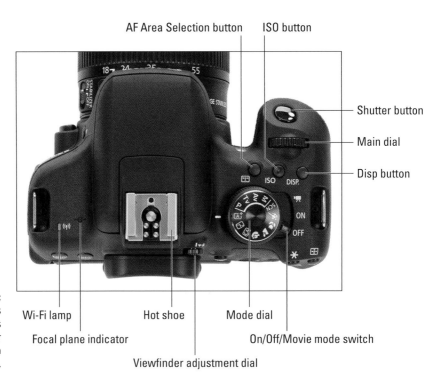

FIGURE 2-3: This Canon has several buttons and other controls on the top.

Figure 2-4 shows the bottom of the same camera. You'll find the tripod socket here, plus the battery or combo battery/memory card compartment. Some dSLRs put their memory cards in the same compartment as the battery.

Tripod socket   Battery compartment cover

FIGURE 2-4:
The bottom of a
typical dSLR.

TIP

Quick-release plates, which screw into the camera bottom and then mount on the tripod head, are great timesavers. These plates are easier and safer to use than having to screw your camera down onto a tripod every time you mount it.

Both sides

You'll grip the camera by the sides. The right side (looking at the camera from behind; shown in Figure 2-5) is where your right hand goes and is completely devoid of buttons and other controls. Most memory card doors are located on the right side of the camera and blend in with the curve of the camera body.

The left side hosts a number of different features, as shown in Figure 2-6. You'll often find the flash button located here, as well as the depth-of-field button. Advanced cameras often have custom buttons and more autofocus controls. You'll also find most of the camera's input and output terminals. Consumer models may only have a few. More advanced cameras have more. Rubber doors swing out of the way but stay attached to the camera. I've digitally removed them (with Photoshop) to make the terminals more visible in Figure 2-7.

Card slot cover   Power adapter cord cover

Flash button   Speaker

Depth-of-Field   Terminal covers
preview button

A/V out Digital terminal

Remote terminal

FIGURE 2-7:
Here are the
terminals
themselves.

HDMI terminal

External microphone terminal

Working the Controls

As you can see, digital SLRs certainly have a lot of parts. Besides knowing the name and function of everything on your camera, you should be comfortable operating the buttons, dials, and other controls. Familiarize yourself with your camera and practice the following actions:

» **Pushing buttons:** Push them with a free finger. The most important button is the shutter button (or shutter-release button). Press it firmly and steadily. Don't jab at it, or you'll shake the camera. Try squeezing it to reduce camera shake. Get used to what it feels like to press the shutter button halfway; you have to do that to autofocus and have the camera evaluate the scene's exposure.

» **Turning dials:** Dials that turn are very knoblike. The largest and most important dial is usually the mode dial. Some mode dials have a locking button in the center. You have to press it in order to unlock and turn the dial.

» **Spinning dials:** Dials that spin are very wheel-like. Most are on the right side of the camera. Spin them with your thumb or index finger.

» **Using the sliders and other controls:** Your camera may have levers and selectors and other controls. Practice reaching and activating them.

>> **Operating the lens controls:** If you're comfortable using your left hand, use it for lens buttons and switches. These controls are normally on the left side of the lens as it faces away from you. You have little choice other than to use your left hand to zoom and focus. Your right hand will hold on to the camera, ready to press the shutter button. Manual focusing takes practice. More on lenses in Book 1, Chapter 3, as well as Book 2.

>> **Opening covers:** When you remove memory cards, change batteries, or make other connections, you'll open a cover on your dSLR. Sometimes a cover has a lever or slider that you need to move to unlatch the cover. This is common with battery compartments. Or, you might slide the cover toward the back of the camera to unlatch it and then swing it open. This is a common feature of memory card covers. Others, like those covering the camera's main terminals, are rubberized and pop in and out of the camera body. It's recommended that you turn the camera off before removing the memory card or battery.

Regardless of the type, *force covers open only as a last resort*. If one feels stuck and you can't open it, check the manual to make sure that you're operating the specific cover correctly; then try again carefully with a little more elbow grease. If it feels impossible to open and you don't want to force it further, search for help online or from a local camera shop.

>> **Connecting cables:** Many cables, like microphones, headphones, some remotes, and older RCA plugs, are very easy to insert. Others, such as HDMI, USB, and some remotes, can be put in only one way. Align these cables with their matching terminal carefully.

Don't force a cable where it doesn't want to go! Make sure that you have the correct cable and are trying to connect it to the proper terminal. Make sure everything is aligned correctly. Inspect the cable and terminal on the camera for damage. Connecting cables can be difficult at night or in dim light, even if you know your camera by touch. If necessary, take a small flashlight with you so that you can see what you're doing.

>> **Changing batteries and memory cards:** Although these actions are simple, they deserve their own sections. I cover them a bit later in the chapter.

>> **Attaching grips:** Grips, sometimes called *battery grips* or *vertical grips*, are very functional. They look cool (see Figure 2-8), house additional controls to make holding the camera vertically easier, and give your camera extra battery power. Attaching one is easy. You may need to remove the battery from your camera, and then load fresh batteries into the grip. Some grips have extensions that slide into the camera's battery compartment. Screw the grip onto the camera's tripod socket.

FIGURE 2-8:
This Sony camera
looks mighty
impressive with a
grip attached.

Vertical grip

Gripping the Camera

Mastering your grip pays dividends of sharper, clearer photos when shooting handheld. You have a more stable platform to shoot from, rely less on image stabilization, and you can use slower shutter speeds and not shake the camera. The following sections talk about positions you can work on.

TIP

No matter what grip you use, try to maintain good posture. Don't hunch, bend over improperly, or hold the camera at arm's length. You'll tire easily and possibly hurt yourself. Hold the camera close so that you can support it easily.

Standard grip

The standard grip is shown in Figure 2-9. Use your right hand to grip and support the camera. Hold the camera's grip with your right hand. Slide your pinky finger underneath the camera and use it as a supporting shelf. Your ring and middle fingers grip and hold the camera, while your index finger works the top controls. Your thumb provides support at times, but also works controls on the back of the camera. Your left hand provides support but also operates controls on that side of the camera and the lens.

Don't forget about operating the flash. I temporarily hold the camera in my left hand and use my right hand to operate external flash controls.

When you're ready to take the photos, support the weight of the lens with your left palm. At times, you may be more comfortable supporting the entire weight of the camera with your left hand so that you can remove your right hand from the grip and work various dials, buttons, and controls. When you're ready to take the picture, move your right hand back into position on the grip to press the shutter button.

To promote good posture and add some stability, lock down your left elbow against your stomach. Look through the viewfinder or watch the LCD screen to frame and focus.

FIGURE 2-9:
Me, holding the camera normally.

Vertical grip

Your hands and fingers stay in the same place, but you twist the camera vertically. If I'm using autofocus and not zooming in and out, I use my left hand to support most of the camera's weight (see Figure 2-10), and my right hand stabilizes the camera vertically and takes the picture. My right elbow is extended in this pose. If you are in a tight space or around other people, you should pull it in close to your body to avoid bumping into them. Your right wrist will cramp a bit, but if you practice at it you'll be fine.

FIGURE 2-10:
Vertical grip.

Over-the-shoulder grip

A well-known photographer promotes a grip style where you point your left shoulder toward the subject, using it to support the weight of the camera. You hold the camera with your right hand, and your left hand comes up to rest on the back of your right hand, stabilizing and securing it. You have to turn your head a bit to face the camera. I've tried this technique and can't quite seem to get comfortable with it, but it is rock-solid.

Live View grip

Gripping the camera when using Live View is a different feeling. You don't hold the camera close to your face and body like you do when you're looking through the viewfinder. Hold the camera away from your face so you can see the LCD monitor. When zooming or focusing, move your left hand back to the lens to operate these controls. Your right hand doesn't change at all. I am checking the composition in Figure 2-11.

TIP

Viewing using the LCD monitor is a much more casual setup, and has some unique benefits. First, it's pretty comfortable. It's possible to use the touchscreen better with this grip because your face isn't plastered up against the camera. You're able to keep track of what's going on around you easier so that you can catch the action or stay safe. You're also able to interact with your subjects better. However, this position is much harder to stabilize, so I recommend keeping shutter speeds a bit higher than you would taking the same photo using the viewfinder.

FIGURE 2-11:
Working in
Live View.

Providing Additional Support

The best way to stabilize your camera is with a good tripod. Using a support lets you set longer shutter speeds and not worry about camera movement blurring your photos. One-legged monopods offer less support but are much more mobile.

You can mount different heads on tripods and monopods. Some pan and tilt. Others are a form of ball joint. Whichever you choose (I have both), look into getting one with a quick-release plate. You screw it into the camera bottom and then lock the plate onto the tripod head. It's far easier to latch and unlatch the quick-release plate than it is to screw and unscrew the entire camera.

You can use a fence, a rock, a vehicle, the ground, or another item if you need to stabilize your camera and don't have a support with you. You can also try kneeling to stabilize the camera. You may find that resting your elbow on your knee is comfortable in this position.

TIP

Tripod

I use a tripod all the time (see Figure 2-12). It's good for ya. When taking macros or close-ups in the studio, formal portraits, or landscape shots, nothing works better at securing and supporting the weight of the camera. Cheap tripods, however, while affordable and minimally functional, are very disappointing. You really do get what you pay for. If you want something that will be stable and last for more than two days, get a name-brand tripod from a camera shop, not a discount store.

TIP

Aside from providing rock-solid stability, using a tripod frees your hands and allows you to concentrate more on camera setup and framing than on supporting the camera and taking a steady shot. You won't grow as tired, either.

FIGURE 2-12:
Tripods provide fantastic support for cameras.

Monopod

Monopods have a single leg that telescopes in and out to the height you want to work at, as shown in Figure 2-13. Most often, you see professional photographers at sporting events using monopods. They stand, sit, or kneel on the sidelines and use the monopod to support the weight of their camera. If using bulky, heavy lenses, you need all the support you can get. You'll mount your telephoto lens right to the monopod.

FIGURE 2-13:
Monopods excel
at supporting
large cameras
and lenses.

REMEMBER

Walking around with a monopod is much easier than lugging around a tripod. They're faster to set up and tear down. Setting the exact height you need with one leg is easier than fiddling around with three. The tradeoff for this convenience, however, is stability and safety. Monopods aren't as stable as tripods, and if you forget they don't have three legs and let go, well, you're in for a nasty surprise.

Handling an Articulated Monitor

Using Live View on an LCD monitor gives you the flexibility of shooting when you can't look through the viewfinder. Having an *adjustable,* also called *articulated,* LCD monitor lets you shoot from a number of otherwise impossible positions. Although the style may vary, they all swing or move up and out from the back of the camera so you can position them. You can get down low, hold the camera up high, or even point it around a corner. Using an articulated monitor isn't difficult. Your main concerns should be:

WARNING

>> Don't whack the monitor against anything. It's easy to forget that the monitor extends a ways from the camera.

>> Don't overstress it by cranking the monitor around like the rearview mirror on a '57 Chevy.

The articulated monitor on the back of the Canon T6i (see Figure 2-14) is a good example of how one type works. This monitor comes stowed, but can flip out from the back of the camera and then tilts, swivel, and rotates. To open a monitor like this, carefully use your thumb or other finger to pull the monitor out from the back of the camera. If you like, you can rotate the monitor. You can also flip the monitor back up and fit it back into the camera with the screen out. In this setup, it acts like a normal LCD monitor on the back of the camera. Rather than flipping out (intentional humor alert), some articulated monitors flip up or tilt.

FIGURE 2-14: Articulated LCD monitors give you a lot of viewing options.

Using a Touchscreen

Touchscreens bring the same type of gestures you use to operate a smartphone or tablet to the digital SLR. Depending on the camera and what you're trying to do, you may tap (see Figure 2-15), touch, swipe, drag, pinch, or expand using one or more fingers. Touchscreens are fun and save you a lot of time and trouble hunting through menus, choosing settings, or reviewing photos. Some cameras even let you use the touchscreen to focus and trigger the shutter. Their one downside is when you accidentally change a camera setting with your nose without realizing it. Always be on the lookout for incidental contact with your touchscreen.

FIGURE 2-15: Use the touchscreen like you would a smartphone.

Working in dusty or wet weather, or in the winter when you have gloves or mittens on, makes using a touchscreen more difficult. Depending on the conditions, you should be ready to revert to traditional controls when necessary.

Changing Batteries

Batteries supply your dSLR with power. Never take that for granted. It's a good idea to have more than one for a backup. Always store batteries in a cool, dry place, and charge them before you need them.

Checking battery power

Your camera has battery status indicators all over it. You should see one in the viewfinder, on the top LCD panel (if your camera has one), and on the back LCD monitor.

You may also be able to look in your camera's menu for a more detailed estimate of remaining power. Look for a menu option related to the battery, as shown on the left image in Figure 2-16. When you select it, the battery information is shown, as illustrated on the right of Figure 2-16. In this case, you learn how much charge is left, how many shots you've taken on this battery, and how well the battery is expected to recharge.

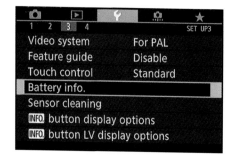
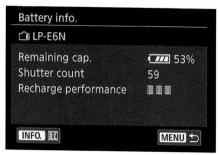

FIGURE 2-16:
This camera gives you plenty of useful battery info.

Inserting a battery

Here's how to insert a battery into your dSLR:

1. **Turn off the camera.**

2. **Release the catch on the battery compartment cover.**

The catch is on the bottom of the camera, as shown on the right in Figure 2-17. If the cover is spring loaded, it will pop open. Some cameras have an unlock knob that you have to twist to unlock the cover.

Some cameras put their memory cards in the same overall compartment as the battery. They go in different slots so you can't mix them up. The only danger is dropping the memory card into an empty battery compartment. If that happens, just turn the camera over and shake the card into your hand.

3. **Orient the battery and insert it into the battery compartment.**

WARNING

New batteries ship with a plastic cover that protects the contacts and keeps the battery from shorting out. Remove this cover before trying to put it in the camera.

Batteries go in contacts first. Many batteries have an arrow that tells you which way they should be inserted. Gently press any locking levers (shown in the center of Figure 2-17) out of the way. I use the corner of the battery to nudge mine.

FIGURE 2-17: Be sure to move the locking lever out of the way as you insert the battery.

4. **Press the battery in or until it locks in place.**

Make sure the locking lever locks the battery in place, as shown on the right in Figure 2-17. If your camera doesn't have a lever, press the battery in and use your finger to keep it from falling out as you close the cover.

5. **Close the battery compartment cover; it should lock in place.**

Removing a battery

Here's how to remove a battery:

1. **Turn the camera off.**

2. **Release the catch on the battery compartment cover.**

   The cover should pop or fall open.

3. **If necessary, press the battery lock lever in until it releases the battery.**

   The battery will spring up a bit, as shown in Figure 2-18. Some batteries just fall out.

4. **Take the battery out of the camera.**

   You can pull it with your fingers or hold the camera so that it falls out.

5. **If you want, put another battery in the camera.**

6. **Close the battery compartment door.**

TIP

   Most manufacturers recommend that you take batteries out of the camera if you aren't going to be using them. Likewise, they don't recommend leaving batteries in the charger after they have been fully charged. Keep your batteries safely tucked away in your camera bag and recharge them shortly before you plan on using them.

Inserting and Removing Memory Cards

Treat your memory cards as though they hold the most precious cargo. They do! Here are some general tips for handling memory cards:

>> **Don't expose memory cards to extreme weather.** That makes sense. Keep them in the camera, in a protective case, or stored in a card wallet.

>> **Normal magnetism is fine.** Contrary to what you may believe, flash drives (which a memory card is a subset of) aren't affected by normal magnetic fields. Notice that I said *normal* magnetic field: If you run the card through an X-ray or MRI machine (the one in your basement?), you may be in for trouble.

>> **Take a load off.** Memory cards aren't indestructible. While it may take a lot of force, they can be crushed. Try not to sit on them, step on them, drive over them, or rest heavy objects on them.

>> **Don't lose them.** At the risk of sounding repetitive, keep memory cards in the camera. Store extras in a protective case or card wallet. Don't scatter them all over your desk or in your vehicle.

Inserting a memory card

To insert a compatible memory card into your dSLR, follow these steps:

1. **Turn off the camera.**

Most cameras suggest strongly that the camera be powered down before swapping out memory cards.

2. **Open the card cover.**

Depending on your camera model, you may have to operate a card cover release latch. Other covers pull out and swing open, as shown in Figure 2-19.

3. **Orient and align the card properly.**

SD cards have a notched corner. You can use this to orient the card the correct way every time. For other cards, try to remember which way the label faces. Your camera may have an illustration that shows you the proper orientation of the card.

FIGURE 2-19:
This cover slides
back and then
swings open
to reveal the
card slot.

4. **Insert the card into the slot and press until it's securely in place.**

   An eject button may pop up, indicating that the card is in position. When inserting Compact Flash cards, be careful not to bend the pins inside your camera or card reader. Gently align the card in the slot and seat it properly on the pins before pressing further to secure it in place.

5. **Close the card cover.**

6. **Turn on the camera.**

7. **Check to see whether exposures register and the card seems to work.**

Removing a memory card

To remove the card, follow these steps:

1. **Turn off the camera.**

2. **Open the card cover.**

3. **Eject the card.**

   Depending on your camera model, press an eject button once to make the card pop up. This is how Compact Flash cards work. Or, gently press the card so that it releases and pops up, as shown in Figure 2-20. SD and Memory Stick cards work this way.

4. **Grab and fully remove the card.**

5. **Insert another card, if you want, and then close the cover.**

FIGURE 2-20:
This card is ready
to pull out.

Cleaning Your Camera

Cleaning your camera and lenses is an important part of the quality-control process. Your equipment will thank you, and you'll take better photos. The camera has lots of different elements to clean, so hang on!

REMEMBER

Check your manual and follow its specific cleaning instructions recommended by the manufacturer. They're generalized here by necessity.

Wiping off the camera body

To clean the camera body, dust it with canned air, a blower, a soft brush, or a lint-free cloth (see Figure 2-21). Photo shops such as Adorama and Amazon sell a number of microfiber products. They're easy to use and require no chemicals or cleaners. For more troublesome dirt, wet the cloth with a *little* water. If your camera is in *really bad* shape (wet, muddy, or stuff you can't clean), be safe and take it to an authorized service center and ask for assistance. I use an old toothbrush, sometimes dry and sometimes moist, to clean dust and other debris off of my cameras. Don't use organic solvents to clean your camera body. That means no thinners, alcohol, or benzene.

TIP

Turn off the camera before you clean its body. That way, you can push buttons and turn knobs without throwing off your settings.

FIGURE 2-21:
Wipe your
camera with a
nice cloth to keep
it clean.

Cleaning LCDs

WARNING

Treat the LCD screen gently. Don't use chemicals or abrasive cleaners when cleaning or you may mar or scratch the surface. In addition, pay special attention to the cloth you use. If it's rough (such as an industrial strength paper towel), you might scratch the LCD monitor. The same microfiber cleaning cloths you might use to clean a lens works equally well on the monitor, as shown in Figure 2-22. As more cameras move to touch-sensitive LCD monitors, get into the habit of turning the camera off before cleaning the monitor.

FIGURE 2-22:
Regularly give
your monitor a
gentle cleaning.

Cleaning inside the camera

Unless you're working in a NASA clean room, dust is going to eventually find its way into your camera. When dust sticks to the image sensor, the results are obvious: Big, fuzzy, dark spots invade your shots. If you're in doubt, photograph a clear blue sky or a white wall and check the photo for spots.

TIP

If your camera needs a serious cleaning inside, call for help. Look in your camera's manual for websites or phone numbers you can visit or call to find the nearest service center. Have your dSLR cleaned by someone trained and practiced in it.

Automatically dusting the image sensor

Many cameras have a *dusting*, or *self-cleaning* (sensor shaking) mode. This is your first line of defense against dust. The camera shakes the dust off the sensor to try to clean it. You don't have to open the camera, blow anything in, or swab anything out. Typically, the camera will clean itself when it starts up or shuts off. You may be able to change when your camera cleans itself, disable the behavior, and even activate it manually (see the left image in Figure 2-23). The image on the right in Figure 2-23 shows the notification you might see when the camera cleans itself.

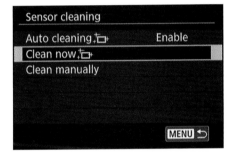 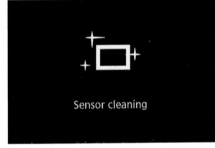

FIGURE 2-23: Initiating an automatic dust-off.

Blowing out dust manually

Some cameras have a feature that locks the mirror so that you can remove the lens and blow dust out of the camera body yourself. This is not an especially hair-raising procedure. I encourage you to give it a try.

WARNING

Make sure to read your camera's manual before attempting this and follow the instructions exactly. With that caveat out of the way, here are the general steps you'll follow to blow dust out of your camera:

REMEMBER

1. **Charge your camera's batteries.**

   Camera manufacturers recommend using fully charged batteries when locking the mirror up. If you have an AC power adapter, you can use it.

2. **Turn on the camera.**

3. **Go to your camera's sensor cleaning menu.**

4. **Turn on the manual cleaning mode.**

It may have any name: Mirror Lock Up, Mirror Up, or Sensor Cleaning. I am choosing that option on the left image in Figure 2-24. The right image shows the informational message the camera displays when it is ready.

FIGURE 2-24:
Setting up a
manual dusting.

5. **Take off the lens or remove the body cap and make sure the mirror is raised.**

If the mirror is still down, replace the lens or cap and turn the camera off. Return to Step 2 and start over. If you can't get the mirror to raise, and you know you're using the right menu, you may need to contact a service center.

6. **Tilt the camera so that the opening faces downward.**

This makes it easier for the dust to fall out of the camera when you blow it.

7. **Take a blower and squeeze-blow air into the sensor cavity three or four times.**

WARNING

- *Don't* push the tip of the blower into the open cavity. It isn't a vacuum cleaner. You get plenty of air movement by hovering the tip even with the lens mount or just outside the camera.

- *Don't* use a canned-air spray blower. Don't use a blower brush, either. Use a blower that you squeeze with your hand.

- *Don't* dally. The more you have the camera open, the more dust can get back in.

8. **Put down the blower and put the camera back together.**

9. **Turn off the camera.**

10. **Turn the camera back on and check to make sure it's working.**

Take a few test shots. Stop down to a small aperture and take a photo of the sky or your ceiling. Can you see any dust spots? If you do, you can repeat this series of steps and hope another round of cleaning works better, try swabbing the image sensor yourself (see the next section), or send in the camera for maintenance.

Swabbing or brushing the image sensor

If your camera needs a serious cleaning inside, send it to an authorized service center. You'll appreciate having your dSLR cleaned by someone trained and practiced in it. It's not the end of the world to pay for a bit of maintenance. You may want to schedule yearly cleanings, or have it looked at before important trips, holidays, occasions, or other very special events.

WARNING

If you insist on cleaning the sensor yourself, look in your manual for the proper procedures, if possible. *Don't open your camera and touch anything inside it unless you're sure of yourself and willing to take the risk.* However, many people swab their sensors, and do it successfully. Look for more information on the Internet or visit your local camera shop if you want to try this.

Protecting Your Camera

Do yourself a favor: Invest in the right protective gear for your camera, lenses, and accessories.

Using a camera strap

Using a strap is an important step toward safeguarding your camera. My straps have saved me and my cameras a number of times. You will feel a tug when you drop your camera, but it won't crash to the ground and ruin your day. Get a comfortable strap. The more comfortable it is, the more likely you'll be to use it for long periods of time. Standard straps come in many styles and with different features. If you're looking for something more adventurous, BlackRapid (`www.blackrapid.com`) makes some very unique sling straps.

TIP

As an additional safety precaution, put the strap over your neck before mounting or removing your camera from a tripod. I learned this lesson the day I triggered the tripod release lever without having a good grip on the camera. The camera took a nosedive off the tripod due to the heavy lens, and I was barely able to catch it.

Getting a camera bag

Camera bags protect your gear and make it easier for you to carry it around. I have several bags and pack the one that matches my needs that day. Look for these characteristics when deciding on a bag:

>> **Type:** Conventional carry bags have a shoulder strap and a handle. Most people put them down when shooting. Large conventional camera bags make

great base camps to work out of. Smaller conventional bags hold less gear but are easier to carry. Sling bags tend to be smaller and slip over your shoulder. They are meant to be worn more, and swing around from back to front when you need access to your gear. Backpacks have two shoulder straps and are great for hiking.

>> **Size:** Most bags let you carry a dSLR and a few lenses. If you need more space, get a bigger bag. If you need less, look for a smaller bag.

>> **Padding:** Bags with more padding protect your gear better.

>> **Strap support:** Look for a bag with a wide, padded, comfortable strap if you're going to be wearing it a lot.

TIP

Be sensible when packing your bag. My experience is that bags are easier to use and more practical if you focus on packing the essentials. Most often, you won't need to take everything with you on every excursion.

Buying extra lens and camera caps

Always secure your camera and lens with the proper caps. Front and rear lens caps go on lenses. Body caps go on the camera body in place of a lens. Consider buying extra caps as backups in case you misplace any. I have a number of extra rear lens and camera body caps (see Figure 2-25). As long as the lens mount is the same, rear lens caps are interchangeable. Likewise, given the same lens mount, camera body caps fit the same, whether the camera's entry level or professional.

FIGURE 2-25:
Extra body and lens caps make it easier to protect your gear.

Buying multiple front lens caps isn't as practical. Lenses with different front filter sizes require differently sized front lens caps. If you use large filters and step-up rings to match lenses with the filters, then you should buy several front lens caps the same size as your standardized filters. In my case, that's 77mm. When the step-up ring is screwed into the lens, it requires the larger lens cap, not the original.

Armoring your camera

You can buy silicon armor to provide extra protection for your dSLR, as shown in Figure 2-26. It's inexpensive and shields the camera from occasional bumps, dings, and scrapes. Everything that needs to be exposed — the lens mount, built-in flash, shutter button, dial, and so forth — is, yet most of the camera is covered, including the buttons on the back. There's even a plastic cover to protect the LCD screen. For a wide range of cases made for specifically dSLR models, check out easyCover (easycover.eu).

FIGURE 2-26:
Body armor gives the camera additional protection.

Dealing with adverse weather

It's not always sunny and 72 degrees outside with no chance of rain. If you want to shoot in bad weather, protect yourself and your camera. Here are some suggestions for being out in different conditions:

>> **Dust:** If you're working in extremely dusty conditions, try putting a rain cover around your camera. That will help keep the dust out. Don't remove your lens in a dust storm. Be wary of scratching lenses and monitors if they are covered with dust and you decide to clean. To avoid scratching your lens, use a blower or soft brush to clean the glass when around dust. Don't use a microfiber cloth or the carbon end of a lens pen.

>> **Heat:** Don't leave your camera lying around in the sun, which is hot and can melt your gear. Not only that, LCD monitors don't like heat and can become discolored. Be prepared to let your camera adjust to the heat and humidity when going outside from an air-conditioned interior. The lens will fog up if you

WARNING

don't let it sit outside with the lens cap on until it warms up. You can also place your camera in a non–air-conditioned room to adjust before leaving.

» **Wet or humid weather:** Rain equals water, and water is bad for your camera. If it's a slow sprinkle, the threat isn't that bad. Monitor the situation and keep your camera wiped dry when it gets too wet. If you're in a full-on rain (see Figure 2-27), don't go out without a rain cover for your camera. You can find inexpensive rain covers online. You can also make your own from plastic bags and duct tape.

Try to keep lens changes to a minimum in wet weather. If you must, seek cover or point the camera away from the spray.

High humidity is a threat to the electronics in your camera. Take shelter in a dry, air-conditioned location as often as you can to keep your camera from picking up too much moisture.

FIGURE 2-27: Take shelter or protect your camera from heavy rain.

» **Cold:** Working in the cold makes everything more difficult. Plastic and metal get extremely cold and uncomfortable to touch. You can't wear mittens the size of boxing gloves and easily press buttons or turn dials. Thin gloves can be slippery or ineffective against the cold.

If you do a lot of cold-weather shooting, check out special gloves designed with silicon "grippies" that make holding the camera easier. Some have finger caps that come off, exposing one or more fingertips to operate the camera with. Some are fingerless.

Always give your lenses and camera time to adapt to the cold. If you don't, the lenses will fog up and you'll be forced to wait anyway. Set the bag outside to adapt while you stay warm inside.

When you're working in the cold, plastics become more brittle. Be careful not to drop your camera or lens. In addition, your batteries don't last as long as in warm weather.

>> **Snow:** Snow is easier on the camera than it is on you. You will have to deal with cold temperatures, moisture on the camera from melting snow, possibly high winds and low visibility, different depths of snow, and slippery footing. Keep your camera and lens wiped dry as often as you can, and be careful. Lens hoods can help protect the lens from blowing snow. Despite the difficulties, shooting in a raging snowstorm (see Figure 2-28) can be very rewarding and yield beautiful photos.

FIGURE 2-28: Snowy conditions are a challenge to shoot in, but worth it.

>> **Underwater:** Buy a special underwater housing that's certified for use with your camera. They vary greatly in capability and price, so shop around. Some are little more than sturdy plastic bags with room for lenses and access for your fingers. Others look like they were invented by Jacques Cousteau.

Make sure to take care of yourself, too. Wear clothing suited to the weather and don't forget about footwear. One of my favorite accessories is the pair of study waterproof boots shown in Figure 2-29. I take them with me whenever I expect to be trudging through mud, in and around rivers and lakes, and even snow.

FIGURE 2-29: These boots are perfect accessories for sloppy conditions.

Chapter **3**

Learning about Lenses

Prepare yourself for an action-packed chapter on lenses. You'll start out learning how to decode lens names, which are packed with helpful identifying information. Next, you'll see how lenses are organized into different categories. After that, you'll complete a course on lens anatomy, and finish up with very practical information on working with and cleaning lenses. Sounds like a winning combination.

This chapter provides an overview on lenses: technical and handling information. I know what you're thinking — what more can I possibly say about lenses? Turns out: a lot! So much more that I devote Book 2 to shooting with different types of lenses. Head there when you're ready to see in-depth practical applications of each lens in action.

Identifying and Naming Lenses

All dSLR lenses share a few basic characteristics, which, like cameras, are listed with the name. For example, the name *Canon EF-S 18-55mm f/3.5-5.6 IS STM* (see Figure 3-1) says a lot about the lens. You just have to know what you're looking at. By the same token, the name of Nikon's *AF-S DX NIKKOR 35mm f/1.8G* lens is packed with information. Each name lists the manufacturer or brand, lens mount, focal length, aperture information, and other identifying characteristics. This section gives you the information you need to make sense of them.

Image Stabilization

Maximum apertures

Mount   Focal lengths

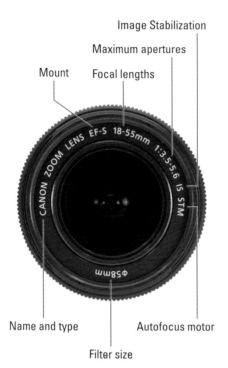

FIGURE 3-1:
Many lenses print
information on
the front.

Name and type   Autofocus motor

Filter size

REMEMBER

Quite often, lens information is printed on the front of the lens. However, some lenses are devoid of any markings up front, as shown in Figure 3-2. You'll need to look for identifying markings and information on the side of those lenses, shown in Figure 3-3.

FIGURE 3-2:
If the lens has
nothing shown
on the front. . .

DX format   G-type

Maximum aperture

Focal length

Brand

Autofocus motor

FIGURE 3-3:
. . .look to
the side.

Brand name

Most lenses list the brand at or near the beginning of the lens name. In some cases it is the same as the camera. Here is a list of the names of popular lens manufacturers that you might see:

>> Canon lenses use the Canon name.

>> Nikon lenses use the NIKKOR brand name.

>> Sony creates its own lenses, but also use the Zeiss brand. Older Minolta A-mount lenses are compatible with Sony A-mount cameras because Minolta created the A-mount that Sony adopted (like the old Remington razor commercial, they liked it so much they bought the company).

>> Pentax lenses are named Pentax.

>> Olympus E-system Four Thirds dSLRs use Zuiko lenses. Its Micro Four Thirds cameras use M.Zuiko lenses.

>> Third-party lenses: Sigma, Tamron, and Tokina all make dSLR lenses that are compatible with the main camera brands. Zeiss makes some manual focus lenses compatible with Canon and Nikon cameras, including the Milvus line. Zeiss has many high-quality lenses with features for both still photographers and cinematographers who use dSLR bodies. There are other brands out there if you look hard enough: Samyang, Rokinon, Vivitar, Yongnuo, and more.

Lens mount

The lens mount is where the lens attaches and locks on to the camera. There is no universal design. Each camera manufacturer creates its own, which means they are naturally incompatible with each other. I cover lens mounts by manufacturer in Book 1, Chapter 1, so I won't duplicate that here, except to say that lens mount is not always present in the lens name. For example, the NIKKOR 35mm f/1.8G lens does not mention the mount because all Nikon dSLRs use the F-mount. Canon EF-S 18-55mm lens indicates that it is an EF-S lens, having the EF lens mount, but not compatible with full-frame bodies.

Focal length

Focal length is the distance between the optical center of the lens and the image sensor. It is expressed in millimeters. Zoom lenses have a focal length range, such as 18-55mm. Prime lenses, on the other hand, have a fixed focal length. You can't zoom in or out with a prime lens.

I won't bore you with all the math and science behind things (even though I am going to sneak some in). What you should know is that, in conjunction with the size of the camera's sensor, focal length affects whether you see a wide or narrow slice of life through the lens. This is technically called the *angle of view*. In the most general terms, lenses with short focal lengths (they have smaller numbers) are considered wide-angle while lenses that feature longer focal lengths (with larger numbers) are called telephoto lenses. For example, 12mm is considered an ultra-wide angle lens while 300mm is a telephoto lens.

Notice that I mentioned that the sensor size plays a role in the angle of view. Photos taken with the same lens come out looking differently, depending on whether the lens is mounted on a full-frame versus a cropped-frame camera. The crop factor (turn to Book 1, Chapter 1 if you need a refresher) helps you figure out by how much:

>> If you mount a 50mm lens on a full-frame camera with a crop factor of 1.0x, photos will look like you took them with a 50mm lens. This is because the full-frame sensor is the reference you use to compare.

>> If you mount the same lens on an APS-C camera with a crop factor of 1.6x, photos will look like you took them with an 80mm lens mounted on a full-frame camera. In other words, the 80mm lens on the full-frame camera would give you an equivalent view as a 50mm lens on an APS-C camera with a crop factor of 1.6x. 80mm is the equivalent focal length.

>> If you mount a 50mm lens on a Four Thirds sensor camera with a crop factor of 2.0x, photos will look as if you took them with a 100mm lens on a full-frame dSLR. In this case, the equivalent focal length is 100mm.

This focal length produced by multiplying the actual focal length of the lens by the crop factor of the camera has a name. It's called the *35mm equivalent* focal length.

WARNING

You don't get free optical zoom with a cropped-frame sensor. The photo is *cropped,* not zoomed. It looks zoomed, but the lens is not providing any additional resolution or detail. You're just seeing it from a different perspective.

TECHNICAL STUFF

If you're interested, here's how crop factor is calculated: Divide a dimension of 35mm film by the same dimension of the image sensor. For dSLR sensors that have the same aspect ratio as 35mm film, you can use width, height, or the diagonal. For example, to calculate the crop factor of a Canon APS-C camera, divide 24mm (the height of 35mm film) by 14.8mm (the sensor height). The result is 1.62, which can be rounded and written as a crop factor of 1.6x. For Four Thirds cameras, I suggest comparing diagonal measurements, which can be calculated by taking the square root of the sum of the squares of the two sides of the sensor (this is the famous Pythagorean Theorem).

The long and the short of it is this: If you know how to put focal lengths in 35mm equivalent terms, you can match the right lenses with your camera to produce the photos you're after. For example, if you are interested in replicating the look and feel of classic 50mm film photography using an APS-C camera with a crop factor of 1.5x, you should use a 35mm lens. The 35mm equivalent focal length of that lens/sensor combo is 52.5mm. Close enough to 50mm for me.

Aperture

Camera lenses have an adjustable aperture — an opening — in their center to allow light to pass through them and into the camera body. The relative size of the aperture is expressed as a number called an *f-number* or *f-stop.* It is not a direct measurement, but a ratio of the focal length of the lens to the diameter of the aperture. F-numbers are written with the letter f, then a forward slash, and then the value. Like this: f/8 or f/5.6. Sometimes the aperture is written with a capital F and without the slash: F2.8. The tricky thing for new photographers to remember is that larger f-numbers let in less light than smaller ones. For example, f/5.6 lets in more light than f/8.

Some lenses are listed with a single aperture, like the NIKKOR 50mm f/1.4G. The f-number shown, f/1.4, is the maximum aperture that the lens can use. You have to look into the specification to find the minimum aperture. All prime lenses list a single aperture. Some high-quality zoom lenses feature a constant aperture. Other lenses, like the Canon EF-S 18-55mm f/3.5-5.6, list a range of apertures. These are the maximum apertures possible at each of the focal length limits. In this case, the first aperture, f/3.5, is the maximum aperture when the lens is zoomed out to 18mm. The second aperture, f/5.6, is the maximum aperture possible when the lens is zoomed in to 55mm.

Knowing the maximum aperture a lens is capable of is important because it gives you an indication of how well the lens performs. Lenses that let in a lot of light give you more flexibility as a photographer.

You can calculate the f-number by dividing the focal length of the lens by the diameter of the aperture. For example, if the aperture were open on a 50mm lens to about 9mm, the f-number at that setting would be f/5.6. From this, you can see that changing the focal length of the lens by zooming in or out changes the f-number without having to touch the aperture control on the lens or camera.

Image stabilization

Some camera manufacturers feature lens-mounted image stabilization while others implement it within the camera body. In the latter case, you will not see image stabilization listed as part of the lens name or present anywhere physically on the lens. In the former case, you can rest assured that companies proudly announce the fact as part of their lens naming scheme. Many wide-angle, prime, some mid-range focal length zoom lenses, and less expensive telephoto lenses do not normally have image stabilization.

Nikon uses the term Vibration Reduction, abbreviated as VR. Canon calls its feature Image Stabilization, abbreviated as IS. Depending on the lens, you may be able to select specific IS modes, from 1 to 3. Each is optimized to counter a particular type of movement. You will not see VR or IS on any Nikon or Canon lens that does not have image stabilization.

Third-party lens manufacturers may or may not have image stabilization technology. Sigma lenses with image stabilization are labeled OS, for Optical Stabilization. Tamron calls its stabilization technology Vibration Compensation (VC). Tokina lenses equipped with a Vibration Correction Module (VCM) are stabilized.

When companies say their image stabilization features reduce shake and vibration by a number of stops, you can lower the shutter speed by that many stops and still take a sharp photo. Of course, it doesn't always work as well as advertised, and there is a limit to how slow you can shoot without a tripod or other support even if you have image stabilization engaged. The effectiveness also depends on what type and how much movement is encountered. I would not expect great results if I were doing jumping jacks.

The old–school rule recommends that you not set a shutter speed any slower than the inverse of your effective focal length. If you're using a 50mm lens on a camera with a crop factor of 1.5x, the 35mm equivalent focal length is 75mm. Therefore, you should set the shutter speed to 1/75 second or faster when shooting handheld (round that to 1/80, which is a common shutter speed on most cameras). Stay with me, because here's where the number of stops comes in. If you use 1/80 second as your unaided minimum shutter speed and then engage image stabilization whose effectiveness is up to two stops, you can theoretically slow the shutter speed to 1/20 second. Not bad.

Other identifiers

There are a number of other lens identifiers that may make it into the name. You can put them into categories to make sense of them:

- **Quality:** Canon L-series lenses are their highest quality product. Sony designates its high-end lens series as G Master.

- **Type:** Nikon identifies the type of lens by a letter that immediately follows the aperture of the lens. For example, the 50mm f/1.4G lens is type G. The latest is E-type, which has a different type of interior aperture mechanism than prior lenses (electromagnetic instead of mechanical), enabling smooth and constant control over the aperture by the camera. Its G-type lenses were the first to do away with a manual aperture control ring. You have to set the aperture from the camera, not on the lens. Older D-type lenses have a combination of new (autofocus) and old (most have a manual aperture ring) technologies and are still very popular.

- **Autofocus motor:** Canon have two autofocus motor technologies: USM and STM. Nikon uses the term AF-S (Auto Focus—Silent Wave) to identify the motor type of its lenses. Consumer-level Nikon cameras do not have internal focus motors and require AF-S lenses for autofocus to function. Pentax lens motors are designated DC or SDM.

- **Glass:** Some companies put additional identifiers in the lens name to showcase their glass quality or coatings. Nikon, for example, uses ED to indicate Extra-low Dispersion glass, which resists chromatic aberrations. Pentax lenses can have special HD or SP coatings.

- **Sensor size compatibility:** Nikon labels lenses designed to work best with cropped-frame dSLRs with DX. DX lenses can be used on FX camera bodies in crop mode. Canon uses the EF-S mount identifier similarly, except that EF-S lenses are not compatible with full-frame cameras. Sony DT lenses can be used with cropped and full-frame cameras (you will get a cropped photo in that case, however).

>> **Macro:** Some lenses are identified by the term *macro*. This means they are designed to get in close to focus and reproduce what they capture nearer to actual size than other lenses. Nikon names its macro lenses *micro*.

I don't have room to put every combination of identifier from all manufacturers. Take the knowledge you've gained from this small section to help you research more lens terminology on your own.

Other lens characteristics

If you look at the supporting product page for a lens or read the manual, you'll run across other specifications that describe even more characteristics. You may be interested in knowing these facts about the lens:

>> **Filter diameter:** Identifies the diameter, in millimeters, of the screw-in filter compatible with the lens.

>> **Minimum focusing distance:** This is the closest distance the lens can focus at.

>> **Minimum aperture:** The smallest aperture you can set. Knowing the maximum aperture is typically far more important. However, minimum aperture gives you an indication of how the lens will perform in some situations.

>> **Construction details:** Information about the number of optical elements in the lens, which are often arranged into groups.

>> **Angle of view/field of view:** Angle of view measures, in degrees, the width of your view through the lens, either horizontally, vertically, or diagonally. Field of view describes the size of the area captured at a known distance. If you shine a flashlight against a wall, the angle of view tells you how wide or narrow the beam is. The field of view is how much wall you can light, which changes if you move forward or back. Angle of view is irrespective of distance.

Older lenses

Older lenses may have different marking than you're used to. The lens in Figure 3-4, for example, has minimal markings on the front. The side, shown in Figure 3-5, has no identifying information. The colorful scales and numbers show the focal distance, depth of field, and aperture. Be prepared to do some extra research to make sure any lenses you look at are compatible with your camera body or any you plan to purchase. Although this lens was manufactured in 1981 or so, it still works on many Nikon dSLRs.

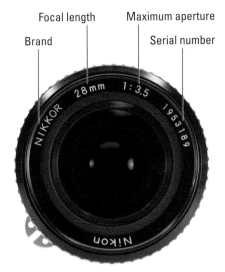

Brand Focal length Maximum aperture Serial number

FIGURE 3-4:
You may have to research old lenses for more information.

FIGURE 3-5:
There are no helpful identifiers on the side of this 28mm prime.

Categorizing Lenses

This section explains and summarizes many of the most-used digital SLR lens categories in use today. It's pretty helpful to get to know how manufacturers categorize their lenses and how photographers use them.

Interestingly, there are a few different ways to categorize lenses. You can organize them into groups based on their focal length (see Table 3-1). You can also organize them around whether they have a fixed aperture or can zoom in and out. There are many types of zoom lenses, ranging from those that specialize in wide-angles, to general purpose zooms, to telephoto zooms.

TABLE 3-1   ## Rough Focal Length Categories

Category	Full-frame	APS-C	Four Thirds / Micro Four Thirds
Ultra wide-angle	20mm and below	15mm and below	10mm and below
Wide-angle	20-40mm	15-25mm	10-20mm
Normal	40-60mm	25-40mm	20-30mm
Near/medium telephoto	60-200mm	40-135mm	30-100mm
Telephoto	200-300mm	135-200mm	100-150mm
Super telephoto	300mm and up	200mm and up	150mm and over

Some specialty lenses don't fit into other categories, while others fit into more than one. For example, a 400mm lens is both a prime and a telephoto lens.

Normal lenses

Lenses with focal length values approximately the same as the diagonal measurement of the image sensor are considered *normal* lenses. They are called normal because they cover the same basic field of view as the human eye. Most kit lenses cover the entire normal focal length range of the camera they are bundled with.

For full-frame cameras, 50mm lenses are the gold standard. There is a history and tradition of fantastic photography built around these lenses. If you're using a zoom lens, anywhere between 40-60mm puts you in the normal range. For cameras with cropped-frame sensors, what appears normal depends on the crop factor. For crop factors of 1.5x and 1.6x, set your zoom lens between about 25mm and 40mm. If you want to use a prime lens, 35mm puts you very close to that classic normal lens look. Figure 3-6 shows a nice portrait taken with a cropped-frame dSLR at 35mm — right in the middle of the normal range. For Four Thirds and Micro Four Thirds cameras with crop factors of 2.0x, zoom lenses between 20mm and 30mm to fit into this category. If you want a normal Four Thirds prime lens, look for something around 25mm.

Wide-angle lenses

Focal length values less than the diagonal measurement of the image sensor are considered *wide-angle*. Wide-angle lenses have impressive angles of view and are able to capture large fields of view. They are, however, prone to distortion. Most kit lenses have the ability to shoot wide-angle shots, although they may not cover the entire range.

For full-frame cameras, wide-angle territory covers everything below 35mm. I took the shot in Figure 3-7 using a full-frame camera with 28-105mm lens set to

28mm. While not extreme, it's still wide enough to capture the river quite nicely. For APS-C sensors, that equates to approximately 24mm. Four Thirds and Micro Four Third lenses are considered wide-angle around 17mm. Some lenses are considered ultra wide-angle lenses. These lenses are incredibly fun to use, and capture sweeping landscapes and interiors of all sizes beautifully. Their focal lengths are roughly 14-26mm for full-frame, 10-17mm for APS-C cameras, and 7-14mm for Four Thirds. For more on shooting with wide-angle lenses, turn to Book 2, Chapter 2.

FIGURE 3-6:
Normal focal lengths produce classic photos.

FIGURE 3-7:
Wide angles capture scenic vistas.

Telephoto lenses

Lenses with focal length values greater than the diagonal measurement of the image sensor are considered *telephoto* lenses. Dedicated telephoto lenses abound, and most everyday kit lenses can reach into telephoto range when they are fully zoomed in.

For full-frame cameras, focal lengths greater than 60mm or so are considered telephoto. I took the photo shown in Figure 3-8 using a full-frame camera. The focal length is 73mm — ideal for portraits. For APS-C cameras, telephoto focal lengths start at approximately 40mm. Four Thirds and Micro Four Thirds cameras begin the telephoto range around 30mm. Initially, the telephoto range is called *near* or *medium* telephoto. As you continue to move into longer focal lengths, the category changes to *telephoto,* and then *super-telephoto* (have a glance back to Table 3-1 to see the focal lengths of these categories). Turn to Book 2, Chapter 4 to learn more about telephoto lenses.

FIGURE 3-8:
Near telephotos are great for portraits.

Prime lenses

A *prime* lens (see Figure 3-9) has a fixed focal length. You can't zoom in or out with prime lenses. When you compose your shots, you have to move closer or farther away to zoom in and out. Its magnification level is fixed from the day you buy it until your grandkids sell it on eBay.

FIGURE 3-9:
Prime lenses do
not zoom in
or out.

Prime lenses specialize. Everything is optimized for the lens to produce the best photos at its focal length. The downside to prime lenses is the major reason why zoom lenses are so popular: People get tired of being limited to a single focal length and the time it takes to swap lenses when they want to change it.

TIP

When shopping for prime lenses, look for focal lengths you find yourself using the most or that meet a particular need that you have to capture photos with a specific look. There are a lot of lenses in this category. You'll find wide-angle primes, normal, *portrait primes* in the near telephoto range, and all kinds of telephoto and super-telephoto prime lenses.

General-purpose zoom lenses

General-purpose zoom lenses (see Figure 3-10), also called *standard zoom* lenses, excel in versatility. Most kit lenses sold are in this category. They include wide-angle, normal, and near-telephoto focal lengths. It's hard to go wrong with general-purpose zoom lenses.

FIGURE 3-10:
General-purpose
zoom lenses are
versatile and take
good photos.

Learning about Lenses

Wide-angle zoom lenses

A *wide-angle zoom* lens zooms in and out, just as general-purpose zoom lenses, but with a focal length range that's limited to wide-angle territory. This gives them a versatility that a wide-angle prime lens won't have. Being able to zoom in and out when you're capturing a landscape or a tight interior is a welcome feature because you're often limited in how you can move in relation to the scene. Ultra wide-angle zoom lenses (see Figure 3-11) give you expanded wide-angle coverage. Wide-angle zoom lenses really are great at what they do and fun to use. I heartily recommend them.

FIGURE 3-11:
A wide-angle zoom lens is an excellent addition to your bag.

Telephoto zoom lenses

Typical *telephoto zoom* lenses operate over a huge range of telephoto focal lengths. There is a lot of variety between telephoto zooms, both in the starting and ending focal lengths. You'll find some that specialize in the near-telephoto range, some that extend into telephoto and super-telephoto focal lengths, and more.

Specialty lenses

Other specialty lenses offer creative and artistic uses:

>> **Macro** lenses specialize in capturing extreme close-up photos of objects. Although they don't generally magnify, macro lenses appear to because the subjects look so much larger than normal. This is achieved because macro lenses have a *reproduction ratio* (the size of an object on the sensor compared to the actual size) as close to 1:1 as possible. Most macro lenses are primes.

>> **Fisheye** lenses capture scenes with an angle of view approaching 180-degrees. The photos are characterized by extreme barrel distortion, which bulges the center of the photo out, often to the point where the entire photo turns into a circle.

>> **Tilt-shift** lenses (see Figure 3-12) can change the orientation of the focal plane by tilting. The effect of angling the focal plane is to completely discombobulate what should be in focus compared to a normal lens. Objects can look surreal and toylike. These lenses can also move the imaging circle of the lens that hits the camera's image sensor by shifting. This allows you to move the subject's location within the photo without moving the camera. The shift effect is useful when photographing subjects that can easily distort if you have to point the camera up or down to capture them.

FIGURE 3-12: Tilt-shift lenses are specialty lenses that capture unique photos.

You might have noticed that I have praised every type of lens I have described. That's because I love them all. Each serves a purpose. Your challenge as a photographer (well, one of many) is to find the lens that suits *your* purpose, whether that's shooting artistic shots, portraits, landscapes, or fast-moving action.

>> **Pinhole** lenses have a small hole in them, about the size of a pinhole (thus the name). They don't actually have a lens, there is no way to zoom in and out, and you cannot focus. Basically, they are a plastic body cover with a pinhole in it. It's pretty easy to make one yourself if you want to try it out. Expect longer exposure times or higher ISO speeds due to the small aperture. Pinhole lenses create soft, dreamy photos.

>> **Creative lenses** break the mold of most traditional lens types. Here are a few popular types:

- *Lensbaby* lenses were originally based around a mechanism that resembled a bellows. Later, the Composer and Composer Pro were released, which were also manual focus, but made using a swivel ball mechanism. The Composer Pro mounts directly to the camera's lens mount and holds different interchangeable optics with varying properties. You can angle the lens in different ways, which moves the focal plane somewhat like a tilt-shift lens does. Optics range from the Sweet 35 to pinhole, plastic, and double-glass. The effects are endless.

- *Holga* cameras are cheap plastic film cameras that have a large following. They create very distinctive photos with dark corners and a soft focus. You can join the fun by mounting a plastic Holga dSLR lens on your camera. Very cool. I love mine.

- *Diana+* are similar to Holga lenses, but have much longer effective focal lengths. For example, the Diana+ fisheye lens acts like a standard lens on a dSLR. Diana+ lenses are meant to be dreamy and artistic.

Looking at Lens Anatomy

Knowing what the different parts and pieces on lenses are is as important as knowing what all the buttons, dials, and displays on your camera body are for. Depending on the lens you have, it might have these features (see Figures 3-13 through 3-16 for reference):

Auto/Manual focus switch

Focus ring

Zoom ring

Lens release button

Image Stabilizer (IS) switch

FIGURE 3-13:
This kit lens has a number of features to learn.

>> **Hood mount:** Many lenses come with a detachable lens hood, which usually rotates on with a quarter- or half-turn. Lens hoods block stray light from entering the lens, but may cause *vignetting* (when the corners of the photo looks darker than the center).

>> **Filter threads:** Most lenses mount screw-in filters at the front. Filter size is measured in millimeters. On some lenses (those with very large front diameters, for instance), filters go toward the rear and are dropped in with special trays.

>> **Focus mode switch:** Switch between manual and auto focus. Some telephoto lenses let you choose a distance region. Not all lenses have this switch.

>> **Zoom ring:** On zoom lenses, the zoom ring changes the focal length, which lets you zoom in and out. Depending on the lens, the zoom ring may be larger than the focus ring. Some lenses do not turn when they zoom in and out, but rather push or pull.

>> **Focusing ring:** Use this ring to focus manually. In the days when manual focus was the only option, focus rings were often larger than zoom rings.

Their importance is generally diminished now, so they've gotten much smaller on lenses that autofocus.

>> **Vibration reduction (VR) or image stabilization (IS) switch:** Turns on the lens's internal vibration reduction or image stabilization feature. When your camera is mounted on a tripod and you are not panning or moving it, you should turn this feature off. Check your lens manual for details. Some Nikon lenses, for example, have a special tripod mode that changes what type of movement the lens will counteract.

>> **Focal length scale:** Zoom lenses show you what your lens's focal length is, as shown in Figure 3-14. Line up the number with the focal length index line.

FIGURE 3-14:
The focal length scale is on top of the lens.

Zoom position index   Focal length scale

>> **Distance or depth-of-field scale:** The scale (see Figure 3-15) shows you the *focal plane distance* (the distance that the lens is focused at, measured from the camera sensor) and sometimes the depth of field. Though this feature is handy at times, it's becoming much less prominent on new lenses.

>> **Lock switch:** Some lenses let you lock in the current focal length. This prevents *focal length creep* when you're pointing the camera down. Some cameras let you lock in the focus, as opposed to the focal length.

>> **Mount:** The rear of the lens is the mount, which locks into the camera. Keep the rear cover on lenses when not in use.

Distance scale

FIGURE 3-15:
Some lenses give distance and depth of field information.

Depth of field indicators

>> **Lens mount index:** There's usually a dot on the side or rear of the lens. Match it up to the corresponding mark on the camera mount before inserting it into the camera.

>> **CPU contacts:** These little gizmos send computerized data to the camera from the lens. See Figure 3-16.

WARNING

CPU contacts are critical to modern lenses. Don't bend them, break them, or otherwise mess with them. Keep them covered.

Mounting index

CPU contacts

FIGURE 3-16:
Modern lenses and dSLRs communicate through these contacts.

Lens mount

> » **Aperture ring:** Older lenses (and some new or specialized lenses) have an aperture ring on the lens. Newer, computerized lenses forego it — you have to set the aperture in-camera.

Working with Lenses

The skills you use when handling lenses are just as important as those you use when handling the camera body. This section covers how to grip your lenses, mount and remove them, how to zoom in and out, switch from auto to manual focus, how to manually focus, and how to activate image stabilization. When you treat your lenses well, they will give you a lifetime of service.

WARNING

Lenses are round and they like to roll. Take care not to lay them on their side next to a table edge. Some lenses are tall and can be knocked over easily. Then they roll off the table and hit the floor. Please secure your flailing arms, loose elbows, cats, flying squirrels, and other forms of clumsiness when you set lenses down. Place your unattached lenses in their cases, your camera bag, or other suitable storage container to secure them.

Getting a grip

This section prepares you to mount and remove lenses by suggesting two different types of grips. I've written the material from the perspective of removing a lens, which is the more perilous task. To use these grips when attaching lenses, put your hands in the same positions. The difference is that when you grab the lens with your right hand, it's not attached to the camera. Your right hand will move it into position while your left hand (and possibly body) steady the camera.

Grip 1

Refer to Figure 3-17 to see one of the recommended grips and follow these steps to execute it:

1. **Hold the camera's left side with your left hand.**

   Press its right side in to your body for additional support.

2. **Put your left thumb on top of the cameras (in this case, on the mode dial) and stretch your left pinky underneath the camera for additional grip.**

   The camera will be facing to your right. Use your left index finger to press the lens-release button when necessary. If the lens-release button is on the side of the shutter button (Pentax cameras), you'll use your right index finger or knuckle instead.

3. **Use an overhand grip on the lens the way you would put your hand on a railing.**

The C formed by your right index finger and thumb grips the lens from the top and faces the camera body.

FIGURE 3-17:
Grip 1 uses your body to help support the camera.

Grip 2

Refer to Figure 3-18 to see the second recommended grip. This grip is similar to Grip 1 in that the camera faces to the right. However, rather than use your body for support, your repositioned left hand does all the heavy lifting. This grip does not work as well with cameras that have their lens-release buttons on the shutter button side of the camera, such as Pentax dSLRs. I'll explain how you should change the grip as I go along.

1. **Angle the camera and grip it in your left hand.**

The main point of initial contact is the skin between the thumb and index finger. Your left palm extends down the camera back while your left thumb wraps over the top of the camera. In this case, the base of my left thumb covers the LCD panel.

Pentax users should place their left thumb on the back of the camera, toward the top, rather than wrapping it around. This gives you the reach you'll need later. If you have large hands, you might be able to put your thumb on top of the camera.

2. **Firmly grip the camera with your left thumb.**

This is where you get most of the strength of this grip.

3. **Reach down with the fingers on your left hand to the back of the camera and grab the bottom.**

Your left index finger rests on the LCD monitor. Use it to stabilize things. You should be able to hold the entire weight of the camera with this hand. (It feels like you're shaking hands with the camera, using your left hand.)

If using a Pentax camera, you should wrap your left fingers farther under the camera than shown. You need to be able to reach the lens-release button with the middle finger on your left hand. Grip the camera with the ring and pinky fingers on your left hand. The strength of your grip comes from the base of the left palm and those two fingers.

4. **Put your right hand on top of the lens.**

Grip the lens near the lens collar (the part of the lens that's nearest the camera body). Your right thumb should be on the side of the lens nearest you.

5. **Use the knuckle on your right index finger to press the lens-release button in when you're removing a lens.**

The last part sounds dodgy until you do it. Then it feels totally natural. If you're using a Pentax camera, use the middle finger on your left hand.

FIGURE 3-18:
Grip 2 requires your left hand to support the camera.

Tips and pointers

Here are some things to keep in mind when using these grips:

>> If you don't feel like you can hold the camera and remove or attach lenses without dropping something, mount the camera on a tripod or set it down. You have no reason to feel embarrassed.

>> Try angling the front of the camera down a bit. Although it may feel awkward at first, this position helps prevent dust and other debris from getting into the camera.

>> Practice so that you can attach and remove lenses without angling the camera up to see what you're doing. After some experience, you should be able to attach and remove lenses while blindfolded.

>> Your grip doesn't have to be as steady when changing lenses on smaller cameras. You can sort of wing it. However, heavy cameras offer more of a challenge.

>> If the camera is mounted on a tripod, most of the handholding and camera-supporting descriptions in this section are moot. The camera should be well supported by the tripod. Hold tightly to the lens, however.

>> If you're using a lens-mounted support (monopod or other), turn the camera instead of the lens to remove it.

Mounting a lens

Although mounting lenses isn't difficult, it can be a little frightening until you get used to it. I remember being a bit nervous about the camera's insides being open to the world while I made a lens swap. Don't be. Unless you're in a dust storm or outside in the rain with no cover when changing lenses, the camera will survive. Just don't drop the lens (no pressure).

TIP

The key is to be quick without rushing and to be firm without being harsh. Got it?

Here's how to attach a lens to a digital SLR camera:

1. **Turn off the camera.**

    If you forget (I do all the time), it isn't the end of the world. Ideally, though, you want the power to be off.

2. **Remove the camera body cap or lens, if one is attached.**

    Most body caps twist off. Some have a locking function. Put away the cap or lens, if necessary. See the next section for how-to steps on removing lenses.

3. **Quickly remove the rear lens cap from the lens.**

    Place the cap on a table, in your camera bag, or in your pocket for safekeeping.

    I take the rear lens cap off most lenses with my right thumb and index finger while palming the lens in the same hand. If I can do it (my hands aren't huge), you can. Caveat: I don't palm heavy or incredibly expensive lenses; just the normal variety, and I don't hold them over a cliff or sea of boiling lava when I do this in case I drop something.

4. Get your grip on.

In other words, grip the camera and lens using one of the previously described hand grips.

5. Line up the mounting index on the lens with the one on the camera body, if it exists.

Sometimes, it's orange, as shown in Figure 3-19. It can be any color.

Index marks

FIGURE 3-19:
Carefully line up
the index marks.

6. Insert the lens onto the mount.

You feel the lens and the camera fit together if they're properly lined up.

7. Rotate the lens in the proper direction until it locks and clicks in place.

You should hear a click or feel it lock. Don't mess with the lens-release button as you mount the lens.

REMEMBER

Nikon lenses rotate toward the shutter release button to lock. Others lenses rotate toward the opposite side, which feels more natural to me because I've said "rightsie-tightsie, leftsie-loosie" all my life.

8. When you're ready, turn the camera on and remove the lens cap from the lens.

Check and set switches on the lens, such as autofocus or vibration reduction. You're ready to shoot.

Removing a lens

Taking a lens off is pretty easy. It feels a bit scarier until you get the hang of it. But that's why you're going to practice, right? Follow these steps to remove a lens:

1. **Turn off the camera.**

2. **Get your grip on.**

In other words, grip the camera and lens using one of the previously suggested methods. Make sure you have a good hold on both camera and lens.

3. **Press and hold the lens-release button.**

Make sure to continue holding the lens as you press the release button so that it doesn't accidentally fall out. I press the button with my left index finger or the knuckle of my right index finger, which is connected to the hand that is holding the lens.

4. **Turn the lens until it releases from the mount.**

Once the lens turns a bit, you don't need to hold the lens-release button. Nikon lenses turn away from the shutter release button when you remove them. Other types turn toward the shutter release button.

REMEMBER

When you've turned the lens far enough, you feel the tension ease and the lens float free within the mount. You might hear the lens come up against the mount stops. The mounting index will line up between the lens and the camera body.

5. **Pull the lens straight away from the camera body.**

If you angle the lens as you take it out, you might damage the sensitive contacts on the rear of the lens, the collar, or the mount.

6. **Secure the lens.**

Put the rear lens cap on quickly and set the lens in a safe place. If that spot is in your camera bag, you're done with it. Otherwise, make sure to pack it away safely when you take care of the camera body. As you do this, keep the open camera body tilted down.

7. **Replace the body cap or attach another lens.**

WARNING

Don't leave the camera open to the elements. Always replace the body cap or mount another lens on the body right away.

Zooming in and out

Use the zoom ring on the lens to zoom in or out. Most lenses have their zoom ring closer to the base of the lens, which is shown in Figure 3-20. Typically, you'll turn the zoom ring toward the shutter release button to zoom out (focal lengths will get smaller) and turn it away from the shutter release button to zoom in (focal lengths will get larger).

Focal lengths are printed on the lens's zoom ring. Read your current focal length by noting the number (extrapolate if you're between printed numbers) lined up with the zoom position index.

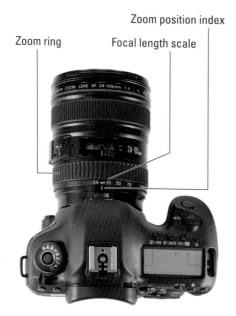

FIGURE 3-20: Zoom lenses have a focal length scale on top.

I'm holding the camera in Figure 3-21 with my left hand on the zoom ring, ready to zoom in or out. This position works well for looking through the viewfinder and using autofocus.

If you're manually focusing, zoom in or out first and then move your hand to the focus ring, as shown in the next section.

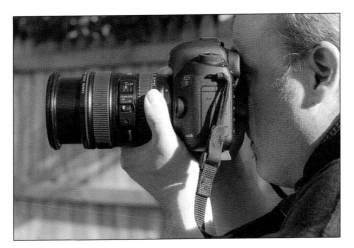

FIGURE 3-21:
Zooming in using
my left hand.

Switching from auto to manual focus

To change to manual focus, simply switch the focus mode switch on your lens to MF, as shown in Figure 3-22. Note that this camera has a second switch on the camera body. That enables the camera to support lenses without a focus mode switch. When set differently (as is purposefully the case here), the switch on the lens takes precedence. That way you don't need to toggle two switches to change the focus mode.

FIGURE 3-22:
Switch to MF to
take total focus-
ing control.

Manually focusing

Despite how powerful modern AF systems are, there are situations when you need to step in and manually focus in order to get the best photo. If you are using a manual-focus lens, this is your only option.

Mechanically, focusing is simple. Turn the focus ring one way or the other until your subject is in focus. If your camera has focus-confirmation, you may hear a chirp or something in the viewfinder will light up when the AF point over your subject comes into focus. Manually select the AF point you want to use beforehand for best results. The challenge to manual focusing nowadays is that dSLR focusing screens are not all that helpful. Old SLRs were designed with viewfinder focusing screen optimized for manual focus. My older Nikon FE 2, for example, has three manual-focus aids that help me see when the subject is in focus: a split-image rangefinder, a microprism collar, and a matte field.

Manually focusing changes how you hold and support the camera because your fingers have to control the focus ring. I'm holding the camera horizontally in Figure 3-23. My right hand is supporting the weight of the camera while the fingers of my left hand focus and assist in weight-relief. In Figure 3-24, I am holding the camera vertically. The fingers of my right hand stiffen and hook around the front of the grip. The camera can almost hang off them. The left hand performs the same focusing task.

FIGURE 3-23:
Manual focus in horizontal hold.

FIGURE 3-24:
Manually focusing in vertical hold takes more practice.

I recommend zooming in and checking your focus using the camera's LCD monitor when you're using a tripod. A magnified view makes it easy to see when things are in good focus, as shown in Figure 3-25.

FIGURE 3-25:
This shot is in excellent focus thanks to magnifying the Live View.

Activating lens-based image stabilization

Turning on lens-based image stabilization is easy. Set the appropriate switch on your lens to On. See Figure 3-26.

FIGURE 3-26:
Engage the stabilizer!

Some lenses may have more than one IS mode. Some Canon telephoto lenses, for example, have several different types. Mode 1 is normal. Mode 2 enables you to pan and follow a subject without the IS system trying to counter the sweeping motion of the camera. Mode 3 engages only when you have the shutter button pressed fully to take a shot. Hybrid IS (available on a Canon macro lens) corrects for shifts more prevalent in macro photography instead of typical camera shake.

Cleaning Lenses

Despite your best efforts, your lenses are going to get smudged and dirty with use. Don't beat yourself up over it. It happens all the time to everyone. Make cleaning your lenses part of your routine, just like charging your camera's battery.

REMEMBER

You should become comfortable cleaning lenses whether or not they are attached to the camera. Also, you will rarely need to clean the rear lens element (it's normally covered by a cap or the camera), but you should check it occasionally. Also make a habit of checking front and rear lens caps as well as the camera body cap for dust and debris. If you must, use the same steps as you would to clean the front of the lens.

1. **Very gently, dust the lens surface clean, as shown in Figure 3-27.**

   The idea here is to remove anything that might scratch the lens when you clean the surface. You can use a soft-bristled lens-cleaning brush or a blower. Do not use canned air, as the propellant can shoot out of the can and damage the lens or camera.

FIGURE 3-27:
Brushing or blowing gently removes grit and other scratchy things.

2. **If needed, apply lens-cleaning solution to your preferred wipe or cloth.**

   Avoid spraying the solution on the lens. You don't want fluid seeping into spots where you can't remove it. And, don't overdo it. A little goes a long way, and you can always reapply and continue cleaning. Some lens-cleaning pads come pre-moistened. If you're using a microfiber lens or glasses cleaning cloth, you may not need to use a solution. You can often lightly dampen it or leave it dry and still achieve great results.

Lens manufacturers recommend against using paint thinner, benzene, or organic solvents when cleaning. Be wary of using other potent chemicals on lenses with coatings.

3. **Clean the lens with a clean wipe, pad, or other lens-cleaning cloth, as shown in Figure 3-28.**

   Some recommend cleaning from the center out. Others recommend wiping from the outside in, using a circular motion. Be firm, but don't overdo it. If the lens is badly smudged and has oil from your fingers, you may need to clean it two or three times. Be patient. The oil will come off.

   You can buy cleaning pens that typically have a brush and a rubbery cleaning tip that wipes the surface of the lens. LensPen (www.lenspen.com) has a number of products. I have a version from Nikon that I use, even on my Canon and Sony lenses. It's handy and works well on lenses and filters.

FIGURE 3-28: Cleaning lenses should be a regular part of your routine.

4. **Inspect the lens.**

   Make sure the lens is clean and dry. Then get back to shooting or put the cover back on.

Always carry a microfiber lens cleaning cloth with you when you're out shooting. Use it to touch up the front of your lens if you need to. If you see dust or debris, brush first.

Learning about Lenses

Chapter **4**

Exploring Menus and Camera Settings

Living in this day and age, it should not surprise you to learn that digital SLRs are sophisticated electronic devices with tons of features and options. Don't let that freak you out. So are HDTVs, smartphones, handheld gaming devices, tablets, landline phones, audio gear, computers, larger video game systems, Blu-ray players, and satellite/cable/fiber television boxes. Even refrigerators, washers, and dryers have gotten into the act. This chapter is about learning to communicate with your digital SLR through the built-in menus so that you can set up and use your camera more effectively. You'll see how easy it actually is to get started as you tell it who you are, set the time, format memory cards, set the image quality, and accomplish a whole host of other chores.

Understanding How Menus Are Organized

Camera manufacturers organize dSLR menus into convenient categories. The goal is to make it easier for you to find things. A large portion of dSLRs sold today share a handful of common menu groups:

>> **Shooting:** Shooting menus are devoted to common photo settings such as Image Quality, White Balance, Noise Reduction, Color Space, ISO, and so forth.

Live View and Movie menus may be located with or at the end of the Shooting menu because they pertain to recording as opposed to playing back or setup.

>> **Live View:** Live View menus have options and settings unique to Live View shooting. This menu includes features like focusing methods, options to configure the display, a metering timer, and so forth. Some cameras do not have a Live View menu, instead preferring to have a single Shooting menu.

>> **Movie:** Some cameras have a Movie menu that groups all the different movie options together.

>> **Playback:** Playback menus house options that relate to image and movie playback. You'll find things like Protect Images, Rotate, Erase, and Slide Show. Sometimes retouching options are located in the Playback menu. Other cameras (the Nikon D7200, for example) have a specific Retouching menu.

>> **Setup:** Setup menus include options such as Language, Help, Battery Information, Sensor Cleaning, Copyright, and more. You'll use some features only once. Others, such as Format Card, you'll use many times.

>> **Custom:** This group includes menus, settings, and other functions.

While common, these categories are not definitive. You may see other menu names in different cameras. Sony cameras, for example, have a few unique menus: Memory Card Tool and Clock Setup being two. You may also see Camera Settings and Wireless menus.

Finally, you may see menus and options change based on the shooting mode you've chosen. For example, Canon doesn't display advanced options when the camera is set to a Basic Zone mode. Some Canon cameras also change the Shooting menus when you're in Movie mode.

The features I describe in the following sections are common to most digital SLRs. You'll find major concepts grouped into separate headings, and a plethora of menu displays to illustrate the points. If you can't find a corresponding option in your camera's menu hierarchy, have a look at your manual's table of contents or index to locate it.

Opening and Using the Menu

Before getting to details about digging through specific menu choices and options to set up and configure your camera, you should familiarize yourself with the basics of accessing and navigating your camera's menu. It's pretty simple and won't take long.

Typically, here's how you get to the menu and make changes:

1. **Press the Menu button.**

Some cameras position the Menu button on the far left side of the camera, next to (Nikon, for example) or just above (Canon and Sony like this position) the LCD monitor. The Canon T6i is illustrated in Figure 4-1. Use your left thumb to press the Menu button when located in either of these spots.

You might see the Menu button placed on the right side of the camera, low and to the right of the monitor (Pentax likes this spot). When on the right, press it with your right thumb.

Menu button

Navigation and Set buttons

FIGURE 4-1:
This camera's Menu button is very conveniently placed.

The menu (shown in Figure 4-2) appears on the camera's LCD monitor until the camera turns the display off (to save power) or you press a button not related to menu navigation or selection (the shutter button, for example). Many menus use color coded tabs or icons so you can tell at a glance what section you're in. If you're using a camera with an electronic viewfinder, such as a Sony dSLT, you can also see the menu through the electronic viewfinder. In either case, if the menu doesn't appear, you may have to press your camera's Display or Info button to turn the monitor on.

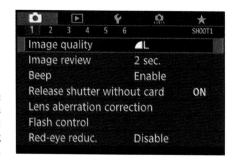

FIGURE 4-2:
This menu is
color-coded:
red for shooting
options.

2. **Navigate to the menu or tab that contains the option you want and highlight an option.**

Use your camera's arrow buttons (also shown in Figure 4-1) or circular controller. Press the appropriate button to navigate up, down, left, or right in menus and settings. If using a touchscreen, simply tap the menu you want to use. I've highlighted the Red-Eye Reduction option in Figure 4-3. Note that the current setting, disabled, is shown next to the option name.

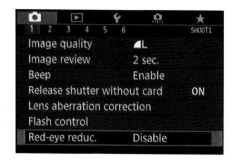

FIGURE 4-3:
Select an option
you want to
change.

REMEMBER

Not all navigation controllers look identical. Some cameras have separate arrow keys (the Canon EOS Rebel line). Many cameras use a round dial that you can press in any of the four directions. Other cameras have a controller that acts like a little joystick. You may also be able to navigate your menu system by spinning a control dial (a.k.a *command dial*). Navigation controllers are also called by different names: *Arrow keys, multiselector, four-way controller, quick control dial, arrow pad,* and *cross keys* are other examples.

You may need to turn other dials or press other buttons to get around and make selections. Check your camera's manual to see if this is the case. For example, some Canon models use the main dial or the Quick Control button to move between tabs in the menu system.

3. **Press the Set or OK button to open the settings.**

After you navigate to the menu you want to use, activate it. Think of it as clicking your mouse. To choose an option, press your camera's Set (Canon) or

OK button (Nikon). Some cameras call it the Enter or Control button. Touchscreen users can simply tap the menu option they want to use.

Now you can choose the setting you want. In this case, only two options are available: Disable or Enable.

TIP

To cancel, you should be able to press the Menu button. You may also be able to press the shutter release button halfway to kick yourself out of the menu system. Touchscreen users often have a return arrow you can tap.

4. **Highlight the specific setting you want to use, as shown in Figure 4-4.**

The current setting (Disable) is shown in blue. The setting that I've chosen (Enable) has an arrow beside it. Your camera, of course, may indicate things differently. Some cameras place checks or bullets next to the currently selected option to show that it is enabled, while others outline the current option in a different color.

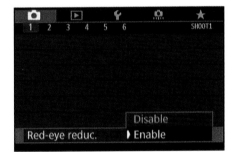

FIGURE 4-4:
Select an option you want to change.

5. **Press Set or OK to change it.**

6. **Press the Menu button to exit.**

REMEMBER

I used a Canon camera to illustrate these steps. Compare it to the other menus sprinkled throughout the chapter.

LOOKING FOR ANSWERS

For more definitive information about your camera, you'll have to turn to your camera's manual. It lists the menus and tells you what all the settings and options are for your specific camera. While the manual won't be as colorful, funny, or as charming as I am, it does have a lot of useful information. If you prefer something with personal insight and examples, look for a *For Dummies* book written for your camera model. I've written and coauthored several.

Setting Up Your Camera

When you get your camera, you'll need to accomplish a few tasks when you first turn it on. Setting the date, time, and language is often required by the camera. The others are my suggestions that will help you get started on the right foot.

Date and time

Set the date and time so that all your photos have the correct date and time imprinted in their *metadata* (data stored in a header that can be accessed and read apart from the image itself; examples data include the camera make and date and time of the exposure). Some cameras show the date and time when turned on. Set the time zone too, making sure to note daylight saving time, if applicable. You often see a snazzy map, like Sony's in Figure 4-5. Sometimes you simply choose your zone from a list.

FIGURE 4-5: Setting the time zone.

TIP

Remember to reset the time zone if you travel, and check it on any cameras you may rent.

Language

Unlike your smartphone or tablet, your camera can't speak to you. I wouldn't be surprised, however, when the day comes that you'll be able to turn on your dSLR and have Siri, Cortana, or Google open the menu and format the memory card. Specifying the language makes it possible to read all the menus. All the options might look interesting, but you should choose the one you can read.

Feature guides and expanded help

If you're a seasoned photographer and don't need your camera continually explaining what features are or giving you photography hints, turn the Feature

Guide (Canon), Guide Mode (Nikon), Mode Dial Guide (Sony), or Guide Display (Pentax) off. If you need a bit of assistance as you operate your camera, leave that option enabled. You can always turn it off when you're comfortable with the camera.

Review time

This feature specifies the number of seconds a photo appears on the LCD monitor immediately after you shoot. If you find yourself pressing the Playback button every time you take a photo to look at it — whether it's to check focus, brightness, or cuteness — turn on auto review and give yourself more than a fraction of a second. If Auto Review is on, and you find yourself continuously pressing the shutter button halfway to get back to taking photos, either reduce the review time or turn it off. You can always press the Playback button to review specific photos. In Figure 4-6, I am configuring Auto Review on a Sony camera.

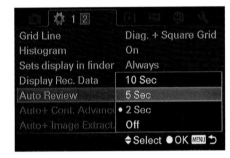

FIGURE 4-6:
Setting Auto Review to 5 seconds.

Auto power off

Have you ever accidentally left your camera on? You can automatically turn it off and save batteries with this option. While some cameras have a "one size fits all" setting, others allow you to customize the time to wait based on what you're doing. Figure 4-7 shows four different options on an inexpensive Nikon dSLR.

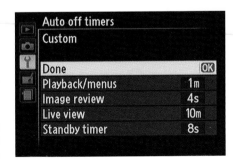

FIGURE 4-7:
Shorten times to save battery life.

Sound

Most cameras give you audio feedback in the form of beeps and boops. You can turn them off, if you like. Touchscreen cameras may beep when you touch them. You can often disable this while keeping other sounds on.

Touchscreen settings

Cameras with touchscreens typically have options that enable you to alter their sensitivity or turn them off entirely. Canon has a Touch Control menu in Setup Menu 3 of the Canon EOS 80D (see Figure 4-8), for example, that has three options: Standard, Sensitive, and Disable. Set it to your liking.

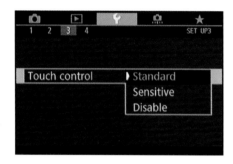

FIGURE 4-8:
Remember to set options like touchscreen sensitivity.

No card

This option, which might be named Release Shutter without Card, determines whether or not you can take photos if there is no memory card in the camera. I recommend setting this option to off to prevent you from taking photos without a card in the camera, even if your camera warns you about the fact. You don't want to accidentally take what you think is a great photo only to realize after it's too late that there is no card in the camera. The only time I allow the camera to take a photo without a card is when I am configuring something and don't want to store the photos. For example, my Fotodiox lens mount adapter requires that I take several shots with different camera settings to program it. I don't want to delete 50 photos from my card when I'm done.

Setting Typical Shooting Options

Your camera's basic still and movie recording settings control how your digital SLR shoots and saves photos and movies, as well as other photo- and exposure-related options. If you're in an advanced mode, you'll have to set (or change) these settings yourself.

Image size and quality

You've got a modern-day marvel in your hands. Your dSLR/dSLT can take magnificently clear, compelling photos. And let me tell you something more: You can get such photos in several sizes, aspect ratios, and qualities. Figure 4-9 shows the Quality option of a mid-range camera from Canon. You can see file size and the pixel dimensions.

REMEMBER

Your dSLR/dSLT has no bad settings. Your camera has good settings and better ones. In general, if you plan on printing large copies of your photos, select the highest quality settings possible. If you're going to use the photos on a computer or make small prints, even the smaller, lower quality settings are fantastic.

>> **Choose JPEG** if you want to use a final product right out of the camera. You don't want to mess with processing the file yourself. You don't need the ultimate in quality and are happy with what the camera produces. You're using JPEGs on your computer or putting them online. (You can't upload Raw files to Flickr, Facebook, your blog, or your web page. Don't even think of tweeting them.)

>> **Choose Raw or Raw + JPEG** if you want creative control over your photos and don't mind processing them yourself. You want the flexibility of making multiple edits throughout the process. For you, saving storage space and transferring photos faster aren't as important as having the flexibility, quality, and creative control that you get with Raw files.

TIP

Don't get too cocky about the superiority of Raw files over JPEGs. Unless you're good at processing Raw files, the JPEGs may look better.

FIGURE 4-9:
Image Quality combines several options in one place.

Using multiple memory cards

If your camera uses multiple memory cards, you should have an option that enables you to configure how they are used. You may be able to use them sequentially, which treats them as one large card, mirror them by saving the exact same data to both cards, or Raw files to one and JPEGs to the other. Figure 4-10 shows the Memory Card Options menu for the Pentax K-1.

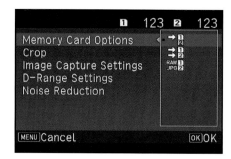

FIGURE 4-10: Set storage preferences if using multiple memory cards.

ISO settings

Typically, you can not only set the ISO, but limit the camera's Auto ISO to minimum and maximum values. Some cameras enable you to control valid ISO settings even when shooting manually. Disable Auto ISO if you want to set the ISO manually in advanced shooting modes. You don't have a choice when using automatic modes. I cover ISO more fully in Book 3, Chapter 4.

Picture control or creative style

This option specifies how the camera processes JPEGs from the image data. You normally have Standard, Portrait, Landscape, Vivid, Neutral, and Monochrome choices. Depending on the camera, you may have more or fewer choices. This setting doesn't affect Raw photos. It's like you're providing guidance to the camera about how to convert the raw data to a JPEG. Figure 4-11 shows some of the options available from a Nikon camera.

WARNING

If you aren't saving raw exposures, *be careful:* When a picture style is applied to the raw data by the camera and saved as a JPEG, you can't change it afterward. Test the settings you like with copies of photos — not the ones you want to keep.

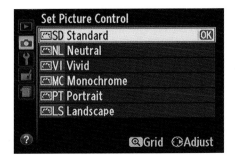

FIGURE 4-11:
Choose an option to control how JPEGs are processed by the camera.

Color space

Specify the color profile assigned to JPEGs file. Raw images *don't have* a color profile; it's assigned by the raw processor when you convert it to TIFF or JPEG format. Choose from two color space options:

TIP

>> **sRGB** defines a smaller color space but is more widely accepted. In fact, sRGB is the de facto standard and so ubiquitous that devices with no color management capabilities at all assume that all colors are defined in sRGB and reproduce sRGB photos perfectly. I recommend assigning this color space to your photos.

>> **Adobe RGB** defines a larger color space than sRGB but is less widely used. The danger is that you may be viewing or editing colors on your system that other people can't display or print. If you work in an environment that's tightly color managed, you may be able to take advantage of Adobe RGB's greater color range.

Highlights and shadows options

These options, also called brightness and contrast or dynamic range options, try to protect you from blowing out highlights and losing details in shadows. It's not a bad deal, but not a free lunch, either. You may lose detail in certain tonal ranges, depending on what the camera has to do to enhance or protect shadows or highlights. You can do the same thing yourself, and enjoy total control over the process, when you process raw exposures and, to a limited degree, edit JPEGs. Canon options include Auto Lighting Optimizer and Highlight Tone Priority (both shown in Figure 4-12). Nikon uses Active D-Lighting. Sony uses the term D-Range Optimizer.

Noise reduction

You can often toggle two types of noise reduction: long shutter speed and high ISO (both shown in Figure 4-13). The camera automatically processes the photo when you take it according to the type of noise reduction settings you've chosen. This

Exploring Menus and Camera Settings

takes a bit of time, so it may reduce your shooting speed. You may also lose some detail in your JPEGs (noise reduction is not applied to raw files). However, if you want cleaner looking photos and don't want the hassle of doing it yourself, these options are incredibly useful.

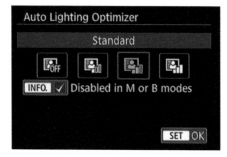

FIGURE 4-12: These options help preserve detail in bright or dark areas of photos.

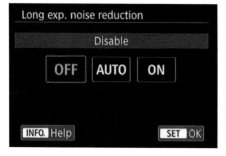

FIGURE 4-13: Set noise reduction options to keep noise under control.

Aspect ratio

Set the aspect ratio you want your photos saved in. Standard 35mm-type photos have a 3:2 aspect ratio. Four Thirds cameras shoot with a 4:3 aspect ratio. You should also be able to select widescreen (16:9) and square (1:1) ratios. When shooting JPEG-only, the camera will only save the cropped photo and discard any additional data. When shooting Raw photos, cropping information is typically stored in the file for you to use in your processing software. Unless you're certain of what you want, I suggest shooting 3:2 photos in Raw and cropping your shots in the camera or using software later. That way you can decide yourself what to keep and what to cut.

Red-eye reduction

Enable your camera's Red-Eye Reduction option if you're photographing people or animals and using a flash. Otherwise, leave it off. Red-eye reduction is often located in a Shooting menu as a separate option, but some cameras consider this a flash option.

Flash options

Some cameras have very few flash options. In this case, you can choose between automatic and manual. If you choose the latter, you can set the flash strength. Other cameras enable you to set up wireless flash, use high-speed sync, and many other advanced flash options. You can find more information on using your camera's flash in Book 4, Chapters 2 and 3.

Movie options

You can typically set up the size, format, frame rate, and compression type for movies from a Movie menu.

Making Other Choices

Read through these sections and complete these setup options at your leisure. I've included important or interesting features that you'll benefit from. This is by no means an exhaustive list of everything your camera has to offer. See the manual for specific details on these and other options.

Display settings

Configure what information you want displayed in the viewfinder or on the monitor. You'll find options like these in a Shooting or Setup menu:

>> **Grid:** This option (shown in Figure 4-14) displays a grid in the viewfinder or on the monitor. In some cases, you may be able to customize the grid by having more or fewer lines. Typical values are 3x3 or 6x4. You may even be able to show diagonal lines.

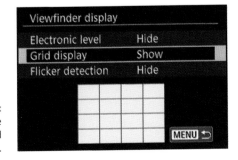

FIGURE 4-14:
Grid lines are
a very useful
option.

TIP

Keep your camera's grid turned on to help level the scene through the viewfinder or on the monitor. You'll be able to frame a better shot.

>> **Electronic level:** Turn on the electronic level or virtual horizon (see Figure 4-15) to show you how your camera is oriented. LCD monitors can look quite snazzy, while viewfinders are typically less impressive.

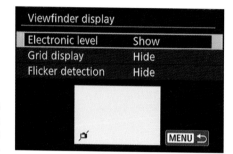

FIGURE 4-15:
Levels help you keep things straight.

>> **Warnings and alerts:** You may be able to display warnings in the viewfinder, such as when there are flickering lights or when the shutter speed is too slow.

When shooting in Live View, you have more options:

>> **Shooting information:** When you're using Live View, you can toggle between a little or a lot of information shown on the monitor, as shown in Figure 4-16. Press your Info or Display button to cycle through these displays.

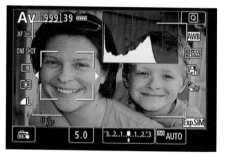

FIGURE 4-16:
You can toggle the display to show very little or a lot.

>> **Histogram:** Decide whether you want to see a live histogram displayed. A histogram is a graph that reveals the distribution of brightness in the scene. This helps you determine the overall balance between bright areas and dark regions, and whether you are in danger of under or overexposing the photo. RGB histograms show color-channel information instead of an overall brightness.

Electronic viewfinders outperform optical viewfinders in terms of the amount and type of information they can display. Basically, it shows what the monitor displays on the back of the camera. Sony users, for example, can adjust the brightness of the viewfinder, change its color temperature, display shooting information graphically, show all shooting information, show none, and even display a histogram in the viewfinder.

LCD brightness and color

You may be able to dim or brighten your LCD monitor. Dim the beast if you're taking photos at night or somewhere in low light, where a super-bright LCD monitor might be distracting. Lowering the brightness of the LCD also decreases battery drain. Figure 4-17 shows the LCD Brightness option on a Canon camera.

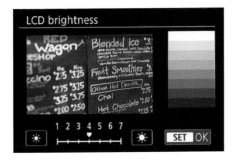

FIGURE 4-17: Brighten the LCD when you're in strong light.

Cameras with electronic viewfinders allow you to adjust their brightness just like you would an LCD monitor on the back of the camera.

Filenaming and numbering

This setting determines how the camera names your files. The camera counts every photo you take, from 0001 to 9999, and puts the number to a preset base filename. You can sometimes change to a different base name and change the camera's behavior when it starts over on the renumbering. Figure 4-18 shows typical file numbering options.

File and folder structure

Some cameras let you change the way folders are named on the memory card from a standard form (sequential numbering) to a date form (based on the date you take the first photo in the folder).

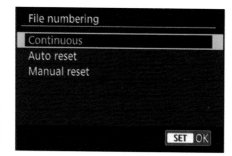

FIGURE 4-18:
Exploring file
numbering
options.

Auto rotate (camera orientation)

This setting records the camera's orientation when you take the picture and stores the information in the EXIF information. When you review the photo or open it in *smart software* (photo management or editing software that looks at the orientation information in the file to correctly display it), the picture is automatically rotated to its correct orientation. The auto rotate option prevents you from having to turn the camera every time you review a portrait-oriented photo. It makes the photo look smaller, though.

Copyright

Enter your name or organization in your camera's Copyright information, if possible. This information gets embedded into your photos and helps to secure your rights. In Figure 4-19, I'm entering my name in a Canon camera.

Wi-Fi connectivity

New dSLRs and dSLTs are ready to connect to networks and other devices right out of the box. That's a wonderful thing! The not-so-wonderful part is getting it to work. You'll have to figure out the settings and, if necessary, have the right password to access your network. If you've ever set up your smartphone or tablet to work on a wireless network, though, you should be able to figure things out quickly.

FIGURE 4-19:
This information
is embedded in
your photos.

Video mode or system

Quite likely, you won't have to set the video mode on your camera because you will have bought it in the same region you live in. If you travel, however, you may need to change it if you want to connect your camera to a television set. There are two video standards to choose from: NTSC and PAL. NTSC stands for National Television System Committee. This standard is used in North and Central America and several countries in South America and Asia (South Korea, Japan, and the Philippines to name three). PAL stands for Phase Alternating Line, and is used in Europe, Russia, China, Australia, much of Africa, the Middle East, and India.

Controlling Playback

Your camera should have an entire menu with a whole host of options devoted to playing back photos and movies. It's an important aspect of using your dSLR.

TIP

Cameras with touchscreen controls make playback a breeze. Instead of tap-tap-tapping on buttons to scroll through photos, swipe as you would using your phone.

Protect images

Use this option if you review your photos and want to keep yourself from accidentally deleting them. Beware: They aren't protected from reformatting. If you're like me, and you *never* delete photos from your card while it's in the camera, this option is somewhat superfluous.

Rotate

You can rotate photos during photo playback if you like. Simply select the Rotate option from your Playback menu, choose a photo, and then rotate the image. This is helpful if you don't have Auto Rotate (which is typically in the Setup menu) on or it gets the orientation wrong. This happens most frequently when you're holding the camera vertically and want to review photos in that orientation.

Erase/delete

WARNING

Erase or delete one or more photo. Be careful! You can typically erase photos as you review them on the back of the camera by pressing the Erase or Delete button. You can also erase them by selecting a menu option (see Figure 4-20) and then tagging one or more shots you want deleted.

FIGURE 4-20:
Delete multiple photos using the menu.

Print order

Identify exposures to print, and the order you want them printed, on a compatible PictBridge printer and many photo-finishing kiosks by setting the *digital print order format (DPOF)* options. Depending on your camera, you can imprint each photo with the shutter speed, aperture, file number, and date the photo was taken.

Slide show

Set up and display an automatic slide show of your photos or movies. Figure 4-21 shows the slide show settings on a consumer-level dSLR from Nikon.

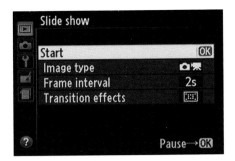

FIGURE 4-21:
Preparing to start
a slide show.

Retouch

Some cameras let you retouch photos. You'll enjoy being able to quickly produce finished photos in-camera. This is a great option if you don't like using your computer or you're on location and need to touch up a photo right away. You can find those settings on the Retouch menu.

Keeping Everything Running Smoothly

There are several menu items that will help you keep your camera running smoothly. Check out these options and incorporate the ones you like into your basic maintenance routine.

Showing battery information

Your camera should have a place in the menu system for you to check the status of your battery. I encourage you to do so regularly, and explain how in Book 1, Chapter 2. Some cameras also enable you to *register* each battery with the camera. For example, the Canon 80D assigns a serial number to each battery you register. It stores this information, and you're expected to label the battery. Once do, you can track their performance by serial number from within the camera.

Formatting memory cards

This option (often listed simply as Format) erases all data on the memory card. Keep these memory card tips in mind:

TIP

>> *Some* cameras toss only the file structure and don't reinitialize the card. If so, you may be able to rescue lost files before you overwrite them. Other cameras give you the option of performing a low-level format if you want, as shown in Figure 4-22. This deeper level of formatting may improve performance on cards that seem sluggish.

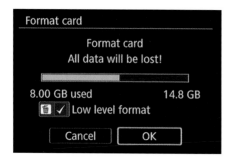

>> To protect your privacy, be sure to reformat your card as aggressively as possible if you ever sell it or give it away.

>> I always format my cards in the camera I'm going to use them in. This trick produces a clean slate, created by the system that will store my photos. I also reformat the card immediately after transferring photos and putting it back in the camera. This prevents the "Have I saved these or not?" dilemma.

Cleaning the image sensor

As explained in Book 1, Chapter 2, you can have the camera automatically clean the image sensor by shaking itself. This menu option may be called Sensor Cleaning or Clean Image Sensor. You can also lock up the mirror and out of the way to blow dust out of the camera body. That menu option may be listed as a form of manual cleaning, but can also be called Lock Up Mirror for Cleaning. Although I don't recommend this, you can also lock up the mirror and clean the image sensor yourself with a cleaner and special pads designed for the task.

Creating a dust reference photo

Depending on the camera, you may have the option of taking a dust reference photo. The menu option may be named Image Dust Off Reference Photo, Dust Delete Data, or something similar. See Figure 4-23 for an example from Canon. Here's how it works: You take a photo of a light, featureless object as a reference photo. The camera appends information to that photo that locates the little dust bunnies that are still stuck to the image sensor. Later, you can use the photo processing software that comes with your camera to automatically remove dust spots.

REMEMBER

There is some debate over the effectiveness of creating a dust reference photo if the image sensor is constantly cleaning itself every time you turn the camera on and off. And, this technique requires more of you than just taking photos. You have to keep the reference photo updated, and you have to load it into the provided software and apply it to your photos for it to work. While this may sound discouraging, your mileage may vary. Give it a shot and see what you think.

FIGURE 4-23:
Creating a dust reference photo for software to use later.

Resetting the camera

Being able to automatically change all options (or a good percentage of them — see your manual for details) to their factory default settings is helpful. It helps you restore the standard camera setup if you change a setting and can't later recall its original values. This option frees you to be wildly creative and experiment with your camera. You typically get a warning, shown in Figure 4-24, asking if you really want to reset the camera. If you made a mistake, cancel the operation.

FIGURE 4-24:
Clear camera settings to reset the camera.

Updating the firmware

Firmware is what runs your camera. The cool thing about dSLRs is that you can change and update the firmware to smooth out bugs or introduce new features. Visit the manufacturer's website to see what the latest version for your camera is (look in the support area, download center, or on a page devoted to your camera), then check that against what your camera shows. Update if necessary. Updating involves either putting the firmware file(s) on your camera's memory card or connecting your camera to your computer. You can see in Figure 4-25 that the Pentax K-1 firmware is version 1.00.

FIGURE 4-25:
Make sure firmware is up to date.

WARNING

Please read all applicable instructions before starting. Be careful when updating your camera's firmware. Do so with a full battery. If something goes wrong, you may have to take your camera to be serviced to revive it.

Exploring Advanced Options

Digital SLRs often have a number of advanced options. They aren't always necessary, but are available when you find that you need them. That's one thing that makes dSLR photography so rewarding — the camera grows with you. I've chosen to highlight a number of different advanced options from different cameras in this section to give you an idea of what's possible. Please refer to your camera's manual for a complete list of your camera's features and how to use them.

Using custom functions and settings

Some cameras place many of their most esoteric options into a group called Custom Functions (Canon) or Custom Settings (Nikon and Pentax). Each setting is typically numbered, and may be grouped into categories. Figure 4-26 shows the first Custom Settings menu on the Pentax K-1.

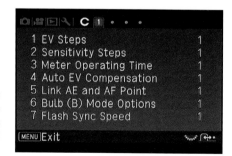

FIGURE 4-26:
Custom settings and functions are advanced options.

Creating custom shooting profiles

More advanced cameras let you create, save, and load different shooting profiles with different settings. For example, you may have one ready for portraits and another for casual photography with your general-purpose zoom lens. The Canon EOS 80D has two Custom Shooting Modes, as shown in Figure 4-27.

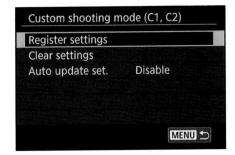

FIGURE 4-27: Customize the camera by saving your settings into a special mode.

Tweaking autofocus settings

More advanced cameras have a plethora of autofocus menu choices. This is one thing that separates professional cameras from amateur models. For example, you can fine-tune focus on more advanced cameras. You might need this option if a lens repeatedly focuses in front of (*front focus*) or behind (*back focus*) where it should. That indicates it needs to be sent to a service center and recalibrated. In the meantime, you can correct its vision. Figure 4-28 shows one such option from a Canon camera.

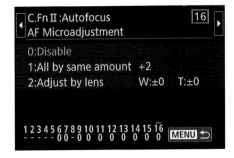

FIGURE 4-28: Look for advanced autofocus options in custom function or settings menus.

Configuring bracketing settings

You often have the ability to fine-tune the way your camera sets exposure and controls autoexposure bracketing. Take advantage of these advanced settings to customize the way you like to work.

Exploring Menus and
Camera Settings

Customizing the controls

You may be able to customize some of your camera's buttons and dials, which is handy at times. Do you want to change ISO when you press the Function button? You can (probably) do that! See Figure 4-29.

Be kind to other people's cameras. If you customize someone else's controls, put them back when you're done shooting. Use the camera's reset feature if it has one.

FIGURE 4-29: Customizing buttons and controls really lets you make the camera work for you.

Creating custom menus

Canon in particular has a My Menu option that lets you create your own custom menu from your favorite menu options, as shown in Figure 4-30. You can even set up the camera to display this menu only, or have it be automatically selected when you press the Menu button. Nikon helps you find options easier by offering up those that you used most recently.

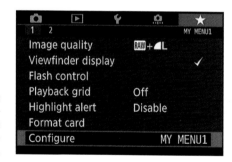

FIGURE 4-30: Create customized menus to collect your most-used options.

IN THIS CHAPTER

» Planning for success

» Starting out on a good foot

» Unpacking and getting ready to shoot

» Configuring the camera

» Taking pictures

Chapter **5**

Taking Pictures with Your dSLR

This chapter is action-packed. I walk you through taking photos with your digital SLR from start to finish. I share tips and tricks for preparing photo shoots, packing things up, setting up when you're ready, choosing a shooting mode, and taking the photos.

Don't hesitate to flip back and forth between chapters and books to find more details about certain subjects, such as menus, lenses, exposure, and handling your camera.

Seeing the Big Picture

Checklists are great organizers. Writing things down helps you focus your attention and not forget things. My purpose for this chapter is to give you a sense of what you need to take care of when you're shooting photos. The big picture. It can be involved, complicated at times, and there are a lot of things to forget. I want you to realize that there's more to it than simply pressing a button.

I've organized this chapter into four main sections. Each plays a part in forming the big picture:

1. **Plan ahead.** Think about what you might need so that you have it when you're out on location (even if it's just in your backyard). Get it all ready.

2. **Unpack and set up.** Unpack, get things assembled, and prepare to configure the camera.

3. **Get the camera ready.** You'll make essential choices in this section: what shooting mode to use, whether to use the viewfinder or Live View, how to tweak the display, and what exposure controls and other camera parameters to set.

4. **Take photos.** Get to the nitty-gritty of photography. Frame the scene, focus, and take the shot. Next, review the photo. If something isn't right, analyze what happened and correct it. If the photo's a keeper, continue to the next one.

REMEMBER

Geek alert: I put a few checklists (based on this one) in the following sections. Some are numbered, and necessarily suggest an order to the process. However, you should feel free to move steps around to suit your own preferences. In the end, they'll be *your* steps.

Planning Ahead

REMEMBER

To save yourself time and potential frustration when you go out to take photos, make sure that you have all these items before setting out:

>> **Batteries:** Charge your camera's battery (or batteries) the day or night before you leave. If batteries have been sitting around long enough, they discharge. Pop them in your camera and see whether they need to be refreshed. I have at least two camera batteries for all my dSLRs. That way, I always have a reasonably fresh battery in the bag in addition to the one in my camera. If the in-camera battery is low the day before a big shoot, I recharge it so that I have two fully charged batteries.

>> **Memory cards:** Transfer photos before you pack up and then format the card using your camera to wipe it clean; see Book 1, Chapter 4.

WARNING

Formatting erases photos and cleans the card. Make sure that you first transfer photos (see Book 5, Chapter 1) to your computer.

>> **Lenses and filters:** Clean lenses and filters before packing them; see Book 1, Chapter 3 for more information.

» **Sensor:** Some time before important shoots, see whether your camera's sensor has a lot of dust. If so, consider getting your camera's sensor professionally cleaned. Otherwise, you can blow dust out of your camera and activate the camera's self-cleaning mode, if it has one. You may also want to take a dust registration shot. See Book 1, Chapter 4 for more information.

» **Basic camera options:** Make sure that the date and time settings are correct. Ensure that fundamental photo options are set, such as the file format you want to use, filenaming conventions, photo quality, ISO settings, and review time. You may benefit from resetting all the camera options. Check the menu to see whether you can do that automatically. Alternatively, you might have a basic setup stored in a custom shooting or memory mode.

» **Camera bag and its goodies:** Check your camera bag to make sure that you have all the items you need. For me, that often includes one or more camera bodies, lenses, extra batteries and memory cards, an external flash unit, extra batteries for that, flash accessories, something to clean my lenses with, reading glasses, a remote shutter release, filters, my cellphone, business cards, model release forms, and a white balance tool. White balance is covered later in this chapter.

At times, I carry different tripod heads (ball, pan, or panorama) and my tripod or monopod. I occasionally pack bug spray, kneepads, waterproof boots, extra socks, a rain cover for the camera, and a tub to put wet boots in.

When I want to keep things simple, I put my camera and attached lens in my sling bag with an extra battery and memory card, and that's it.

TIP

If possible, pack your camera body with lens attached to minimize the amount of dust and debris that can get into things on location. Don't forget to put the rear lens and body caps in your bag for safekeeping.

Unpacking and Readying Your Gear

When you have your gear and you're on the scene, follow these steps to prepare yourself and your dSLR to take pictures:

REMEMBER

Not all the steps are required in every instance. You may swap them around if you like.

COPING WITH OLDER DSLRS

Old dSLRs may only use the monitor on the back of the camera to display menus and for photo playback. For example, my Nikon D200 (an excellent camera for its time; I still use it) has no Live View mode, doesn't shoot movies, and doesn't display any shooting information on the monitor. It's shocking, really, compared to dSLRs that came soon thereafter. If you have a camera like this and are reading through this chapter, you won't be able to check settings as easily as you see shown in many of the figures. You'll need to look at the physical position of knobs, switches, and buttons, and view information on supplementary LCD panels and through the viewfinder.

TIP

1. **Unpack your camera.**

   Start with your camera. Don't unpack everything and spread things around on the ground. Wait until you need something to take it out of the bag.

   I always have a strap on my cameras, so I immediately secure it around my neck, even when I plan to use a tripod. Quickly inspect the camera and lens for damage.

2. **If necessary, attach or swap lenses.**

   Don't forget to keep track of any caps you remove.

3. **Mount the camera on your tripod or monopod.**

   If using a tripod or monopod, I prefer to get the camera mounted and secured quickly so that it is supported as I dial in my settings. You can choose to perform this later if you like.

4. **Remove the lens cap.**

   When removing caps, store them in a consistent location. It doesn't matter where, as long as it's relatively convenient. You might prefer a particular pocket in your sling bag. This approach helps you quickly grab caps and reattach them when you need to.

5. **Attach an external flash, if necessary, and turn it on.**

   You may also rely on your camera's built-in flash, if it has one.

6. **Attach the remote shutter release, if desired.**

   Keep the cord out of the way, unless it's a wireless remote. In that case, you just need to get it out and have it handy.

7. **Turn on your camera.**

   Quickly make sure everything is powered on and working properly. If you haven't already, inspect for damage.

Setting Up Your Camera

Now that you've unpacked and gotten everything attached and ready, it's time to set up your camera to take the shots you want. While I can't suggest every possible setting that you might need in every possible circumstance, I've tried to list the major options and settings that you should pay attention to when starting out.

Performing an initial checkup

First, perform an initial checkup. Quickly check these things:

›› **Battery level:** Note the battery level to make sure you didn't accidentally load a bad battery. Replace it, if necessary.

›› **Exposures remaining:** Check to see if you're starting out with an empty memory card (like you should be) or not. If not, note how many shots you can take before running out of space. You can continue using it, of course, or swap it out for an empty card. If you are certain that you've downloaded the photos already, you can format it.

›› **Knobs and buttons:** Make sure that all knobs and switches are set where you want them.

›› **Lens:** Configure the lens. Set switches such as auto or manual focus and image stabilization to your preference.

Preparing for still photography

While digital SLRs and SLTs enjoy robust movie-making modes, this chapter is about shooting still photos. If necessary, turn your capture mode switch to still photos. Some integrate this function into the power switch. In that case, make sure you've powered on using the correct mode. If your camera has a Movie mode on the Mode dial, you just need to set a still photo shooting mode, which is described in the next section. Some cameras have no separate movie mode. Instead, they have a Start/Stop button, which begins recording a movie in whatever shooting mode you've chosen.

Choosing a shooting mode

It's time to decide on a shooting mode. What you decide affects how much control you can exert over the camera, and to what purpose. There isn't a wrong choice here. Some people prefer to let the camera handle most of the work. Others prefer exercising more creative control. Decide on the mode you want to use based on your subject, creative goals, camera, experience, location, and environment. Table 5-1 summarizes typical shooting modes, most of which are directly on the Mode dial. You may need to press and hold an unlock button in the center of the Mode dial to turn the dial and change modes. Note that not all cameras have all the same shooting modes.

TABLE 5-1 Typical Shooting Modes

Name	Description
Automatic (Basic Auto)	The typical automatic mode is basically point-and-shoot. You have very little input over the settings the camera uses.
Flash Off	A quick way to disable the flash from the Mode dial and still take advantage of the camera automatically handling the other settings.
Advanced Auto	Advanced, or Intelligent Auto, modes detect the type of lighting or scene and configure the camera appropriately.
Guided/Creative Auto	In guided or creative auto modes, you give the camera information about what you're shooting, whether you want sharp or blurred backgrounds, and whether or not to use the flash. It handles everything else.
Scenes	Scenes allow you to identify the specific scene you're shooting. This enables the camera choose the best settings to use for that scene. Typical scenes are Portrait, Action, Close-up, and Landscape. Many cameras have even more creative scenes, such as Food, Candlelight, Night Portrait, and more.
Specialty Modes	Specialty modes enable you to shoot panoramas, HDR, time-lapse shots, and more. They are unique to specific cameras or brands.

Name	Description
Filters and Effects	The camera processes shots according to the filter or effect you choose. Some cameras place them conveniently on the Mode dial. You typically have little to no control over other camera settings.
Programmed Autoexposure (P)	This mode bridges the gap between the basic automatic modes that give you no control over the camera and advanced modes that enable you to change settings. In this mode, you need not worry about setting the aperture or shutter speed but can configure anything else you like.
Aperture-Priority Autoexposure (A or Av)	In aperture-priority mode, you set the aperture you want to use (larger for more light and blurred backgrounds; smaller for less light and sharper backgrounds). The camera figures out the other settings needed to reach the best exposure. Unlike basic modes, you have total access to all other camera settings.
Shutter-Priority Autoexposure (S or Tv)	In shutter-priority mode, you set the shutter speed you want to use (faster for action, slower for more light and still subjects). The camera figures out the other settings needed to reach the best exposure. Unlike basic modes, you have total access to all other camera settings.
Manual (M)	Manual mode is just that. You're in charge of everything, especially exposure. The biggest difference between aperture-priority and shutter-priority modes is that after you meter the scene, you must adjust both controls to get the exposure you're after.
Bulb (B)	Bulb mode is a manual mode that enables you to keep the shutter open as long as you hold the shutter button down.

This decision affects the rest of the checklist. If you choose a more automated mode, you don't have to do certain tasks, such as setting the exposure controls. On the other hand, if you're more inclined to shoot manually, you'll be *required* to adjust those settings.

REMEMBER

You don't need to worry about setting the correct exposure yourself unless you're in manual or Bulb mode. The camera does it for you. If it can't reach the correct exposure for some reason (if it can't set the shutter speed fast enough or widen the aperture, for example), it will try to get your attention by beeping or flashing the shutter speed or f-stop display.

Automatic modes

Automatic shooting modes are fantastic helpers. The camera takes most of the load off your shoulders and lets you concentrate on framing the shot. Whether you're more experienced or just beginning, I encourage you to try out your camera's automatic modes, including scenes. Most automatic modes are right on the camera's Mode dial, as shown in Figure 5-1. Simply dial one in and start shooting.

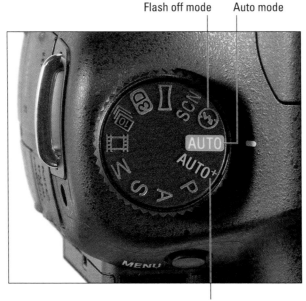

Flash off mode   Auto mode

Auto+ mode

FIGURE 5-1:
Automatic mode
symbols are often
a different color.

Here's a rundown of the types of automatic modes you might come across:

>> **Auto:** This mode (see Figure 5-2) probably needs the least explanation. You point the camera. You press and hold the shutter button halfway to focus, and then press the shutter button down fully to take the photo. The camera does the rest. Simple.

Several cameras have advanced auto modes that are smarter than basic Auto. Sony calls it Intelligent Auto, formerly Auto+. Most Canon cameras have a Scene Intelligent Auto mode. The camera senses the shooting conditions, not simply the exposure, and chooses the best settings for you to take the photo.

FIGURE 5-2:
Auto mode allows
you to focus on
photography
instead of the
camera.

>> **Flash Off:** This mode is Auto without the flash. It may even be called Auto (Flash Off) on your camera. Use it when you want to be in Auto mode but want to keep the flash from firing. See Figure 5-3.

FIGURE 5-3:
Flash Off is an automatic mode that prevents the flash from firing.

Ego is the number-one reason people bypass Auto modes in favor of something more complicated. That's a shame, because no matter how smart or technically driven you are, it can be fun to just take pictures.

Guided creativity modes

This section features modes that share an important feature: They actively help guide your creativity. You don't have to do a lot of camera wrangling when using these modes. These modes are often located on the Mode dial (see Figure 5-4), but you may have to make several selections or choices before you can start shooting.

GUIDED/CREATIVE AUTO

Guided Auto and Creative Auto modes are automatic, but give you several options for how the photos should turn out. Some consumer-level Nikon cameras have a Guide mode that walks you through a series of situations (similar to scenes) or goals (soft backgrounds and the like) to get to the right camera setup; this mode is highly interactive — not hands-off like a standard Auto mode at all. Canon's equivalent is the Creative Auto mode. It's less interactive than Nikon's Guide mode, but has some of the same goal-driven choices.

SCENES

Basic Auto modes have a significant drawback: The camera doesn't know what you're photographing. You could be taking a photo of a running child or a potted plant and the camera may not be able to tell the difference. Scenes are different. You remove the guesswork from the camera by telling it what you're shooting.

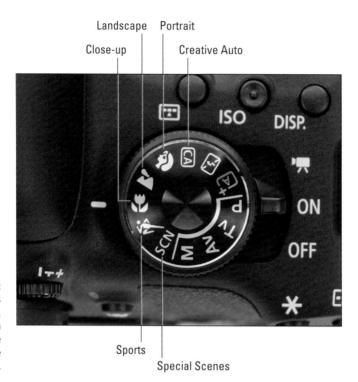

Landscape Portrait

Close-up Creative Auto

FIGURE 5-4:
This dial has
Creative Auto,
scenes, and a
special scene
mode with more
options.

Sports

Special Scenes

Many cameras represent scenes on the Mode dial with small symbols. You may need to refer to your camera manual to decode them the first few times. Other cameras include a few scenes on the Mode dial itself, plus a Scene mode on the Mode dial to access more scenes. Yet others may just have a Scene mode on the dial instead of individual scenes. Select this mode using the dial and then choose a specific scene from the camera display.

Here's a list of some typical scenes your camera may have:

>> **Portrait:** Use when you want to take a nice solo or group portrait. The lens is set so that the background will be nicely blurred, as shown in Figure 5-5. Skin tones are natural.

>> **Landscape:** This scene captures scenery in vivid colors and with a large depth of field.

>> **Macro/Close-up:** Use this mode to capture close-ups.

>> **Sports/Action:** Optimized to photograph moving subjects with a fast shutter speed, as shown in Figure 5-6. You can also use this scene when *you're* moving in order to reduce camera shake by implementing a fast shutter speed.

>> **Child:** A cross between action and portrait. Use when photographing children.

FIGURE 5-5:
Portraits often
have soft
backgrounds.

FIGURE 5-6:
The object here is
to capture action
without blurring.

>> **Sunset:** You got it. This scene is ideal when photographing sunsets. It brings
out the red, orange, and yellow colors well.

>> **Night View/Scene:** Think landscape at night with city lights, as shown in
Figure 5-7. Some cameras recommend using a tripod with this scene.

FIGURE 5-7:
This mode doesn't attempt to brighten the background at night.

>> **Handheld Night/Twilight:** Shoot at night without a tripod.

>> **Night Portrait:** Shoot portraits in the dark. The idea is to allow the overall scene to remain darker than normal, but still expose the subject properly. The flash may fire.

>> **Candle:** Shoot scenes lit by candlelight, as shown in Figure 5-8.

FIGURE 5-8:
Special modes like this enable you to capture subjects in different settings.

>> **Food:** For all you "foodies" out there, a special scene to help you photograph those tasty treats you've proud of making.

>> **Others:** You may run across more scenes ranging from Blue Sky, Forest, Pet, Kids, and Surf & Snow.

SPECIALTY MODES

Some cameras have a few specialty modes that deserve consideration:

>> **Sweep Panorama:** Instead of manually photographing several frames of a panorama and then using software to stitch them together into a single, large photo, Sweep Panorama handles everything. All you do is point, shoot, and pan. I positively love this mode. A finished photo is shown in Figure 5-9. Sony also has a special 3D Sweep Panorama mode, which saves the panorama in two files: a standard JPEG and a 3D data file.

Panoramas are saved as JPEGs only. You can't get Raw files. Individual frames from the panorama aren't saved either.

REMEMBER

FIGURE 5-9:
Automatic panoramas are fun photography.

>> **Continuous Advance Priority AE:** This Sony-only mode sets the camera to rattle off photos as fast as possible by locking the aperture open. This removes the delay from resetting it between shots. The camera also determines the shutter speed. It's great for sports, but also when someone's opening a present or blowing out the candles. Photograph pets or children as they play.

>> **HDR/Dynamic Range:** HDR, or *high dynamic range,* modes (sometimes located with scenes) are designed to capture multiple exposures (normally three) with a higher dynamic range than a single frame, and then automatically process them into a single finished image. Book 5, Chapter 6 has more information on shooting HDR images.

>> **Multiple exposures:** Shooting multiple exposures is a creative challenge. The fun part is experimenting with different scenes to come up with two or more that look good together. Figure 5-10 is an example of a dual exposure shot using the Canon 5D Mark III.

FIGURE 5-10:
Creative use
of multiple
exposures.

FILTERS AND EFFECTS

Your camera may have a special filter or effect mode. Some even have these modes right on the Mode dial. For example, the Canon 80D has a special Creative Filter mode, which enables you to shoot photos with the filter effect applied. There are many different types of filters. To name a few: Soft focus, Fisheye, Toy camera, Miniature, HDR, Water painting, and so forth.

I strongly encourage you to play around with creative filters and effects. This is fun and creative photography. You can also shoot photos normally and apply special effects later, either using the camera or special photo-editing software.

Classic autoexposure modes

Three classic autoexposure modes are shown on a Mode dial in Figure 5-11. They evaluate the exposure automatically, but allow you to control everything else (metering mode, autofocus options, white balance, drive, and so on).

The modes are:

>> **Program Auto (P):** Also known as Programmed Auto, Program AE (for autoexposure), or programmed autoexposure. Program Auto is basically an advanced Auto mode. The camera is set on automatic exposure and selects an aperture and shutter speed combination that it thinks is best. You control all other settings. It's great for snapshots.

Most cameras have modes called either Program Shift or Flexible Program mode. This mode let you choose a combination of shutter speed and aperture that you want to use. Use this mode if you have a particular aperture or shutter speed you want to achieve a certain depth of field (for aperture) or to freeze action (for shutter speed). You have more creative input this way. Figure 5-12 shows a camera display in Program Auto mode.

Aperture-priority mode

Shutter-priority mode

FIGURE 5-11:
Classic modes
P, A, and S.

Programmed autoexposure mode

FIGURE 5-12:
Programmed
auto screen with
typical options.

>> **Aperture-priority (A or Av, which stands for Aperture value):** Also known as aperture-priority auto or aperture-priority AE. In aperture-priority mode, you set the aperture and the camera determines the shutter speed needed to reach the proper exposure. This mode is good when you want to control the depth of field. Use it for portraits, landscapes, and close-ups. Aside from expo-sure, you control all the other settings. Figure 5-13 shows a camera display in aperture-priority mode.

>> **Shutter-priority (S or Tv, which stands for Time value):** Also known as shutter-priority auto or shutter-priority AE. This mode works the same as aperture priority, only you set the shutter speed instead of the aperture. It's best used when you need control over the shutter speeds. Use it for sports, action, and when you are moving. Aside from exposure, you control all the other settings yourself. Figure 5-14 shows a camera display in shutter-priority mode.

Manual mode

Switch to manual mode when you want full control over exposure. While "manual mode" sounds intimidating, you can exercise as much or as little control as you want in other areas. I recommend using manual mode when aperture- or shutter-priority modes aren't able to capture photos with the exposure you want. You also benefit from manual mode when you want the exact same settings for every photo in a session. There are two manual modes, which are shown on a Mode dial in Figure 5-15:

>> **Manual (M):** You control all camera settings, including the exposure controls. Auto ISO may not be available in manual mode. Manual mode is shown on a camera display in Figure 5-16.

Bulb mode

Manual mode

FIGURE 5-15:
Manual is always
M; Bulb (B) may
or may not be on
the dial.

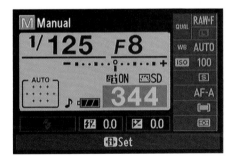

FIGURE 5-16:
In manual mode
you can play
around with
custom expo-
sures without
the camera
interfering.

>> **Bulb (B):** Bulb mode is a special type of manual mode. You select an ISO and
aperture normally, but the shutter is untimed. When you press the shutter button, the shutter opens, and when you release the button, the shutter closes.
This mode is great for long exposures and fireworks. If your Mode dial doesn't
have a B setting, try entering manual mode and lengthening the shutter speed
until it reads B (Bulb). A camera in Bulb shooting mode is shown in Figure 5-17.

CHAPTER 5 **Taking Pictures with Your dSLR** 139

<figure>
FIGURE 5-17:
In Bulb mode the
shutter duration
is up to you.
</figure>

Setting the image quality

If you're in an advanced mode, set your image quality now. The Image Quality option is located on a Shooting menu for most cameras. Your dSLR will have a number of options. I prefer to have the camera record Large/Fine JPEGs and Raw images simultaneously because it gives me a high-quality JPEG right out of the camera. I can process the Raw version later at my leisure. In fact, all the photos in the book using advanced exposure modes were shot this way, whether they are photos of cameras or something more picturesque. You may not need the largest, highest-quality images. Book 1, Chapter 4 has more details.

Choosing a viewing mode

Digital SLRs offer two ways for you to view the scene through the lens: using a viewfinder (optical or electronic) or the monitor on the back of the camera. Using the viewfinder is a time-honored tradition that harks back to the days of manual focus SLRs. It's still here because viewfinders are very effective. The latter is generally called Live View mode, Live View, LCD mode, or sometimes Live Preview. There are unique benefits to using the monitor on the back of the camera instead of the viewfinder. Which one you choose depends on the situation at hand and your personal preferences.

Viewfinder

The viewfinder is a great way to compose and take photos, as shown in Figure 5-18. I like it for most situations because it pulls my attention into the scene and keeps it there with minimal distractions. Some dSLRs have large, bright viewfinders that make looking through them a joyful experience.

You will see a number of exposure settings as well as autofocus points and possibly metering aids. You may be able to turn on grid lines and other indicators (a level, for example) that will help you line things up in the viewfinder. Use everything at your disposal if you need to.

FIGURE 5-18:
Use your viewfinder for the classic photography experience.

REMEMBER

In general, I find that viewfinders (electronic and optical) focus my attention better in most situations than when I use the LCD screen. I tend to hold the camera steadier because I'm able to support it with my body. However, I often use the LCD monitor in the studio or when I can't hold the camera and look through the viewfinder.

Live View

If you prefer to compose shots using the LCD monitor, switch to your camera's Live View mode, as shown in Figure 5-19. To make this choice, you may need to use the menu, press a button, or move a switch. You may need to enable Live View from the menu. In some cases (Sony's electronic viewfinders, for example) you simply pull back from the viewfinder. The Eyepiece sensors recognize this and switch viewing to the monitor. If you have an articulated LCD monitor, swing it out to an appropriate position if you need to.

Live View works great in the studio, where you can mount your camera on a tripod and take the time to precisely compose the scene and focus. Live View, especially in tandem with an articulated monitor, makes it easier to shoot in some funky positions where the viewfinder is inconvenient. You can hold the camera over your head and shoot over obstacles, or hold the camera down low without having to lay down on the ground. Be prepared to turn up your monitor brightness when using Live View outside in bright daylight. Look in your camera's menu system (see Book 1, Chapter 4 for more information on menus) for Live View settings.

FIGURE 5-19:
Live View shooting is a very effective photography style.

TIP

When using Live View, you can zoom in when focusing (generally by pressing some sort of zoom button, depending on the camera). The magnification, which is far more than you can get through a viewfinder, makes getting the precise focus a snap. In addition, some cameras have focus helpers. Sony dSLTs, for example, have a feature called *Focus Peaking.* When on, edges in the area in focus are highlighted with the color of your choice. It's a very nice visual indicator to have.

Configuring the display

Quickly decide if you want to change the display. As shown in Book 1, Chapter 4, you can turn on a grid, use an electronic level, and show or hide different warnings and alerts. You can also change the amount of information shown.

TIP

When you're setting up your camera using Live View and working out the exposure, it helps to have everything turned on and at your fingertips. However, when you're framing, turn off everything except the grid.

Setting exposure controls

If you're using one of the advanced shooting modes, you need to set the exposure controls to the values you want before shooting. Aperture and shutter speed are normally set by a dial, or graphically using a shooting information screen. ISO often has its own button, but can also be changed graphically or from a menu. Here is a quick review of the controls:

» **Aperture:** The opening in the lens, as expressed by an f-number. I cover aperture more in Book 3, Chapter 2.

» **Shutter speed:** How long the shutter stays open, measured in fractions of a second or seconds. For more information on shutter speed, turn to Book 3, Chapter 3.

» **ISO:** ISO controls how sensitive the image sensor is to light. Most of the time you can leave it on Auto. If you need to set it manually, use the lowest ISO you can. You'll get less *noise* (graininess). You may need to raise the ISO if you can't open the aperture on the lens any more than it is and need a fast shutter speed. When necessary, set your camera to Auto ISO and specify a maximum ISO for your camera. I cover ISO in Book 3, Chapter 4.

For more information on exposure, turn to Book 3, Chapter 1. Here are some guidelines for each shooting mode:

>> **Program:** Setting exposure controls isn't necessary, but you may want to use your camera's Program Shift feature to choose a specific shutter speed/aperture combination.

>> **Aperture-priority:** Set the aperture to achieve the effect you're after. Large apertures (small f-numbers) let in more light and are very useful in low-light situations. They also create pleasingly blurred backgrounds. Small apertures (large f-numbers) let in less light and take photos with sharper backgrounds.

>> **Shutter-priority:** Set the shutter speed based on the conditions. Faster shutter speeds let in less light but capture action without blurring. Slower shutter speeds let in more light, but your subjects (and you) need to be still.

>> **Manual:** Set the aperture and shutter speed to achieve the exposure and creative side effects that you want.

>> **Bulb:** Set the aperture that you want and time yourself or guess how long you need to keep the shutter open when you take the photo.

Setting other parameters

Depending on the mode you're in, you may need to set a number of other parameters, some of which are outlined in this section. If you choose an automatic or guided mode, the camera does most of this work for you. That's the idea, and why those modes are very popular. They remove a lot of the guesswork for people who don't know how to set up everything.

Flash

Configure the flash if you're in a mode that allows you to. If you're using the camera's built-in flash and in an advanced mode, open it pressing the Flash button. For more information on setting up and using a pop-up flash, or using a flash, refer to Book 4. I'll wait for you here. If you're using an external flash, make sure it's mounted and turned on. Attach any flash modifiers, such as a diffuser. Set the flash type you want to use: Slow Sync, Red-Eye Reduction, or Rear-Curtain Sync. Use your experience as a guide, or take a few test shots and compare. Don't forget about using flash compensation or controlling the flash's output manually in certain situations.

Drive (a.k.a release) modes

Set the drive/release mode (see Figure 5-20) to match the type of shooting you're doing. Some cameras have a Drive button. Others require you to set the drive from a shooting settings screen.

» **Single shot:** Take one shot at a time (also known as *single-frame* shooting). Use this deliberate mode whenever you just need a single picture.

» **Continuous (a.k.a. sequential or burst):** Continuous modes (there are two types: high-speed and low-speed) fire off exposures for as long as you hold the shutter button down or until the memory card is full. Capture speeds slow down as the camera's buffer gets filled and images wait to be stored on the memory card. How quickly this happens depends on the image size and quality, type (JPEG+Raw, or just one format), and size of the buffer. Choose low-speed when you want to capture a few shots in sequence but don't need 50. Depending on the action or the moment, you may want to switch to high-speed continuous. It's perfect for capturing fleeting moments and slices of action. Use continuous mode when you're shooting brackets of any kind (white balance or exposure brackets for HDR).

» **Self-timer:** Many cameras have 2 and 10 or 12-second timers. These are great if you want to take a self-portrait or if you want to minimize camera shake when using a tripod.

» **Remote:** By the same token, if using a wireless remote, set the drive to the correct mode to support it.

FIGURE 5-20:
Set the drive/
release mode
to take single,
consecutive,
timed, or
remote shots.

Focus mode

Choose a focus mode using the switch on the lens. Some cameras also have this switch on the camera body. Here are your options:

» **Autofocus (AF):** Most people prefer using autofocus. If you do, you have options of changing the AF point selection method (manual or some form of automatic) and the AF mode of operation (single versus continuous).

» **Manual focus (MF):** If you want to switch to manual mode, now is a good time.

AF modes

If you've decided to use autofocus, you have quite a bit of control over how the system works. Your camera has *AF modes* (sometimes called AF Operation), which determine whether the camera focuses once and then beeps or continues to focus while you have the shutter button pressed and held halfway. You can change them using your camera's menu or shooting information display. See Figure 5-21. Here are three common types of AF modes:

>> **Single focus:** The camera focuses once and beeps at you. The AF point used might light up in the viewfinder. This works well for portraits and other non-moving subjects. Also called *one shot* or *single-servo AF.*

>> **Continuous focus:** The camera focuses continually for as long as you hold the shutter halfway down. Use this mode to track moving subjects, or if you're moving. Continuous focus is also called *AI servo* or *continuous-servo AF.*

>> **Automatic switching:** In this mode, the camera automatically switches between single focus and continuous focus as the need arises. Also called *AI focus* or *auto-servo AF.*

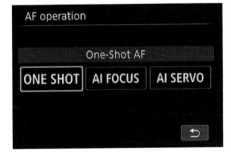

FIGURE 5-21:
This mode determines whether or not the camera keeps autofocusing.

AF point selection methods

Another way to refine how the autofocus system works is to change how it determines what *AF points* (specific points in the camera's viewfinder it uses to focus) to use. Some cameras have an AF Point Selection button. Others require you to use a function or settings screen, as shown in Figure 5-22. There are two broad categories that define how AF points are selected:

>> **Automatic AF point selection:** You let the camera decide which points to use. Most of the time, it does a pretty good job. However, it does have a tendency to focus on the closest object, whether that's what you intend or not.

TIP

Automatic AF point selection may not be precise enough when you're working with extremely shallow depths of field (the area that appears in focus) or when needing to focus on one of several objects at different distances.

>> **Manual AF point selection:** You select the AF point yourself. You generally have to press an AF Point Selection button or make a menu choice to make your selection. Depending on your camera, you may be able to choose a point, a zone, a group of points, a dynamic group of points, or other AF point selection methods.

TECHNICAL STUFF

More expensive cameras have additional AF point selection options. The Canon 5D Mark III professional-level full-frame camera has no fewer than six AF area selection modes. They are: Single-point Spot AF (Manual selection), Spot AF (Manual selection), AF point expansion (Manual selection, 4 surrounding points), AF point expansion (Manual selection, 8 surrounding points), Zone AF (Manual selection of zone), and 61-point automatic selection AF.

FIGURE 5-22:
You can allow the camera to decide or take control of the AF points yourself.

Live View focus modes

Most cameras use different autofocus routines when using Live View. Newer Canon cameras, for instance, offer three ways to use autofocus in Live View: Face Detection + Tracking, FlexiZone Multi, and FlexiZone Single (see Figure 5-23). Each mode has its pros, cons, and quirks. Cameras like the D3400, on the other hand, offer four AF area modes when in Live View: Face-priority AF, Wide-area AF, Normal-area AF, and Subject-tracking AF. You can change focus modes generally from the menu or the Live View shooting display.

FIGURE 5-23:
Investigate your
camera's Live
View focusing
modes.

Metering modes

Your camera should have a number of metering modes that enable you to prioritize how it reacts to light in different parts of the frame. Pattern, Evaluative, Matrix, or Multi-segment metering modes evaluate the entire frame to determine how bright the scene is. Center-weighted Average uses the entire frame but gives priority to the center of the frame. Partial covers a large area in the center of the frame. Spot metering meters a small circle in the center of the frame or the selected autofocus point (depending on the camera). Check your camera for specific metering modes. Some cameras have a Metering mode button. Others require you to access the menu or a shooting information display. I go into more metering detail in Book 3, Chapter 1.

White balance

When your camera's white balance is set correctly, you won't even notice it. Photos will look good and that's that. When white balance is off, photos will have an unnatural-looking color cast to them. Here's what's happening: Digital cameras assess light based on temperature (daylight, for example, has a color temperature that's different from shade or man-made lighting) and use that information to make recorded colors and shades of gray look correct.

I advise changing the White Balance setting on your camera only if you notice that photos look overly blue, yellow, or have a distinctly odd look to them. If you want to experiment, change the White Balance setting to match the lighting conditions of your subject. Some cameras have a White Balance button. Others require you to access them from the menu or a shooting information display. Typical presets shown in Figure 5-24 and described in this list:

>> **Auto:** The camera figures out the conditions and sets a color temperature. This setting works well outdoors and when you're using a flash, but not so well indoors without a flash.

FIGURE 5-24:
There are a
number of white
balance options
to choose from.

REMEMBER

Auto isn't foolproof. The camera can get it wrong. When working with Raw files, you can reset the white balance as if nothing ever happened, without any loss of image quality. This is one of the best reasons to shoot Raw photos.

» **Direct sun:** Use this White Balance setting whenever you're outdoors in the sunlight.

» **Flash:** When you're using flash, choose this setting.

» **Cloudy:** Use this setting on cloudy days.

» **Shade:** The Shade setting is used differently from the Cloudy setting.

» **Tungsten lights:** Use it when you're indoors, working with normal "old-fashioned" light bulbs with a tungsten filament in them.

» **Fluorescent lighting:** You may have a few options for fluorescent lights. For example, higher-level Nikon cameras offer Sodium-Vapor Lamps, Warm-White Fluorescent, White Fluorescent, Cool-White Fluorescent, Day White Fluorescent, Daylight Fluorescent, and High-Temp Mercury-Vapor.

TECHNICAL STUFF

» **Custom/Set temperature:** Set the color temperature based on a photo of a white object you take on location (see Figure 5-25), or manually, in (geekazoid alert) degrees Kelvin.

FIGURE 5-25:
The camera
evaluates the
light and sets a
custom white
balance.

MAXIMIZING PRODUCTIVITY

You don't have to complete a 48-point checklist before you take every photo. The process of checking settings goes pretty quickly once you get started. If your subject remains the same and the lighting is consistent, you won't have to make many changes at all.

That assumes things are going well. Problem solving is the task that slows you down. In that case you need to relax, focus on the problem, and find the solution. For instance, if you're taking action shots and the photos are a bit blurry, the problem may be that you don't have the shutter speed set fast enough. Reset it and try some more.

REMEMBER

However important, don't confuse a good White Balance setting with reality. I noticed this effect when sitting in church one day. I could see the pastor in person and a Live Video display of him at the same time. He was in warm light and had a nice golden glow on his shirt and skin. The video, whose white balance had been set to counteract the color of the light, negated the golden glow and made him "cooler" than he actually was. It looked nice, but wasn't a totally accurate depiction of the scene.

Configure other parameters

Make sure to configure any other features or parameters that are important for this sequence of shots. They are available from your camera's menu or a shooting information display. Here are a few things to think about:

- **»** **Exposure helpers:** If necessary, set or change options like the Auto Lighting Optimizer or Highlight Tone Priority (Canon), D-Lighting (Nikon), Dynamic Range Optimizer (Sony), and any others.

- **»** **Noise reduction:** Set any noise reduction options your camera has for using long exposures or high ISO speeds.

- **»** **Lens corrections:** Ensure any automatic lens distortion or chromatic aberration correction features on your camera are enabled if you desire.

- **»** **Brackets:** Set the number of brackets and any other parameters now. You may be able to shoot either white balance brackets or auto exposure brackets (AEB). Some cameras shoot other types of brackets. The Sony A77, for instance, has a special Dynamic Range Optimizer bracketing mode. For more information on brackets and HDR, see Book 5, Chapter 6.

- **»** **Mirror Lockup or Mirror Up setting:** This setting (see Figure 5-26) reduces camera shake caused by mirror slap, which are vibrations created when the mirror swings up and out of the way to take the photo. When this setting is enabled, the camera flips up the mirror and delays the shutter for a moment. You don't need this feature unless you're using a tripod or another type of support and want the most stable, shake-free shot possible. On some cameras, you'll get a mirror lockup indicated on the camera display or top LCD panel.

Don't forget to revert to normal mirror operation when you finish. I've used mirror delay and forgotten about it, and then wondered why a delay occurred between the time I pressed the shutter button and when the camera took the photo the next time I went out.

Taking and Reviewing Photos

Are you ready to take photos? I bet! Follow these steps:

1. **Confirm the camera is ready and check shooting options.**

   Make sure the lens cap is off and out of the way, the camera and any powered attachments are on, you're in a still photography mode (as opposed to movie), you've set the correct shooting mode, and the focus mode is set correctly. Nothing hurts more than not realizing the camera was set to manual focus mode after shooting 20-30 photos.

   Double-check settings for image quality (see Figure 5-27), exposure controls, color space, noise reduction, red-eye reduction, image review, creative styles, and so forth. Your specific checklist depends on your camera.

   • Canon users should check Picture Style, Auto Lighting Optimizer, Creative Filters, and the like.

   • Nikon users should look at Picture Control, Auto Distortion Control, Active D-Lighting, and so forth.

- Sony users should check settings like Creative Style, Picture Effect, and D-Range Optimizer.

These options are dependent on the shooting mode you're in. The more automatic modes keep you from changing certain settings.

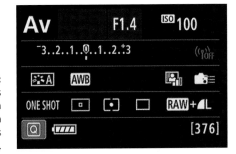

REMEMBER

After completing this step, you need not obsessively check these options before every photo. This step is to make sure the camera is set up the way you want before continuing.

Unless you're engaging in tripod-mounted landscape, macro, or other studio-type photography, it will take longer for you to read through the next few steps than it will to actually accomplish them. That's because composing, focusing, and metering can take place almost simultaneously.

2. **Compose the scene.**

Aim the camera at the subject and place it in the frame of the viewfinder or monitor. If desired, zoom in or out to alter the composition. If you're using a prime lens, you can move yourself closer to or farther away from the subject to change how the photo is composed.

When shooting certain types of shots (animals, people, or action shots), this step may only take a moment. When you're setting up a portrait or shooting macros in a studio, you'll spend more time perfecting the scene.

If things are totally out of focus and impossible to see, quickly press the shutter button halfway to autofocus or turn the focus ring on the lens to manually focus. Otherwise, you'll be looking at blobs and vague shapes. You need to see your subject with some clarity to compose, even if you have to refocus later.

REMEMBER

There's a tried and true framing rule you should know about. It's called the *Rule of Thirds*. The rule suggests that you divide the frame vertically and horizontally into thirds — like a Tic-Tac-Toe board (see Figure 5-28). The idea is to place dominant vertical or horizontal lines in the scene (like building edges, the horizon, people, and so forth) on the dividing lines. You should place important objects at the intersection of those lines or within them. You can also work along the diagonals.

FIGURE 5-28:
Visualizing using
the Rule of
Thirds.

TIP

An advantage of using the Rule of Thirds is being able to align or balance objects in the scene against each other and the empty space. Balancing a scene involves weighing things in the frame (take size, shape, color, brightness, texture, and other factors into account) and positioning them so that most things average out. You can train your eye to see balance well enough that it becomes more of a gut feeling than a conscious act. You'll start to frame photos with balance because they "just feel right."

Do you have to use the Rule of Thirds? No. Should you? Mostly. Although there are always exceptions, humans find it more visually pleasing when things are arranged this way.

3. **Focus.**

If using autofocus, press the shutter button halfway to establish autofocus. Don't stab at the button — press it smoothly. Practice a bit to know what halfway feels like, and how much more pressure causes the camera to take a photo. If you're focusing manually, use the focus ring.

If you're using Live View, focus according to the procedures for your camera. That may involve moving a focusing frame over the subject you want to be in focus. If using Live View and a tripod, you can zoom in and check focus very precisely. I use this technique all the time when shooting close-ups in my studio.

Metering also occurs when you press the shutter button halfway. The camera quickly evaluates the brightness of the scene and calculates the correct exposure to produce a good photo. If desired, enter exposure correction now. If you're in manual mode, make changes to the exposure controls now. Watch the exposure index to see what affect they have on the exposure (more on this in Book 3, Chapter 1).

When you've focused and the exposure looks good, you may have time to quickly adjust your aim. At times, you won't have this luxury. If you only get one take at it, make it a good one. However, many types of photography give you plenty of time to compose the scene, focus and meter, adjust exposure settings, think about it for a while, fine-tune the focus, and then readjust the composition of the scene.

Here are some thoughts to keep in mind when focusing and metering:

- You may be able to press a different button than the shutter button to autofocus. This reduces the chances of accidentally taking photos when focusing. You may also be able to change button assignments.

- In low light, you may have an AF-Assist beam shine out from the camera or flash to help the camera lock onto the target. If this bothers you, you may be able to disable it. Other cameras use a pulse from the built-in flash to help autofocus.

- If you're using autofocus and there is a problem focusing on the subject you want, change focusing modes or focus points if necessary.

- If you're using AE lock, you'll compose the scene differently than normal. Center your subject, focus, and then press and hold the AE Lock button. While holding the AE Lock button down, recompose and take the photo.

4. **Reality check.**

   Check focus indicators, exposure settings, and, if possible, depth of field. This may take only a fraction of a second. Get used to working quickly. For example, if you see the ISO spiking and don't want a noisy photo, you may want to make changes before you take the shot. By the same token, if you're photographing people and notice that the shutter speed is so low that they will be blurred, change it. See Figure 5-29.

FIGURE 5-29:
Quickly confirm that everything is within normal parameters.

5. **Press the shutter button fully to take the photo.**

   If you released the shutter button earlier, press it halfway again to focus and meter. When focus is confirmed, press the shutter button fully to take the shot.

6. **Review the photo.**

   I like reviewing every photo unless the action is fast and furious. Then I review the first few and glance at the rest until there is a break in the action. At a minimum, you should periodically review sample shots to make sure you're not wasting your time.

   Check to see that photos are in focus, well-lit, have good color, and framed the way you want them to be. If necessary, use the zoom in or zoom out buttons in

Playback mode to look closely at the photo, and the left, right, up, or down buttons to pan. This is also a good time to look at the histogram. Figure 5-30 shows the final shot.

FIGURE 5-30:
Review photos to ensure they captured what you intended.

7. **Correct problems.**

REMEMBER

Correcting problems is an important step. If you identify problems when reviewing photos, make changes to correct them.

You're looking to solve these general issues:

- *Composition:* Level, even, or as planned.
- *Exposure:* Good, with details in bright and dark areas, or as intended. Check metering mode if necessary to get a better reading of the scene.
- *Focus:* Sharp, unless you're after a special effect.
- *Color:* Good, with correct white balance.
- *Subject-related:* Eyes open, looking at the camera or where you intend.

8. **Rinse and repeat.**

Depending on what you're shooting, you may be able to quickly cycle back to Step 2 and keep at it. If you want to make dramatic changes to your setup, such as changing lenses, trying different shooting modes, or changing other major settings, return to the earlier section "Setting Up Your Camera" and reconfigure the camera.

2 Looking Through Lenses

Contents at a Glance

Chapter **1**

Appreciating Standard Zoom Lenses

N ormal or *standard zoom lenses* are the first digital SLR lens most people handle. These lenses are widely used because inexpensive models (up to a few hundred dollars) are packaged with consumer-level dSLR kits. Hence, they are often called *kit lenses.* Standard zoom lenses are also used because they are incredibly versatile. You can shoot anything from wide-angle landscapes to telephoto portraits simply by twisting the zoom ring. As I show you in this chapter, there's not a lot you *can't* do with zoom lenses! Standard zoom lenses are not just for amateurs, though. Even professional photographers use zoom lenses.

Embodying Versatility

Standard zoom lenses, also known as a *multipurpose zoom, zoom, normal zoom,* or *general-purpose zoom,* are designed to be versatile enough to be useful in a wide variety of circumstances. The name sort of gives that away.

There are other types of zoom lenses, of course. Some cover wide-angle or telephoto territory exclusively. Others have a wider range of focal lengths than general-purpose zoom lenses. Standard zoom lenses, though, cover the focal length range that you need most of the time for everyday photography. In other words, the "sweet spot." They dip into wide-angle territory, fully encompass normal focal lengths, and extend into the telephoto range. This makes them very handy lenses to have.

Standard zoom lenses come in all price ranges. Most kit lenses are relatively inexpensive. Manufacturers try to keep costs down when bundling the camera and lens together. There are also mid-level zoom lenses and professional models that cost upwards of $2,000. Pro-level lenses, like that shown in Figure 1-1 (AF-S NIKKOR 24–70mm f/2.8G ED), are fantastic. They have better optical qualities and construction than less expensive models, can stand the rigors of shooting without breaking as easily, and take outstanding photos. To see more examples of standard zoom lenses, have a look at some of the cameras and lenses shown in Book 1, Chapters 1 and 3.

Here are some points to ponder when using a standard zoom lens:

>> **Experiment with different shooting modes:** You can use any of your camera's shooting modes with a standard zoom lens. Scenes and Auto are real helpers if you're just beginning.

>> **It's fun and pretty easy:** You don't have to be a rocket scientist to use a general-purpose zoom lens. Walk around, point your camera at things you see, zoom to frame the shot you want, and then snap the picture. Having a zoom lens lets you flexibly frame subjects at different distances.

REMEMBER

In the sections that follow, I make sure to mention the brand of the camera I used for each photo, the sensor size, and the focal length the lens was set to when I took the photo. This is enough information for you to calculate the 35mm equivalent focal length for cropped-frame dSLRs on your own, should you want to.

At times, I include that to emphasize a point. Refer to Book 1, Chapters 1 and 3 for more information on image sensor sizes, crop factors, and 35mm equivalent focal lengths.

Taking Wide-Angle Shots

Wide-angle photography captures a greater angle of view than normal or telephoto focal lengths. Sometimes you perceive the photos as being very expansive. At other times, you hardly notice it. It all depends on the subject and how you frame the scene.

Figure 1-2 shows a farmland scene that I took using a Sony APS-C camera and a standard kit lens zoomed out to 18mm. The scene is clearly wide, but not in the extreme. When shooting wide-angle landscapes, you should zoom all the way out to capture as much of the scene as possible. That approach captures breadth, while the details in the scene, and where they are located, add depth. In this case, the corn and the clouds take up most of the frame. They also provide color and interesting details that liven up the photo. The homestead sits in the distance, intriguing, and yet purposefully small. That's exactly what wide-angle shots are good for. Notice that I employed the Rule of Thirds in this shot. Typically, wide-angle landscape shots do not look as good when angled or out of balance.

FIGURE 1-2: Standard zoom lenses are very effective at capturing wide, expansive scenery.

Don't think that you always need a super, over-the-top-ultra-mega wide-angle lens. If you like, you can take several shots with your kit lens set to the wider angles and create panoramas.

Figure 1-3 shows a very different type of wide-angle shot. This is an interior scene that I photographed with a standard zoom lens and Canon APS-C camera. It's a unique wide-angle perspective that almost hides that fact. I zoomed all the way out to initially frame the elevator doors, then angled the camera a bit and zoomed in slightly to 20mm to take the shot.

FIGURE 1-3:
Get close and zoom out to capture interior scenes in detail.

The fact that I angled the camera adds some quirkiness to the photo. It's not meant to be a serious shot of the machinery or architecture, but rather a fun look at the red doors. Because I was using a standard zoom lens, I was able to zoom in and out as I photographed objects and scenes around the doors, even inside the elevator, without having to change lenses.

Not all wide-angle shots have to be landscapes or interiors. In Figure 1-4, I was standing behind a protective fence, photographing my youngest son running toward home plate. I was using the same APS-C camera and lens, and even focal length (18mm) that I used in Figure 1-2. I was much closer to my main subject, however, and composed the scene differently.

This shot has a number of wonderful elements. Sam, the coaches, the other kids, the ball in the air, and the scenery all capture the essence of the action as it was happening. Although action shots look great when shot at zoomed-in telephoto focal lengths, some — such as this one — work as wide-angle photos.

TIP

Standard zoom lenses give you the ability to tell complete stories. You can take wide-angle supporting shots, zoom in and take normal shots of particular elements of the scene, and then zoom in further for close-ups of details.

Here are some tips to consider when shooting wide-angle shots with your standard zoom lens:

>> **Try it.** Most people like zooming in more than they appreciate zooming out. Don't fall into the trap of not using the wide-angle range of your zoom lens. Zoom out, Luke.

>> **Use smaller apertures.** Combine a wide angle of view with a deep depth of field by using an aperture of f/8 or smaller. This makes more of the photo appear to be in focus.

>> **Composition is more challenging.** The more you put in the frame, the harder it is to get everything to work well together. Pay attention to the background and edges of the frame, how things are aligned, how they are balanced, and distractions like power poles and cables.

Working with Normal Focal Lengths

Normal focal lengths (those about the same as the diagonal measurement of your sensor) are the bread and butter of traditional photography. They are very pleasing to the eye because they look very much like what you see. I took the shot shown in Figure 1-5 on an incredible snowy day by a lake. I walked up to an overlooking deck with the intent of photographing the water and far bank, and realized the snow on the railing would make an interesting subject. I used a Canon APS-C camera and standard zoom lens set to 33mm.

I'm convinced this photo works as well as it does because the focal length is within the normal range (about 58mm in 35mm equivalent terms). Had I zoomed out, the railing would have shrunk and taken a less dominant role in the photo. The background would have become more important, which was not the point. Had I zoomed in and framed a tight shot of the railing, the bigger picture would have been lost.

REMEMBER

Figure 1-5 was a casual, spur-of-the-moment shot. Having a zoom lens gave me the flexibility to quickly choose just how to frame the scene. I didn't have to move closer or farther away — I simply gave the lens a twist and took the photo.

FIGURE 1-5:
Not every land-scape has to be captured with a wide-angle focal length.

Figure 1-6 shows an entirely different scene, shot using a Canon APS-C camera and kit lens set to 32mm. As a family, we had been out playing in the yard. I took some casual shots of everyone and then gave the camera to my wife so that she and the kids could review them. While they enjoyed the photos, I grabbed another camera and took this shot.

For this scene to work, I needed to select a focal length that would capture every-one in the shot (it's a group photo, after all). I zoomed out initially to see what that would look like. Too wide. I quickly zoomed in and stopped when I was satisfied with the composition. Just right. The final focal length was 32mm (about 51mm in 35mm equivalent terms). Zooming in further would have ruined the composition.

TIP

When shooting portraits, zoom in to minimize the background.

FIGURE 1-6:
Use normal focal
lengths to keep
people from look-
ing distorted.

Finally, I took the shot in Figure 1-7 using the Nikon APS-C camera and professional lens shown earlier in Figure 1-1. I composed the scene using a focal length
of 40mm. That was close to the middle of the focal length range of the lens, and
right on the edge between normal and near-telephoto focal lengths. In this case I
wanted the attention focused mostly on the tree, and yet I didn't want the tree to
totally obscure the lake and other scenery in the background. Given my distance
to the tree, a normal focal length achieved the right effect. Zooming out would
have overemphasized the background, and zooming in would have eliminated it.

FIGURE 1-7:
Zoom in and out
to find the right
balance between
foreground and
background.

Keep these things in mind when shooting in the normal focal length range:

>> **Everyday use:** Normal focal lengths are perfect for everyday photography.

>> **Normal look:** These focal lengths produce the most normal-looking photos. Use them when you want a classic 35mm feel to your shots.

>> **Less distortion:** Normal focal lengths tend to produce photos with less distortion than wide-angle focal lengths.

TIP

>> **Use the vertical:** Hold the camera vertically at times to change the composition.

Zooming In

Most people want to get larger or closer shots of their subjects. I know I do, and my wife and kids are the same way. I've got great news for you: Zoom lenses are perfect for this. They enable you to increase the focal length of the lens by zooming in, whether you are near your subject or far away. How much you can zoom in depends on your lens, of course.

When zooming in, consider these points:

>> **Shutter speed:** The more you zoom in, the harder it is to take sharp photos. Camera shake becomes more of a problem. Make sure image stabilization is enabled and select a faster shutter speed if needed to keep things from getting blurry.

>> **Portraits:** Taking shots of people in the near-telephoto range of your standard zoom lens can result in very effective portraits.

>> **Distance matters:** Using the telephoto focal lengths of a standard zoom lens at close range will produce very tightly framed shots. When outside or shooting something farther away, the same focal lengths will produce very different results.

Capturing telephoto shots

Telephoto shots share two distinct characteristics: They use focal lengths greater than the diagonal size of the image sensor and are taken some distance from the subject.

Figure 1-8 shows my three boys (Sam, Ben, and Jacob) in costume one Halloween. I used the zoom ring on the kit lens of a Sony APS-C camera to frame the shot how I wanted it, which came out to a focal length of 45mm. That doesn't sound like a lot, but you should remember that a crop factor of 1.5x makes this the equivalent of 68mm on a full-frame camera. That puts this shot just inside the near (or medium) telephoto range. Compare this photo to the group shot in Figure 1-6. I'm standing farther back in this shot and have zoomed in more. While the aperture in both photos is f/5.6, the background is more attractively blurred in this photo. You get that by using a longer focal length.

FIGURE 1-8:
Longer focal lengths enable you to stand farther back and still capture great portraits.

Picture this: One day my family and I heard an odd sound coming from outside. We all ran out the front door (there are six of us, so that is an event in and of itself) to see what it was. Lo and behold, it was *the Goodyear Blimp!* I ran back into the house and grabbed the camera (Canon APS-C). Thankfully, the lens I was using had a maximum focal length of 135mm. I zoomed in fully and captured the blimp before it flew away. See Figure 1-9.

FIGURE 1-9:
Zoom all the way in to capture objects at a distance.

In cases like this, having a camera with a healthy number of megapixels really helps. While you clearly want as much zoom as you can get out of your lens, the pixel count gives you the option of cropping out extra space without compromising the photo's quality if you decide to get a large print made.

Finally, Figure 1-10 is a casual portrait of my wife outside prepping for a family dinner on our picnic table. I shot this with a Canon full-frame dSLR using a 24-105mm lens set at 105mm. That makes this a near (or medium) telephoto portrait. Aside from marveling at just how pretty she is (natural smiles and laughter make for great photos), notice the background in this scene compared to Figures 1-6 and 1-8. This one is by far the most pleasing. Part of the reason is the lens, but it's also the fact that the focal length in this photo (105mm) is the longest. On an APS-C camera with a crop factor of 1.6x, you would have to use a focal length of 65mm or more to have the same effect.

FIGURE 1-10: Zoom in to capture stunning near telephoto portraits.

REMEMBER

Unlike the group shot of the boys, having a single subject enables me to focus entirely on her. The result is a great photograph — shot with a really nice zoom lens. However, near telephoto focal lengths on standard zoom lenses are quite effective at shooting group *and* individual portraits.

Capturing close-ups

Close-up photography is another category that you can pursue very effectively with a standard zoom lens. As with telephoto shots, you zoom in to magnify the subject. The key difference between the two, however, is that you are typically closer when shooting a close-up.

Figure 1-11 is a classic close-up of a bowl full of radishes sitting on a table, taken with a Canon APS-C camera and standard zoom lens. I set up this classic "foodie" shot from start to finish. I chose the subject, the lighting, the placement, the distance I stood at, and the focal length I used (55mm). I was able to get the shot I wanted without having to resort to any special equipment or a macro lens. While that is sometimes necessary, it's very nice to be able to grab your camera and a zoom lens and just take photos.

FIGURE 1-11:
Get close to your subject and then zoom in and out to compose the shot.

Portraits shot as close-ups also work well. Figure 1-12 in a fun shot of one of my kids. We were all out in the backyard one hot August day playing with water balloons, hoses, and shaving cream (we run a fun household). Jake has on goggles to protect his eyes and is lathering himself up before his mom turns the hose on. Nothing says "close-up action-portrait" more than that!

FIGURE 1-12:
Step closer and zoom in if you need to capture a nice close-up.

While he was getting ready, I zoomed in to 44mm with my Nikon APS-C dSLR. I wasn't standing far away to begin with. The combination of being relatively close and zooming in resulted in a wonderfully nice, tight shot of his face and pleasantly blurred background. Compare how I framed this photo to the one in Figure 1-10. While their faces take up similar space within the frame, I consider this an effective *close-up* because I was standing much closer and the focal lengths, while both in the near telephoto range, were very different.

REMEMBER

You want a nice, shallow depth of field in a portrait. You can get that by choosing focal lengths in the telephoto range as well as using a wide aperture.

Finally, flowers make fantastic close-up subjects. They are beautiful, colorful, easy to find, and don't blink. Figure 1-13 is a nice close-up of a vase of flowers I shot on a table in my studio. I mounted my Canon APS-C dSLR on a tripod, composed the scene using the camera's Live View mode, and kept camera-shake to a minimum by using a wireless remote shutter release. Taken with an inexpensive kit lens at 55mm, this shot is simply gorgeous.

FIGURE 1-13: Shoot a close-up to capture as much detail as you can.

Chapter **2**

Enjoying Wide-Angle Lenses

Wide-angle photography is fun, and possibly more versatile than you might think. You can shoot sweeping landscapes and large cityscapes, of course, but can also capture great-looking shots of other interesting subjects, including buildings, interiors, people, and more. It's easy to fall in love with this type of photography, and it's a refreshing change of pace from stalking the cat around the house. Join me in this chapter as I walk you through how to take great wide-angle shots of different subjects.

Wide-Angle Whatzit

A *wide-angle lens* is a lens whose focal length is greater than the diagonal size of the image sensor in the dSLR. If you've shot with a standard zoom lens, you've already been exposed to wide angles — maybe without even realizing it. Here is a summary of what lenses are able to take wide-angle photos:

> » **Cropped frame:** Most cropped-frame kits for consumer-level APS-C cameras have zoom lenses with focal lengths from 18–55mm. That means you're equipped and able to shoot wide angles, as long as you zoom out from 18mm to 25mm.

Four Thirds cameras with kit lenses from 14–42mm should zoom out to at least 20mm to enjoy wide-angle photography.

>> **Full frame:** If you're a full-frame user with a standard zoom lens, you probably have good wide-angle capability built into your lens. For example, the Canon EF 24–105mm f/4L IS USM lens operates in wide-angle territory (when mounted on a full-frame camera) from 24mm to about 40mm.

Aside from standard zoom lenses with wide-angle focal lengths, there are a number of different types of dedicated wide-angle zoom and wide-angle prime lenses available from most lens manufacturers. You can also pick up an ultra wide-angle zoom lens, as shown in Figure 2-1. Turn to Book 1, Chapter 3 for more information on focal lengths and how wide-angles compare to everything else.

TIP

When you're deciding whether a focal length is wide angle or not, it's important to consider the camera as well as the lens. For example, 35mm is considered a normal focal length on an APS-C camera because of its crop factor, but wide angle on a full-frame camera.

FIGURE 2-1:
Ultra wide-angle lenses capture amazing scenes.

REMEMBER

In this chapter, I mention the camera and sensor size along with the focal length of each photo. With this information, you can calculate 35mm equivalent focal length if you like, and compare it to your setup if you're using different gear. Book 1, Chapters 1 and 3 have more information on how to do this and why it's sometimes necessary.

Looking at Landscapes

You can find few better tools for shooting landscapes than a digital SLR with a wide-angle lens. Throw in a tripod and a remote shutter release and you're set. The tripod lets you take longer exposures without worrying about keeping the camera steady. I recommend using a remote in these instances to minimize camera shake.

I photographed the sunset in Figure 2-2 using just those tools. The weather was ideal. The sun was just about to set behind the trees. The glow reflected off the river, which extended into the distance. It was amazing to see in person, and amazing to photograph with my Sony APS-C dSLR. I set the lens to 10mm to capture as much as possible.

FIGURE 2-2:
A beautiful sunset photographed with an ultra wide-angle lens.

Figure 2-3 shows a totally different scene, shot using the same basic techniques to photograph this scene. I used a Nikon APS-C camera, set the lens to 11mm, mounted the camera on a tripod, and used a remote to trigger the shutter. The entire scene was well lit by the evening sun, which is to the left of the frame. The clouds add welcome texture and detail to the sky.

Keep these tips in mind when shooting wide-angle landscapes:

>> **Great shots are about great locations.** There are a lot of pretty places in the world, but a lot of them have elements like power poles, lines, and signs that take away from the natural beauty. I've discovered that the landscape shots that I like the best are free from these distractions. It's not always easy to find these locations, but you will if you keep an eye out.

FIGURE 2-3:
The wind-swept plains of Oklahoma captured near sunset.

TIP

>> **Keep the camera level.** Keep the camera as level as possible unless you want to spend time aligning all your shots in Photoshop. You should activate your camera's electronic level to orient the camera. Having a tripod really helps.

>> **Compose using the Rule of Thirds.** It's even more important to remember the Rule of Thirds when framing wide-angle shots, especially landscapes with the horizon. Notice that in my two examples the horizon is at the bottom third of the photo. If you like, compose your shots so that the land, rather than the sky, dominates.

REMEMBER

Wide-angle lenses *vignette* quite often, which means their corners are darker than their centers. You can correct this problem in software or with special in-camera lens correction options, if available. I sometimes use vignetting purposely to make the photo look interesting.

Capturing Wide-Angle Cityscapes

Wide-angle lenses also excel at capturing entire cities (or reasonably large parts thereof). Figure 2-4 shows one way to capture an expansive view. I took this shot from inside the top of the Gateway Arch in St. Louis, Missouri. The sun is off to the left of the frame and made shooting in that direction very difficult. I chose to angle the camera to the north for this shot. Notice that this photo is an example of not strictly following the Rule of Thirds. The horizon is in the center of the frame, which is sometimes bad. In this case, I think it works. The city below leads your eyes along the diagonal toward a point to the right and below the center of the photo. The window frame also accentuates this line.

This photo is particularly interesting because you can see about 30 miles (48 km) toward the distant horizon, yet the buildings in the city below are nice and detailed. The highway angling away from the Arch is a great element. The cars and trucks travelling on it are mostly dots. This is a stunning location to shoot from. I took this shot using a Nikon APS-C camera and ultra wide-angle lens set to 14mm.

Not every city has a good vantage point from which to photograph. Of those that do, not all are equally accessible. You should, however, be able to find some interesting buildings to photograph. Look at your downtown area near the city center. If that doesn't work, look at other parts, perhaps well outside. These are often photogenic. Schools, museums, memorials, and government buildings are often ideal subjects. When you find the right subject, make sure you have your wide-angle lens with you, because you'll need it.

Figure 2-5 shows a small part of downtown Detroit. I am standing on Brush Street, looking southeast toward the Renaissance Center. This street reminded me of a canyon, so I got in the middle and used the buildings on both sides to frame the far end of the street. I set the lens to 20mm and took the shot with my Sony APS-C camera. Notice that I'm a few blocks away from the subject of the photo. This is a testament to how tall the building is. In situations like this, you may have to physically move to the right distance for your shot to work.

TIP

When you're shooting cityscapes, keep these tips in mind:

>> **Do a walkabout.** Choosing the right vantage point is probably the most challenging aspect of capturing cityscapes. In some cases, you may not be able to find a good view at all, especially if the terrain is flat and there are no surrounding hills or heights. You can often find a good spot to shoot from if the city is bordered by water on one or more sides.

Enjoying Wide-Angle Lenses

>> **Watch the horizon.** A crooked horizon can be distracting unless it's a purposeful design element of the photo. If you can't eyeball it, use a level.

>> **Check the foreground.** Pay attention to what's close to you as well as what's off in the distance.

Focusing on Single Buildings

You don't always have to photograph as much of a city as possible. Single buildings are often easier and more convenient to capture. Figure 2-6 shows the former Dearborn Hyatt Regency (now Edward Village Michigan) located just across the road from the Ford Motor Company world headquarters. It's a large, curved, 14-story building. I took several shots of the entire building, but then moved in close to the entrance and held the camera vertically to capture this photo. It showcases the curve of the top very nicely, along with the restaurant on top. The white car in front of the door was a matter of fortunate timing that I took advantage of. I used a Sony APS-C camera for this photo, and set the lens to 10mm.

Figure 2-7 shows another close-up of a single building. This time it's the Allen County War Memorial Coliseum (named well before the 140-character limit imposed by Twitter), located in Indiana. Originally built in 1952, this large arena was updated in 2001 when they literally raised the roof over 40 feet. They made other extensive renovations and improvements at that time, and have since added on almost 50,000 square feet of additional conference and event space adjoining the arena. It's totally impressive.

FIGURE 2-6:
Single buildings
are natural
subjects for
wide-angle
photography.

FIGURE 2-7:
Point the camera
up to capture cre-
ative viewpoints.

The building is so large you have to step well back to photograph it, even using wide angles. For a more dramatic, artistic presentation, I chose to get close to it for this photo and point the camera up. This side of the Coliseum faces west, and light from the setting sun is bathing it in golden hour goodness. I used a Sony APS-C dSLR and ultra wide–angle lens set to 10mm. This shot would be impossible without using wide angles.

Find out as much as you can about what you're photographing. Learning draws you closer to your subjects and gives you stories to tell.

Photographing Interiors

Believe it or not, a wide-angle lens is indispensable when shooting indoors, whether you're in a large or small location.

I took the photo shown in Figure 2-8 from the balcony of a local church. The modern sanctuary is large and open, and ends in a stage rather than a pulpit. The room invites you to photograph it with a wide-angle lens. In fact, it really requires it. I had to move to the back of the balcony and zoom out to 10mm with my Nikon APS-C camera to fit the entire room in the frame.

FIGURE 2-8:
Interiors, large and small, are captured nicely by wide-angle lenses.

The problem with large interiors, however, is normally lighting. While the scene may look fine in person, photographing interiors usually requires more light than you think, and larger rooms have a tendency to be even darker. The situation is made even more difficult if you want to stop down and use a smaller aperture to increase the depth of field. To cope with the lighting and capture a reasonable shot, use a longer shutter speed, higher ISO, additional lighting, or a technique like HDR (high dynamic range) photography.

Wide-angle lenses can be incredibly practical. Take your digital SLR and a wide-angle lens (a zoom lens may work fine) with you when house shopping. When you review the photos, you'll see *rooms* instead of corners. That will make it easier to plan how you will furnish and decorate.

Keep these points in mind when shooting wide-angle interiors:

>> **Watch for vertical distortion.** Pointing the camera up or down will introduce vertical distortion, which is particularly unappealing in interior shots. As you compose the scene, pay attention to vertical lines. If they tip toward or away from you, you know you have a problem. Unless you have an overriding artistic purpose, keep the camera pointing straight away from you (as opposed to up or down).

>> **Use a tripod if possible.** Although you may think you don't need a tripod when shooting inside, exposure can be a real challenge. Being able to use slower shutter speeds will help you keep the ISO low, which will in turn keep noise from overwhelming an otherwise good shot.

Shooting Wide-Angle Portraits

My wife took the shot shown in Figure 2-9 of me and our three boys as we were dropping one of our kids off at summer camp. We're proudly displaying our sunglasses and having a great time hamming it up for her. She was using a Canon APS-C dSLR and standard zoom lens set to 18mm. That's right in the middle of the wide-angle range for an APS-C camera. While not an impressive landscape, this is nonetheless a very valuable wide-angle shot to show. You can capture artistic shots or photos of everyday life, including portraits of people, using wide angles. Simply put, this is one of my favorite photos, and it was shot spontaneously.

FIGURE 2-9:
Wide-angle portraits capture groups of people very effectively.

One key to using wide angles when photographing people is not to be too far away. Unless you're photographing a large group of people, stay close. Another important point is to makes sure the shutter speed is quick enough to capture guys who are giggling and being silly. My wife set the camera to shutter-priority mode with a shutter speed of 1/500 second. That was possible because we were outside in bright sunlight.

Not every wide-angle shot requires a special lens, tripod, remote, or other extra gear. Keep your standard zoom lens attached and zoom out when you need to.

REMEMBER

Improving Your Wide-Angle Shots

Wide-angle photography is incredibly fun, and there are many ways to improve your photos. When you go out to take wide-angle shots, try to use wide-angle focal lengths to your advantage. You will be rewarded with special photos if you recognize and emphasize elements of the scene that cry out to be photographed with wide angles.

Frame tall objects from afar

When shooting a scene and you want to make sure and get it all in, step back and use a wide-angle lens. Figure 2-10 is an exterior shot of the Gateway Arch. My family and I had just arrived for a visit and were walking down the trail from the now-demolished parking garage toward the Arch. I took a series of shots as we got closer. In this one, I estimate my position to be about 100 feet away. It looks closer than that in the photo, but the Arch is huge and distances can be deceiving in wide-angle shots. The legs, for reference, are 54 feet wide at the base. The moral of the story is this: Distance can make the world of difference when shooting in wide-angle territory. I was able to capture the entire Arch with very little apparent distortion because I stood back and used an ultra wide-angle lens set to 14mm on a Nikon dSLR (APS-C).

Pointing the camera up or down when you're working with focal lengths in the wide-angle region causes vertical distortion. At times, you have no choice. In this case, though, I moved back to photograph the Arch. That kept vertical distortion in this photo to a minimum.

Some wide-angle scenes confuse automatic focus modes. If yours is complex and you have a specific point that you want in focus, consider choosing the specific AF point yourself or switching to manual focus.

TIP

FIGURE 2-10:
This shot
features large
and small
subjects
simultaneously.

Get up close and personal

I took the photo shown in Figure 2-11 from a low perspective, but more importantly, up close and personal. The camera is about 18 inches away from the front wheel of this gorgeous yellow Harley. I used a Sony APS-C dSLR and set the focal length of the lens to 10mm.

The point here is that I was able to feature the entire bike and still have room for the building and the sky by getting pretty close. In fact, I was sitting on the ground when I took this shot. The result? Everything fits without making the motorcycle seem small. In fact, it dominates the frame. This would not have been possible with another lens. I would have had to photograph a particular part of the bike or move away to fit it all in.

TIP

You don't always have to be standing up when you take a photo. Likewise, if you continually set your tripod to the same height, your shots will end up looking similar. Shake things up — consider using the ground for support, instead — even when you're using a wide-angle lens.

FIGURE 2-11:
You can get close
with wide-angle
lenses.

Use the vertical

Don't be afraid to switch your camera to a vertical (portrait) orientation, even when shooting wide-angle shots. The photo in Figure 2-12 is an effective example. I took this shot using a Nikon APSC-dSLR and wide-angle zoom lens set to 10mm. I didn't need to hold the camera vertically, but after taking a series of shots holding the camera normally I decided I wanted a change of pace. I therefore switched to portrait orientation (holding the camera vertically). The result is a compelling shot that enabled me to capture much more of the lake and sky than I would have otherwise. Instead of the photo extending left and right, it goes out and up.

Combine different elements into one shot

Sweeping landscapes and impressive cultural monuments aren't the only beautiful scenes out there to capture in wide angles. Figure 2-13 shows a local park. It's simple, but still very compelling. I took this shot with a Nikon (APS-C) dSLR and an ultra wide-angle lens set to 11mm. The scene has several elements that make it work. The colorful brick path is covered with a scattering of small leaves and is very important to the photo. It extends away and disappears as it sweeps to the right in the distance. That creates a feeling of mystery. The trees on each side add color, and the lamps, bench, and fences add interesting details. The clouds and the sky are equally important. I was able to capture all these different elements in one shot without making the photo look cramped. In fact, it feels nice and relaxed.

FIGURE 2-12:
Frame some sub-
jects vertically for
a change of pace.

FIGURE 2-13:
Beautiful scenery
is everywhere
around you.

Emphasize height

Use wide-angle shots to emphasize height. The photo shown in Figure 2-14 is of the Cadillac Tower in Detroit, Michigan. This building is 40 stories tall and 438 feet high. Although that is 192 feet shorter than the Gateway Arch shown earlier, it still looks quite impressive in this shot.

Enjoying Wide-Angle Lenses

FIGURE 2-14:
Wide-angle lenses
can emphasize
height as well as
width.

I used a wide-angle lens set to 10mm and held the camera (Sony dSLR with an APS-C image sensor) vertically to fit the entire building in the shot. That's the beauty of using wide-angle lenses. You can fit in so much more than normal lenses, including very tall buildings. The reason this shot appears to have quite a bit of vertical distortion is that I had to point the camera up to get the top of the building in the scene. While I could have stood farther away and held the camera closer to horizontal, I chose to get right next to the building and look up. I wanted to fill the frame with as much of the building as possible for artistic effect and to emphasize its height.

DEALING WITH DISTORTION

Depending on the subject, wide-angle lens distortion can go unnoticed. However, some scenes shot with extremely wide angles bring it to the forefront. This is particularly true of people. If distortion (including odd perspectives) bothers you, try easing up on the focal length. See if you can find a sweet spot where the distortion is minimal. You can also try removing or minimizing it with your photo editor or Raw converter. Not all wide-angle lenses perform the same. If you have a lens with particularly bad distortion, you may consider returning it to the store for a different brand or model of wide-angle lens. For more on image processing and editing, turn to Book 5.

Chapter **3**

Capturing Macros and Close-ups

M acros and close-up photos tend to evoke "oohs" and "aahs" from us because they give us a vantage point we don't normally see. Small bugs become huge. Hidden details become visible. The mundane becomes magical. You can literally see the hair on a fly's backside. I've packed this chapter with information about macro and close-up photography so that you can see it in action. Take advantage of the tips and techniques I share to help you get started and capture amazingly cool photos. Finally, shop for accessories that will help you shoot close-ups with normal lenses. Enjoy!

Defining Macro and Close-up Photography

Technically, macro photography relies on special lenses called *macro* lenses. (Nikon calls them *micro* lenses.) Macro lenses have two defining characteristics:

>> **Reproduction ratio:** Macro lenses focus objects on the sensor closer to their actual size than non-macro lenses. This is called the *reproduction ratio*. Ideally, macro lenses should have a one-to-one ratio. Some even enlarge objects by having a greater than one-to-one ratio. However, many macro lenses

don't offer this type of reproduction ratio; if they do, it may not be available throughout the lens's entire focus range.

TIP

Not all macro lenses have the same reproduction ratios. When you're shopping for a macro lens, look carefully at its specifications. That way you avoid buying a lens labeled "macro" that falls short in the reproduction ratio category.

>> **Close focusing distance:** Macro lenses can focus at very close ranges. Most normal lenses have close focusing distances around a foot, or between one and two feet. Telephoto lens close focusing distances may be several feet. Macro lens close focusing distances may only be a few inches.

TIP

Both of these characteristics make focal length less obviously important to macro photography than other types. Focal length is still important in determining the angle of view you will get, and therefore you should pay attention to it. However, unlike telephoto lenses, focal length isn't a good measure of how powerful a macro lens is. Therefore, you can find *macro primes* (those with a fixed focal length) in a whole range of focal lengths.

Close-up photography is a less technically restrictive pursuit. Anything you photograph from a relatively close perspective qualifies. As with macro photography, the point of a close-up is to zoom in or get close enough to the subject to make it appear large. You can use any lens you want.

TIP

Regardless of how you take your macros and close-ups, you can always zoom in even further when you process the photos in software. That's a great advantage of having a camera with a few million pixels to spare around the edges.

Shooting at Close Ranges

Macro lenses and normal lenses fitted with the right accessories can focus on objects much closer than standard zoom or prime lenses. Depending on the lens you're using, you may be able to position yourself exceptionally close to your subject.

I've done just that in Figure 3-1. This is a photo of one of my kids' toys (just like the ones I used to play with). He's the one throwing the hand grenade. I put him down on the table and snuck up on him real close to take this shot. He appears to be happy with his work and his uniform fits him like a glove. I took this photo in a studio setting, so I had a lot of bright lights shining from several angles.

FIGURE 3-1:
Gung Ho for
macros.

TIP

Light and using the viewfinder can sometimes be problematic when this close. If you can't see what's happening through your viewfinder, switch to Live View. You may have to increase the ISO speed to brighten the scene on the monitor. This also helps if you manually focus, if needed.

Managing Depth of Field

When you move close to your subjects, aperture isn't the only factor that affects depth of field. At these ranges, the depth of field shrinks, regardless of what setting you choose. Keep in mind that the settings you're used to won't produce the same results.

When shooting macros or close-up work I often work with apertures set to f/16 or smaller. This increases the depth of field enough so that my subjects are reasonably sharp. The depth of field is still small, however. When it's a problem, I rely on positioning to manage depth of field. Rather than shoot at an angle, I try to flatten my angle so that what I am interested in is on the same plane. Figure 3-1 is a good example of this.

Capturing Macros and Close-ups

Of course, you can have fun either way. Figure 3-2 shows rain droplets on a leaf. The depth of field is incredibly narrow — only a few small water droplets deep. In this case, that makes the photo much more interesting.

REMEMBER

Working with very shallow depths of field can make focusing difficult. Add in camera weight and subjects that may not stay still for long, and you've got a real challenge. When that happens, relax and take a deep breath. Switch off your targeting computer and trust yourself, as Obi-Wan suggests. Focus the lens as best you can, then take your hand off the focus ring. Move the camera until the scene looks best, and take the photo.

Shooting Handheld (with a Flash)

You can set up a base camp and mount your camera on a tripod to shoot flowers, but bugs move. They flit here and there. When I set up my camera on its tripod and zero in on a flower, all the bugs chose the other flowers to land on. Hmm. If that happens to you, ditch the tripod and stalk bugs on foot with a long focal length macro lens.

Figure 3-3 illustrates a good example of a handheld shot where everything seemed to work perfectly. The image of the fly is sharp, colorful, and in focus. If you look carefully, you can see my reflection in the fly's body segments. The brighter spots are from the external flash I used to help light the scene, which I shot in the late afternoon. I set the aperture to f/11 as a compromise between having a decent depth of field and needing more light, and I raised the ISO marginally. Even with those changes, the shutter speed was a paltry 1/60 second. Thankfully, the macro lens had vibration reduction.

The long focal length I used helped, too. I had the amazing Micro-NIKKOR 105mm f/2.8G lens mounted, and if that wasn't enough, the TC-20E III 2x teleconverter attached. The total 35mm equivalent focal length was 210mm. This let me position myself and the lens farther away from the fly than, say, a 60mm macro. A longer macro is better for photographing skittish, stinging, or dangerous insects that are likely to fly away or attack you when you're too close.

TIP

Exposure can sometimes be a problem when you *stop down* (set a smaller aperture). If necessary, raise ISO or use a flash, if possible.

TIP

Take breaks more often when you're shooting handheld macros, especially if you're outside in the heat. The weight of the camera and macro lens will tire you out faster. While this may not seem like such a big deal, remember that you're focusing on such tiny items that any camera movement can knock you out of the focal plane. Keeping elements steady is difficult, even with fast shutter speeds and vibration reduction turned on.

If you're patient in the right situation (for example, you have a bird feeder within close range that gets regular visits) you can set up your camera on a tripod and pretend that you're on safari.

Maximizing Shutter Speed

If you're shooting bugs, you have to be able to handle movement. One bee I tracked flitted diligently from flower to flower to flower. (That's what bees do.) Every time she landed, I had to locate her, reposition myself and the camera, and then frame, refocus, and shoot before she buzzed away.

If you're shooting either inanimate or slow-moving objects, tracking, framing, and focusing get easier. Figure 3-4 shows a bug that moved more deliberately. I was able to follow him for quite some time before he left. I stopped down to f/22 to maximize the depth of field and increased shutter speed to 1/400 second. This kept most of the beetle in focus and froze his movement. To make up for the lost light, I increased ISO to 1600. I didn't use a flash. The morning light was very strong.

FIGURE 3-4: Even with close-ups, you freeze movement by increasing shutter speed.

Shooting in Controlled Conditions

When you're working inside your studio (refer to wherever you shoot as your *studio,* whether it's your dining room table, kitchen counter, a corner of the basement, or a 20x20 outbuilding), you have much more control over your setup and lighting. You don't have to worry about the sun, wind, flying bugs, or a camera that grows heavier with every photo you take.

Figure 3-5 shows a close-up of my class ring that I took with a Holga digital SLR lens and 60mm macro attachment. I perched the ring in a ring box with a black velvet interior to stabilize it for the photo. You're seeing about an inch (2.54 cm) from left to right. Interesting rings and other jewelry make great subjects for macro photography.

FIGURE 3-5:
Shooting in a
studio enables
you to design the
shot you want
more precisely.

REMEMBER

When you're in the studio, mount your camera on a tripod to ensure stability. This also lets you make the shutter speed as slow as you need.

My preferences when shooting in-studio run like this:

>> **Continuous lighting:** I've rigged up several homemade *soft boxes* (a soft cover than diffuses light) to light the scene. I know exactly what the ISO, shutter speed, and aperture need to be before I even turn on the camera. This comes from shooting hundreds of shots in the same location with the same lighting and setup.

>> **Manual focus:** The best way to focus in a studio setting, with the camera mounted on a tripod, is to switch to your camera's Live View mode and zoom in using the LCD monitor's controls. This enables you to very precisely focus using whatever part of the scene you wish. If you use autofocus, you should select and use a single AF point. Position it over the spot that you want to be in the area that is in focus.

>> **Focus rail:** 2- and 4-way focus rails are ruler-looking devices that incorporate racks, pinions, and rails that enable you to focus very accurately. Mount your camera to the rail and focus using the rail's fine-focusing adjustment knobs. Use with a tripod for best results. 2-way rails move forward and backward. 4-way rails also move side to side, enabling you to alter the composition slightly.

Figure 3-6 shows an inexpensive 4-way rail that I picked up to experiment with. If you're on the fence and want to try it out without spending hundreds of dollars, I encourage you to take this approach to see whether or not you like working with it. If you do, you can always go out and buy a better model.

**Capturing Macros
and Close-ups**

>> **Dusting and taping:** I always brush and blow dust off my subjects, but it's impossible to remove all traces of dust and miscellaneous fibers. Use blown air and masking tape as well. When you're shooting small subjects, be prepared to remove a lot of dust using your favorite photo editor.

Your other challenges are mainly lighting and depth of field. Here are some additional lighting pointers:

>> **No flash:** You can shoot macros in a studio without using a flash. The character of the lighting is different than with a flash, though, and you may struggle to find the right white balance. Try setting a custom white balance or take several test shots to get it right.

>> **Pop-up flash:** Don't even bother unless you have a very short macro lens. The longer the lens and the shorter the distance to the subject, the more distance you need to move the flash away from the camera to keep the lens from casting a huge shadow over everything. Pop-up flashes won't work in these cases.

>> **External flash:** Seriously consider investing in an external flash or Speedlight/Speedlite. When you mount one on your camera's hot shoe, the flash can clear the lens in most situations. You can also get a *ring light,* specifically designed to light close subjects unobtrusively.

Ideally, you can position the flash away from the camera but stay connected using a sync or flash cord. (Wireless is even better.) From there, creatively design the photo and position the flash away from the lens. When you're working at very close ranges, it can mean the difference between lighting your subject or not.

REMEMBER

> » **More complicated lighting setups:** The possibilities that arise from using extra gear are endless. You'll be able to patiently work your craft and *design* the shots you want. It's incredible fun and very rewarding!
>
> Because your goal is to shed light on your subject, be as flexible as possible.

Relaxing Your Angle of View

Not all macros or close-ups need to be microscopic wonders. Depending on the lens you're working with and the distance you are from your subject, you may enjoy shooting close-ups of larger subjects. Figure 3-7 is a shot of my son's Raspberry Pi, an amazing little computer packed onto a small circuit board. While smaller than a typical computer, it's far larger than a bee, ring, and many other close-up subjects.

FIGURE 3-7:
Step back for a change of pace.

Shooting Close-ups with Everyday Lenses

While true macro photography requires special lenses, you can shoot close-ups with just about any lens you have. All you need to do is look for scenes that you want to zoom in on. Figure 3-8 is a shot I took with a very nice 50mm prime lens and inexpensive Nikon camera. I arranged the candles on a tray and set them on my bed (of all places) to take the shot. I set the aperture to f/1.4 and was pretty close to the candles, which kept the depth of field nice and shallow. The background candles are pleasantly blurred. Overall, this is an excellent illustration that proves that it's possible to shoot great close-ups with what you have on hand.

FIGURE 3-8:
Shooting close-ups with everyday lenses is easy.

Using Telephoto Lenses

Although telephoto lenses excel at photographing distant objects, you can also use them to take nice-looking close-ups. Figure 3-9 is a close-up of a succulent we bought one summer to liven up our home. I was using a 300mm telephoto lens to take other photos, and on the spur of the moment decided to try some close-ups. I grabbed this plant and put it on our picnic table outside. I had to stand away from it to get the lens to focus, but the result is one of my favorite photos. The strong light enabled me to use a low ISO and quick shutter speed of 1/500 second. Fast shutter speeds are important with lenses that have very long focal lengths because they help you shoot shake-free photos.

FIGURE 3-9:
A fast shutter speed allowed me to take this photo with a long focal length.

Using Holga Lenses

I'm a huge fan of the Holga digital SLR lens and accessories. The Holga lens is a cheap, plastic, fixed-aperture manual focus lens developed for the popular Holga film cameras. You can customize the basic lens with macro and close-up attachments like those shown in Figure 3-10.

FIGURE 3-10:
Close-up and macro attachment sets for the Holga dSLR lens.

While shooting with Holga lenses requires a lot of manual effort (focusing and calculating exposure), it's worth it for me. Figure 3-11 shows a stunning macro taken with the 30mm macro attachment. It really shows off the capabilities of attachments like this. I have more on Holga lenses in Book 2, Chapter 5.

Capturing Macros and Close-ups

FIGURE 3-11:
Holga photos are softer compared to typical lenses, but brimming with personality.

Shooting with Special Accessories

If you don't have a macro lens, I recommend looking into some special accessories for standard lenses. They typically make shooting close-ups easy and rewarding by making a standard lenses act like a macro lens. Most of the techniques used to shoot with these accessories are the same or similar to what you would do with a macro lens. You can use many of these accessories with your favorite macro lens for even more macro-tastic power.

Using a teleconverter

Teleconverters are tubes with optical (and sometimes electronic) elements that attach between the lens and your camera. Attach the lens to the teleconverter, and mount the combined unit to the camera. They increase the focal length of your lens by a set amount — normally between 1.4 and 2 times. Because light must pass through another lens, you may need to raise the exposure to offset the loss of light if shooting in manual mode. Figure 3-12 shows an older TC-201 2x teleconverter from Nikon.

REMEMBER

Teleconverters can be finicky. Make sure your lens and camera are compatible. Newer and better versions communicate information between the camera and lens and even autofocus. Cheaper versions may not have very good optics.

However, you can take great photos with teleconverters, especially if you're using a decent lens. Figure 3-13 shows a photo of some BBs I took with the TC-201 2x teleconverter and vintage (1981) Zoom-NIKKOR 35-70mm f/3.5 AI-s manual focus lens. That adds up to 140mm of old-fashioned macro goodness mounted on a new digital SLR.

FIGURE 3-12:
Teleconverters
increase the focal
length of the lens.

FIGURE 3-13:
Cool shot, but I
had to put every
single one back
in the bottle
afterward.

Using extension tubes

Extension tubes are open tubes. One end connects to your lens, extending the front toward the subject. The other end connects to the camera. This has the effect of shrinking the close-focus distance you're able to achieve and increasing the reproduction ratio of the lens.

Despite what it seems, extension tubes don't merely increase the lens's focal length. That's what teleconverters do. It also isn't like putting a magnifying glass up to the lens. That's what diopters do. Extension tubes move the focal plane of the lens away from where it should be, which means that you have to move closer to the subject to compensate. This has the effect of increasing the reproduction ratio.

Capturing Macros
and Close-ups

Because extension tubes don't have lenses inside them, you don't have to worry about degrading the optical quality of the lens you mount them to. You may, however, experience pronounced light falloff (where more distant objects quickly become darker) and vignetting (where photo corners are darker than the center) when using a tube. When using an extension tube, you are also unable to focus out as far as you could without it. This is the opposite of how lenses normally work. Typically, you're always able to focus on infinity but can't get too close to your subject. Extension tubes reverse this.

Figure 3-14 shows an inexpensive extension tube set from Zeikos. Most sets come with three different size tubes. This set has a 12mm, 20mm, and 36mm. You can mix and match them to create different magnification ratios. For example, if you use the 12 and 36mm tubes with a 50mm lens, the magnification ratio is just over 1.0 if the focus is set to half a meter. Figure 3-15 shows a macro taken with a 50mm lens on a cropped-frame camera and extension tubes. It's George Washington's face from a dollar bill.

FIGURE 3-14: Extension tubes turn any lens into a potential macro lens.

FIGURE 3-15: He cannot tell a lie: Macros are worth shooting.

REMEMBER

One consequence of how the magnification factor is calculated (I won't bore you with the formulas) is that it decreases as you increase the focal length of your lens. In other words, if you use the same extension tube with a 35mm lens and then a 50mm lens, the 35mm photo will have the greater magnification. Therefore, remember to use shorter lenses to get greater magnification when paired with extension tubes (the same rule applies to reversing rings, discussed in a later section).

Using diopters

If you don't want the hassle of putting extension tubes between your lens and the camera, try screwing in one or more diopters on the front of the lens. A diopter is like corrective glasses that magnify the subject. Diopters work with any lens that can accept screw-in filters. They don't interfere with shooting modes, autofocus, or other camera features that rely on communicating with the lens (unlike extension tubes and some teleconverters). They can be mixed and matched to increase the amount of magnification. As with all filters, though, they can cost a lot. You either need a step-up adapter or a complete set of diopters for any lens you may want to use that takes a different filter size.

Figure 3-16 shows a Hoya close-up filter set. It came with three filters of different strengths: +1, +2, and +4. In this shot, one is mounted on a Nikon 18–55mm lens with the help of a step-up ring. This allows me to standardize all my filters to 77mm. All I need to do is get another *step-up ring* (an adapter that mounts a larger filter on a smaller lens) if I get a new lens that doesn't match what I already have.

FIGURE 3-16: Diopters are like corrective lenses for lenses.

Capturing Macros and Close-ups

As you can see, a diopter *is* an optical element. The glass is very important. Take care of them by always keeping them in a protective case and cleaning them regularly. Cheaper filters will degrade your photos more than a high-quality set.

Figure 3-17 shows a nice shot of some flowers I took with a diopter attached to the standard kit lens mounted on a Canon dSLR. I zoomed in to 55mm and the diopter took care of the rest.

FIGURE 3-17: Diopters are easy to use and produce great close-ups.

Using reverse rings

Reverse rings are a totally cool way of having fun with macro and close-up photography. They enable you to mount a lens on your dSLR *backward*. One side of the reverse ring adapter (see Figure 3-18) has very fine threads that screw onto the front of your lens just like a filter. They aren't necessarily fragile, but it's possible to cross-thread the ring when screwing it onto your lens. If you feel it resist before it's fully screwed in, back the ring out and restart to make sure you have it threaded correctly. As long as you handle it with the same care as a filter, you'll be fine. The other side, which is a lens mount, attaches to your camera like a lens.

If you want to pick up a reverse adapter rings, match the adapter with the filter size on the lens you want to use.

Despite being awesome, however, there are a few caveats to reverse rings: Because the lens is mounted backward on the camera, the camera and lens are not able to communicate mechanically or electronically. Therefore, autofocus is not an option — you must manually focus or move either yourself or your subject. Focus rails are a great help because you don't have to mess with the lens or move anything around to get a good solid focus.

FIGURE 3-18:
This 58mm reverse ring mounts lenses backward on Canon EOS cameras.

One beneficial quirk of this type of approach is that you can use any lens that has the same filter diameter as the reverse adapter you're using. This is exceptionally liberating. Use old NIKKOR lenses on Canons, Pentax, or Sony cameras. Pick up as many inexpensive reverse adapters as you need to mount your best lenses in reverse.

Lenses that do not have a manual aperture control are more difficult to use because the camera can't communicate with the lens when it's mounted backward. Because of this, older manual focus lenses with aperture rings are ideal. It's easy to change the aperture by twisting the right ring. I have a few old Nikon AI and AI-s lenses that I use all the time for this purpose. Their aperture rings make controlling exposure easier. I took the shot in Figure 3-19 using this setup: a Canon dSLR and an old Nikon 50mm manual focus lens.

FIGURE 3-19:
Reverse ring adapters are fun and totally worth trying.

Canon users have developed a unique workaround that allows you to lock in an aperture. Here's how: Mount the lens, turn the camera on, and then select aperture-priority mode. Set the aperture you want to use. Then, if your camera has one, press and hold the Depth of Field Preview button. While holding it down, press the lens-release button and carefully remove the lens — with the camera still powered up. The aperture will remain set in the lens. Yes, it's clunky. Yes, it's inconvenient. If you want to shoot with a stopped-down aperture, however, it works. I recommend experimenting and finding a favorite aperture that you want to use for most of your shots, and sticking with it. That way you won't have to go through this process more than one or two times during a shoot.

Using a macro bellows

Macro bellows work just like extension tubes but are made of flexible material and can be extended to varying distances. One end of the bellows mounts to your camera like a lens would. You mount your lens to the far end and extend it to the distance you want. Professional-level bellows are very expensive. There are inexpensive models, however, that you can use to decide whether or not this is something you want to experiment with.

IN THIS CHAPTER

» Learning about telephoto focal
  lengths

» Enjoying action photography

» Setting up telephoto close-ups

» Capturing portraits

» Photographing animals with
  telephoto lenses

Chapter 4

Reaching Out with Telephoto Lenses

Don't think that telephoto lenses are just for professional photographers photographing sporting events or giraffes in the wild. They (plus zoom lenses set to telephoto focal lengths) make great lenses to have with you wherever you are. Telephoto lenses enable you to photograph everything from distant objects like the moon without leaving your backyard to portraits of your loved ones at summer camp. The photos you can capture are simply amazing. You won't get the same perspective from a wide-angle lens or a lens that uses normal focal lengths. I want to show you what's special about telephoto photography in this chapter. You'll learn what makes a telephoto lens unique, and how to take advantage of the versatility that they have but we often overlook.

Learning the Lingo

Telephoto lenses have a focal length greater than the diagonal size of the digital SLR image sensor they are attached to. Although most people think of large telephoto lenses, you don't have to have one to shoot using telephoto focal lengths.

Most standard zoom lenses sold with dSLRs in kits have some telephoto capability. Here's a quick summary of what telephoto focal lengths are:

>> **Medium (also called near) telephoto:** On full-frame dSLRs, lenses set from 60-200mm are considered medium telephoto. This translates to 40-135mm on APS-C bodies and 30-100mm on Three Fourths cameras.

This is the most practical and least expensive telephoto region. It's where most people begin taking telephoto shots.

>> **Telephoto:** The telephoto range extends from 200-300mm on full-frame cameras, 135-200mm on APS-C dSLRs, and 100-150mm on Three Fourths cameras.

This focal length range is where you start taking photos that feel more like classic telephoto shots, as opposed to shooting close-ups, macros, or portraits. You can find zoom lenses that reach well into this range as well as dedicated telephoto lenses.

>> **Super telephoto:** The super telephoto range begins where the standard telephoto range ends: 300mm and up for full-frame, 200mm and up for APS-C, and 150mm and up for Three Fourths cameras. You can find some zoom lenses that extend into these focal lengths, but telephoto zooms and primes dominate the market. They are extreme lenses that excel at what they do.

As you shop for lenses, remember that not all zoom lenses are considered telephoto lenses, even if they have telephoto focal lengths. For example, the AF–S NIKKOR 28–300mm f/3.5–5.6G ED VR lens is in the Normal Zoom category on Nikon's website. This lens has a tremendous range, reaching the super telephoto category when fully zoomed in. You have to browse around to find it. Canon's EF 28–300mm f/2.5–5.6L IS USM lens, on the other hand, is in its Telephoto Zoom category. (You have read the lens chapter in Book 1, right? It will help you decode these ridiculously long names.) The bottom line is that you should take the time to look in several different categories for lenses with telephoto focal lengths, including zoom, telephoto, and prime.

REMEMBER

As I do elsewhere with different lenses, I make a point of mentioning the camera and sensor size along with the focal length of each photo in this chapter. This allows you to calculate the 35mm equivalent focal length for each shot if you like, and compare it to your setup. Book 1, Chapters 1 and 3 have more information if you need to brush up on the hows and whys.

TIP

RENTING LENSES

If you want to experiment with lenses with different features, focal lengths, and prices, try renting. You can also rent camera bodies. Rent something that's an upgrade or check out the competition. If you have a Nikon, for example, rent a Canon. Or, if you have a Canon, rent a Sony.

I use www.lensrentals.com for most of my rental needs. The site's employees are polite, professional, and trustworthy. Its services are timely and the list of available gear is impressive. The site offers flexible plans based on the amount of time you rent items. I recommend getting the insurance.

Using a Super Telephoto Lens

Lenses are considered super telephoto if they have a focal length of 300mm and longer when used with a full-frame dSLR, 200mm and up on an APS-C camera, and 150mm and over on a Three Fourths model. Super telephoto lenses come as primes, but you can also shoot in those focal lengths with zoom lenses.

Super telephoto lenses are truly awesome. They're big, and they mean business. Unless you have a lightweight zoom lens, you should use a monopod to help support it. You'll last longer and your photos will be sharper as a result. You can see a picture of the AF-S NIKKOR 300mm f/4D mounted on my monopod in Book 1, Chapter 2 (look for Figure 2-13).

With large lenses like super telephotos, the lens attaches to the monopod, not the camera body. This keeps the weight of the lens, and therefore the center of gravity of the whole setup, directly over the monopod instead of in front of it. If your monopod has a handy strap attached to it, use it. It's protection against losing an expensive lens.

REMEMBER

Hold your monopod at all times. I sometimes keep the camera strap around my neck for added protection so that if I accidentally release my grip the strap will keep the camera and monopod from crashing to the ground.

These lenses are also expensive, which means that most people won't have one lying around the house. Don't let that stop you from looking into renting one and seeing what the fuss is about. Look at prices and be choosey. Some models can be relatively inexpensive to rent, but you will probably pay top dollar for the cream of the crop.

Now for some photos. Figure 4-1 is a photo of a North American P-51 Mustang taxiing out to the runway at an airshow my family and I attended. I used a 300mm lens on a Nikon APS-C camera. This was a short break in the rain (tell me about it). Visibility wasn't the greatest and the sky was gray. In the end, the plane never took off. I got a few shots of it taxiing and nothing else.

The beauty of using a super telephoto lens is that this photo looks like I was standing right next to the plane and using a normal lens. Details really pop out. The prop is cutting through the moist air, leaving contrails behind. You can also see the name of the plane and other markings very clearly. If you zoom in a bit, you can even see the screws holding the body panels on the frame of the airplane.

FIGURE 4-1:
Telephoto lenses bring out small details on subjects that are nearby or far away.

Figure 4-2 shows a moment after a harness race. The driver and his horse were returning to the paddock when I turned and saw them. Covered with sand, he has to lean to the side to see where he's going.

I quickly put the driver under my active AF point and focused on him, knowing that they were too close to get both in focus. Shooting with a super telephoto lens gives you shallower depths of field than similar apertures on normal or wide-angle lenses. The other elements provide context (his horse, of course, and the horse in the background) and balance the fact that he is very far to the right of the frame.

Super telephoto lenses let you take photos from a safe vantage point that seem to put you right in the action. Although it looks like I am about to be run over, I was actually a good distance away with my 300mm lens and Nikon APS-C dSLR.

One side effect of using a telephoto lens is called *telephoto lens compression.* Photos appear to lack the depth they would if taken using a wide-angle lens. Background objects are enlarged. This is how photographers take photos that make the moon look huge compared to the rest of the scene. In this case, the horse and driver in the background are far more prominent when seen through a 300mm lens than they would be with another lens. They look closer to the horse and driver in the foreground and take up more space in the photo. The technical explanation of the effect has to do with the relationship between the camera-to-subject distance versus the subject-to-background distance and how they change at longer focal lengths.

FIGURE 4-2:
This shot is a great example of how telephoto lens compression affects the background.

Finally, to show you that telephoto lenses are indeed similar to telescopes, I present you with Figure 4-3: the moon. I took this photo using a 300mm super telephoto lens and Nikon APS-C dSLR. I also used a 2x teleconverter, which doubles the focal length. When teleconverter and crop factor are taken into account, this photo is the equivalent of a 900mm lens on a full-frame camera. Because the moon is not in full phase, more crater details stand out in relief from shadowing on the left side. Simply astounding.

To set the shot up, I mounted the camera and lens on my tripod in the back-yard, entered aperture-priority shooting mode, and switched to spot metering. I didn't want the dark sky affecting how the camera evaluated the exposure. I played around a bit with different combinations of shutter speed and ISO to see whether it made any difference, and settled on an ISO of 100 and shutter speed of 1/90 second. I could have done the same thing in manual mode, but I would have been looking at the exposure index as I took the shots anyway, so it didn't make that much difference which mode I was in.

FIGURE 4-3:
The moon, shot
with a 35mm
equivalent focal
length of 900mm.

Capturing Action with Telephoto Lenses

Action shots and telephoto lenses and focal lengths just go together. Although most sports photos you'll see are taken from quite a distance, they don't have to be. Figure 4-4 is a shot of my son, Sam, jumping off the sidewalk of a walking bridge that overlooks a river onto the main roadway. It's an old, decommissioned bridge that is now a scenic spot for tourists and photographers so he's in no danger.

I took this playful action shot using a nice zoom lens set to 52mm and a Nikon APS-C dSLR. 52mm? Yes. On a cropped-frame camera, that comes out to a 35mm equivalent focal length of 104mm. Even moderate telephoto focal lengths are great at capturing action, because you can stand out of the way and get a good shot. When dealing with family, friends, or strangers, it's nice to let people enjoy themselves without breathing down their necks.

Of course, super telephoto lenses also excel at action. You've probably noticed professional photographers at sporting venues photographing athletes in action. You can too. For example, Figure 4-5 is another photo I took at the horse track, this time as a harness race was unfolding. I was using a 300mm lens on a Nikon APS-C dSLR.

FIGURE 4-4:
Use zoom lenses
to capture
telephoto action.

TIP

I chose this vantage point because I was able to capture the action as the horses and drivers made the turn toward the home straight. I was standing off the track, pretty far away. A telephoto lens is your ticket to success at venues like this. You can stand pretty far back and still get good photos.

The lens enabled me to capture the intense look on the drivers' faces. The horses are in mid-air, solving the riddle of whether or not a horse leaves a foot on the ground and at what point during its gait (look up the 1878 series of photographs called *Sallie Gardner at a Gallop*).

Figure 4-6 is another shot from the rainy day airshow in Figure 4-1. At this time, the rain had let up and an A-10 Thunderbolt was performing a demonstration flight. I was using my trusty 300mm super telephoto and Nikon APS-C dSLR.

TIP

As you might expect, action shots like this are not all about the focal length. They require fast shutter speeds. I took this photo with a shutter speed of 1/1000 second. You can read more about shutter speed in Book 3, Chapter 3.

FIGURE 4-5:
Telephoto lenses
put you in the
middle of the
action.

If you look closely, you can see the patches on the pilot's uniform and small details on the plane. The rain makes the photo look a bit noisy, but isn't able to rob the photo of all of its sharpness. Remember, I was standing on the ground, several hundred feet below and away from the line of flight. This kind of moment is when you want the best telephoto lens you can get your hands on. I also used a monopod for support. I also discovered that panning the camera to track fast moving objects like jets at extreme focal lengths is challenging. Expect to take several photos of moments like this as you try to center the plane in the viewfinder and get a good focus.

FIGURE 4-6:
Super telephoto
lenses are
the pinnacle
of telephoto
photography;
they can capture
scenes no other
lens can.

Using Telephoto Lenses for Close-ups

In standard telephoto photography, you stand at a distance from whatever it is you're photographing. While that distance varies from photo to photo, the point is that the telephoto focal length enables you to capture the subject with some detail. When shooting close-ups, you stand much closer, and the fact that you're using telephoto focal lengths accentuates this fact.

I took the photo shown in Figure 4-7 with this idea in mind. It's a close-up of a cactus plant set up in my studio. I shot it with a Canon full-frame camera (the fantastic 5D Mark III) and excellent EF 24-105mm f/4L IS USM lens set to 105mm. This is a classic close-up. It's not powerful enough to be a macro, but not far enough away to be a normal photo. It's a fantastic middle ground.

FIGURE 4-7:
Telephoto focal lengths are great for close-ups too.

Figure 4-8 is a close-up I shot in the field. The front turn signal lens on an old, abandoned Chevy C-60 dump truck caught my attention and I decided to get in close and then zoom in for this shot. I framed it on the edge of the photo to make room for the background, which is interesting, but intentionally not the focus of the photo.

I used a Sony APS-C camera and standard zoom lens set to 60mm. Unlike the last photo, I didn't use a tripod and there was no setup involved. I simply had to be aware of my surroundings. Bam. Telephoto focal length close-up.

Finally, what section on close-ups would be complete without a flower? Not this one, I tell ya! Figure 4-9 shows a colorful flower that I shot using a Nikon APS-C dSLR and 300mm lens. It's ridiculous using that sort of lens for this kind of close-up, I agree, but as I tell my kids, "I specialize in ridiculous." Notice the *bokeh* (the aesthetic quality of the unfocused area) in this photo. Good super telephoto lenses can make backgrounds look very nice.

FIGURE 4-8: Always be on the lookout for interesting subjects to zoom in on.

The key to this shot is having enough light so that the shutter speed can be reasonably fast. Telephoto lenses tend to need good light, and shooting close-ups accentuates the importance of having a crisp photo. In this case, 1/250 second was fast enough to prevent camera shake from blurring the photo.

On the other hand, you will have to deal with very narrow depths of field when shooting close-ups at very long focal lengths. You can try to use smaller apertures, but the light may not cooperate. If that is the case, you will need to raise the ISO to compensate or try using a flash.

FIGURE 4-9: Telephoto close-ups make for very attractive bokehs.

Capturing Portraits

If you can get away with *not* lugging around a 300mm telephoto lens, do it. You can even use your standard zoom lens to capture nice portraits in the near-telephoto range.

Figure 4-10 shows a group portrait of my kids after the last was finished with summer camp. I know this doesn't feel like a telephoto shot, but it is. I took it with a Canon APS-C camera and basic zoom lens set to 45mm, which is just inside the near-telephoto range.

I set up this shot using the telephoto instead of the wide-angle or normal focal lengths of the lens by standing back and zooming in. The kids are nice and sharp while the background is blurred. Everyone looks natural with no discernable distortion from the lens, which can happen when you stand too close and shoot your portraits using wide-angles. I also made sure they stood in a line. This helped me keep them all in focus, despite having a shallow depth of field due to the aperture and focal length.

FIGURE 4-10:
Stand back to shoot group portraits with telephoto focal lengths.

Telephoto lenses and focal lengths are very useful for individual portraits. When you're photographing a single person, you can afford to stand closer. Figure 4-11 is a playful shot of my wife, who has Easter Bunny ears on her head. I shot this using a Nikon APS-C camera and fast 50mm prime lens.

Better, more expensive lenses like the AF-S NIKKOR 50mm f/1.4G I used will have more attractive *bokeh* than average kit lenses. They will also have larger maximum apertures, which helps let in a lot of light and blur the background.

Finally, I took the photo in Figure 4-12 using the full-frame Pentax K-1 dSLR. I set the zoom lens to 95mm for this shot of my oldest son. That's near the ideal 85mm look that people really like, and the longest focal length (or equivalent) of the three photos in this section. To frame the shot, I stood back at a comfortable distance and zoomed in so that I would get him and the fence in the background.

TIP

Many photographers like using 85mm telephoto lenses on full-frame cameras for portraiture. Shooting 50mm on an APS-C camera puts you right in that ballpark. I would not go above 135mm on full-frame or 85mm on cropped-frame cameras for portraits because at those focal lengths you'll run into lens compression and people's faces will appear flatter than they are.

FIGURE 4-12:
Classic telephoto portraiture with a nice lens on a full-frame camera.

Photographing Animals

People love taking photos of animals. It doesn't matter if it's a lion on safari, giraffes at the zoo, or your own pets. Using telephoto lenses and focal lengths will make your photos really stand out.

Figure 4-13 is a nice photo of one of our cats. He was looking out the window when I took this. It was very bright outside, and the natural sunlight makes this photo shine. I took it with the full-frame Pentax K-1 dSLR and nice Pentax HD D FA 28-105mm f/3.5-5.6 standard zoom lens. I zoomed in to 80mm to frame his face. Remember, on full-frame cameras you get what you pay for with focal lengths, so 80mm is 80mm. That's into the near/medium telephoto range by 20mm. A comparable lens on an APS-C camera would be something in the range of 18-65mm.

FIGURE 4-13:
Use telephoto
focal lengths to
photograph pets.

Figure 4-14 is a photo of a wild kit (the technical name for a baby rabbit) we rescued. She's up on a table with a white background and some red cabbage to keep her occupied (a departure from her normal diet of timothy hay). I was using a Canon 5D Mark III full-frame dLSR with the lens set to 105mm. Although I was in my studio, I didn't use a tripod because I had to react to and track a moving rabbit.

This photo was taken with a longer focal length than the preceding photo, but is still something you can easily take with a standard zoom lens. Focus and aperture control are vital in shots like this. I set the aperture to f/8 to give myself more depth of field to work with, and had to raise the ISO to 2500 to compensate. The shutter speed was 1/60, which is on the slow side for a photo like this, but fast enough to capture brief pauses in the action. Having a good lens with image stabilization helped keep the photo nice and sharp. Had she run around more, I would have had to set the shutter speed faster, enlarge the aperture, and increase the ISO.

FIGURE 4-14:
Use long focal lengths to photograph animals you don't want to frighten.

Finally, having a telephoto lens is a must when photographing close-ups of dangerous animals like this crocodile. I took the photo shown in Figure 4-15 at our local zoo using a Nikon APS-C dSLR and 300mm super telephoto lens. Although I was outside the enclosure, I was able to get this low perspective by positioning myself on a sidewalk leading downhill from the side toward the front.

REMEMBER

This shot would have been impossible without a 300mm lens. The great thing about using a telephoto lens is that you can be far away from the action and still feel like you're right in the middle of it. (That last sentence is brought to you by Mr. Obvious.)

FIGURE 4-15:
Long focal lengths enable you to capture dangerous animals in the wild or animals in captivity from a distance.

Chapter **5**

Exploring Other Lenses

Before I finish the minibook on lenses, I would like to encourage you to seek out alternative designs. Even though a lens must fit your camera body, not every lens has to fit the same mold. In fact, you can have a lot of fun with creative lenses or accessories like the ones I showcase in this chapter. The wide range of different and sometimes exotic lenses really sets dSLRs apart from smartphones, tablets, and other types of digital imaging devices.

One note: You may want to mount your camera on a tripod or monopod for support when using some of these lenses. It depends on what you're photographing, whether the shutter speed is too low for handheld shots, and when you want to take your time composing the scene or focusing precisely. For example, I typically use a tripod when shooting macros with Holga lenses, setting up detailed tilt-shift shots, when shooting long-exposure shots with a pinhole lens, and when I'm in my studio.

Fisheye Lenses

On the extreme end of the wide-angle spectrum are fisheye lenses. Just like their wide-angle relatives, they're incredibly fun to use. The (roughly) 180-degree diagonal angle of view puts a whole new twist on taking unique photos.

Be careful when looking for fisheye lenses to use on a cropped-frame dSLR. Fisheye lenses have been around for a long time, and they were designed with full-frame cameras in mind. This means that you *will not* get the complete, circular, fisheye effect when you mount a full-frame fisheye lens on your APS-C image sensor. It takes more oomph than many lenses have to squeeze the scene onto a smaller sized sensor. For example, the AF Fisheye-NIKKOR 16mm f/2.8 lens sounds nice, but it has an effective focal length of a whopping 24mm when mounted on a cropped-frame Nikon dSLR, and therefore only a 107-degree angle of view. The AF DX Fisheye-NIKKOR 10.5mm f/2.8G ED, on the other hand, was designed specifically for DX (cropped-frame) Nikon cameras, and has a 180-degree picture angle. Having said that, the 10.5mm fisheye lens is called a "frame-filling" fisheye lens by Nikon, which means that you won't see the circular fisheye effect with this lens either. Because I really like the circular image that some fisheye lenses produce, I looked for an alternative solution.

Although not traditional fisheye lenses (from stem to stern, so to speak), you can purchase screw-in fisheye optics that widen the field of view so much that they achieve a fisheye or near-fisheye effect. They range in price, but all are relatively inexpensive. The Opteka HD2 0.20x AF Fisheye Lens, shown in Figure 5-1, lists for just under $40. I heartily recommend trying out this solution in lieu of buying an expensive fisheye lens. In fact, all the fisheye photos in this chapter were shot with this optic. There are a few things you should be aware of, however, before you start:

» **Screw-in optics mount to the front of existing lenses.** You must buy one that is compatible with the filter size of the lens you want to use. Some optics have multiple step-rings that enable you to mount them to different lenses. For example, the Opteka set I purchased has a native thread of 52mm and comes with three rings (one of which is shown in Figure 5-1 leaning against the main lens): 55 to 52mm, 58 to 52mm, and 67 to 52mm. I can use any lens in my closet that has one of these four filter sizes (52mm, 55mm, 58m, or 67mm).

» **You'll need to find the effective focal length of the optic.** Multiply the magnification factor of the optic by your camera's crop factor by the focal length of the lens you want to attach it to. For example, a 0.20x optic mounted on a 1.6x Canon cropped-frame camera using a 16mm lens equals 5.12mm. If you zoom in to 55mm, the resulting effective focal length is 17.6mm.

From this you can see that you should purchase an optic with a low magnification factor and use it on a wide-angle lens (or in that range of a zoom lens) to achieve the greatest fisheye effect you can.

FIGURE 5-1:
This Opteka
fisheye lens
screws on to your
existing lens.

Figure 5-2 shows a scenic lake scene I shot looking out along a pier. I was stand-ing on the beach and took special care to not show any sand. With such a vast angle of view it's harder than you might think to keep your feet and other items you don't normally have to worry about out of the photos. The far side of the lake shows off the curve of the lens while the pier looks relatively normal, although it looks small because the wide angle seems to push it away from the camera.

FIGURE 5-2:
Shoot unique
landscapes with
fisheye lenses.

Figure 5-3 shows off the circular effect of the fisheye lens. It's our shower curtain, which certainly sounds like an odd thing to photograph for a book. However, the small squares on the curtain provide a great point of reference because they illustrate what should be straight. They are 11/16 of an inch, or about 18mm square, and arranged in relatively orderly columns and rows.

TIP

Don't lock yourself into one mode of thinking. Take your fisheye lens and photograph everything you can with it.

The fisheye lens causes the center of the photo to bulge out. It also bends all the vertical and horizontal lines toward a central vanishing point along each axis. While not the greatest tool to take precise architectural photos, I love it.

FIGURE 5-3:
Use objects that show off the lens distortion.

The flower I photographed in Figure 5-4 shows what happens when you get really close to an object. It dominates the center of the scene, but because the lens has such a wide effective focal length, there's plenty of space on the sides for everything else. My feet are almost in the photo at the bottom, and the bottom quarter of our neighbor's garage is visible at the top. Notice that even though I'm using a standard kit zoom lens and inexpensive screw-in optic, the flower looks sharp and very clear.

TIP

Although I have not shown this aspect of using a fisheye lens, another completely viable approach is to take extreme wide-angle shots with a fisheye lens and remove the distortion in software. You'll get nice photos with extreme angles of view that are impossible to take with most other lenses.

FIGURE 5-4:
Fisheye lenses
are great at
close-ups.

Tilt-Shift Lenses

Tilt-shift lenses are special-purpose lenses with two distinct features:

>> **They tilt.** The front of the lens swivels, or tilts, to point at an angle. This angles the focal plane so that the area of sharp focus is no longer perpendicular to the axis of the lens. The depth of field changes from rectangular, running at an equal depth across the image, to a wedge shape. The wedge actually gets larger as it extends farther from the camera, causing the depth of field to increase.

>> **And shift.** The lens shifts up or down while pointing in the same direction. Tilt-shift lenses have a larger *image circle* than normal lenses. This means they project a larger image of the world (you guessed it — it's circular) inside the camera that goes well past the borders of the image sensor. It's like putting a large round tablecloth on a small rectangular table. Shifting the lens moves a different part of the view as seen by the lens onto the camera's image sensor to be captured during an exposure.

Figure 5-5 shows the Canon TS-E 24mm f/3.5 II, tilted to the left, but not shifted. Notice the knobs and markings on the lens. Operating a tilt-shift lens requires you to set the amount of tilt and shift you want applied and then lock it down. If you're using a tripod or shooting in a studio you can set up the lens very precisely using all the helpful information on the lens. Tilt-shift lenses require you to use manual focus. I took all the tilt-shift photos in this section with this lens. It's an amazing, although heavy, lens that captures great photos even when not tilted or shifted.

REMEMBER

Manually focusing is probably the greatest challenge to using this type of lens unless you are already proficient in it.

Canon also offers 17mm, 45mm, and 90mm versions. Nikon has three tilt-shift lenses at these focal lengths: 24mm, 45mm, and 85mm. Other manufacturers offer various tilt-shift lenses, such as Rokinon and Samyang. Often, they are the same lens, simply rebranded. Arax also makes tilt-shift lenses in several focal lengths.

REMEMBER

Remember, tilt-shift lenses were originally created for 35mm film cameras. The range of available focal lengths are therefore optimized for full-frame dSLR image sensors. The 45mm Canon tilt-shift lens acts like a 72mm near-telephoto lens on a Canon cropped-frame dSLR. The 24mm lens, on the other hand, sits at 38mm on a cropped-frame camera, so it feels like a normal lens. The 17mm lens would allow you to shoot wide-angle shots with an effective focal length of 27mm.

Tilt-shift lenses have long been used by photographers to photograph buildings and other scenes to eliminate perspective distortion. When you point your camera up, vertical lines in the scene converge rather than run parallel. Shifting a tilt-shift lens helps counteract this effect. Shifting the lens also enables you to shoot panoramas without ever having to move the camera.

Tilt-shift lenses have an artistic nature to them as well, which is what I want to focus on. You can create interesting depth of field effects using the tilt feature of the lens. Figure 5-6 shows a friendly game of sand volleyball underway at camp. The sun was shining nicely. A nice breeze was blowing. It was an idyllic scene. I tilted the lens so that the girl in the pink shirt was the primary focal point. You can see the depth of field extending from her to the opponents on the other side of the net and into the trees.

FIGURE 5-6:
Tilt-shift lenses create unique focal points.

Figure 5-7 is a totally different shot. I took this photo of the first floor elevator doors at my favorite parking garage at a local university. I was able to get the left door to be nicely in focus while blurring the right door by tilting the lens. The unusual depth of field plays mind games on us. We think what we're seeing is from a model or small diorama when in fact it's a full-sized set of elevator doors.

FIGURE 5-7:
This set of elevator doors looks like it's from a model.

Finally, the scene in Figure 5-8 presents another shot that looks miniaturized. Rather than a close-up of a set of elevator doors, this scene (shot with the same lens) features buildings that I photographed diagonally from across the street in a quaint little town in Michigan. I tilted the lens, angled the camera a bit, and focused on the building on the corner.

Holga Lenses

Holga makes digital SLR lenses (available from different outlets) that are simple, inexpensive, and plastic. In 1981, Holga began manufacturing a 120mm medium-format film camera called the Holga 120S. It was so unlike anything else that people considered it a toy camera. However, that toy camera that often leaked light took amazingly cool, analog, sometimes messy photos.

The Holga digital SLR lens is derived from the lens on the original camera. It has a rough focal length of 60mm (in full-frame terms), a fixed aperture of f/8, and has very rudimentary manual focus. You'll have to use your camera's manual shooting mode too.

Aside from the main lens, shown in Figure 5-9, Holga makes a remarkable number of attachments that mount onto the front of the lens. They include macro and close-up lenses, telephoto, wide-angle, fisheye, and filter accessories. There is even a pinhole lens. Pick things up à la carte or buy kits with the add-ons you want.

I have to say that, although these lenses are cheap plastic and you have to guess at the initial exposure settings and experiment some, I love playing around with them. I've taken many photos with my Holga lenses and feature several of them in this book.

FIGURE 5-9:
The Holga plastic dSLR lens mounts directly to your dSLR.

TIP

Pay attention to the focus distance set on the lens. There are five different symbols, each representing different subjects and distances. Focus before you frame the shot, as it's hard to turn the lens when looking through the viewfinder. Basically, I set the focus distances that matches the scene I plan on shooting, take the shots I want, and only change the focus distance when I change scenes.

Figure 5-10 is a scene from a local university. I was taking photos of buildings and other things when I decided to station myself along one of the main walkways and photograph the students coming and going. Although this shot doesn't have many people in it, the main focus of attention is a young woman in silhouette walking away from me. This is one of my favorite shots that I have taken with the basic Holga lens.

I boosted the ISO to 800 to have a quick exposure time of 1/500 second. That guaranteed a crisp photo of moving subjects and no camera shake from me. I used an additional in-camera filter to blur portions of the scene, accentuate the color, and boost the contrast.

FIGURE 5-10:
I processed this Holga shot through a creative filter for additional effects.

The bridge shown in Figure 5-11 shows a completely different scene shot with the same basic digital Holga lens. I got up early one foggy morning and was taking photos around the base of a bridge near where I live. The water level is low and the light is very subtle. I framed the scene from behind some tree branches, which adds to the moody effect.

Holga lenses need a lot of light. If you're not out in bright sunlight, expect to raise the ISO. I had to raise the ISO to 6400 to take this shot, and still couldn't make the shutter speed any faster than 1/60 without underexposing the scene.

FIGURE 5-11:
Holga lenses are a great change of pace from traditional lenses.

Finally, Figure 5-12 shows an example of a macro shot. I slipped the 30mm macro attachment onto the front of the basic Holga lens, and used a tripod to set this shot up. When working with close-ups and macros, it helps to frame the scene using Live View. I raised the ISO through the roof so that I could see and focus, then switched to the viewfinder and lowered the ISO to take the shot. Of course, focusing with a Holga lens is harder than a normal lens, so more often than not I use a 4-way focus rail (see Book 2, Chapter 3). If you don't have one, you can also move the subject (I have, and it's pretty effective). Shooting macros and close-ups with Holga lenses is incredibly fun and very rewarding.

FIGURE 5-12: Shoot macros and close-ups with additional attachments.

Lensbaby Lenses

Lensbaby (visit `www.lensbaby.com` and have a look 'round) has created several unique and creative lenses and accessories for digital SLRs. Its main creative lineup features the Composer Pro, shown in Figure 5-13, which is a manual focus tilt-swivel lens body that accepts removable add-ons like the Double Glass, Single Glass, and Plastic Optics. They continually come out with additional lens bodies and optics, like the Composer Pro II (an upgrade to the Composer Pro, featuring metal body), Edge 50 Optic, Sweet 35 Optic, Circular Fisheye, and Velvet 56. These aren't traditional lenses, but they aren't toys. They act and feel solid.

FIGURE 5-13: Lensbaby has a wide array of creative lens products.

I shot Figure 5-14 using the Composer Pro with the Double-Glass Optic installed. Tilting the lens up and to the right a bit let me move the circle of sharp focus where I wanted it. The words in this poster of the United States Declaration of Independence that aren't in this sweet spot are blurred, which is the main effect this lens offers.

FIGURE 5-14:
This poster
shows off how
the lens creates
a selective focus
effect.

While the newer optics feature built-in apertures, part of the charm of the older optics is that you control the aperture by manually swapping out aperture disks. While changing from f/4.0 to f/2.8 might be a hassle to some, it allows you to use creative aperture disks with cutouts for special effects. Figure 5-15 shows a star effect caused by light reflecting off of several silver votive holders.

FIGURE 5-15:
Additional
aperture rings
create unique
special effects.

Pinhole Lenses

Pinhole lenses aren't really lenses at all. They are simply covers with small holes that allow light into the camera to strike the image sensor. Figure 5-16 shows a pinhole lens that I picked up from Lenox Laser.

FIGURE 5-16:
This pinhole "lens" is a precision-machined body cap.

You can, of course, create your own. I've found a very effective approach that involves drilling a larger hole in the cap, then taping aluminum foil over it (you can also use part of an aluminum can that you cut for the purpose). I then use a small straight pin to carefully prick the foil in the center to make the hole. There are technical details about this that I won't go into. However, the size of the hole matters, depending on the brand of camera you're using and the size of the image sensor. Make sure to use an extra body cap that you don't mind putting a hole in.

REMEMBER

Once again, I should point out that you will experience a pretty big difference between using a standard pinhole lens on a full-frame dSLR versus a cropped-frame body. Normal pinhole lenses have a wide-angle look on full-frame cameras. They appear normal and in some cases approach telephoto angles of view on cropped-frame cameras. The pinhole lens shown in Figure 5-15 has a focal length of about 45mm. I took a ruler out and measured the distance from the image sensor plane mark on top of the camera to the lens mount. This comes out to a focal length of almost 68mm in 35mm equivalent terms.

The idea of using a hole this way can be traced back to the beginnings of photography in the form of a camera obscura, close to a thousand years ago. At some point it became clear that smaller holes created sharper images.

The challenges of pinhole photography are twofold. First, the aperture is so small it's hard to see the scene in order to compose. Second, you have to determine the proper exposure for each scene by trial and error. However, given the same conditions, once you settle on an ISO and an exposure time, you can easily repeat them for follow-on shots.

Figure 5-17 shows a photo I took with the Lenox Laser lens on a Nikon APS-C dSLR. It's soft, but not to the point of distraction. I processed the photo in Adobe Lightroom to make it look a bit older. I also left in the dark spots, which are caused by dust on the image sensor. Normally these spots are fuzzy and you may never notice them. I think they add to the nostalgic effect in this photo. It was a bright day, so I used a shutter speed of 1.3 seconds and an ISO of 100.

Diana F+ Lenses

Plastic Diana cameras were introduced in the 1960s and have made a real comeback in recent years. While the cameras themselves use film (just like Holga cameras), you can mount the lenses on a dSLR with the right adapter. Figure 5-18 shows the fisheye lens mounted on a cropped-frame dSLR.

TIP

One note of advice regarding the Diana lens focal lengths: Use the widest angles possible for normal fields of view. The Diana lenses are designed to be used on film cameras whose 120 film is much larger than a cropped-frame dSLR sensor (in fact, far larger than 35mm film and full-frame image sensors). You're only going to see a small portion of what the lens can truly capture. I recommend the fisheye lens as a most practical focal length for dSLRs.

FIGURE 5-18:
Attach the Diana F+ lens adapter to your dSLR and then add the lens of your choice.

I took the photo shown in Figure 5-19 with the fisheye lens attached to a Nikon APS–C dSLR and Nikon F-mount adapter. I used an external flash held to the side with the help of an off-camera hot shoe cord (see Book 4, Chapter 3). The result is amazing, and I hope inspires you to try out creative lenses like Diana F+ with your dSLR. I've certainly had fun!

FIGURE 5-19:
The Diana F+ fisheye lens has a good field of view and captures soft, dreamy scenes with a retro vibe.

3

Taking Creative Control

Contents at a Glance

Chapter **1**

Making Sense of Exposure

Photography is the process of exposing the image sensor in your digital SLR to light. Understanding how this works, and more importantly, how to manage the process, will greatly improve your skills as a photographer.

This chapter also covers the technical aspects of accomplishing this: learning about exposure, tracking exposure on your camera, knowing the different metering modes, reviewing photos, analyzing histograms, and troubleshooting exposure.

Understanding Exposure

The word *exposure* is used several ways in photography. Each of the following sections explains how.

REMEMBER

Although I don't address this further, photos can be referred to as exposures. This usage is diminishing as digital cameras have taken over and the vast majority of people no longer use film. Digital camera users typically refer to exposures as shots, photos, images, or even files.

Qualifying exposure

Exposure describes whether the photo has enough light. Photos can be underexposed, overexposed, or properly exposed. Figure 1-1 shows an example of each. As a photographer, your goal should be to take properly exposed photos unless the artistic merits of taking the path less traveled call for you to do so.

>> **Underexposed:** Unacceptably dark photos are underexposed. For whatever reason, too little light hit the image sensor to make a good photo.

>> **Properly exposed:** When everything comes together and you're able to capture just the right amount of light and produce a good photo, it's been properly exposed.

>> **Overexposed:** Photos that have been overexposed are too bright.

REMEMBER

Overexposed photos often have *clipped* or *blown highlights*. When this happens, the pixel turns pure white. There are no details at all. Likewise, underexposed photos often have clipped shadows. These are dark areas that turn black and lose all detail.

FIGURE 1-1: These photos illustrate the broad range of possible exposures.

Underexposed   Good exposure   Overexposed

The amount of light that can cause a photo to be under- or overexposed can be a little or a lot. It depends on the scene and camera. If the exposure is off by a relatively small margin, you may be able to rectify the situation using photo-editing software (see Book 5, Chapter 2 for help with this). If the amount is great enough, the photo is truly ruined.

Controlling exposure

Controlling exposure is an important part of photography. Your camera has exposure (also called shooting) modes that determine whether you or the camera control exposure, and how. Figure 1-2 shows a dSLR Mode dial.

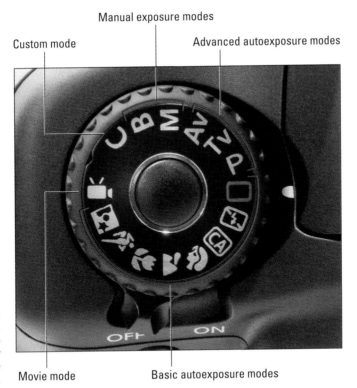

Custom mode

Manual exposure modes

Advanced autoexposure modes

Movie mode

Basic autoexposure modes

FIGURE 1-2:
Your camera's
Mode dial is
dominated by
autoexposure
modes.

REMEMBER

Autoexposure modes put the camera in charge of exposure. The type of input you have depends on the mode you've selected. Basic autoexposure modes require no input from you. Advanced autoexposure modes let you set one or more exposure controls for creative purposes and the camera sets the other controls for the best exposure.

You have total control over exposure in two modes: manual (M) and Bulb (B). The camera still evaluates the scene and displays what it thinks the best exposure is, but you're responsible for setting all the controls. While this may sound intimidating, it gives you the ability to override the camera with very little hassle.

REMEMBER

Your camera is not foolproof. Even in the autoexposure modes, it sometimes gets it wrong. That's why there is an exposure troubleshooting section at the end of the chapter.

Making Sense of
Exposure

In addition to exposure modes, your camera has three exposure controls, each with its own unique settings, for the aperture of the lens, the shutter speed, and ISO sensitivity. They limit the amount of light that you allow into the camera in space, time, and sensitivity. Each of these settings is important enough to warrant a chapter of its own here in Book 3. You can also control exposure by using the flash (Book 4, Chapters 2 and 3) and filters (Book 3, Chapter 5).

Comparing exposure intervals

Finally, various combinations of camera settings create different exposures. They're compared to each other in terms of stops and exposure values (EV). (You may be familiar with the term EV if you've ever shot exposure brackets for HDR or dialed in exposure or flash compensation. That's because all those methods use EV to quantify and compare exposures.)

Stops are a traditional way of describing exposure intervals. They are mechanical. The term comes from how photographers changed apertures and shutter speeds on their film cameras. They would widen the aperture by a physical stop on the lens or make the shutter speed faster by turning a knob to the next stop (see Figure 1-3). This doubled or halved the amount of light that the film was exposed to. The term therefore made its way into the lexicon of photography as a way to double or halve light.

Selected shutter speed

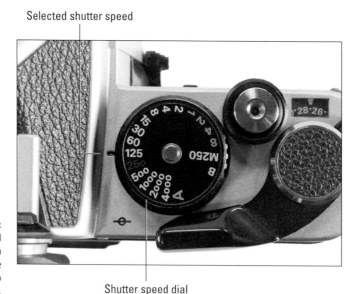

FIGURE 1-3:
The mechanical stops on a film camera were the precursor to exposure values.

Shutter speed dial

Exposure value is a number that represents a given amount of light. You can change the EV by altering the camera's exposure settings (aperture, shutters speed, or ISO) however you like. Each EV is the numerical equivalent of a mechanical stop. For example, raising the ISO by a stop increases the EV by +1.

Figure 1-4 shows the relationship between newer camera settings and stops. Each numbered division represents a stop of exposure, as on the older dial. Each stop is divided into thirds by smaller, unnumbered marks. Each stop is also a whole EV.

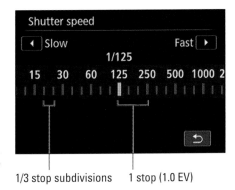

FIGURE 1-4:
This display shows stops of shutter speed.

1/3 stop subdivisions   1 stop (1.0 EV)

The standard exposure is placed at 0 EV on a scale representing possible exposures. This position indicates the combination of exposure settings that will create a properly exposed photo. Doubling the light creates an interval of +1.0 EV. Halving the light creates an interval of –1.0 EV. This interval is known as an exposure value. Exposure values are most often measured in thirds and whole numbers. You can often set your camera to control exposure level increments in halves.

REMEMBER

Stops and EV are so powerful because you can exchange units of exposure without worrying where they came from. A stop is a stop, whether it comes from changing the shutter speed, aperture, or ISO. In terms of exposure (but not necessarily creativity), it doesn't matter if you get a 1.0 increase by opening up the aperture, slowing the shutter speed, or increasing the ISO.

Keeping an Eye on Exposure Information

Keeping tabs on exposure information isn't hard. Your camera makes sure to display it for you in several handy places, including the viewfinder. You just have to know where to look. If you don't see anything, press the shutter button halfway. The camera will meter the scene and display the information. The camera may hide detailed exposure information from you if you're in a basic or automatic shooting mode because you don't control the exposure in those shooting modes. If you want to follow along with this section, place your camera in an advanced mode.

Reading the exposure level

Your camera has an *exposure level indicator* scale (a.k.a. *exposure scale* or *exposure meter*), shown in Figure 1-5. The center of the scale (sometimes labeled with a 0 but often with just a slightly different mark) indicates a *standard exposure* — the combined exposure value with inputs from all the camera's exposure settings that the camera thinks will produce the best photo.

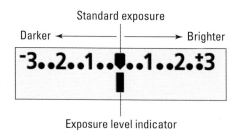

FIGURE 1-5:
The exposure
level indicator
scale shows the
exposure.

REMEMBER

The numbers to the left and right of center tell you how many stops — or levels of exposure value (EV) — you are away from the center. As you know by now, negative numbers indicate values that would underexpose the photo. Positive numbers indicate values that would cause overexposure.

The size of the scale may vary, but cameras usually show a minimum of +/- 2.0 EV from the center. Some cameras have displays that read +/- 5.0 EV. Normally, the vertical bar under the scale, known as the *exposure level indicator,* predicts a photo's exposure, relative to the standard exposure, taken with the current meter reading and using the current exposure settings.

In autoexposure modes, the exposure level indicator stays pegged in the middle. After all, that's the point of autoexposure. In manual mode, the exposure level indicator moves depending on your exposure settings. If you set your exposure settings so that the exposure level indicator is on 0, you'll take the standard exposure. The exception to that is when you are in manual mode and have set the camera to Auto ISO. As you make changes to shutter speed and aperture, the ISO will automatically adjust to keep the exposure at 0 EV.

TIP

After you set the exposure in manual mode, the settings won't change between shots, even if the meter displays a slightly different light level. Shooting in manual mode is an excellent way of making sure that your photos consistently use the same exposure settings, which is to your advantage when processing them the same way later.

The indicator can move left or right when you're in an autoexposure mode by a process known as exposure compensation (described later in the chapter). When you're shooting with autoexposure bracketing, each bracket's exposure is often marked with a tick mark.

Viewing exposure settings

Aside from paying attention to the overall exposure, shown on the exposure scale, you should track the three exposure settings: aperture, shutter speed, and ISO. Shutter speed and aperture are often paired; ISO tends to be off on its own. You can find them here:

>> **Viewfinder:** The exposure settings often appear prominently at the bottom of the viewfinder, as shown in Figure 1-6.

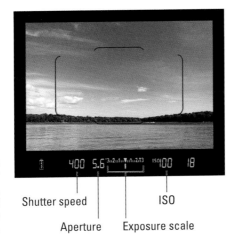

FIGURE 1-6: The shutter speed, aperture, and ISO speed all appear in the viewfinder.

Shutter speed

Aperture

Exposure scale

ISO

>> **LCD monitor:** The exposure settings also appear in the various information displays, as shown in Figure 1-7. In this case, the shooting information display is along the top.

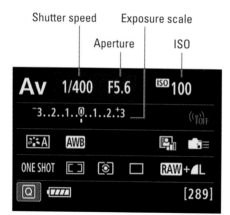

Shutter speed · Exposure scale · Aperture · ISO

FIGURE 1-7:
The shooting information display also shows the shutter speed, aperture, and ISO speed.

>> **LCD panel:** If your camera has a top LCD panel, you can check the exposure settings there. See Figure 1-8.

>> **Live View:** When you're using Live View, exposure data often appears at the bottom of the monitor and looks similar to what you see in the viewfinder. See Figure 1-9.

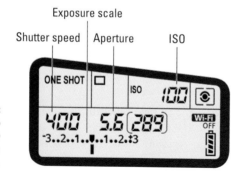

Exposure scale · Shutter speed · Aperture · ISO

FIGURE 1-8:
Don't forget to look at the LCD panel, if you have one.

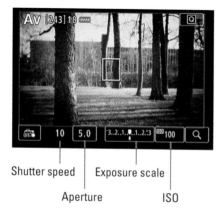

FIGURE 1-9:
Live View displays also show exposure information at the bottom.

Shutter speed · Exposure scale · Aperture · ISO

Paying attention to warnings

REMEMBER

Your camera may have several exposure-related warnings that let you know it can't take a good photo the way the camera is currently set up. For example, you may have the shutter speed set so fast that the camera can't open the aperture wide enough to take a properly exposed photo. Typically, the setting that is the problem will blink. See Table 1-1 for a summary of problems and solutions.

TABLE 1-1 ## Exposure Warnings and Their Solutions

Setting	What's Happening	Solution
Aperture and shutter speed	If both the aperture and shutter speed values blink, the camera can't select a combination that will properly expose the image. This most often happens in program autoexposure mode.	Adjust the lighting or change the ISO setting.
Aperture only	The aperture blinks if the camera can't set the aperture to expose the image properly at the selected shutter speed. This happens in shutter-priority mode.	Change the shutter speed or ISO.
Shutter speed	The shutter speed value blinks if the camera can't select a shutter speed that will produce a good exposure at the aperture you selected. This happens in aperture-priority mode.	Choose a different f-stop or adjust the ISO.

Measuring Light by Metering

Metering is the process of sensing how much light is in the scene you want to photograph. The amount of light helps determine what aperture, shutter speed, and ISO sensitivity you or your camera need to set in order to take a good photo.

General metering methods

There are two different ways to measure (or meter) how much light is in a scene: using *reflected* or *incident* light.

Measuring reflected light means that you collect light that bounces off stuff and finds its way into your camera or *light meter* (an external accessory that measures light). Cameras use this metering method exclusively. The upside to measuring reflected light is that you're able to meter distant objects. You can also meter specific objects in the scene, like a person's face. The downside to the approach is that not everything reflects the same amount of light, which can fool the metering sensor. This can become a problem when photographing people of different skin colors and tones. Reflected metering can also be called spot metering.

Incident light meters work differently. Rather than sensing reflected light, an incident light meter sits *in the scene* and measures how much light is falling *where it is*. Most incident meters have a white-colored dome or disk that bulges out from the meter's body. Ambient light passes through the dome and is measured by the meter. Cameras can't do this without special attachments. The upside to this method is that, overall, it is less prone to being spoofed by objects with different reflective properties. The problem with incident light meters is that they don't take reflectivity into account. If you're photographing something very bright and reflective, an incident light meter will not take that into account, and therefore may recommend setting the exposure too low.

REMEMBER

The long and the short of it is this: Your camera has a reasonably good reflective light meter built right in, but it's not perfect. You have to be able to switch metering modes (explained next) or manually compensate if the camera misjudges the scene. If you want a more realistic gauge when shooting portraits and other studio-type shots, as well as many landscapes, consider buying a light meter.

Camera metering modes

Digital SLRs have several ways to measure reflected light. They are called *metering modes*. Your camera will have three or more modes for you to choose from. They differ in how they evaluate different areas of the scene. One mode takes the entire frame into account. Other modes measure the center or very small spots. Refer to Figure 1-10 as you read the next few sections. The green areas in the viewfinder represent the areas the camera uses when metering in each mode.

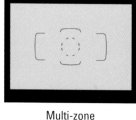  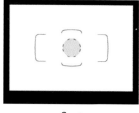

FIGURE 1-10: Metering modes enable you to customize how the camera meters.

Multi-zone   Center-weighted   Spot

Multi-zone

When this mode is selected, the camera divides the scene into zones and evaluates the brightness of each separately. Each manufacturer has its own system for how it weighs each area and combines the information into a single overall exposure. Camera manufacturers call their multi-zone metering modes by different names: 3D color matrix metering (Nikon), evaluative metering (Canon), and multi segment metering (Pentax and Sony). You may also hear it referred to as segment or multi-pattern metering.

Multi-zone is a good general-purpose metering mode and is the default for most cameras. You need not switch from it unless you're dealing with strong backlighting or want to measure light reflecting off of specific objects or areas in the scene.

Center-weighted

Center-weighted mode meters the entire frame but gives more weight to elements in the center than around the edges. Though the bias varies, it's in the range of 70 percent center to 30 percent edges. Canon refers to this as center-weighted average metering mode.

Center-weighted metering is a good mode for portraits and other photos with relatively large subjects in the center of the frame.

Spot

Spot metering measures light in a small circle in the center of the frame and ignores everything else. This metering mode is useful if you need to measure reflected light from a specific object or point in the scene. Some cameras let you change the size of the spot circle. Canon has an extra mode that covers a larger central area, called partial metering. Some cameras (more expensive Nikon models) enable you to link the spot meter to the current AF point, which is very handy.

Spot metering is good when you want the camera to calculate the exposure from a very precise spot in the scene. This can be your main subject, or an object that you don't want under or overexposed.

Changing metering modes

More expensive cameras have dedicated metering mode buttons. This makes changing metering modes a snap. Press the button and pick a new mode, as shown in Figure 1-11. Other cameras display metering mode information in the shooting information display from where you can often change it relatively quickly. As a last resort, you can always change metering modes using the camera's menu.

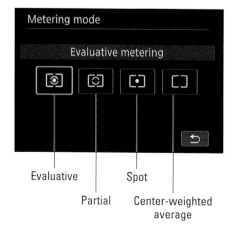

FIGURE 1-11:
Learn your
camera's
metering mode
symbols.

Evaluative

Partial

Spot

Center-weighted
average

Metering the scene with your camera

To meter the scene with your camera, follow these steps:

1. **Frame the shot you want to take.**

2. **Press your shutter button halfway.**

   You don't have to hold the button down. The camera remembers the light measurement for a moment (this is called the *metering timer* or *AE Lock time*) and suggests exposure settings based on your current shooting mode. However, most people hold it there briefly to focus before continuing to press all the way down and take the photo.

   Check your camera's manual for metering options. You may be able to press a different button to meter the scene, which lets you separate metering from autofocusing. You may also be able to reprogram the metering/autoexposure function to a new button of your choice. See Book 1, Chapter 4 for more on that topic.

Using an external light meter

An external *light meter* is a separate gizmo that measures the amount of light in a scene. Figure 1-12 shows mine. That's all it does. It doesn't take pictures. More expensive light meters can measure incident light with a dome and reflected light through a spot metering lens. Some light meters only measure incident light. While not strictly necessary, a light meter can be a valuable addition to your kit.

Look up your light meter's manual for specific instructions. In the meantime, I can tell you the general process works like this: After you set up your light meter to measure incident or reflected light, you need to enter two of the three known exposure settings you have set on the camera (ISO sensitivity, aperture, or shutter speed). Then take a reading. The meter figures out what the third exposure setting should be and shows it to you. Enter that value (aperture or shutter speed) in your camera.

Spot lens

Lumisphere

Eyepiece

FIGURE 1-12:
This Sekonic light meter is ready for action.

Reviewing and Analyzing Your Photos

Reviewing photos is one of the most important aspects of digital photography. You've got that fancy high-res monitor on the back of your camera: Use it to check whether your photos are exposed the way you want them to be.

If you don't review your shots, you won't be able to analyze the histograms or use any of the troubleshooting techniques described later in this chapter because you won't know what's there and what may be wrong.

Delving into photo playback

There's more to photo playback than you might think. It's an especially useful tool that enables you to check the exposure and color of every photo you take. There are two ways to go about playback. With auto review, the camera displays the photo for a specific amount of time. You may already have auto review enabled. Turn to Book 1, Chapter 4 to find out how to customize that feature. You can also initiate playback by pressing your camera's Playback button. Figure 1-13 points out the Playback button on a typical dSLR, and other buttons you might use during playback.

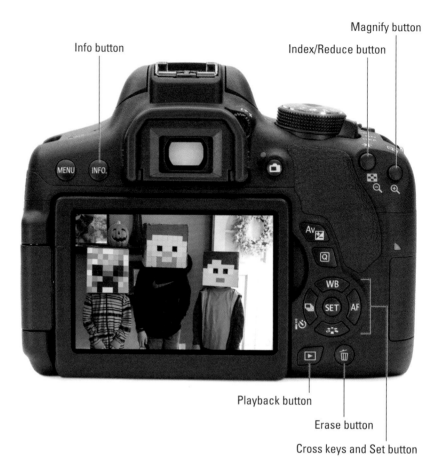

FIGURE 1-13:
The Playback
button is some-
where on the
back of your
camera.

I hit the highlights in this section. You'll have to turn to your camera's manual to see how to use specific features. Pressing the Playback button allows you to do the following:

» **Display different amounts of data.** You can change what information you see during photo playback by pressing your camera's Display or Info button. If you want a general sense of the photo, turn off everything. If you want a reminder of the settings you used, increase the amount of information, as shown in Figure 1-14.

» **Zoom in and out.** Press your camera's Zoom button to go in and closely inspect your photos.

» **Pan back and forth.** When you're zoomed in, use your camera's controller or cross keys to move back and forth in the photo.

FIGURE 1-14:
A range of
information is
available during
playback.

 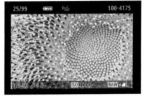 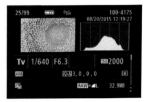

No information   Basic information   Detailed information

>> **View indices.** You can often show small thumbnails of your photos: 4, 6, or 9 — sometimes as many as 100 — at a time.

>> **Check the histogram.** Examine the photo's histogram to check general exposure and color.

>> **Check for clipped highlights.** See whether you have clipped highlights with the Highlight Alert (Canon) or Highlights (Nikon) display during photo playback. When this feature's on, overexposed areas will blink. If you see large areas blinking (and that isn't your creative goal), rethink the camera's exposure and take another shot.

There is one caveat to this feature: Areas of the photo that are clipped in one or two color channels, but not all three, may not register as clipped highlights. This means they won't blink. Examine the photo's color histograms for exposure across the board. (All photos have three layers of color information: red, green, and blue.)

>> **Delete the bad ones.** Don't save obviously bad photos. Delete them from your camera's memory card to save space, time, and trouble. This should involve pressing your camera's Delete or Trash button and confirming.

>> **Protect the good ones.** Alternatively, you can protect the photos you want to keep so they don't accidentally get deleted. You might be able to press a specific button to protect a photo or use the menu in Playback mode.

>> **View playback on a TV (HD or otherwise).** If you haven't already, view playback on a large HDTV. Photos (and movies, but that's another story) look fantastic and it's easier to spot focus, color, and exposure problems. Look at the terminals on the side of your camera. HDMI terminals, located on the side of your camera under a rubberized cover, enable you to connect your camera to an HDTV. Older dSLRs use analog audio/video connections.

Interpreting histograms

Simply put, *histograms* are charts. Digital SLRs display two different types of histograms: brightness and color (sometimes called RGB). Brightness histograms show the number of pixels in an image arranged by their brightness, while color histograms chart each color channel (red, green, and blue) separately. Live View histograms give you this information before you take the photo. You can also view the histogram of each photo during playback.

Cycle through your camera's Live View and playback displays to see the histograms. You may need to turn them on from the menu.

Brightness histograms

Brightness (sometimes called *luminance*) histograms are pretty easy to understand. As shown in Figure 1-15, they arrange pixels along the horizontal axis according to their brightness. Dark pixels appear on the left and bright pixels are plotted to the right. Pixels at the edges are at the minimum or maximum level, respectively. The vertical axis shows how many pixels share that same brightness. High peaks and mounds represent large numbers of pixels. Dips and valleys show fewer pixels, and bare spots show that no pixels have that brightness. You can divide the histogram into five tonal regions. Moving from left to right, they are: very dark, dark, medium, light, and very light. Pure black is on the far left; pure white is on the far right. Some cameras put lines on the histogram to help you make sense of these general areas.

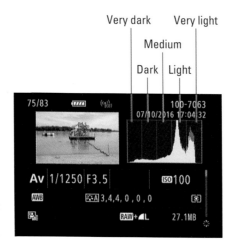

FIGURE 1-15:
This histogram charts brightness.

In the case of the photo shown in Figure 1-15, there is a range of brightness levels, but light and very light tones dominate. Nothing appears to have been clipped on either end.

The trick with brightness histograms is to realize that they weigh the brightness of each pixel in relation to how the human eye perceives it. Information from the green color channel is the most important, followed by red, then blue. This makes them great at showing you how the tonality is distributed, but less good at judging exposure. Exposure doesn't run on perception. A photo's appeal, however, often does.

Color histograms

Color histograms (see Figure 1-16) plot pixel brightness for each color channel (red, green, and blue) on a separate part of the chart. The horizontal axis plots color brightness. Bright colors are pure color (red, green, or blue, depending on the channel) while dark colors turn black. The vertical axis displays how many pixels are at that brightness level, just as a brightness histogram does. Peaks and mounds represent large numbers of pixels at that color brightness. Dips and valleys show fewer pixels, and bare spots show that no pixels have that brightness. The photo in Figure 1-16 has nice, strong colors with different brightness levels: dark reds from the berries, green leaves in the middle, and bright blues from the sky.

Color histograms may be displayed in black and white or in their respective color. Unlike brightness histograms, perception plays no role in how pixels are treated.

It's very easy to look at individual color channels and tell if there's clipping on either end. What can be tricky is looking at all three channels together and not overdrawing conclusions. For example, when peaks in each channel align, that's an indication of strong neutral tones, whether they are dark (blacks), medium (grays), or bright (whites). When there are strong peaks of color that don't line up, that's an indication that there are distinct colors in the photo that differ in brightness. It's *not* an automatic indication of a white balance problem.

FIGURE 1-16: Color histograms show color channel brightness and clipping.

Putting it all together

Histogram shapes give you important information about your photo. Knowing how to interpret these shapes is central to effectively using a histogram.

REMEMBER

>> **Peaks and mounds** show a larger numbers of pixels. If you see a peak, the pixels are concentrated over fewer brightness levels. If you see a mound, then the pixels are spread out across a larger range of brightness levels.

>> **Dips and valleys** reveal fewer pixels at those brightness levels.

>> **Empty areas** mean that there are no pixels at that brightness.

>> **Spikes at the edges** tell you that those pixels are clipping. The chart has run out of room to display their brightness levels, whether dark or light.

Different people use different terminology to refer to clipping. Some say that details get *lost in shadows* and that highlights are *blown out.* Each can also be described as *clipped* because the chart looks cut off, or clipped, at that point.

Figures 1-17 through 1-23 are histogram displays. To save space, they aren't full sized. The point is to quickly compare the histograms with the photo thumbnail, as you would on your camera, and to see at a glance what is going on. You don't need to zoom in 1,000 percent when evaluating histograms.

>> **Clipped shadows:** Figure 1-17 shows a scene shot from shadows in trees looking toward a lake. Some details in dark regions have been clipped and are lost. The bright areas of the sky make this a very high contrast scene, which is always a challenge to photograph. The photo was underexposed to keep the highlights from blowing out.

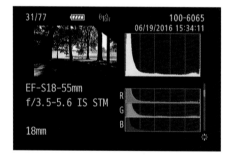

FIGURE 1-17: Underexposed with clipped shadows.

>> **Very dark tones:** The lighthearted photo in Figure 1-18 shows my wife and daughter. The photo is dominated by very dark tones from their hair and clothes. Their skin tones show up as very light reds in that color channel. Overall, the contrast is good, with tones in all regions.

FIGURE 1-18:
Very dark tones,
but a great photo.

>> **Dark tones:** Figure 1-19 shows a scene I shot at a small river. I stood right at the riverbank. The water glimmers with reflected light from the sun but the rest of the scene is largely dark. This shot has very smooth brightness and color histograms.

FIGURE 1-19:
The light sky and
reflections keep
the rest of this
photo dark.

>> **Medium tones:** I took the photo in Figure 1-20 from the top of a five-story parking garage with a tilt-shift lens. Medium tones of the road dominate, followed by lighter tones from the sidewalk and the dark grass. This photo is probably a tad underexposed, as there are few very light tones. Tilt-shift lenses sometimes have unexpected effects on exposure.

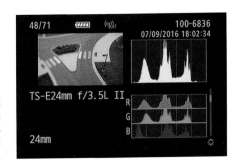

FIGURE 1-20:
This photo has
a lot of tones
concentrated in
the middle.

>> **Light tones:** Figure 1-21 shows the same parking garage from ground level, this time with a different lens. The brightness histogram shows the photo has a lot of bright tones, but seems to end there. If you look closely at the color histogram you can see that the blue channel is close to, or possibly has, clipped. Very bright single colors can cause this type of problem in a scene. It's better to underexpose a little so that you don't blow out color highlights.

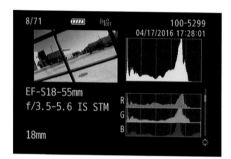

FIGURE 1-21:
Protect color
channels from
blowing out.

>> **Very light tones:** I set up the photo shown in Figure 1-22 in my studio. As you might expect, I have been able to dial in a great exposure and overall contrast through experience. The very bright tones of the white background show up in the brightness histogram. However, the flowers are not too dark relative to the rest of the scene. They sit very nicely in the medium to bright tonal region. The bump of dark blues comes from the shadows in the arrangement.

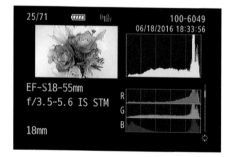

FIGURE 1-22:
Studio settings
enable you
to fine-tune
exposure.

>> **Clipped highlights:** Figure 1-23 is another casual shot of my wife and daughter. While they are well lit, the sky is blown out. This is another example of how bright skies can be so troublesome. They extend the contrast ratio of the scene beyond the camera's ability to capture. Had I accounted for the sky and lowered the exposure, they would have been too dark. Another option would have been to use a fill flash to brighten their faces with a lower exposure.

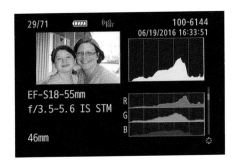

FIGURE 1-23:
Bright skies are very hard to control.

Troubleshooting Exposure

If everything always went as planned, you wouldn't need to read this section. The trouble is, the real world is a complicated place and even the most sophisticated dSLR can misjudge the scene, or your intent.

After reviewing your photos and looking at their histograms, you should have a good idea whether they are under- or overexposed, and why. Thankfully, dSLRs are designed with plenty of tools to help you correct any trouble you might be having and nail the next shot.

Using exposure compensation

Although it may seem obvious, when you have the camera in an autoexposure shooting mode (which includes everything but manual and Bulb modes), it sets the exposure for you. To make corrections, you have to override the camera. Changing the exposure controls won't actually change the exposure, as the camera will just work around you. The way to successfully change the exposure the camera sets is to use *exposure compensation (EC)*. Here's how it works:

1. **Review each photo after you take it and look to see how it's exposed.**

   You don't have to get too technical about it. Does someone's face need to be brighter? The photo's underexposed; raise the exposure. Is the sky too bright? The photo's overexposed; lower the exposure.

2. **Press and hold your exposure compensation button while you dial in exposure compensation. See the left image in Figure 1-24.**

   - Choose positive values, as shown in the figure, to raise the exposure and brighten the scene.

   - Choose negative values to lower the exposure and darken the photo.

REMEMBER

As shown on the right image in Figure 1-24, your camera's shooting information screen always shows how much EC you have entered.

3. **Release the EC button and take another shot.**

4. **Review it to see if it's closer to what you want.**

Exposure compensation stays locked in many cameras even after you turn them off, so be careful to reset to 0 after you've taken the shot.

WARNING

+1.0 EV Exposure compensation

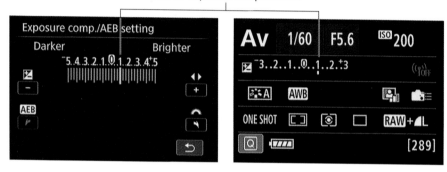

FIGURE 1-24:
Exposure compensation moves the exposure up or down.

Your camera should allow up to two stops of both positive and negative exposure correction. Some enable you to dial in as many as five stops either way.

Setting the exposure manually

One of the most powerful exposure tools in your arsenal is you. Given an understanding of what you want to accomplish creatively, combined with the limitations of your equipment and the lighting on hand, you can effectively troubleshoot exposure by bypassing the camera's autoexposure modes and handling it yourself.

REMEMBER

Each photographic stop has the same effect on exposure, whether it comes from shutter speed, aperture, or ISO. You can swap one for another to get to the exposure you need.

Here are some suggested steps to setting exposure manually:

1. **Select your camera's manual mode.**

2. **Decide what exposure control you want to set first.**

Let your creative goals guide you to limit one of the three exposure controls:

- *Aperture:* Smaller is better for landscapes. Larger is better for portraits. Read Book 3, Chapter 2 for more about aperture.

- *Shutter speed:* Set a fast minimum (this is the point you're not willing to shoot slower than) for action and dim light when going handheld. If you try another mode first and the shutter speed is too low, switch to shutter-priority mode. Set the shutter speed high enough to avoid blurring.

- *ISO:* For shooting still subjects from a tripod, set to lowest ISO and slow shutter speed. If your camera shoots relatively noise-free photos up to ISO 800, use anything from ISO 100 to ISO 800.

3. **Set the first value.**

   Typically, this will be aperture or shutter speed. Setting the aperture guarantees you the depth of field you want. Setting the shutter speed helps you capture action or prevent yourself from taking blurry photos.

4. **Set the second exposure control.**

   Quite often, you may have set the aperture first but now bring in shutter speed to guarantee a crisp photo. You may want to set the ISO sensitivity now to keep noise to a minimum.

5. **Adjust the third exposure control to get the right exposure.**

   This is what I call the "floating" control. It has to be able to move around so that you can set the exposure. The exposure scale tells you whether the camera thinks you're under- or overexposing the photo, or right on the mark (see Figure 1-25). When you're troubleshooting, you may need to ignore the camera meter. If you've already taken a shot and it was too bright, tone down the exposure by a third, a half, or a whole stop. Raise the exposure if the photo was too dark.

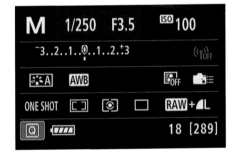

FIGURE 1-25:
Setting manual exposure for a properly exposed photo.

TIP

Don't make wild changes unless the other photos were significantly off, too. Keep changes small and try to be methodical about it.

6. **Take a photo.**

7. **Review it.**

REMEMBER

This is the most important step. I know you want to get back to shooting, but you can't rush this step.

- Look at the photo on your monitor and decide if it appears underexposed (too dark) or overexposed (too light). Be aware that your perception may be affected if you're looking at the photo in extreme conditions (bright or dim), or if you've altered the brightness level of your LCD monitor. The histogram is helpful in these situations.

- Check the color histograms to see if any colors are clipping.

- Zoom in, if necessary, to check details.

If the exposure looks good, this photo is in the bank. You may be able to use the same settings for more photos, provided the scene and lighting don't change much.

8. **Continue adjustments, if necessary.**

If the exposure is off, return to Step 5 and work with your floating exposure control. You may also return to Step 4 and revise the second control. If your exposure solution won't work for more drastic reasons — you can't set the right shutter speed to avoid blurring or you're concerned about too high an ISO, go back to Step 2 and reset your priorities. You may have to live with more noise or a shallower depth of field.

REMEMBER

Shutter speed is generally the least forgiving exposure element. It's easier to accept different depths of field or noise levels, but camera shake and motion blur caused by slow shutter speeds provide little artistic leeway.

Using AE Lock

Autoexposure (AE) Lock lets you handle situations where your subject is strongly backlit and you want to offset them in the shot.

You'll meter and focus on one area of the scene, lock the autoexposure reading into the camera, recompose the shot, and then take the photo with the locked exposure settings. This works wonders if your subject is backlit. Simply change to spot or center-weighted metering mode and engage AE Lock. Here's how:

1. **Change the metering mode to spot or center-weighted metering.**

Although you can use any metering mode, switching to spot or center-weighted metering is a quick way to make the camera meter where you want it to. Some cameras enable you to manually select an AF point and use that for AE Lock when in certain metering modes. For example, new Canon cameras apply AE Lock to the selected AF point when you set the camera to Evaluative metering mode. Read your camera's manual for specifics.

2. **Center the subject in the viewfinder, as shown in Figure 1-26.**

Unless you are able to use a specific AF point with AE Lock. See Book 1, Chapter 5 for information on selecting individual autofocus points.

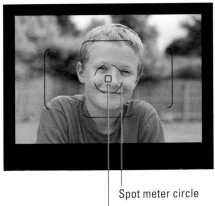

Spot meter circle

Center AF point

FIGURE 1-26:
Center the
subject to use
spot metering.

3. **Press and hold the shutter button halfway down.**

This meters the scene and gets things in focus, unless focusing manually.

4. **Press and hold the AE Lock button, shown in Figure 1-27.**

This locks the exposure into the camera. You may release the shutter button once the exposure is locked, but keep pressing the AE Lock button. Press the AE Lock button again if you want to update the exposure.

Some cameras have AE Lock on a timer that lasts a few seconds. If that is the case, you don't have to hold the AE Lock button down unless you want to lock that specific exposure in the camera for longer than the timer allows.

TIP

You might feel like you have too much to do with too few fingers. Use your left hand to support the weight of the camera while pressing the shutter and AE Lock buttons.

5. **Recompose the shot, as shown in Figure 1-28.**

While this is optional, it's the reason most people use AE Lock. AE Lock enables you to choose any metering point in the scene and then compose the shot the way you want. If you have a camera that enables you to use any AF point when spot metering, you can skip this step.

If your camera requires it, continue to hold down the AE Lock button.

Making Sense of Exposure

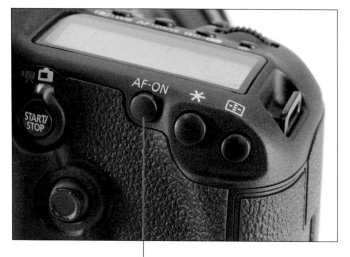

FIGURE 1-27:
Press the AE Lock and hold it with your thumb.

AE Lock button

FIGURE 1-28:
Recompose after metering and focusing.

AE Lock

6. **Take the picture (see Figure 1-29).**

AE Lock is a great way to make sure people's faces are exposed correctly when shooting portraits. Whether it makes a huge or minimal difference, it forces the camera to prioritize the center of the frame when you meter. This keeps dark and bright elements in the background from throwing the camera's exposure off.

If you want to take more shots with these specific exposure settings, note the shutter speed, aperture, and ISO; then switch to manual mode and dial in those values yourself.

FIGURE 1-29:
AE Lock is especially effective when shooting portraits.

Autoexposure bracketing (AEB)

Despite recent trends, your camera's *autoexposure bracketing (AEB)* feature isn't useful solely for *high dynamic range (HDR)* photography. If the lighting is giving the camera trouble, try turning on AEB and shooting several exposure-bracketed photos.

Set up your camera's AEB feature, as shown on the left in Figure 1-30. Tell it how far apart to set the exposure of each bracket, and how many you want to take. It may seem haphazard, but sometimes it's the best you can do. You can choose the best photo of the set. The right image in Figure 1-30 shows the brackets on the shooting information display.

For more information on bracketing (within the context of HDR), see Book 5, Chapter 6. The mechanics of using AEB are the same.

Autoexposure brackets

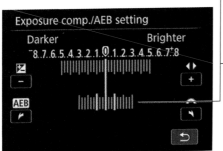

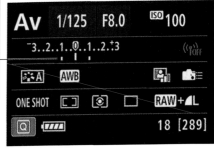

FIGURE 1-30:
Autoexposure brackets give you the option of choosing the best exposure.

Using other exposure tricks

Camera makers use several other exposure tricks to help you solve exposure problems. Most have to do with overcoming a camera's limited capability to photograph very high-contrast scenes.

The names of the tricks differ from brand to brand, and not every camera in every company's lineup will have all the features. However, after reviewing them, you'll see that most of these exposure solutions are similar.

Look for these features on Canon cameras:

>> **Highlight Tone Priority** improves details in highlights by expanding the camera's dynamic range from mids to highs. Doing so enables you to capture more information in bright areas.

>> **Auto Lighting Optimizer** is a processing function the camera uses to automatically adjust brightness and contrast. You can modify the strength.

>> **HDR mode** takes a number of shots and combines them into a single finished image.

Nikon dSLRs have these features:

>> **Active D-Lighting,** when on, adjusts exposure to maximize the camera's dynamic range, protecting highlights and shadows in high-contrast scenes.

>> **HDR** automatically takes exposure-bracketed photos to increase the camera's dynamic range and then combines them into a single, tone-mapped image.

Sony cameras also have several tricks up their sleeve:

>> **D-Range Optimizer** is Sony's method of protecting highlights and shadows in scenes with high contrast. You can choose from several strengths.

>> **Auto HDR** combines AEB with auto tone mapping to provide a single-step HDR capability.

Chapter **2**

Setting the Aperture

This chapter is about the aperture of your lens and how to use it to control exposure and the *depth of field* (the area in focus) in your photos. You'll learn what apertures are, how they affect exposure, how to tell what apertures a lens is capable of, and how you can control them. You also learn how the size of the aperture contributes to defining the scene's depth of field. Armed with this information, you can move beyond your camera's automated shooting modes (if you like) and purposefully take photos with different creative goals in mind.

Investigating f-numbers and Apertures

The opening in every lens that lets light shine into the camera, guided and focused by the optical elements, is called the *aperture.* Larger apertures let in more light. Smaller apertures let in less light. The aperture plays an important part in exposure, and it's expressed as an f-number, which I explain next.

REMEMBER

An aperture is part of the lens, not the camera body. This is one reason the lenses you choose are an important part of your overall dSLR experience.

Learning about f-numbers

The numbers f/5.6 and f/8 and f/16 describe an aperture's effect on exposure. Why are apertures represented by f-numbers? Because f-numbers factor in focal length in addition to the physical size of the aperture. Both things matter when describing how much light passes through the lens.

An *f-number,* also known as an f-stop, is the relationship between a lens's focal length and its aperture diameter. In plain(ish) language, you can calculate the f-number by taking the current focal length of the lens (in millimeters) and dividing that by the aperture's diameter (in millimeters). If you know the lens's focal length and its f-number, you can figure out the diameter of the aperture by dividing the focal length by the f-number.

By convention, f-numbers have two digits. That's why you see f/4.0 and f/8.0 here in the book and displayed by your camera, but not f/11.0 or f/16.0, which are instead shown as f/11 and f/16. The exception to this involves lens names. Quite often, if you run across a lens with a single-digit whole number maximum aperture, it will be simplified. The Canon EF 100mm f/2 USM lens is one example.

Figure 2-1 illustrates this concept. I set the same NIKKOR 50mm f/2 Ai prime lens to four different f-numbers: f/2.0 (the largest aperture shown), f/4.0, f/8.0, and f/16 (the smallest aperture shown). The fact that it is a prime lens, with a constant focal length, simplifies the situation. The only thing that changes between each photo is the f-number, which increases by a full stop each time. The focal length remained constant

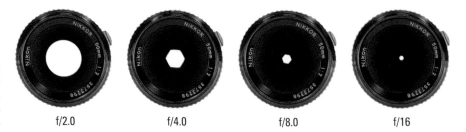

FIGURE 2-1: As f-numbers increase, aperture sizes decrease.

f/2.0   f/4.0   f/8.0   f/16

Remember, the f-number is also dependent on the focal length the lens is set to. To illustrate that point, I've photographed my Zoom-NIKKOR 35-70mm f/3.5 AI-s lens with the aperture set at a constant f/3.5. As Figure 2-2 shows, as I increased the focal length, the physical size of the aperture also increased. The f-number stayed at f/3.5 in each shot.

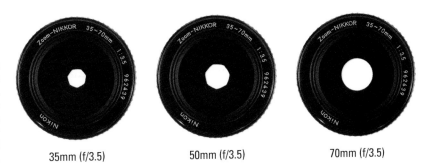

FIGURE 2-2:
As focal length increases, aperture size does too, but the f-number remained the same.

35mm (f/3.5)   50mm (f/3.5)   70mm (f/3.5)

Lenses and apertures

Because apertures are described by f-numbers (ignore the fact that focal length plays a role in determining the f-number for the moment), it stands to reason that the name of the lens will tell you something about its capabilities, and those capabilities are shown in terms of f-numbers. That's exactly how it works. Standard dSLR lenses list their maximum aperture as part of their name.

Constant maximum aperture

Many lenses list a single maximum aperture in their name. This means they have a *constant maximum aperture*, regardless of the focal length. Two types of lenses have a constant maximum aperture:

» **Prime lenses:** All prime lenses have constant maximum apertures because they never change focal length. For example, the maximum aperture of the AF-S NIKKOR 50mm f/1.4G prime lens is f/1.4.

» **Zoom lenses:** Some high-quality zoom lenses have a constant maximum aperture across their focal length range. These lenses cost more and are better than those with variable maximum apertures because you can collect the same amount of light whether you're zoomed in or out. The Canon EF 24-105mm f/4L IS USM is a good example. Although it's a zoom lens, the maximum aperture is f/4.0. It doesn't change, no matter what the focal length is.

Variable maximum aperture

Lenses with *variable maximum apertures* list two f-numbers in their name. For example, the Sigma 17-70mm F2.8-4 DC Macro HSM zoom lens sports apertures listed at f/2.8 and f/4.0. What gives? The maximum aperture changes depending on the focal length the lens is set to. You're given the two extremes: At 17mm, the maximum aperture is f/2.8. At 70mm, the maximum aperture is f/4.0.

You may look down at your camera, after having set the aperture to f/3.5, and see that the camera has changed it without your permission. You've zoomed beyond the range where it can support your chosen aperture.

Minimum aperture

To find the minimum possible aperture, you have to look into the specification sheet or manual for each lens. You can also figure it out pretty quickly by attaching the lens to your camera, entering aperture-priority or manual mode, and setting the aperture to the largest f-number possible. Common values range from f/16 to f/32.

Fast lenses

Lenses with small f-numbers in their name (hence large maximum apertures) are known as *fast* lenses. The Canon EF 50mm f/1.2L USM is a good example of a fast prime lens. The Canon EF 24-70mm f/2.8L II USM is a fast standard zoom lens. When open, fast lenses let in a lot of light. It's why they excel in low-light situations. It also means that you can use a faster shutter speed with a fast lens than with a lens with a smaller aperture. Fast lenses are prized for their ability to pleasingly blur the background when their apertures are open.

Table 2-1 puts lenses into speed categories based on their maximum apertures. Table 2-1 applies to most lenses below 400mm. When you're working with super telephoto lenses at 500mm and 600mm, f/4 is considered fast. For super-duper-ooper-schmooper telephoto lenses (800mm), f/5.6 is considered fast.

TABLE 2-1 ### Fast versus Slow Lens Speeds

Speed	Maximum f-number range	Notes
Very Fast	f/1.8 and below	Professional lenses; very fast compared to all other lenses; companies often field more than one fast prime lens with different price points and slightly different maximum apertures; can be expensive; cost goes up as focal lengths increase
Fast	f/2 to f/2.8	Very expensive telephoto and zoom lenses; very good in low light; zoom lenses at this range are considered professional caliber
Medium	f/3.0 to f/4.0	Moderately expensive, but still reasonably affordable; can be used in low-light with higher ISOs and longer shutter speeds; very good outside
Normal	f/5.6 and above	Often inexpensive; come as kit lenses on consumer and some midrange dSLRs; hard to use inside without elevating ISO or using flash; fine outside; great lenses for amateurs but limited by aperture

Setting the Aperture

Setting the aperture on your lens is pretty straightforward. You don't need to, though, unless you're in your camera's manual or aperture–priority mode. Other modes take care of it for you. The main reason why you might want to handle it yourself is that it allows you some control over the depth of field in the scene.

There are two primary ways to set the aperture. Set it in the camera if using a modern lens. Older lenses (and some new ones) have aperture rings that you may need to turn to set the aperture. The following sections explain how.

In camera

Most modern lenses *don't* have aperture rings, which means you have to set the aperture using the controls on the camera.

Set the aperture with these methods:

>> Enter your camera's manual or aperture-priority modes and dial in the aperture of your choice (as shown in Figure 2-3). Use one of the controls (normally the front or rear dial) to adjust the setting.

>> Use your camera's program mode and then shift the aperture/shutter speed combination via Program Shift or Flexible Program.

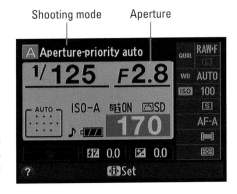

FIGURE 2-3:
The aperture is displayed only in the camera.

If you're using a more automatic scene or mode, you choose the depth of field you want and the camera selects an appropriate aperture. For example, if you choose Landscape, you're telling the camera that you want a large depth of field. It'll stop down accordingly. When you understand why certain scenes call for certain depths of field, you might want to start setting the aperture directly yourself.

Some cameras have shooting modes that let you select the amount of background blur you want in the photo. Canon calls its mode Creative Auto, while Nikon uses a shooting mode called Guide.

Aperture ring

All SLR lenses used to have an aperture ring. Canon has done away with aperture rings altogether, although you will find new lenses from various manufacturers that have them for some lens mounts.

Nikon still offers elements of old (aperture ring) and new-school (computer chip) technology in its D-series lenses. Figure 2-4 shows the AF-S NIKKOR 300mm f/4D IF-ED I've used for many photos throughout this book. It's a relatively low-cost super telephoto lens that performs quite well. It also has an aperture ring. To use D-series lenses on new camera bodies, lock the aperture ring on the lens to its highest f-number (smallest aperture), and control the aperture from the camera. Ignore the aperture ring in this configuration. When using an old, manual focus lens on a modern dSLR, set the aperture on the lens.

FIGURE 2-4: Notice the aperture ring on this modern Nikon lens.

Aperture ring

More advanced Nikon dSLR bodies let you enter the focal length and maximum aperture of old lenses, called *non-CPU* lenses, in the camera's menu, as shown in Figure 2-5. Entering the data enables the camera to meter, recognize the aperture set by the lens, and control the flash better. Check your manual for specifics.

Some specialty lenses, like certain Lensbaby optics, do not have traditional aperture rings. They require you to change the lens's aperture by swapping aperture discs with a special magnetic tool. It sounds clunky, but it's sort of fun.

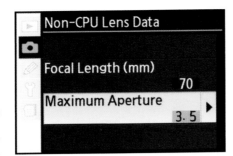

FIGURE 2-5:
Setting non-CPU
lens data in the
camera.

Digging into Depth of Field

Each of the three primary exposure elements (aperture, shutter speed, and ISO) has an effect on the photo's exposure. They also have a side effect.

REMEMBER

The aperture's creative side effect is *depth of field.* Depth of field is the area of the photo that appears sharp when focused. Everything outside the depth of field area, whether foreground or background, will look blurred.

Figure 2-6 illustrates depth of field with a shot taken at f/1.4. The white knight in the center was the point of focus. It, and the brown pawn to the right of it, are in the center of the depth of field. The board and pieces nearer to the camera are out of focus because they're in front of the depth of field. The background, beyond the depth of field, is also out of focus.

FIGURE 2-6:
Illustrating a
shallow depth
of field.

Setting the Aperture

Controlling the depth of field

One of the aspects of photography that makes it so interesting is that you have control over the size of the depth of field. You can, with relative ease, make it larger or smaller.

Several factors determine how large or how small the depth of field is:

>> **Circle of confusion:** The circle of confusion is, frankly, a circle of confusion. It's a subjective value that decides, essentially, how out-of-focus something has to be before you notice it. If there were no circle of confusion, the depth of field would be infinitely small because you could spot the least little bit of blur.

Unless you want to calculate depths of field yourself, you can completely ignore the circle of confusion. DOFmaster (www.dofmaster.com) has online and downloadable depth of field calculators.

>> **Distance to subject:** This is the distance at which the lens is focused. Focusing on nearby objects results in *shallow* depths of field. Focusing on faraway objects gives *greater* depths of field. Some lenses have distance scales on them.

>> **f-number:** You may be most familiar with this factor.

- Smaller f-numbers (large apertures) result in shallow depths of field.

- Larger f-numbers (small apertures) result in deeper depths of field.

At very close ranges, however, even very large f-numbers (small apertures) have shallow depths of field. Figure 2-7 shows the difference between using shallow and larger depths of field. I took both photos from the same distance with the same lens and focal length. I used an aperture of f/1.4 in the photo on the left, and f/11 in the photo on the right. There are three stops of difference between the two settings. Notice that at f/1.4, the only thing in focus is the center candle and the berries to the front of it. The depth of field is very small. Unrelated to that, but significant, is the fact that the bokeh is very nice. At f/11, everything has sharpened up.

>> **Focal length:** The longer the focal length the shallower the depth of field for a given aperture. This is why telephoto lenses produce shallower depth of field than normal or wide-angle lenses. Telephoto lenses create wonderful *bokehs* (the aesthetic nature of the out-of-focus areas of the photo, discussed later). This, in turn, makes near/medium telephoto lenses very effective portraiture and wedding lenses.

FIGURE 2-7:
The depth of
field changes
dramatically
based on the lens
aperture.

f/1.4   f/11

Previewing the depth of field

Modern dSLRs keep the lens wide open while you frame, meter, and focus the scene. When you press the shutter button to take the photo, the lens quickly changes to the aperture set in the camera. That means you don't normally see what the depth of field will be.

To correct that, many digital SLRs have a *Depth-of-Field Preview* button. When you press it, the aperture on the lens changes to what is set in the camera, enabling you to see the depth of field as it will be when you take the photo. Look for the button somewhere on the front, either on the right or left side near the lens mount. Reach around to press it after you focus on your subject. Figure 2-8 shows the Depth-of-Field Preview button on the Canon EOS Rebel T6i. This camera has the button on the lower-right front of the camera body, just beneath the lens-release button.

TIP

Checking the depth of field is most effective when the aperture is set to a value *smaller* than the lens's maximum aperture.

While not a preview, many prime lenses have depth-of-field scales printed right on the lens, somewhere near the distance scale. This gives you a quick estimate of how large or small the depth of field will be. The depth is based on your current f-number and the focus distance.

Setting the Aperture

Depth-of-Field button

One caveat: Be careful when you're using a full-frame compatible lens with a depth-of-field scale on a cropped-frame body. The scale on the lens will overestimate the actual depth of field by a factor equal to your camera's crop factor. For example, if your camera has a crop factor of 1.6x, then the depth of field on the lens will be 1.6 times larger than it should be. This is enough to throw off a carefully planned shot and produce photos with depths of field much larger than you intended. To get the proper value, divide the depth-of-field distance given by the lens by your camera's crop factor.

Paying attention to the blurry parts

What lies outside the depth of field is generally called the *bokeh*. Technically speaking, bokeh refers to the aesthetic quality of the blurred area, not its size. You either have *good bokeh* or *bad bokeh*, not large or small bokeh. However, many people refer to the blurred area in general as the *bokeh*. The size of the blurred area, or the blurred area in general, may be referred to as the area outside of the depth of field.

Photos with great-looking bokeh are very desirable. Figure 2-9, shot with the AF-S NIKKOR 50mm f/1.4G, has a bokeh that looks like a painting. Lights and reflections make good bokeh, but you will see smooth, creamy bokehs when the background is uniform. A great bokeh is a telltale sign that a photographer is using a high-quality professional lens. When it comes to bokeh, the lens really does matter.

FIGURE 2-9:
Nice bokehs are
otherworldly.

Aperture has no direct impact on bokeh, other than its effect of the size of the depth of field. Photos with deeper depths of field may have no blurry parts. Landscape photos, for example, generally remain in focus from a distance reasonably close to the camera to infinity.

Being realistic

REMEMBER

Beware of obsessing over trying to get the shallowest depth of field possible, thinking it will make all your photos better. Shallow depths of field make focusing much harder. You may also end up with a photo of a person who has one eye in focus and the other, which is slightly out of the depth of field, blurred.

The reverse is also true. When the aperture is very small (depending on the lens, aperture smaller than f/22), diffraction starts to become a problem. *Diffraction* happens when light waves get bent as they go around the edges of the aperture. This results in softness or fuzziness in areas of the photo that should be sharp.

If you're shooting at close distances (food or product shots, for example), take test shots at different f-numbers and compare sharpness. Choose the photo that best meets your depth of field (small aperture) and sharpness (an aperture not so small that you run into diffraction) needs.

TIP

If a shallow depth of field is giving you fits, try this:

>> **Step back from the subject.** Don't just zoom out. That doesn't increase the distance between you and what you're shooting. Actually step back.

>> **Zoom out.** If you can't step back, try zooming out.

>> **Stop down.** For example, if you're shooting at f/1.4 (I've learned my lesson and rarely shoot here anymore), try f/2.8 or f/5.6. Not many people care what aperture you use; they're interested in what your photo looks like.

If you're after a shallow depth of field, do the opposite: Step in, open your aperture more, and zoom in.

Designing with Depth of Field

Because of its effect on depth of field, the aperture plays an important part of how photos look. The point of this section is to show how it all comes together in practice. Read through the following sections and look at the sample photos to see examples of how different apertures work with different scenes. Then go out and experiment with your own.

TIP

I throw a lot of numbers at you in the following sections. If you need to, skip them and focus on the narrative and the photos. If you want to, take a notepad and write down the f-number. Ask yourself what setting you would have used or how the depth of field would have changed. Then go online for a depth of field calculator (the one I use is at www.dofmaster.com) and crunch the numbers. You'll need the camera, focal length, aperture, and subject distance.

Landscapes

When shooting landscapes, you typically want a large depth of field. This keeps as much of the scene in focus as possible. Remember, the depth of field has depth. There is a near distance at which things appear sharp, then comes the depth of field where everything looks fine, and a point where that ends. Anything past the far limit will be out of focus unless you're taking advantage of something called the *hyperfocal* distance. The hyperfocal distance is the distance you focus at which causes the depth of field to extend infinitely away from you.

Figure 2-10 illustrates the point. To take the photo, I used a Sony APS-C dSLT with an ultra wide-angle zoom lens set to 10mm. My aperture was set to f/8 and I was focusing far out into the distance. Given those parameters, the hyperfocal distance is just over 2 feet. That means that everything in this photo beyond 2 feet from the camera is in focus. It's a physical impossibility for it to be anything less. It's clear from this photo, because you can see so far into the distance. The tree line on the far side of the river is nice and sharp all the way to the point where it disappears around the bend.

Now, if you play around with the aperture, you'll still get an infinitely wide depth of field with larger apertures, as long as you focus on a far point in the scene. However, you will move the hyperfocal distance away from you by a few feet if you select something like f/2.8. This may make the foreground appear obviously out of focus. To play around with smaller depths of field when shooting landscapes, you should focus on something nearby or use a longer focal length (near telephoto or longer). To guarantee an immense or infinite depth of field, focus as far away as possible with shorter focal lengths (wide angles).

To find the hyperfocal distance for the camera, aperture setting, and focal distance you're using check out online or printed depth of field calculators.

FIGURE 2-10: Maximize depth of field when shooting most landscapes.

Approach buildings and cityscapes the same way. I took the shot of downtown Detroit shown in Figure 2-11 with an aperture of f/8. I also was not focusing as far away as I did with Figure 2-10 and had a different lens, set to 50mm. In this case, the near edge of the depth of field starts out farther away (about 37 feet, or 11 meters), but the depth of field is still infinite.

FIGURE 2-11:
Buildings and cityscapes benefit from large depths of field.

Portraits

Your goal when photographing people will generally be to limit the depth of field so that they are in focus, but nothing else. Subjects almost pop out of the photo it they're the only thing in focus. The apertures you use to photograph them will be larger than for landscapes. Longer focal lengths and closer distance to your subject also play a role in making the depth of field smaller. As I've mentioned, though, beyond a certain point, shrinking the depth of field too much makes it impossible to capture a good photo.

Figure 2-12 shows a group portrait of me and my sons in the kitchen. My wife had just given me a haircut and the kids were next. We were playing around, so she grabbed the camera and took this shot with a Nikon APS-C dSLR and 50mm lens. The aperture was f/2.8. This combination made the depth of field about a third of a foot, or 10 cm. As you can see, the background is nicely blurred.

FIGURE 2-12:
Line up people
when shooting
group portraits.

TIP

The challenge when taking group shots with a shallow depth of field is to get everyone lined up so that all of them are about the same distance from the camera. If the distance varies too much, they won't be in focus. To increase the depth of field, use a smaller aperture or step back. For every stop of aperture, you double or halve the size of the depth of field too (this may be one of the more important sentences in this chapter). This means that had my wife used a setting of f/5.6, the depth of field would have been about two-thirds of a foot, or 20 cm.

You don't have to worry about lining up people when shooting individual portraits. Figure 2-13 shows a nice photo of my son, Sam. I used a Canon APS-C dSLR with lens set to 42mm and an aperture of f/5.6. In this case, the depth of field is about 1.5 inches, or 4 cm. How can this be smaller than the last photo? Even though I took the photo with a smaller aperture and the focal length was a bit less, the fact that I was closer to the subject more than makes up for it.

Believe it or not, f/5.6 was the perfect aperture to use in this situation. If I had been using a better lens and been tempted to set the lens to f/2.8 or f/1.4, the smaller depth of field might have been disastrous. As it is, Sam's nose and eyes are sharp and in focus, while his ears are not. This is about as shallow as you want to be unless you're going for a special effect.

Setting the Aperture

FIGURE 2-13:
Aim for a shallow
depth of field
when shooting
portraits, but be
careful.

If you want to be meticulous with your portraits, I encourage you to calculate the depth of field you want, then reverse-engineer the aperture, focal length, and distance from the subject; that will help you achieve your goals. Base the size of the desired depth of field on things you're going to photograph:

>> **A person's face:** Aim for a depth of field of a few inches, or about 15 cm.

>> **A person's head:** Set the depth of field to about a foot, or approximately 30 cm.

>> **A group of people:** You want the depth of field to be 2 or 3 feet, or something like 60-90 cm.

Over time, you'll know what to expect and be able to work more on the fly.

Macros and close-ups

With landscapes you want a large depth of field. When photographing portraits you generally want a small depth of field. Macros are another story entirely. You'll generally struggle to overcome microscopic depths of field.

Have a look at Figure 2-14. It's a small beetle that I photographed using a Nikon APS-C camera and lens. The focal length was 105mm and my distance to the beetle was about 16 inches, or 42 cm. I had the aperture set to f/22. This created a depth of field of .4 inch, or only 1 centimeter (10 millimeters) . That's right, a centimeter, even with a small aperture of f/22. Had I used something more typical of standard photography, like f/5.8 or f/8, the depth of field would have been impossibly small. As it is, the front of the beetle and parts of the leaves are nice and sharp. The background is very smooth and nicely blurred. It's a great photo.

Treat close-ups like you would portraits, with distances that are generally closer. You should use large apertures to create nice blurred backgrounds, as long as there is depth in the photo. Some shots are relatively flat.

You can create this distance yourself. I set up the shot in Figure 2-15 for precisely this reason. Photographing a piece of pie is one thing, but showing a cup of coffee and the rest of the pie in the background created a much more appealing photo. I used a Nikon APS-C dSLR with the 50mm lens set to f/2.8 to capture the front face of the piece of pie in focus and blur everything else.

As you can see, focusing on a precise point is very important when shooting macros and close-ups.

Action

Shooting action forces your hand a bit. You naturally want fast shutter speeds and low ISOs. This drives the aperture to open in order to expose the photo properly, which then reduces the width of the depth of field. Using a telephoto lens also gives you less depth of field. If you're working in bright light you may be able to use a smaller aperture. If not, raise the ISO or see if you can use a slower shutter speed.

Figure 2-16 is an example where everything worked out. I used a Nikon APS-C dSLR and 300mm super telephoto lens to capture this scene. I set the shutter speed to 1/1000 second and ISO of 100. The aperture was f/4. Given that I was about 100 feet away, or 30 meters, the depth of field was just over 5 feet, or 1.5 meters. That was enough to capture the horse in the center and his driver sharply, along with the horse and driver to their right. Had I reduced the size of the aperture by one full stop (f/8 instead of f/4), the depth of field would have doubled. I could have offset this by raising the ISO to 200 or more, if I needed to. Those are the creative decisions you'll have to wrestle with.

Setting the Aperture

FIGURE 2-15:
Use a small depth of field to your advantage when shooting close-ups.

FIGURE 2-16:
Action shots generally have moderate to small depths of field.

Tilt-shift lenses

Unlike standard lenses, tilt-shift lenses enable you to play with the shape and orientation of the depth of field. This opens a whole new world of creative possibilities.

Figure 2-17 shows a scene I took from the top of a parking garage at a local university. I tilted the lens to the left in order to skew the depth of field. Notice that the area that appears in focus does not run from side to side, as it would normally. In this case it runs from the bottom of the photo toward the top, expanding like a wedge. The in-focus area begins in the near bushes and crosswalk, runs through the central crosswalk, and continues past the people on the sidewalk, building, and far sidewalk in the distance. Everything else is blurred to one degree or another. Tilt-shift lenses are utterly remarkable and fun to play with. I shot this with a Canon APS-C dSLR and Canon TS-E 24mm f/3.5 II lens. See Book 2, Chapter 5 for more information and photos taken with tilt-shift lenses.

FIGURE 2-17:
Tilt-shift lenses can create unique depth of field effects.

IN THIS CHAPTER

» Shutters 101

» Translating shutter speeds

» Setting shutter speeds

» Reducing blurring and noise

» Having fun with shutter speed

Chapter **3**

Choosing a Shutter Speed

I used to look down my nose at shutter speed. I have come to appreciate how important is it, though. Fast shutter speeds enable you to capture blur-free photos and fast action. Slow shutter speeds may be important for exposure and for creative effects.

This chapter explains how dSLR shutters work, shows you how to read them, explains how to set the shutter speed, and then discusses how to combat blur caused by camera shake or subject movement and noise caused by long exposures. I finish up with a large section with several examples of how to use shutter speed in different situations.

Decoding Shutter Speed

Shutter speed is one of the most important settings on your camera. If shutter speeds are too low, and someone is moving, photos that could have been sharp won't be. Blurriness is hard, if not impossible, to correct in photo-editing software.

Learning about the shutter

The shutters used by dSLRs are mechanical devices in the body of the camera that keeps the sensor hidden until you expose it to light by pressing the shutter release button. Figure 3-1 shows the shutter of a professional-level Canon 5D Mark III full-frame dSLR. You don't normally see your camera's shutter because the mirror is in the way. Most people think of shutter speed as how long the sensor as a whole is exposed. However, for technical reasons, the *shutter speed* is how long each pixel of the sensor is exposed to light.

TECHNICAL STUFF

The shutter isn't a single door that opens and shuts. Focal plane shutters (named thusly because of their proximity to the focal plane, where the image sensor is) are made up of shutter *curtains*. These curtains act a lot like moving horizontal blinds. During an exposure, the front (also called the *first*) curtain moves down, which starts to uncover the sensor. At the right time, the *rear* (or second) curtain follows and covers the sensor back up. The elapsed time between when the front curtain uncovers and the rear curtain covers the same spot on the sensor is called the *shutter speed.* If you look closely at Figure 3-1 you can see the individual curtains that make up this shutter.

FIGURE 3-1:
The hidden dSLR shutter.

Slow shutter speeds fully expose the entire sensor all at once. Faster shutter speeds don't. Instead, a small opening moves down the sensor, exposing a slice of it at a time. (This is why the camera has a *flash sync speed*, which is the fastest speed that exposes the entire sensor at once; see Book 4, Chapter 2.)

Shutter speed values are fairly standardized. Maximum speeds range from 1/4000 second (read as "one four-thousandths of a second") for consumer-level dSLRs and 1/8000 second on more advanced models. The longest timed shutter speed is almost universally 30 seconds.

ELECTRONIC SHUTTERS

Not all shutters are mechanical. Compact cameras, smartphones, tablets, and some mirrorless cameras use an electronic shutter. Some older dSLRs (the Canon EOS 1D, for example) also feature an electronic shutter.

Rather than rely on curtains to expose the sensor, electronic shutters either scan pixels from the top of the image sensor to the bottom (rolling shutter) or measure them all at once (global shutter) for the duration set by the shutter speed setting. Global electronic shutters are far more complicated and expensive.

Electronic shutters have many advantages over their mechanical counterparts. They are silent, are capable of faster shutter speeds, enable you to shoot more frames per second, don't shake the camera, and will never wear out or break.

On the other hand, electronic shutters sometimes have slower flash sync speeds than mechanical shutters. Rolling electronic shutters are also prone to distortion when photographing fast-moving subjects or when panning quickly.

Some mirrorless cameras (the Sony A7S II) and dSLRs (the Nikon D810, for example) have an electronic front curtain shutter. When enabled, the exposure is begun electronically (this is why it is called an electronic front curtain shutter) and ended mechanically by the second curtain. This speeds up shooting and reduces camera shake.

Expect to see more electronic shutters in high-end mirrorless cameras in the future. It's possible that dSLRs may move in this direction, but not en masse until technical obstacles related to capturing action and other fast-moving subjects without distortion economically are overcome.

Reading the speed

In the days of film SLRs, shutter speeds were printed on the shutter speed dial. Although somewhat cryptic, they were pretty easy to understand. You could easily see each shutter speed in relation to the others. Today, shutter speeds may appear in any one of several formats and pop up in different displays. You also can see them while you're playing back photos.

A few twists sometimes make it confusing to interpret and understand shutter speeds. The following sections translate for you.

Fractional

Shutter speeds less than a second in length are most often displayed as fractions of a second. For example, 1/30 equals 1/30 of a second. If you're scared of fractions, think of it this way: If you divide a second into 30 equal parts and set aside one of those parts, you'd have 1 out of 30 equal parts of a second, or 1/30 second, as shown in Figure 3-2.

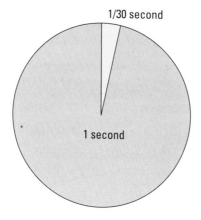

1/30 second

1 second

FIGURE 3-2:
The fractional number 1/30 second is one of 30 equal parts of a second.

To make things confusing, fractional shutter speeds often appear as a single number. The first number of a fractional shutter speed is always 1, so you can assume it's there. You would see 1/30 displayed as 30. This shortcut often happens in viewfinders where space is at a premium. If you don't see a quotation mark (covered shortly), assume what you're seeing is a fractional shutter speed.

REMEMBER

Fractional shutter speeds are the most common shutter speed, whether they're in fractional form (1/30) or not (30).

Seconds

When you see quotation marks after a number, read the shutter speed in seconds, not as a fraction of a second. For example, 4 seconds is shown as 4". Two and a half seconds is displayed as 2.5", as shown in Figure 3-3.

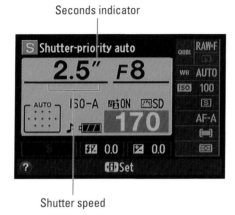

FIGURE 3-3: The quotation mark indicates this number is in seconds.

Seconds indicator

Shutter speed

Decimal

When some cameras get near a 1-second shutter speed, they start to flake out and go decimal on you. Remember that 0.5" means a half a second (1/2), not 1/5 of a second; see Figure 3-4.

TECHNICAL STUFF

Seeing 1/2.5 can be confusing. Is it a fraction or a decimal? Both. It represents one out of two-and-a-half (divide 1 by 2.5 on a calculator), or four-tenths of a second (0.4").

FIGURE 3-4: This fractional speed has a decimal denominator.

Numerator may not be present

Shutter speed

Bulb mode

There is one untimed shutter speed (or mode, depending on your camera) available to you: Bulb. It's named for the way old camera shutters worked. Photographers used a pneumatic bulb to operate the shutter, and timed the exposure themselves. It works the same way on your dSLR, minus the actual bulb. You determine its length by pressing the shutter button as long as you want the shutter to remain open. Release the shutter button to close the shutter and end the exposure.

TIP

Do you really want to press and hold a button on your camera for 2 minutes? I don't! Use a locking remote shutter release cord, infrared remote, or wireless remote app when using Bulb. It can save your finger and help prevent camera shake.

Shutter speed and exposure

Shutter speeds have the same effect on exposure that a lens's aperture and the camera's ISO speed/sensitivity have: A stop of shutter speed either doubles or halves the amount of light entering the camera.

Full-stop shutter speeds from 1 second to 1/4000 second are shown in Table 3-1. Each shutter speed is *half as long* as the one before it and *twice as long* as the one after it. This is the essence of being a full stop apart.

TABLE 3-1   **Full-Stop Shutter Speeds**

Fractional Second	Also Shown As
1	1"
1/2	.5"
1/4	.25"
1/8	8
1/15	15
1/30	30
1/60	60
1/120	120
1/250	250
1/500	500
1/1000	1000
1/2000	2000
1/4000	4000

You'll often see shutter speeds 1/2 or 1/3 stop apart. Fractional stops give the camera greater precision and make it more likely to hit the exact exposure you need. You can often set this difference in the camera's menu. Look for a setting called something like *EV Steps* or *Exposure Level Increments.*

Setting the Shutter Speed

If you want to control the shutter speed yourself, you have to get into a shooting mode that lets you change it. Two modes are best for this task:

>> **Shutter-priority:** The quintessential mode for the shutter speed aficionado. Set your camera to shutter-priority mode and then set the shutter speed yourself, as shown in the left image in Figure 3-5. Your camera meters the scene and then adjusts the aperture and ISO (if you're in Auto ISO mode) to set the proper exposure. It's simple yet effective.

>> **Manual:** It's a bit harder to juggle shutter speed in manual mode, but you can do it.

1. *Choose manual shooting mode.*

2. *Set the shutter speed based on the conditions and how fast you think it should be, as shown on the right in Figure 3-5.*

3. *Meter.*

4. *Choose an aperture and ISO that reach the right exposure.*

5. *Take a shot and review it.*

   If you see blurring, set it to a faster speed and then readjust your aperture and ISO.

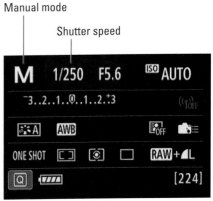

FIGURE 3-5: Set the shutter speed directly in these two modes.

Combating Blur and Noise

Shutter speed is just like other exposure elements: It has an additional effect on your photos that has nothing to do with exposure. In this case, shutter speeds prevent or accentuate blur. Most of the time, of course, you want to capture sharp photos. At times you may want longer exposures for creative effects. Long exposures can also cause photos to have elevated noise levels.

Camera shake, rattle, and roll

Camera shake, a form of blur that affects the entire photo fairly uniformly, is caused by motion on your part. Although long shutter speeds are a major culprit, instability in your grip or stabbing the shutter button like it's the last button you'll ever press also make for camera shake.

The following sections explain ways to fight camera shake.

Faster shutter speeds

In general, try to use moderately fast shutter speeds for most subjects when not using a tripod, even when you don't think you need to. This helps keep photos sharp and in focus. For example, I took the photo shown in Figure 3-6 of a stationary Disc Golf basket at 1/250 second. It's not going anywhere, and I wasn't running about, but the shutter speed made sure this photo was captured crisply by the camera.

TIP

You should also establish minimum speeds. For basic handheld photography with a full-frame camera, a good rule is to set the shutter speed at least as fast as the reciprocal of the focal length you're using. In other words, put a 1 over the focal length to get the fractional shutter speed and then round that speed to a convenient number.

For example, if you've zoomed in with your lens to a focal length of 60mm, shoot with a shutter speed no slower than 1/60 second. You can use slower shutter speeds when shooting with shorter focal lengths. For example, you should use a minimum shutter speed of 1/30 second if the lens is set to 28mm. If you're shooting with a cropped-frame camera it gets a little more complicated.

TECHNICAL
STUFF

To use this guideline when shooting with a cropped-frame camera, use the 35mm equivalent focal length to determine your minimum shutter speed. For prime lenses, this is easy to figure out and remember. Zoom lenses require a bit more effort to figure out, but with practice you will easily remember. Start out by calculating the minimum shutter speeds for both extremes, and then one for a middle-ground focal length.

FIGURE 3-6:
Fast shutter speeds minimize handheld camera movement.

For example, you can quickly figure out three focal length and shutter speed combinations for the Canon EF-S 18-55mm f/3.5-5.6 IS II lens and have them ready any time you want them. Say you choose 18mm, 35mm, and 55mm. Canon APS-C cameras have a crop factor of 1.6x. At that crop factor, these three focal lengths can be expressed in 35mm equivalent terms as 28.8mm, 56mm, and 88mm. The minimum shutter speed at these focal lengths turns out to be 1/30 second, 1/60 second, and 1/90 second (all times rounded a bit).

Once you calculate things, shutter speeds become less intimidating. It's actually pretty easy to remember those three speeds and realize when you're in danger of letting the shutter speed drop too low for a particular focal length. If your camera or lens has image stabilization, you may be able to get away with a bit slower shutter speed.

See Book 1, Chapters 1 and 3 for more on crop factors and 35mm equivalent focal lengths.

Sony cameras have a camera shake warning that flashes when you're in an automatic shooting mode and the camera sees that the shutter speed may be too low for a steady shot. Sony also has a SteadyShot scale, which is a series of bars that appear when the camera shakes. More bars indicate more shakery.

In some cameras (most notably, Nikons), you can set a minimum shutter speed when shooting in program- and aperture-priority modes. This option is tied to Auto ISO. If the shutter speed dips below the minimum setting you establish, the ISO increases, which enables the camera to use your minimum shutter speed and still get a good exposure. For more information about ISO, including this feature, turn to Book 3, Chapter 4.

Vibration Reduction (VR) or Image Stabilization (IS)

Two features that come with your camera also help reduce camera shake: Vibration Reduction and Image Stabilization. When you turn them on, these features may let you slow your shutter speed from one to three stops or more without blurring the photo. Figure 3-7 is a close-up of an unconventional birthday cake my wife made for one of the kids. Ben suggested chocolate and peanut butter, and she made this gorgeous (and oh, so tasty) chocolate cake with peanut butter frosting, topped with chocolate ganache.

I took the photo inside on the dining room table. Although the table is right next to three windows, the light was not very strong. I was very close to the minimum suggested shutter speed. Because I had Image Stabilization enabled, the lens helped account for subtle movement on my part. This meant that I could allow the shutter speed to be no faster than 1/100 second without risking camera shake too much. I didn't want a faster shutter speed because the ISO was already at 1000.

FIGURE 3-7:
Use VR/IS to help reduce shake and use slower shutter speeds.

To turn on lens-based Image Stabilization, look for a switch on the side of your lens and turn it on. Enable camera-based image stabilization from the menu if there is not a switch or button on the camera body. Book 1, Chapters 1 and 3 have more information about Image Stabilization.

Steadying the camera

There are several ways to effectively steady the camera. Most of these are only effective when shooting long exposures with a tripod. Lens or camera-based Image Stabilization features are the exception. They should be used when shooting handheld and turned off when using a tripod (switch to the special tripod mode if your lens has it). Try these techniques then to steady the camera:

TIP

>> **Mirror lockup:** One source of camera shake that isn't your fault is caused by the mirror. Digital SLR (not dSLTs) mirrors rotate up out of the way to unblock the sensor. It flips back so powerfully that it can shake the camera.

Use your camera's mirror lockup feature (also called *Mirror Up mode* or *Exposure Delay*) to combat this type of camera shake when using a tripod. While it can be effective when holding the camera by hand, the delay it introduces can really throw you off. If your camera has a mirror lockup option, turn it on from the menu system; see Figure 3-8 for a Canon (left) and Nikon (right) screen.

FIGURE 3-8:
Raising the mirror early lets the vibrations settle before you take the shot.

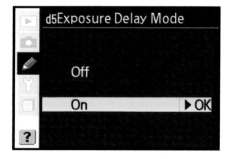

>> **Self-timer:** Believe it or not, your camera's self-timer has other uses besides self-portraits. It's also an effective way to steady the camera if you don't have a remote and are using a tripod (not so much when handheld). Set this function from your camera's Drive or Release mode menu, as shown in Figure 3-9. Assuming you're using a tripod, take your hands off the camera after you press the shutter button. The timer counts down and the camera takes the photo. Combine this technique with mirror lockup for greater effectiveness. If your camera doesn't have a mirror lockup function and you aren't using a remote, this is the most effective way to reduce camera shake when shooting with a tripod.

>> **Remote shutter release:** If your finger is causing the camera shake, increasing shutter speed won't help solve the problem. Connect a remote to your camera so you can activate the shutter button without touching it. You can also switch to the self-timer and try that if you don't have a remote.

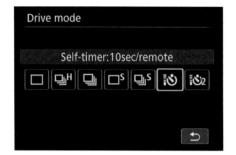

FIGURE 3-9:
Use the self-timer
if you don't have
a remote.

>> **Physically support the camera:** Make sure your grip is stable and that you aren't moving around when you take photos (kids are very prone to shooting on the move). Tripods steady the camera very effectively when using long shutter speeds. Monopods are more mobile and make supporting a heavy camera and lens far easier. In a pinch, you can use any kind of support that's handy: a fence, car, wall, tree, or another person. They all work.

Shooting moving targets

You get *motion blur* (also called *subject blur*) when your subject is moving too fast for the shutter speed to freeze. The subject looks blurred. Unlike camera shake, this type of blur affects only the subject, not the background. Avoid this effect by choosing a faster shutter speed, if possible.

REMEMBER

You can get good shots of a fast–moving subject:

>> **Pan with that person as you shoot.** *Panning* means you follow the subject with the camera as it moves across your field of view. You wind up blurring the background instead.

>> **Move to another spot.** It's harder to capture a racehorse moving directly across your viewfinder than one traveling toward you.

>> **Try catching moving objects in moments when the action pauses.** Such as a tennis player at the height of her backswing, or your wife at the top of her swing (see Figure 3-10). Every time a moving object changes direction, you can time your shot to the moment your subject's relative motion is smallest.

>> **Pay attention to your camera's autofocus (AF) modes.** Set AF to Continuous-servo (also called AI Servo AF) rather than Single. You may be able to select a specific AF point and place it on your target, or you may want to use zone AF if something is moving erratically. Autofocus modes, points, and capabilities are where more expensive dSLRs differentiate themselves from entry- and mid-level consumer models. The Canon 5D Mark IV has no fewer than two focus

modes (manual and auto), three AF modes (One-Shot AF, Predictive AI Servo AF, and AI Focus AF), six different AI Servo cases to choose from, and several AF Point Selection modes. Just setting up the AF system can take your breath away! Regardless of which method you use, practice before it counts.

Focal length matters when you're shooting moving targets, because your field of view is narrower and the subject is magnified greater than normal focal lengths. This tends to emphasize herky-jerkyness. Whatever's in your viewfinder can jiggle, jostle, and move much more than when you're using a normal or wide-angle lens, which causes blurring. Try a higher shutter speed.

Enabling Long Exposure Noise Reduction

Many dSLRs have noise-reduction routines that automatically kick in to clean exposures you've taken with long shutter speeds (a second or longer, normally). Canon and Nikon call it the same thing: *Long Exposure Noise Reduction.* Pentax and other cameras call it *Slow Shutter Speed NR,* as shown in Figure 3-11.

REMEMBER

Noise reduction is applied to JPEGs by the camera as they are saved. If you use Raw files, you can reduce noise during editing.

The one drawback to this form of noise reduction is timeliness: It can delay your return to shooting. However, if you want a more-or-less finished product right out of the box (JPEGs), keep it turned on. Turn off long exposure noise reduction in your camera's menu system.

Designing with Shutter Speed

I finish off this chapter with some interesting examples of how you can use shutter speed to your advantage. You can take all sorts of interesting photos in different conditions and of different subjects by varying it. Even when you're in an autoexposure mode that doesn't allow you to control shutter speed, you'll be able to troubleshoot by paying attention to how long the shutter stays open and making sure it's not too slow, or too fast.

REMEMBER

As you experience different conditions, you'll see how specific shutter speeds, f-numbers, and ISOs differ from scene to scene. You should be able to quickly trade off aperture and ISO for shutter speed to solve exposure problems.

Shooting crisp photos

Nice, crisp photos are a hallmark of good photography. It took me a while to learn this. As I mentioned in the introduction, my first love was the aperture. The problem was, every time I tried to take photos at birthdays and other occasions, they would be a bit fuzzy if not downright blurry. I came to the conclusion that I needed to figure out why I couldn't take a sharp photo of someone standing 6 feet away from me (about 2 meters). The answer was that I wasn't paying attention to the shutter speed.

Figure 3-12 shows how I've grown. This is a nice close-up of my son, Jacob, on his birthday. To ensure that I'm in control of shutter speed, I set the camera to shutter-priority mode and dialed in something reasonably fast. I took this photo at 1/125 second. Bam — crisp photo. If people are playing around, I may bump the shutter speed up to 1/250 or faster.

REMEMBER

The challenge when shooting inside will be controlling the ISO if your aperture can't open very wide. At f/5.6, this inexpensive standard zoom lens limits my options. This shot was taken at ISO 1250.

FIGURE 3-12: Fast shutter speeds ensure nice, crisp portraits.

Animal photography also requires you to pay attention to shutter speed. Figure 3-13 shows a funny photo I took of a giraffe at our zoo (you know, as opposed to our backyard). Animals have a habit of moving around, which means you should expect to use faster shutter speeds when photographing them. This will help make sure your photos are nice and sharp.

You should also use faster shutter speeds when the focal length of your lens is in the telephoto range. I took this shot using a 300mm telephoto lens on a Nikon APS-C camera. I used shutter-priority mode and set the shutter speed to 1/1000 second. While that may sound like overkill, the conditions were bright enough to support that without having to raise the ISO too much (it is 220 in this photo). The result is a tack-sharp photo.

Finally, Figure 3-14 shows a situation where you want to have a fast shutter speed: When you're moving. I took this photo of a water trampoline by wading out into the water. I was neck-deep by the time I reached the rope and float line that separated the swimming area from the rest of the lake. My wife looked on, hoping I wouldn't trip or lose my balance and drop the unprotected camera into the water.

I was in aperture-priority mode, which sounds backward, I realize. However, I knew the day was bright enough that I could set a narrow aperture and have a very fast shutter speed. In other words, have the best of both worlds. Had it not been so, I would have used shutter-priority mode and set the shutter speed first. The speed for this photo is 1/1600 second, which is very fast indeed.

FIGURE 3-13:
Photograph animals with fast shutter speeds too.

FIGURE 3-14:
Use fast shutter speeds when you're moving around.

Accounting for flash sync speed

Figure 3-15 raises another issue: the sync speed between your camera and built-in flash. The sync speed (covered more in Book 4, Chapter 2) is the fastest shutter speed you can set and fire the built-in flash. When you want to use a fill flash on a bright day, as I did here, you may run into this limit. In this case, I could go no faster than 1/250 second.

This can be a problem if the scene is too bright. Be prepared to switch to a smaller aperture to let in less light, use high-speed sync with an external flash (this enables you to use faster shutter speeds), or attach one or more ND filters to the lens to darken the scene.

FIGURE 3-15:
The sync speed limits how fast you can set the shutter speed and use flash.

Photographing action

Capturing action requires fast shutter speeds. There really is no compromising. If you don't want blur, you must use a fast speed and not worry about the aperture or ISO so much.

I took the photo shown in Figure 3-16 of my son Jacob in our backyard. It was a hot summer day and we were playing with the hose, water balloons, and shaving cream. It sounds fun, and it was fun. We all had a blast, and I got to photograph the action.

My first task was to set the camera in shutter-priority mode and take a few test shots to see what sort of shutter speed I could use to capture the action and still get a nice exposure. I settled on 1/500 second. That was fast enough to capture the action nicely. The ISO stayed at 100 throughout and the aperture varied slightly to take up the exposure slack. In this case, it was f/5.3. After that, I was free to focus on getting the best photos of the action and not worry so much about the camera settings.

REMEMBER

It's always easier to photograph action outside on bright, sunny days. Shutter speeds can be high and ISOs can be low. If you're inside, you have to rely on the lighting at the location or venue to be strong.

Figure 3-17 shows another action shot. This time we were at the track, watching a friend of the family race his horses. After checking out different positions, I settled on a spot that enabled me to capture good photos just as horses and drivers were coming out of a turn. This location was great because I didn't have to constantly pan the camera to follow the action. I was able to get a nice, solid focus very quickly each time they came around the bend.

Obviously, you want a very fast shutter speed in instances like this. How fast will depend on the lighting conditions. I set the camera to shutter-priority mode and used 1/1000 second. This caused the aperture to open to its maximum value of f/4. The ISO rose to 160 for this shot, which was very acceptable.

Being creative with water

You can have fun with fast shutter speeds and water. Freeze-frame moments often produce very distinctive photos. Figure 3-18 is a photo of my son having some fun in the splash pad at a nearby park. A bucket (out of the frame) fills with water and then tips over on you. It creates a lot of force and almost knocks you down. I shot this with a shutter speed of 1/2500 second. Had the shutter speed been slower, the water wouldn't have been frozen in mid-deluge, which is one of the elements that makes this photo so interesting.

FIGURE 3-18: Fast shutter speeds can freeze the action for effect.

Slow shutter speeds are equally fun to use with water. Figure 3-19 shows a waterfall I photographed one afternoon. I wanted the water to be misty and blurred, so I entered manual mode and set all the controls myself.

After some experimentation (I can't emphasize how important that is at times), I found that a 2 second shutter speed, with the camera supported by my tripod, made the falling water look nice and dreamy. I set the aperture to f/11 and the ISO to 200 to get the right exposure.

Working with slow shutter speeds

Slow shutter speeds can be practically and artistically effective in other situations as well.

FIGURE 3-19:
Slow shutter
speeds make
water look soft
and misty.

REMEMBER

Try shooting water, fog, or clouds with slow shutter speeds. The movement is smoothed and looks very dreamy. While you can often shoot fast action handheld, slow shutter speeds require a tripod or other stable support.

Figure 3-20 is a shot over the Dr. Martin Luther King, Jr., Memorial Bridge. I set up the camera on a tripod and turned it away from the oncoming traffic so I could catch the vehicles' taillights as they travelled over the bridge. I had to time the shot to the traffic flow and experiment with different shutter speeds. This one, at 5 seconds, is spot on.

While slow shutter speeds normally require that you use a tripod, not all do. I took the photo in Figure 3-21 at a friend's house. He and his wife invited us over for a "3rd of July" party. We and a few dozen other people visited, played volleyball, ate hot dogs, enjoyed the apple pie and homemade ice cream, and played cards. When it got dark we broke out the sparklers.

At times like this you only have a moment to set up the camera. This was not a shot I got to plan out. I quickly set the camera to shutter-priority mode and entered a speed of 2.5 seconds. I pointed the camera at the sparkler, pressed the shutter button, and hoped for the best.

While the flag is slightly blurred, the effect actually contributes to the photo. The sparkler is fantastic.

FIGURE 3-20: Moving lights are classic subjects for slow shutter speeds.

FIGURE 3-21: Use slow shutter speeds on the spur of the moment around sparklers.

Using Bulb mode

Here's an homage to your camera's Bulb mode. This mode is great for shooting fireworks or lightning, as shown in Figure 3-22. All you need to do is set up your camera on a tripod and set the shutter speed or shooting mode to Bulb. It helps to have a remote. When you're ready, open the shutter and wait for the fireworks. You can capture them singly, or hold the shutter open for more than one. Experiment to find your preferred method. The exposure time for this photo was 9 seconds.

Shooting macros

Finally, it's time for a guest appearance by macros. You wouldn't think this subject would be in a shutter speed chapter, but I want to point out that lighting some scenes when shooting macros can be very difficult. You'll find yourself needing to shoot with long exposure times, especially if you don't want to raise the ISO through the roof.

FIGURE 3-22: Fireworks are a great way to practice shooting in Bulb mode.

I took the macro in Figure 3-23 in my studio. It's an extreme close-up of a marigold. Of course, it's important to use a tripod in these situations. It helps you focus and steady the camera for a longer exposure. I set the shutter speed for 1 second for this shot, and used an ISO of 400.

FIGURE 3-23: Some macros require longer shutter speeds.

IN THIS CHAPTER

» **Decoding ISO sensitivity**

» **Configuring and setting ISO**

» **Enabling Noise Reduction**

» **Determining an ISO strategy**

» **Viewing an ISO gallery**

Chapter **4**

Selecting an ISO

SO sensitivity is a subject that can get lost in the mix. Controlling your camera's ISO speed doesn't offer you the same creative possibilities that you get by setting the aperture. Nor does ISO play the same role as shutter speed in capturing crisp photos. However, you'll find that ISO is just as important.

This chapter is devoted to ISO: explaining what it is, what effect it has on exposure, and how you can set and manage it. You see some examples of photos with lower and higher ISOs, and I share some tips on keeping ISO speed and noise levels under control.

Understanding ISO

Technically speaking, ISO is the term we use in photography to characterize the amplification of the analog signal coming out of a camera's image sensor. Most people think of ISO as how sensitive the image sensor is to light. In fact, the image sensor is no more or less sensitive, regardless of what the ISO is set to. It's just that the ISO control allows you to turn up the signal coming out of the image sensor before it is converted from analog to digital.

The confusion between the two schools of thought is due, in part, to the fact that the International Organization for Standardization (or ISO) sets the sensitivity standard for all photographic recording media. Which means that it's okay to use the term sensitivity when describing ISO.

Practically speaking, all you need to know is that turning up the ISO is akin to increasing the exposure. ISO is sometimes called *ISO sensitivity* or *ISO speed*.

Varying ISO speed

ISO (sometimes referred to as *ASA*, but that's another story) was originally a measure of *film speed* — the speed at which film in a camera reacted to light when exposed.

>> *High-speed*, or *fast* film, is more sensitive to light and needs less to expose the photo. It has higher ISO numbers and tends to look grainy, because it literally is.

>> *Slow* film is less sensitive to light and needs more to expose the photo. It uses lower ISO numbers. The size of the light-sensitive crystals in the film has to be larger to catch the light faster. Slow film is created using much smaller grains, and therefore has a very fine-grained, attractive look that captures small details.

Figure 4-1 shows the ISO dial on an older 35mm film camera. The numbers themselves don't actually do anything but remind you what the ISO was for the film you loaded into the camera. The index lifts and turns so you can put the mark by the ISO speed. To the right is an exposure compensation index and scale. When you press the small button and turn the dial, you dial in exposure compensation, which adjusts the camera's meter. Notice that exposure compensation is measured in EV even on this old film camera.

Film speed index

ASA/ISO film speed

FIGURE 4-1:
ISO on film cameras is set for the entire roll.

Forgive me for prattling on about old film cameras, but I want you to realize that you set the ISO the moment you loaded the roll of film into the camera and could not change it for the entire shoot. The amazing thing about digital cameras is that they give you *real-time* ISO control.

You or your camera can react to changing lighting or creative impulses by adjusting the ISO on the fly — from picture to picture, if you want. Your camera displays the ISO setting in the usual places: in the viewfinder, displayed on the monitor when in Live View, and on your camera's shooting information display (see Figure 4-2).

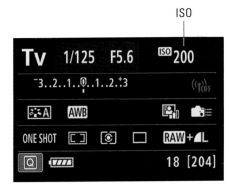

FIGURE 4-2:
The ISO is displayed with the other exposure control settings.

Inside the numbers

In terms of exposure, ISO works just like shutter speed and aperture — only the numbers are different.

Every stop of ISO equals a stop of exposure (1.0 EV). Raising the ISO a single EV, or photographic stop, doubles the sensitivity of the sensor. By the same token, lowering the ISO a single EV, or a stop, halves the sensor's sensitivity.

Unlike shutter speed or aperture, ISO is very peculiarly related to the camera body. What model you have, by whom, and its age will influence what ISO settings you can use and what affects they'll have.

Take some time and look through your camera's manual. Keep these tidbits in mind as you do so:

REMEMBER

» ISO speeds don't have commas or other punctuation. For example, ISO 12800 *isn't* shown as 12,800.

» Most cameras *start* at ISO 100, but not all.

» ISO speeds are a good way to evaluate dSLR categories and to judge performance of cameras in the same general price range. For example, if you're shopping for an entry-level consumer dSLR, take a look at ISO performance between the cameras that interest you. If one clearly stands out as a winner, give it more serious consideration.

» Read the fine print when it comes to ISO capabilities. For example, many cameras restrict ISO to a certain range when you're in Auto mode. In addition, you may be able to expand ISO speed beyond the native values.

» Some dSLRs (notably, Canon dSLRs) have something called *ISO expansion,* which is a way to boost the camera's ISO capability. You must turn on ISO expansion in the camera's menu system, as shown in Figure 4-3. While this unlocks higher ISOs, ISO expansion gives you an indication that you're working at sensitivity levels that the manufacturer considers outside the recommended range.

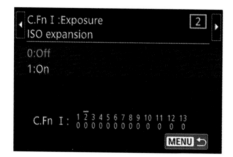

FIGURE 4-3:
Turning on ISO
expansion lets
you get to the
really high ISOs.

» Many cameras display extremely low and high ISO sensitivities using a label rather than a standard ISO number.

For example, Canon uses L to indicate an expanded low ISO setting, which is often the equivalent of ISO 50. It identifies some high ISO expansion settings with H1 and H2.

Many Nikon dSLRs also use identifiers for low and high ISOs. For example, low ISO settings are commonly shown as Lo 0.3, 0.5, and so on. High values are displayed as Hi 1, 2, 3, and so forth. Like Canon ISO expansion, working in the Hi ISO range on a Nikon dSLR tells you that you've exceeded the optimum ISO range for that camera. It will still work, but you may not like the amount of noise you see.

These ISO sensitivities have an equivalent ISO number that depends on the camera. Check your manual to find it.

>> You can often adjust the ISO speed step value from a full stop to 1/3 (as shown in Figure 4-4) or 1/2 stop.

>> Some cameras let you reprogram the ISO button to other functions.

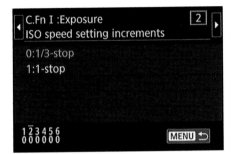

FIGURE 4-4:
Changing ISO
increments.

Generating noise with high ISOs

The effect of raising ISO is *noise* (small discolored artifacts in the photo made apparent by a low signal-to-noise ratio). Too much noise causes the photo to look grainy when you put it onscreen or print it at larger sizes.

Figure 4-5 shows the same scene shot at a low ISO versus a much higher setting. Notice that at the low setting, the photo looks perfect. The colors are bright and there is, for all intents and purposes, no noise. At low ISOs, noise is essentially invisible. You can't detect it, unless you have super powers. However, when the ISO is elevated, the photo turns into a noise-fest. The colors, sharpness, and quality of this photo are all compromised.

Being able to increase the ISO comes with a certain amount of danger to it. As you can see, ISO sensitivity isn't free. Every time you or your camera ratchet it upward, you're also turning up the bad with the good: noise! Noise takes away a photo's clarity and roughs up smooth areas of color. Notice the noise in the leaves in Figure 4-6. The naturally smooth surface of these leaves is overwhelmed with noise. It looks terribly grainy at this level of magnification. When zoomed out (look ahead to Figure 4-17), the photo looks much better.

Up to a certain point, you don't notice increased noise. There's an inevitable tipping point, however, where noise begins to compromise the photo until it overwhelms the shot.

High ISO   Low ISO

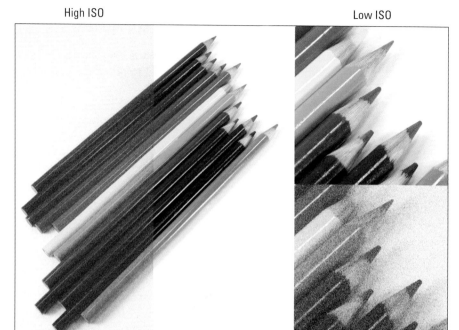

FIGURE 4-5:
High ISOs
generate much
more noise than
low ISOs.

Low ISO   High ISO

FIGURE 4-6:
You always see
more noise
zoomed in.

REMEMBER

The point at which noise becomes a problem in your photos varies from camera to camera and from year to year. Consumer-level cameras tend to generate more noise starting at lower ISO levels than more expensive models. In addition, cameras keep improving. Today's inexpensive dSLRs can operate at ISO levels only dreamed of some years ago. The takeaway is this: You have to experiment with your camera to find the point where noise becomes a problem for you.

The funny thing about noise

Although photos have more noise as ISOs rise, the noise level doesn't affect every photo the same way. Light areas tend to hide noise. So do complicated textures. Smooth, dark areas tend to reveal noise.

In addition, you may not notice noise at all until you try to brighten the photo in your favorite photo-editing software. In effect, you're turning up the volume again, which increases the intensity of the noise along with everything else in the photo. You may also not realize noise levels until you zoom in and "pixel peep" at a photo, as shown in Figure 4-6. Be careful of viewing your work magnified too much. You may get freaked out by noise that would only be apparent when printed at an outrageous size.

REMEMBER

Don't let noise scare you. Try to keep your ISO setting under control, but know that you can sometimes ignore it.

TIP

Test your camera to evaluate its noise performance and determine where your limits are. Shoot a number of photos of the same subject in the same lighting with different ISO speeds. Compare the photos on your computer. You'll be able to quickly see when noise becomes a problem.

Setting ISO

Unlike the other exposure controls (aperture and shutter speed), ISO doesn't have a dedicated shooting mode (the exception to this are Pentax cameras). That means you have to pay a different kind of attention to ISO and how it affects your photos.

You can do that in one of two ways:

» Control ISO speeds yourself.

» Turn control of ISO over to the camera via Auto ISO.

Controlling ISO yourself

If you've set the camera to a basic shooting mode, you don't have to worry about setting the ISO yourself or even enabling Auto ISO. It's done for you. The camera automatically enables Auto ISO and won't let you set the ISO manually in these modes. That's one of the advantages of using them. You don't have to turn automatic features on individually.

To set the ISO manually or enable Auto ISO, follow these steps:

1. **Enter an advanced shooting mode.**

   P, A, S, M, and B always work. You may be able to set the ISO manually in other modes, depending on the camera. Pentax cameras have a sensitivity-priority mode that operates like aperture-priority and shutter-priority modes except you set the ISO.

2. **Press the ISO button, or equivalent.**

   This is the simplest and quickest approach to setting the ISO. An ISO display appears and you can immediately make changes to the setting.

   You can also set the ISO manually and enable Auto ISO from your camera's shooting display or menu system.

3. **Set the ISO to Auto ISO or dial in the ISO you want.**

   The image on the left in Figure 4-7 shows Auto ISO enabled. The image on the right shows the ISO being set to 800. You may be able to set ISO in whole stops, half stops, or even thirds of a stop. Check your camera's menu system to see what your options are.

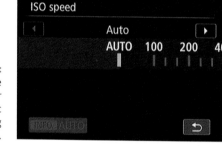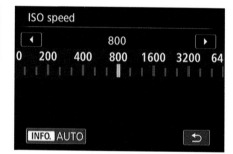

FIGURE 4-7:
You can set the ISO to Auto or choose a specific sensitivity setting yourself.

TIP

If you're particular about ISO, manually control it when you can. This will help you be aware of what ISO you're using and know that it isn't changing from one photo to another. This control is critical if you want all photos from the same photo shoot to have the same noise characteristics.

Using Auto ISO

Using Auto ISO is very simple: Make sure it's on and start shooting. The camera raises or lowers the ISO based on the scene and the other exposure settings. When you're concerned with getting the shot and don't mind that the ISO might rise dramatically or change from shot to shot, Auto ISO is a great solution.

Get familiar with some particulars:

>> **Shooting modes:** Check your camera's manual to see what shooting modes have Auto ISO and whether restrictions exist. When your camera is in an Auto mode, Auto ISO is on by default; see Figure 4-8. When you're shooting in a Scene mode, you may be able to set Auto ISO or switch to manual. You should be able to use Auto ISO or you can switch to manual ISO when you enter program, aperture-priority, or shutter-priority shooting modes.

FIGURE 4-8:
ISO is set to Auto in this mode and cannot be changed.

Most cameras allow you to enable Auto ISO and shoot in manual mode, which effectively unlocks a hidden shooting mode. However, some older dSLRs require you to set the ISO manually when you're in manual mode.

>> **Auto ISO limits:** Most cameras limit the ISO range in Auto ISO mode. In other words, the camera's entire ISO range isn't available when you're in Auto ISO mode. You may or may not be able to expand or contract this limited range. Check by looking in the menu.

>> **Configuring Auto ISO:** Most dSLRs allow you to set up Auto ISO (see Figure 4-9) by selecting a maximum Auto ISO setting. You may also be able to set a minimum shutter speed; if it hits bottom, your camera starts raising the ISO. Setting up Auto ISO is covered in an upcoming section.

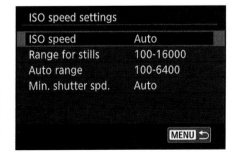

FIGURE 4-9:
Being in an advanced mode gives you more Auto ISO options.

>> **Display peculiarities:** In Auto ISO, some cameras round the ISO to the nearest round number (200 or 400, for example) when displaying the setting in the viewfinder or on the LCD screen. When you review the photo, you'll see the exact ISO.

>> **Auto ISO tip:** When shooting action (inside or out), switch to shutter-priority mode and turn on Auto ISO. This strategy puts a premium on allowing an adequate amount of light into the camera while keeping shutter speeds high enough to avoid blurring everything. If you need more ISO, switch out of Auto ISO (you may have to change shooting modes to do this) and set the ISO yourself.

Restricting Auto ISO

Take some test shots and see how much noise your camera shows at different ISOs. You may decide that you simply won't ever use photos taken at or above a certain ISO. In that case, you can restrict Auto ISO by changing its boundaries. This gives you some control over an otherwise automated process.

Depending on your camera, you might be able to modify some or all of these settings:

>> **Minimum sensitivity:** You can sometimes specify the minimum ISO. Raise this only when necessary. For example, you may want to limit the total range to keep the noise level relatively uniform.

>> **Maximum sensitivity:** The highest ISO that you want the camera to use. Set this to a value that reflects how much noise you're willing to work with, as shown in Figure 4-10.

FIGURE 4-10:
Set a maximum
sensitivity.

>> **Minimum shutter speed:** I encourage you to use this fantastic setting. It tells the camera the minimum shutter speed you're willing to accept before it raises the ISO to keep the photo from being underexposed. The camera lowers the shutter speed below the minimum only if it can't raise ISO enough to get the necessary exposure. You can leave it on Auto in some cases, as shown in Figure 4-11, or choose

a specific value manually. As shown in this figure, you may be able to adjust the range of the Auto setting to have a slower or faster minimum shutter speed.

FIGURE 4-11: Setting the Auto ISO minimum shutter speed.

Using High ISO Noise Reduction

Many dSLRs have noise-reduction routines that automatically kick in. Canon calls it *High ISO Speed Noise Reduction*; Nikon calls it *High ISO NR.* Even if you do need to shoot with high ISOs, you can set the camera to reduce the noise level as it creates and saves JPEGs on your memory card.

Enable or disable long exposure noise reduction in your camera's menu. Some cameras may have only one noise reduction setting. You either turn noise reduction on or leave it off. Some dSLRs enable you to configure high ISO noise reduction strength. Typical Canon settings are Standard, Low, Strong, and Disable, as shown in Figure 4-12. Nikon prefers Off, Low, Normal, and High. The curious thing about ISO noise reduction is that it's always applied, even if you tell the camera to turn it off; it's just applied minimally.

TIP

The drawback to high ISO noise reduction is that it can delay your return to shooting. However, if you want a finished JPEG right out of the camera, use the Standard/Normal setting.

FIGURE 4-12: Check out your camera's high ISO noise reduction options.

Managing ISO

I have good news for you. Under normal conditions, I recommend using Auto ISO, even in advanced shooting modes. Test the exposure before getting started so that you have a sense of what ISO the camera wants to use based on the lighting and the other exposure settings. Then, once you start shooting, simply monitor the ISO each time you meter and take a photo.

I've come to the conclusion that I don't really have to worry about noise with new dSLRs until the ISO gets toward the upper end of a camera's ISO range. This is around 3200 or so in new consumer-level cameras and much higher in professional modes. Most cameras take stunning low-ISO photos and obsessing about it will only slow you down.

If you find the camera setting the ISO in this range, start asking yourself what you can do, if anything, to keep noise from getting out of hand.

TIP

Use these tips to keep ISO low:

>> **Shutter speed:** Within reason, lower the shutter speed to let in more light. Every stop of shutter speed that you can slow down saves you a stop of ISO. For example, rather than raise ISO from 400 to 800, try lowering the shutter speed from 1/250 to 1/125 second.

>> **Aperture:** Enlarge the lens's aperture (lower the f-number) to let in more light. Opening the lens wider by an additional stop keeps the ISO a stop lower. For example, rather than raise the ISO from 200 to 400, increase the size of the aperture by changing the f-number from f/8.0 to f/5.6.

>> **Image stabilization:** This feature helps you lower shutter speeds and prevents blurring from camera shake by one or more stops, depending on the camera and lens. For every stop you can lower the shutter speed without shaking, you save yourself a stop of ISO.

>> **Tripod or monopod:** If your subject lends itself, mount your dSLR on a tripod or monopod. This eliminates camera shake and opens slower shutter speeds and lower ISOs. I rarely raise the ISO above 100 when shooting with a tripod in a studio.

>> **Flash:** Using a flash changes the game quite a bit. Raise ISO when you need to extend flash range and to brighten the background.

>> **Reflectors:** If you've ever had your photo taken professionally in-studio, you probably saw large light reflectors (that look like umbrellas or screens) pointed at you. These reflectors bounce light onto the subjects. You can use reflectors to balance light and brighten a scene. Brighter light means a lower ISO.

>> **Shoot outdoors during the day:** You can't always do this, but try taking photos outdoors in nice daylight. You won't have to raise the ISO as much, if at all.

>> **Other lighting:** If you're indoors, open the drapes and turn on the lights. All the light you can bring into the room helps lower the need to raise the ISO.

TIP

>> **Limit Auto ISO:** Set your camera's Auto ISO settings to a range you're comfortable with. If it's between ISO 100 and 400, make it so. If you're comfortable going to ISO 1600, then by all means set the high end of your Auto ISO range there.

>> **Invest in fast lenses:** If you're shooting indoors a lot, ditch your slow lens and get one with a lower f-number. If you're shopping for zoom lenses, try finding an affordable one that you like that has the same performance throughout the focal length range. For example, if you're using the Canon EF-S 17–85mm f/4–5.6 IS USM, consider moving to the Canon EF-S 17–55mm f/2.8 IS USM or EF 24–70mm f/2.8L USM. If you can't afford a new Canon lens of this caliber, look for a used lens or one from a third-party lens manufacturer (Sigma or Tamron, for example).

>> **Get a newer and better camera:** This step may seem dramatic, but you can often buy a brand new dSLR with improved ISO performance for less than the price of a good lens. If you're able to spend more and jump up a category (for example, from consumer-level to mid-range), you'll gain even more performance.

When getting a good exposure with your chosen shutter speed or aperture becomes a problem, use ISO to take up the slack.

In the end, if you've taken all the steps you can to keep the ISO low but you or the camera need to raise it, do so, and *don't feel guilty about it.* It makes no sense to lose the shot because you're afraid of raising the ISO. A grainy, noisy photo is much better than no photo at all.

ISO Gallery

The photos in this section illustrate certain conditions you may experience that require higher ISOs than normal. Although I list the specific ISO that I used, I want you to key in on why it was raised. This will enable you to be on the lookout for elevated ISOs as you take your photos.

By and large, even these high ISO shots look remarkably good. Remember that as you try to determine the range of ISO settings you allow and the level of noise you are willing to live with. I took most of the photos in this section with relatively inexpensive cameras and lenses. My goal is not to show you the best high ISO performance on the market, but to show you a range of photos with higher and higher ISO levels.

One final note: Although I was tempted to, I did not apply any noise reduction to the photos in this section. They are what they are. I did make corrections to the brightness, contrast, and color. Speaking of processing, you should know that dramatically increasing the brightness of a dark photo in software makes noise more apparent, as does increasing the saturation and sharpening.

Elevated ISO

Although the numbers will change from camera to camera, I start noticing ISO levels when they rise to ISO 1600 or higher.

Figure 4-13 is a shot of one of our family cats. He's orange, and he's big. At times, he likes napping on the back of the couch. As you can see, the door is open in the background and it's nice and sunny outside. You would think it would be bright enough to take a nice photo with low ISO levels.

FIGURE 4-13:
Some elevated
ISO shots have
barely any noise.

Not necessarily. Interior shots are always more difficult than they seem. Our eyes adapt to the light and think the conditions are bright, but they aren't. Additional factors that put pressure on the ISO were the fact that shooting handheld prevented me from setting a low shutter speed and that the lens I used had a maximum aperture of f/5.6. The result? ISO 1600.

Figure 4-14 is another photo with moderately elevated ISO. This time, ISO 2000. Again, it's an inside shot. You can see that the room was bright and that light should not have been too much of a problem. It was. Get used to ISO rising to these levels when shooting inside.

FIGURE 4-14:
Don't be afraid
to let the camera
increase the
ISO beyond the
minimum.

The good news? Neither of these photos appears to have problems with noise unless you zoom in to ridiculous levels. Both can be reduced, if desired, with a minimal amount of noise reduction if you process the Raw photos yourself.

High ISO levels

High ISO levels are higher than your camera's mid-range but not to the point where you've maxed out ISO. I look at ISO 3200 as the beginning point of high ISOs for many cameras.

Speaking of 3200, Figure 4-15 is a close-up of a foosball player I took in the game room at a summer camp. Foosball is a fast-paced, fun, action-packed game based on the principles of soccer (a.k.a. football). I spent hours upon hours playing foosball with my friends at college. Now I amaze my kids with my super-fast bounce shots.

You can start seeing noise in this photo. Look at the green surface of the table. It should be smooth and even-toned. It looks mottled a bit by the noise.

Moving up to ISO 4000, Figure 4-16 is a funny photo of my son, Sam, putting the cat's tail up to his nose as if it were a mustache. He's wearing his camo bathrobe, but he'd grown enough by the time I took this photo that it looks like a dinner jacket.

FIGURE 4-15:
Noise is evident
in the green
surface of this
photo.

FIGURE 4-16:
This shot
requires some
noise reduction
to smooth his
skin and the
background.

This is another example of how hard it is to light interior scenes. The room seems decently lit, and you can see the light shining on the side of his face. However, even with an aperture of f/5.6 and a shutter speed of 1/80 second, the ISO had to go up to get a good exposure.

On consumer-level cameras, ISO 4000 is getting up there. This particular model has only a few higher settings. The noise is fairly apparent in this shot. It's visible on Sam's face, and robs his eyes of some sharpness. The background noise is less apparent when zoomed out, but clearly mottles the photo when you look closely. This shot needs some noise reduction to help smooth out the grain. With a modest amount of noise reduction, it will look as good as new.

Figure 4-17 is a shot of leaves at ISO 5000. I took this photo while riding in a wagon towed by an old firetruck at the camp I keep mentioning. I was bouncing around in the back quite a bit so I entered shutter-priority mode and set the shutter speed to 1/500 to take sharp photos. The aperture setting was f/6.3.

FIGURE 4-17: This photo has barely any recognizable noise from a distance.

Due to the nature of the subject, you can't see any noise at all in this photo when viewed as a whole. The texture is very detailed and a lot of edges basically mask the noise. The surface of the leaves reveals the most noise, but you have to zoom in to see it.

Extreme ISO settings

Extreme ISO settings push your camera to its limits. Although they will vary between cameras, anything at or over ISO 6400 on just about anything but a professional model is extreme.

Figure 4-18 is a bowl full of radishes. I love radishes, and they make great subjects to photograph. Their bright red color stands out and they have details that are interesting to look at.

FIGURE 4-18:
High noise levels
do little to mar
these radishes.

At ISO 6400, you can see that the surface of the radishes is a bit mottled. They could look smoother. This is a better camera than the one I took the last shot with so the noise level looks about the same. It's not that bad, even though it's there.

I took this shot with an aperture setting of f/5.6 (again, wide open on inexpensive lenses) and a shutter speed of 1/50 second. That's about as low as I could go and still get a decently sharp photo.

Figure 4-19 shows a nighttime bridge heading toward downtown. Although the bridge is lit and some other lights are present, it's still a very dark scene. I wanted a relatively fast shutter speed of 1/60 second to artificially limit the amount of light entering the camera, which meant that the ISO had to take up the slack. I raised it to 6400 and hoped for the best. As you can see, it's a pretty noisy photo!

FIGURE 4-19:
Dark scenes
really bring the
noise out.

Finally, Figure 4-20 shows a shot that I took with a professional camera set to ISO 12800. We were inside a bowling alley. This is Sam again, who had just let a ball loose down the rails and was showing off his form. I had the camera in shutter-priority mode to capture the action. The shutter speed was 1/250 second (I dared go no faster) and the aperture was f/4.

The combination of using a great camera with a great lens still had difficulty capturing this photo without raising the ISO quite a bit. The result is noise that can be bothersome unless handled in software.

FIGURE 4-20: Professional cameras shoot at extreme ISO levels very effectively.

Chapter **5**

Using Filters

I n digital photography, everything seems to revolve around advanced computer technology. I'm not necessarily complaining. It's just that this reality can lull you into thinking that there was never any other way to take a picture. There were, and there are, and it has nothing to do with the Stone Age. Filters, although decidedly analog, are *real.* You can hold them in your hand. They clink musically and take up space in your camera bag. When light passes through them, something physical — not modeled, simulated, or programmed — happens to the light. I don't know about you, but that fascinates me. I want to know more.

Learning about Filters

The trouble is, standing in front of a large filter display in a camera shop, or going online and browsing, can be highly intimidating. Questions course through your gray matter. What are these gizmos? How do they work? Should I bother? Which ones are best for me?

In many ways, filters are decidedly simple. You put a filter on your camera's lens and then take photos. Grasping the entire range of possibilities, however, is more of a challenge.

Looking at how filters work

Filters (sometimes called *optical* or *physical filters*) work by literally getting in the way. You stick filters on the front of or in your lens (see Figure 5-1) so that light from the outside world has to pass through on its way to the camera's image sensor — simple stuff. As light passes through a filter, something magical happens.

Filter   Lens

FIGURE 5-1:
Light must pass through the filter for it to work its magic.

That magical something is different for each type of filter. Knowing what filters do will help you decide whether to invest the time and energy required to use them. They may solve one or more problems you've been having with your photography.

REMEMBER

>> **Change color, tone, and contrast** by holding back certain wavelengths of light. Filters can either enhance contrast or reduce or soften contrast. When used in black-and-white photography, color filters transform some colors into dark tones and other colors into lighter tones in the black-and-white image.

Red filters look red because they partially block light from the other side of the color wheel. Red light is allowed to pass through. Blues, greens, and yellows are not, to different degrees.

>> **Darken a scene** by making it harder for all light to pass through. You can reduce or balance the exposure. ND filters do this.

>> **Enhance color and contrast** by blocking polarized light. A polarizing filter makes it harder for reflected light to pass through by reducing glare and reflections from water, metal, glass, and other smooth surfaces.

COLOR FILTERS FOR WHITE BALANCE

It's debatable whether using color filters on a dSLR for white balance is necessary. After all, you have perfectly good white balance controls on your camera. However, some people feel that correcting select light sources improves your camera's dynamic range and reduces the chance of overexposure. This has a ring of truth to it because unfiltered light does have an effect on metering and exposure, which happen before you take a shot. White balance is a processing step that happens after the fact, even when performed in the camera.

>> **Reduce haze** by absorbing UV light.

>> **Create different special effects** by diffusing or diffracting light.

>> **Create other effects;** filters can soften focus, add mist, add a radial zoom, mask areas, add lens reflections, and magnify.

TIP

If you're familiar with software filters and effects, and with common photo-editing tasks, you can make the switch to physical filters quite easily. Think of the tasks you perform using software, and match that up with the physical filter that does the same thing.

Going over filter pros and cons

You don't have to go out and buy every filter at once. Start with one or two different filters and see what you think.

TIP

Having a circular polarizer filter to block annoying reflections is a good first choice if you shoot a lot of these subjects:

>> Landscapes with water

>> Buildings with glass sides and windows

>> Portraits of people who wear glasses

If you shoot inside, or shoot mostly portraits, you'll benefit from filters that correct white balance.

Consider these benefits to using filters:

>> **They work:** *Neutral density (ND)* grads actually affect the balance of light in the scene. (*Grad* is a fancy shortening of the term *graduated*, which means

the filter transitions from clear to shaded.) It's real and not emulated, which means you're getting the actual effect. Someone didn't have to program it to come *reasonably close* to the real thing in software. Having said that, there may be quality differences between filters and brands of filters that affect how well they perform.

>> **Time:** Using the right filter on the scene means that you can often spend less time processing and editing your photos.

>> **Creativity:** The amount of creativity you can express with filters is staggeringly large. It's like having a Hollywood special effects division supporting your photo shoot.

>> **Protection:** Many use clear or UV filters to protect lenses. It's cheaper to replace a scratched, cracked, or broken filter than it is a lens. Not only that, if you break a filter you can toss it in the trash and keep shooting immediately. Not so if you scratch your lens.

And consider these challenges:

>> **Quality:** Many question the benefit of putting a $20 (or even a $100 filter) in front of a $1,500 lens. Think about it.

>> **Compromise:** Some question whether it's worth potentially degrading a photo by making light pass through more stuff to get to the camera's sensor when you can perform most filterlike adjustments in software.

>> **Convenience:** You have to carry filters around and they take up space in your camera bag. Software filters are much lighter by comparison.

WARNING

>> **Fragility:** Optical filters (unlike their software counterpart) can get scratched or broken. I've picked up a variety of filter cases to safeguard my investment; you can see them in Figure 5-2. All offer reasonable amounts of protection, just in a different package. Some filters come with soft cases. Others are shipped in hard plastic cases. In my experience, it's harder to fit more than a few hard plastic cases in your camera bag and get at them with any ease.

FIGURE 5-2:
Buy the type of case that fits your needs and your camera bag.

>> **Cleanliness:** Filters can get smudged and dirty, as shown in Figure 5-3. It's easy for this fact to weigh on you and make you not want the extra hassle. I totally understand.

FIGURE 5-3:
The one photo
I didn't dust
for you.

>> **Cost:** Filters cost money, which always seems to be in short supply. You're limited in the number of filters you can buy, the number of lenses you can support with filters, and the number of times you can replace or upgrade them. With programs like Adobe Photoshop, software filters work on every photo in your collection, whether you took it today or five years ago.

>> **Interoperability:** Different lens sizes need different filters. Software filters don't.

>> **Time:** Setting up and swapping out filters takes time and effort. Don't underestimate this. To use filters, you really must want to.

>> **The X factor:** When you're using a real filter, you have one chance to get it right. In software, you can try a lot of different filters and effects with the same photo until you're happy with the result.

Using filters with dSLRs

Using filters is easy enough. You may spend a few moments getting set up and deciding what filter you want to use, but you'll soon start taking shots more quickly. When you get the hang of it, you get faster with filters.

Clean your filters at home before heading out on your shoot.

1. **Evaluate the scene and choose a filter.**

   Decide whether you want to control exposure, color, or use a filter to achieve a special effect.

   Most people agree that using more than two or three filters at the same time degrades image quality. Every pane of glass, resin, or polyester is another layer between your expensive lens and the image sensor.

2. **Slide or screw in the filter.**

   Depending on your filter system, either screw your clean filter into the end of your lens or slide it in the holder. You can find more details in the next section.

3. **Compose, meter, and adjust exposure.**

   Your filter's documentation might give specific metering instructions. Experiment and take test shots to fine-tune the exposure.

   For graduated filters, the center of the scene should be properly exposed, even with the filter in place. If you're using spot metering, you may see better results from pre-metering the scene and then mounting the filter. Be prepared to review your photos and adjust, if necessary.

4. **Take the photo and review the photo.**

   Check exposure, color, glare, and whether the filter has the desired effect.

5. **Correct and start over or stay on course.**

   If the photo looks good, you're good to go. If not, try to figure out what's causing the problem. Is the filter on the lens correctly? Is this filter right for this scene? Re-examine your starting assumptions, if need be, and question whether you need *this* or *any* filter.

Taking Shape with Filter Systems

Filters come in two main flavors:

>> Circular filters screw into the lens.

>> Rectangular filters slide into a frame mounted on the lens.

Circular (screw-in)

Circular filters are quite popular and easy to work with. Figure 5-4 shows a small collection of Hoya 77mm black-and-white filters. (I suppose that the terms *circular* and *screw-in* are redundant. Can you even turn a square or triangular screw?)

FIGURE 5-4:
Circular filters
screw into the
front of the lens.

Circular filters have three main characteristics:

>> **They are round.** This circular piece of glass (some filters are made from other materials) is mounted in a frame. Higher quality filters use metal frames that are quite sturdy.

WARNING

>> **They screw in.** Circular filters screw into the front end of dSLR lenses. Don't incorrectly thread a filter when you're mounting it. You might ruin the filter or, worse, damage the threads on your lens. Take your time and, if necessary, back out the filter by turning it counterclockwise until you feel it correct itself. Then get back on track.

Getting filters on isn't as much of a problem as getting them off. Handle tough filters with a filter wrench, shown in Figure 5-5. I can't tell you how many times this wrench has saved me.

WARNING

>> **They have a specific size.** Filters are sized by their diameter (the distance across, going through the center), which is measured in millimeters. This is important. *You must match your filter size with your lens.* Many lenses have their filter size printed on the front or top. If it's not in either of those places, check your manual.

If you want to use filters on multiple lenses that require different filter sizes, buy a single, large filter size and use step-up rings to modify its size. This means you buy a step-up ring for each differently sized lens, but only one size filter. I have four step-up ring sizes (52–77mm, 55–77mm, 58–77mm, and 62–77mm) that let me fit one filter size (77mm) on several lenses, as shown in

Using Filters

Figure 5-6. If you go this route, make sure to get step-up rings that are large enough to fit your largest lens.

Figure 5-6.

FIGURE 5-5:
This filter wrench makes removing filters a snap.

Lens with step-up ring mounted

Lens with no filter

Filter screwed onto step-up ring

FIGURE 5-6:
Step-up rings reduce the number of filters you have to buy for multiple lens sizes.

Step-up rings for differently sized lenses

Rectangular frame slide-in

The other main filter type relies on a frame mounted to the lens that enables rect-angular filters to slide in and out. The advantage of this system is similar to that provided by step–up rings. You buy the frame and enough adapters to mount it on your lenses, but only one set of filters. As long as you have the right adapter ring, you can use the same filters on lenses of many different sizes.

Figure 5-7 shows a filter from Cokin's Creative Filter System (www.cokin.com) attached to a 35mm lens, along with an extra adapter and filter. Rectangular filter systems have these main parts:

>> **Adapter ring:** This piece screws into the filter ring on your lens and has fittings to slide on the filter holder and make a secure attachment. Simply buy the correct adapter for each of your lenses and you're ready to rock. Read the manual to make sure this type of filter system works with the lenses you want to use it with. Most normal dSLR lenses work fine. You may have to buy a different system for wide-angle lenses.

>> **Filter holder:** This element holds one or more filters. The holder slides onto the adapter and snaps securely in place. Filters slide into the holder rather than screw onto the lens, which makes changing them extremely easy. It also makes the filters compatible with many different lenses. Notice in Figure 5-7 that there's room for three filters in this particular adapter.

>> **Rectangular filter:** The reason for the entire setup is the filter. It's larger than a screw-in filter and is rectangular. Most rectangular filters don't have frames around them, so be careful when handling them. You can buy filter wallets, sleeves, and boxes for storage.

Filter holder   Filter slid into holder

FIGURE 5-7:
Rectangular filters slide into a holder mounted to an adapter that screws onto the lens.

Filter   Adapter ring

Using Filters

REMEMBER

All in all, the rectangular system is ingenious if you have several lenses that take different filter sizes. Having a rectangular filter holder makes a robust filter library more cost effective. However, the size of the mount with filters is bigger and bulkier than the traditional circular screw-in variety.

Using Filters for Different Purposes

This section has information on several different filter types. Browse through them to see what excites you. Think about the photos you normally shoot as you consider whether a filter type is right for you.

TIP

The sheer number of filters and filter types can be overwhelming, and getting this straight in your mind can take some time. I summarize many of the problems that filters help solve in Table 5-1. Have fun experimenting with different brands, makes, models, and strengths!

TABLE 5-1   **Problem Solving with Filter Types**

To Do This	Try These Filters	Notes
Protect your lens	Clear or UV filter	UV filters also cut haze.
Control exposure	ND filter	Available in different strengths.
Balance exposure	ND grad or color grad	Use ND grad for a neutral effect, or a color grad to emphasize certain colors.
Reduce glare or reflections	Circular polarizer	Rotate to dial in desired effectiveness.
Reduce haze	UV filter	Can also keep on the lens to protect it.
Enhance color	Color or color grad	Effect depends on the color of the filter.
Correct color	Warming, cooling, balancing, or color compensating	Use to adjust white balance or correct tints.
Tone black-and-white photos	Black-and-white filters	Special colored filters that affect how colors are translated into black-and-white tones. Common colors include red, green, yellow, blue, and orange.
Alter contrast	Contrast or other filters	Many filters affect contrast. There are also contrast-specific filters.
Special effects	Fog, haze, stars, mask, close up, mist, diffusion, and more	Experiment with many different types of filters for a range of special effects.

Protective

A *protective filter* is clear, high-quality glass that protects the lens. You can leave it on your lens all the time. As long as the filter is clean, the photo shouldn't be affected. The filter essentially serves as a clear lens cover.

REMEMBER

If you put a clear protective filter in place, you don't have to constantly clean your lens. You clean the filter instead, which keeps the lens (and its irreplaceable coating) from accidentally being scratched.

Circular polarizer

Polarized filters act like a good pair of polarized sunglasses: They filter out distracting reflections and glare. The details of how this type of filter works and why are somewhat technical and, honestly, irrelevant to using them. Polarized filters block *reflected* light (which can even happen in the sky) while allowing natural light to pass through them.

TIP

You have to tune, or *dial,* a polarizing filter by rotating it so that it rejects the reflections you want.

Figure 5-8 shows two photos. I took them looking down at the water in a slow-moving river. The image on the left shows the photo I took without the polarizing filter. The blue sky is reflected in the water. The image on the right shows the photo I took with a circular polarizer filter. The effect is to block the reflections of the sky, which enables you to see details beneath the surface of the water. I find the difference between the two shots amazing.

TECHNICAL
STUFF

For complex and technical reasons having to do with beam splitters and the nature of linear versus circular or non-polarized light, digital SLR metering and auto-focus sensors are compatible with circular polarizer filters, not linear polarizers.

Ultraviolet (UV)

Sunglasses with ultraviolet (UV) protection are better for your eyes because they block a lot of haze. If exposed to too much UV radiation for too long, you can damage your eyes. Ditto for UV filters: They block UV light, which causes blue haze when you're shooting around water, into the air, or into the distance. (Think of the phrase *purple mountains majesty* in the hymn *America the Beautiful.*) UV filters appear clear. That's because you can't see ultraviolet light.

FIGURE 5-8:
Without polarizer:
The blue sky
reflects off the
surface of the
water. With
polarizer: Details
visible beneath
the surface.

Without polarizer   With polarizer

There's some debate as to whether digital cameras need UV filters, because most manufacturers build UV and IR protection into their image sensors. In addition, many lenses are coated to reject UV wavelengths. There's no doubt UV filters work at blocking UV light, but if the lens and the camera can do as good a job, you may not need the filter. Frankly, I took several shots hoping to illustrate how amazing these filters were for this chapter, and I couldn't tell any difference between using a standard UV filter and not. Some people recommend using UV filters as clear lens protectors, just in case.

Neutral density (ND)

Neutral density (ND) filters darken the scene by blocking light. ND filters come in different strengths, called densities. The density tells you how may exposure stops of light they block. For example, an ND filter with a density of 1.2 blocks 4 EV of light. That means that an aperture of f/1.4 acts like f/8 or a shutter speed of 1/60 acts like 1/1000 second. ND filters are, in essence, a negative exposure control. While that may sound counterintuitive (you're normally interested in capturing light, not turning it away), it becomes very helpful in at least two situations.

First, they enable you to use large apertures in bright light. For example, if you're outside during the day and want to take a flash photo, your camera's flash sync speed limits how fast you can set the shutter speed. If you're already at ISO 100 and want a wide open aperture for creative reasons, you're stuck unless you have an ND filter to tone down the lighting. I took the photo of my wife shown in Figure 5-9 to illustrate the worse-case scenario. I used an aperture of f/2.8 to blur the fence behind her, and I didn't want to compromise. I also used the camera's built-in flash. I wanted to provide some direct light because the sun was partly behind her. The ISO was at 100 and the flash sync speed limited the shutter speed to 1/200 second. The result? Massive overexposure.

FIGURE 5-9:
Using a flash overexposed the scene.

I took another shot, shown in Figure 5-10, with a 0.9 density ND filter screwed into the lens. The result is stunningly obvious. The photo is perfectly exposed. The filter blocked enough light so that the shutter speed could come down to 1/160 second. I kept the aperture at f/2.8 and the ISO at 100. If you want to take creative portraits with fill flash and wide apertures, and don't have high-speed sync available, use an ND filter.

The second reason to use ND filters is that they help you set long exposure times. For example, you may want a long exposure that emphasizes moving water, as shown in Figure 5-11. If that's the case, grab your ND filters and set the shutter speed as slow as you want.

ND graduated

ND graduated (or *grad*) filters resemble cool-looking aviator sunglasses with a gradient. As you can see from Figure 5-12, they're darker at the top to tone down light from the sky, and they're clear toward the bottom.

TIP

With an ND grad filter, you can set longer exposure times for the land.

Using Filters

FIGURE 5-10:
She obviously approves of the filter.

FIGURE 5-11:
Use ND filters for long exposures in bright daylight.

FIGURE 5-12:
ND grads are useful in controlling the exposure of bright skies.

Figure 5-13 shows part of a late afternoon scene looking out across a river. I shot the photo on the left without a filter and the one on the right with a 0.6 density ND grad. I processed each photo the same. There is not a huge difference, but if you look closely at the water and the bushes, they are brighter in the photo on the right. The filter blocked enough light from the sky to enable the camera to bring up the exposure for the darker areas of the scene. Details are lost in the bushes in the photo on the left, and the reflections of the sky in the water are less clear.

Without ND grad filter   With ND grad filter

Color filter

Color filters change the color of a scene. I include *cooling* (making things look bluer) and *warming* filters (making a scene look more golden) in this color category. Think of them as white balance correction on the front end of your lens.

Color grad filter

A color grad filter combines elements of both color and ND grad filters. Imagine an ND grad filter that isn't gray, but in color. Tiffen makes color grads designed to add color to normal or washed-out shots. Many work at sunrise or sunset, but you can also use them to create special color effects.

Other filters

TIP

A ton of filter types are available, in addition to the ones I describe earlier. If you catch the filter bug, visit a store in person or online and check them out. Download a brochure to see before-and-after photos for each type of filter.

In-camera filters

Many dSLRs offer in-camera processing options that mimic optical filters or *soft-ware filters* (some are computerized imitations of photo filters, others are more creative special effects) and retouching techniques that you might do in programs like Adobe Photoshop. Software filters are normally found in an Effects or Filters menu. You can have a lot of fun with the filters that come with applications like Photoshop, and if you want more choices, you can find many more filters online in the form of plugins.

Sony's Picture Effects has several filterlike effects, including High Contrast Mono, Soft Focus, and Rich-Tone Mono. Some Canon dSLRs use Creative Filters, which aren't identical to most filters, but nonetheless creative. Nikon also has post-processing options called Filter Effects.

Black-and-white filters

Black-and-white filters enhance contrast and emphasize certain tones by blocking or limiting specific colors (which ones depend on the filter color). They come in several different colors. Red is popular for increasing contrast in landscapes, yellow for balancing contrast between reds and yellows, and green for shooting outdoor monochrome portraits.

The left image in Figure 5-14 shows the monochrome image of a scene I shot without a filter. I took the photo on the right in Figure 5-14 using the red filter. I processed the photos the same. It's clear that the photo on the right has added contrast and detail in the sky and water.

FIGURE 5-14: The photo on the right, shot with a filter, has additional contrast and detail.

No filter   Red (25A) filter

TIP

Set your camera to shoot monochrome images when shooting with black-and-white filters. The camera spits out a black-and-white JPEG so you don't have to do anything else. If you like, save that photo in Raw format also and convert it to black and white yourself (see Book 5, Chapter 4).

Infrared filters

I've got good news and bad news for you. First, the good news: *Infrared (IR)* filters turn your photos into surreal works of art by blocking everything except infrared wavelengths, which are invisible to the naked eye. The bad news is that dSLRs filter out infrared light by varying degrees, which makes it hard to capture infrared images, even with an IR filter.

TIP

If you're curious about IR photography, you can experiment by mounting your camera on a tripod on a bright, sunny day, composing the shot, and then attaching an IR filter (the Hoya R72 is a good IR filter). You'll have to use long exposure times and raise the ISO. You'll have to edit the resulting shot to make it look cool.

As an alternative, the folks at Life Pixel Infrared (`www.lifepixel.com`) can convert your camera so it can shoot handheld IR photos (much like standard photography) without the filter. They take your camera apart and replace the IR-blocking filter that covers the sensor. If you feel up to the do-it-yourself challenge, they also have conversion kits.

Creative filters: Stars, mist, or haze

Use these filters to exercise your creativity. The sky is the limit. Figure 5-15 shows a photo I took with a Hoya Star-Six filter. The filter is engraved with lines. When light strikes the lines, it produces six-sided stars. I took this shot at night looking out at a well-lit bridge. The filter has transformed the lights on the bridge, the distant buildings, and the water reflections.

FIGURE 5-15:
Star effects are very cool; use them wisely.

Using Filters

4

Lighting the Scene

Contents at a Glance

IN THIS CHAPTER

» Shooting at different times
   of the day

» Handling different weather

» Working inside

» Dealing with other situations

Chapter **1**

Working with Ambient Light

The light the sun gives off is tremendous in so many ways. It's exceptionally strong, naturally white, and freely available. And yet, you won't capture the same photos at noon as you would during the morning or evening golden hours. Recognizing this is important. My skills as a photographer took tremendous leaps and bounds the day I realized that light from the sun changes based on the time of day, and different times were better than others.

I invite you to learn this lesson with me as you read about photos I've taken at different times of the day, in different weather, inside and out. Finish off by examining photos shot during different conditions, including indirect light, hazy days, and high-contrast scenes.

Working in Natural Light

The time you choose to go out and photograph people and other scenes plays a very important role in how the photos turn out. Light changes during the day, and it's not all equally good. For example, morning light isn't the same as the light you see at noon or in the evening. Knowing this, you can plan your trips more effectively and capture the photos you want.

Shooting in the early morning

I don't go out in the morning to take many photos. However, I drive by this bridge on the way to church enough Sunday mornings that I know how beautiful it is at that time of the day. The light from the rising sun kisses it on the side. Think about that for a minute. Objects that are normally lit from above during the day and shaded on one side or another are often beautifully and unconventionally lit during the morning or evening. I eventually decided that I had to take some shots of it, so I grabbed my camera the next Sunday morning and we stopped on the way so that I could take the photo in Figure 1-1.

REMEMBER

Mornings are often clear and calm. The day is just starting and the light feels fresh. The hour or so after sunrise and before sunset is called the golden hour because of the great light.

Notice the still water of the river. It's so quiet that the bridge, sky, and foliage cast amazing reflections. You get two scenes for the price of one. Not all mornings are like this, of course. Some will be blustery, wintery, stormy, hot, muggy, or rainy. However, on a good day like this, it's a joy to take photos early in the morning.

One note of caution when shooting in the morning. Once the sun starts to come up, pay attention to the contrast levels in the scene. You may struggle to preserve details in areas of deep shadow without blowing out highlights. If you need to, choose a middle ground by using exposure compensation or manual shooting mode, and then work to bring out details in software. In this case, I had to work hard to tame the highlights in Adobe Lightroom.

FIGURE 1-1:
Sunlight on a clear morning illuminates scenes from the side.

Fighting with the light at noon

As I looked through my catalog of photos, I realized I don't have that great a selection of photos taken around noon. The reason is that it's the worst time of day to photograph people, nature, and buildings.

The sun is the most intense during this time and casts very harsh shadows. Because of this, I won't even take photos of people at noon. They squint and the photos look horrible because half their faces are in deep shadows while the other half of their faces look too bright.

REMEMBER

You're not a bad photographer if you can't take perfect shots at noon. That's just the way it is. Unless you work with a tremendous amount of portable diffusers and other gear to soften the light, it's just not worth it.

So what I have for you is a nice shot overlooking the lake at our favorite summer camp shown in Figure 1-2. The reason this photo is even close to passable is that it's a bit past noon and the sun is off to the right a bit. There are enough clouds in the sky that I took this shot while the sun was briefly obscured. Although the clouds acted as a giant diffuser, it's still very bright.

FIGURE 1-2:
Mid-day lighting is harsh and often difficult to photograph well.

Going out in the early evening

Early evening is a good time to photograph things. The harsh afternoon sun has passed and been replaced by more forgiving light. It's still bright, but not normally overpowering unless you look right at it.

While you're waiting for the golden hour (visit www.golden-hour.com to find when golden hours starts and ends each day; there's also an app), look for interesting subjects and scenes. Many will be large and scenic, but don't overlook the small things. The petunias in Figure 1-3 are a great example. I shot this photo at a park near where we live while testing a new camera.

You can see that the flowers are well lit and the colors in the scene are nice and vibrant. This isn't just me or about my skill, it's the time of day I chose to photograph it. That makes a huge difference in how your photos look.

FIGURE 1-3:
Early evening light is bright without being too harsh.

Prizing the golden hour

The best time to photograph landscapes and many other outdoor subjects is during the evening golden hour. This is the hour or so before sunset. There is a corresponding golden hour in the morning too, right after sunrise.

TIP

If the weather is decent, go out tonight before the sun sets and look at the sky. Take note of how the light softens and everything is lit from the side, not the top. If there are clouds, they will be beautifully colored and lit. On special days, the entire sky glows a gorgeous golden color, which deepens and may appear red or purple as the sun sets. It really is magical without the magic.

I took the photo in Figure 1-4 looking southwest as the sun was close to setting. It's off to the right of the photo. The Oklahoma pasture is well lit, but not blindingly bright. The clouds are bright overhead and more colorful in the distance. It's a great example of how the light appears during this time of the day.

FIGURE 1-4: The golden hour is a stunning time to be out with your camera.

Photographing the sunset

Sunsets are a special treat. If you've been shooting during the golden hour, don't pack up and leave until you've photographed the setting sun. The challenge is finding the right location. I particularly enjoy photographing rivers that run east-west because they form a natural avenue that points toward the setting sun, as shown in Figure 1-5.

In this case, I set up my tripod on some rocks in the river. I used a Sony APS-C dSLR using an ultra wide-angle zoom lens set to 10mm to capture as much of the surrounding scenery as possible.

I also included the sun in the shot. That point is debatable. I love the flares and the interaction between the sun and the lens, but you may not. When shooting toward the sun, you may wish to use an ND grad or graduated filter to dim the light a bit. I stopped down to f/22 for this shot, which kept the shutter speed to a leisurely 1/80 second.

Working with Ambient Light

FIGURE 1-5: Capturing the setting sun produces memorable photographs.

Capturing twilight

The time after the sun sets and before it gets completely dark is called twilight, or sometimes dusk (technically the darkest part of twilight). You would not think this would be that interesting of a time to be out, but you can capture some amazing shots.

Figure 1-6 shows a scene I took looking west about a half hour after the sun set. If you're interested in these things, the time was a minute into the phase called nautical twilight. Clearly, the light is very dim. The light from the setting sun has faded, and it's hard to distinguish any details in the trees nearby as well as across the lake.

This photo features the last little bit of glow on the distant horizon. The lake doubles the effect of the golden light and the cloudless deep blue sky. I shot this using a tripod and had the shutter speed set to 1/5 second.

FIGURE 1-6: Look for the glow left over from the setting sun when photographing twilight scenes.

Shooting at night

Shooting at night is sort of a ridiculous concept. There is no light to see with. Why would you take a photo at night? Well, for stuff that is actually lit.

I took the photo in Figure 1-7 in Detroit. It's the 40-story tall Cadillac tower downtown right by Campus Martius Park. This area is filled with sights and attractions like Woodward Fountain, lots of cool buildings, restaurants, and much more.

Despite the darkness, the building and street are well lit. I took this handheld shot using the camera's Night View scene mode. The camera chose an aperture of f/3.5 and ISO 1600. The mode recommends using a tripod because the shutter speed is lower than normal. In this case, it was a paltry 1/4 second shutter speed. That's on the super-low side and hard to keep steady. However, I didn't have a tripod with me so I just held the camera as steady as possible.

FIGURE 1-7:
Skies are dark at night but this building and the foreground are well lit.

Dealing with Weather

While sunny days with cloudless blue skies are great to be shooting in, they are not guaranteed. What's more, they offer little variety. Different weather conditions can spice up your photography. I've put together this small section to highlight a particular type of weather that isn't impossible to shoot in but affects the light you have available.

Capturing clouds

Clear skies are normally pretty boring. As a rule, I try to go out on cloudy days when photographing landscapes. It's not always possible, of course. And yet, clouds are amazing. They liven up the sky with interesting details. At sunset, they turn into the most beautiful things you've ever seen. Light reflects off their sides and, as the sun sets, it shines up to illuminate them from below.

Figure 1-8 was one of those times when everything seemed to work out just right. I was at a place that offered a scenic look toward the setting sun. Rivers and lakes seem made for photos like this. I had my tripod set up and was ready for this exact moment. The clouds were stunning and the light was profound.

REMEMBER

Do yourself a favor. When clouds are out, get your camera ready.

FIGURE 1-8:
Clouds make skies much more interesting, especially during the golden hour and at sunset.

Working in the snow

Shooting in the snow is completely different than running around in shorts and a t-shirt in the summer taking pictures of the lake. It's cold, windy, possibly wet, and can be hard to walk around in. Depending on the conditions, it can even be dangerous. Make sure to bundle up with the appropriate protective gear for yourself and your camera. See Book 1, Chapter 2 for some pointers on dealing with bad weather. If you're alone, tell people where you're going and when you expect to be back. Be careful not to get hurt or lost, and make sure your phone is charged and you have service if you need to make an emergency call. Can you tell I'm a dad with four kids?

And yet, snow is magical. You'll get stunning photos in the winter that aren't possible to capture at any other time of the year. The scene in Figure 1-9 is of a rather mundane path leading off into the trees. There is a fenced-in area to the left. In the summer, this particular location doesn't seem all that special. In the winter, with the trees and fence covered in snow, it's marvelous. The cool thing about being in a snowstorm, as I was, is that everything looks different.

TIP

At times you need to be careful when processing these scenes so that you don't let contrast get too high. I toned it down a bit so that the dark areas of the trees didn't make the photo look too aggressive.

FIGURE 1-9: Snow reduces overall contrast but can reveal details normally hidden.

Using fog

Fog is wonderful to shoot in, the same way snowy days and some cloudy conditions are. Fog blocks direct sunlight, and replaces it with a diffuse glow of its own. It's a chance for you to enjoy shooting in low contrast conditions.

Figure 1-10 is a case in point. I don't normally go out with my camera in the morning. It was the fog on this particular day that got me moving. I drove to a river fairly close to our house and literally got in it to shoot this ultra wide-angle shot. I was facing west, but you can't really tell that from the photo. It was just past 9:00 in the morning, but you can't tell that either. The fog blankets the entire scene. It's lovely.

FIGURE 1-10: Fog acts like a giant diffuser on the sun.

Shooting Inside

When inside, don't immediately pop the built-in flash on your dSLR. Give natural light a try. It's not just available outside. Although much dimmer inside, you can use it to assist you as you photograph people and spaces indoors.

Working in large spaces

Large interior spaces are a challenge to shoot in because they require a lot of light to look good. Depending on the design, you may be in a space with large windows. That is ideal, but you can't count on it.

I took the photo in Figure 1-11 using a tripod, which I set up very low. The camera is about shoulder-level to a person sitting down. I set the aperture to f/8 to have a good depth of field. I wanted a noise-free photo, so I left the ISO on 100. That meant I needed a full second to take this shot.

There are windows to either side of me. They provide much of the ambient light in the room. The chandeliers add more, with sconces on the wall giving some mood lighting. Spotlights on the stage complete the setup. All-in-all, that's a decent amount of light in the right places for a room like this.

TIP

It's best to shoot scenes like this one using a tripod, but you won't be able to comfortably include people if you have to use long exposures. If necessary, raise the ISO.

FIGURE 1-11: Natural light from the sides helped me photograph this large space.

Photographing in living spaces

Shooting inside using natural light is rewarding, but demanding. Unlike large commercial or public spaces, most living spaces have windows close at hand. Open the blinds and let as much natural light in as possible. Unless you use a flash, you often have to raise the ISO. If your lens is fast enough, open the aperture, but not so wide that you have a microscopic depth of field.

I took the whimsical close-up photo shown in Figure 1-12 of my wife's and daughter's hands one day after they painted their nails together. Their hands are on the floor and the windows are open. No flash, just the natural light. I had the aperture set at f/4 and used a shutter speed of 1/60 second. That's slow, but not impossible. I made sure vibration reduction was enabled on the lens. The ISO did rise to 560. Overall, this is a nice, natural shot.

Working with Ambient Light

Depending on the color of the room and furnishings, you may need to tweak white balance to render colors as they should look. Use the same techniques when shooting portraits inside. You should be ready to switch to shutter-priority mode and use faster shutter speeds if you want to photograph people more casually.

FIGURE 1-12:
I used natural light exclusively for this interior shot.

Using stage lighting

This is the one section where I'm going to break the rules a bit. The rest of this chapter is about natural, ambient lighting from the sun. I want to cover a different type of interior scene briefly; one that relies on artificial light.

Photographing performers on stage is fun, but can be quite challenging. Normally, the auditorium or venue is dark. The performers are lit by stage lighting, which can vary quite a bit. If they are under bright spotlights, it's easy to shoot nice, crisp photos with fast shutter speeds and low ISOs.

If the lighting isn't cooperating, the dark conditions push your camera to the limit. I took the photo in Figure 1-13 with a decidedly average zoom lens. It was not ideal. As a result, I could only open the aperture to f/5.6. While I set the shutter speed to 1/125 second (I wish it were faster), the ISO rose to 1600, which is getting into noisy territory for the camera I was using. In the end, this photo is balanced on a knife edge. A bit slower or a bit noisier and it would not work.

Processing shots like this can be tricky. You can't always rely on automatic routines. Adobe Lightroom, for example, thinks this photo is seriously underexposed. It wants to brighten the background, which ruins the photo.

FIGURE 1-13:
Stage lighting
brightly
illuminates
performers
but leaves the
background dark.

Coping with Different Situations

Not all light is alike. Depending on the scene, even shots taken during the same time of day can be different. Use this section to give you some ideas of how to take advantage of (or deal with) certain lighting situations. Seek out conditions that are to your advantage and avoid, or prepare for, those that aren't.

Working with indirect light

Indirect light is a pleasure to work with. This light is available on cloudy or overcast days and often in the morning and evening. It's ideal for portraits, actually, because the light evenly illuminates faces and does not cause harsh shadows.

Figure 1-14 is a photo of my son, Jacob. He's smiling as he looks off in the distance, undoubtedly happy that he was not being blinded by the light. Your subjects will thank you for this. It's hard for them to constantly try to keep their eyes open while being blinded by the sun. In addition, even lighting on faces makes processing the photo much easier. Shadows are essentially impossible to remove without making a person look worse than when you started. You may be able to alleviate some of the harsh contrast, but not all.

Working with
Ambient Light

FIGURE 1-14:
Indirect light
outside produces
incredibly
natural-looking
portraits.

Capturing reflections

Reflections make for great artistic possibilities. When possible, capture them in water or on other reflective surfaces. I've noted them throughout this chapter, but the photo in Figure 1-15 is a special one.

Except for the plants in the foreground and the leaves on the surface of the water, the photo is entirely reflections. The clouds and trees on the far bank are reflections on the water. The clouds are shining with beautiful light from the sun, but they are not uniform. Some have bright areas while some are much darker.

REMEMBER

I took this in October during the golden hour of evening sunlight. The time was 6:39 p.m., which sounds too early for the golden hour. However, sunset was less than an hour away! Remember, unless you live close to the equator, these times and their durations change throughout the year. Search using the term *sunset* and Google reliably tells you when it's scheduled to occur at your location. There are many other apps and services like `www.golden-hour.com` that also provide this information. `Weather.com` is great because you can check the weather after looking at the times for sunrise and sunset.

Rather than try to take a wide-angle photo of the river, I purposefully took this photo to feature the reflections. I zoomed in to 29mm on my Canon APS-C dSLR, which put the lens close to the middle of the normal focal length range.

FIGURE 1-15:
Be on the lookout
to capture
reflections.

Dealing with glare and haze

While I love photographing water, it's prone to glare through the afternoon and into the early evening. When photographing objects in the distance, you also have to combat haze.

Figure 1-16 shows the problem glare and haze present. I took this photo of Detroit from Belle Isle, which sits in the middle of Detroit River just to the east of the downtown area. I had to face west to capture this photo, toward the direction of the sun, which is just above the frame. It was late afternoon, so the sun was still pretty high.

TIP

From a technical perspective, you can try to combat glare by using a circular polarizing filter on your lens. Dial it to cut out unwanted reflections off the water and make your skies and clouds look better. You can try using a UV or Haze filter to cut through the haze. The UV filters themselves do work, but your results may not be discernable. This is because digital SLRs and coated lenses are already pretty resistant to UV light. For what it's worth, I did have a Sigma DG UV filter on the lens.

You can also try to process the haze out of the photo using Adobe Lightroom or another application. Lightroom, as well as Adobe Camera Raw, has a Dehaze setting that is promising.

Shooting high contrast scenes

High contrast scenes are normally an anathema to digital cameras. It's exceedingly hard if not impossible to capture a scene's deepest darks and the brightest brights in one photo if the *contrast ratio* (how far apart the darks and brights are from each other) is out of control. This is why HDR (High Dynamic Range; see Book 5, Chapter 6) photography has taken off the last several years.

Rather than fight it, you can sometimes take advantage of a scene with too much contrast artistically. I took the photo in Figure 1-17 at one end of a tunnel that allows people to go from one side of camp to the other without having to cross the road (this is really helpful when you're dealing with a lot of kids). My wife and one of my sons are at the other end. I thought it would make a great photo, and it does. In this case, high contrast between the dark sides and the light at the end of the tunnel (yes, I actually got to say it!) makes the scene.

TIP

If you're after a creative shot like this, you may have to switch metering modes from multi-zone or pattern to spot or center-weighted to get the camera to meter the scene the way you want it.

Photographing low contrast scenes

By contrast, scenes with *low contrast ratios* (the distance between the darks and lights) are relatively easy to photograph. I took the photo in Figure 1-18 during a snowstorm. The sky is overcast and gray. As a whole, the contrast in the scene is between the dark surface of the lake and the white snow on the beach. The wood and snow on the floating platform in the water also contrast with each other. It can help to have something of contrast to keep the scene from looking too desolate.

FIGURE 1-17:
It's possible to
photograph some
high-contrast
scenes very
creatively.

REMEMBER

When processing photos like this, you can leave the contrast where it is, reduce it even further, or try to accentuate it. Which approach works best depends on the scene and your sensibilities. I think we have a modern tendency to over-emphasize contrast.

FIGURE 1-18:
Scenes with
low contrast
have a different
emotional impact.

Using shadows

Use shadows in scenes when possible. They add detail and can make some photos more interesting. Use your judgment, of course. Shadows can also distract and take attention away from where you want it.

Figure 1-19 shows a scene where they work but don't dominate. I took this photo inside a pedestrian bridge that connects the main campus at a local university to a student housing area, which is located on the other side of a busy road. I used my digital Holga lens.

The walkway surface is a fairly dull-looking concrete. The shadows cast by the supports in the bridge tie in with the structure itself, making the scene of students walking to and fro even more interesting.

FIGURE 1-19:
Shadows add extra details and geometry to some photos.

IN THIS CHAPTER

» **Introducing the built-in flash**

» **Using the flash in automatic modes**

» **Popping the flash manually**

» **Tips, tricks, and techniques**

» **Exploring advanced flash settings**

Chapter **2**

Exploring Basic Flash Photography

This chapter is devoted to demystifying the built-in flash that most digital SLRs have on top of the camera. Photography gets much more enjoyable if you know when and how to control your camera's flash. You'll be able to take photos in many more situations than without it. For example, flash comes to the rescue when the lighting is dim and your camera is struggling with the exposure. It's also a great way to make sure people's faces are well lit, even in good lighting.

I show you how to use the flash, how to tweak the settings, and how to prevent it from firing when the camera is in an automatic shooting mode. You'll also learn how and when to activate it yourself when you're using an advanced shooting mode. I also cover tips on how to effectively use the built-in flash and introduce you to more advanced flash technique.

Finding the Flash

All but the most expensive digital SLRs have a built-in flash on top of the camera. Professional-level cameras rarely have a built-in flash, as these photographers almost always rely on other lighting techniques. They use external flash units (see the next chapter) quite often, or shoot in a studio with remote strobes and other bright continuous lighting units.

The built-in flash is normally locked in place and hidden, as you've seen in most of the photos of dSLRs in this book. When called upon, it unlocks and flips up a few inches above the camera, as shown in Figure 2-1.

If you have the camera set to an automatic shooting mode, the flash pops up automatically. If you're using an advanced shooting mode, you'll press a flash button to raise it (annotated in the figure). You can read more on the specifics of how this happens next.

Built-in flash   Flash button

FIGURE 2-1:
The pop-up flash extends above the camera, ready for action.

I have two important points to make before continuing.

>> **Whether you activate the flash automatically or manually, the strength of the flash is determined automatically.** The only time it isn't is when you specifically change the flash mode from automatic to manual strength. In other words, don't confuse manually activating the flash with manually setting the strength.

>> **Using the pop-up flash limits the maximum shutter speed your camera can use.** This speed is called the *sync speed* or *flash sync speed*. It's related to

how camera shutters work. Only at speeds at and below the flash sync speed is the entire image sensor uncovered at some point during the exposure. This can be a real inconvenience.

Using the Flash Automatically

Using a digital SLR's built-in flash doesn't have to be complicated or hard. If you like, you can set it to pop up and flash whenever the camera needs more light to expose the scene. The key to automatic flash is selecting the right shooting mode.

Setting a flash-friendly shooting mode

Most automatic shooting modes sense when the camera needs more light and automatically raises (pops up) and fires the built-in flash. It can be a bit of a surprise if you're not expecting it.

Most automatic modes and scenes fire the flash automatically. The left image in Figure 2-2 shows a Canon camera in Scene Intelligent Auto mode. Note the automatic flash symbol. It shows that the flash is available in this mode. The key is to find the exceptions. The right image in Figure 2-2 shows the Landscape scene in the same camera. There is no flash icon, and flash is unavailable in this mode. Check your camera's manual for specific modes, but in general, here are the types of scenes that won't fire the flash: landscapes, some sports and action modes, night scenes, many HDR scenes, and some of the more esoteric scenes like candlelight and food.

If in doubt, set the camera to the mode you want to shoot and look for an indication that the flash is available from your camera's shooting display.

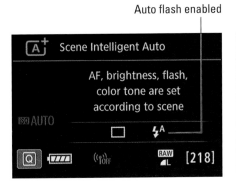

FIGURE 2-2:
The built-in flash is not available in all automatic modes and scenes.

When you're finished shooting, remember to press the built-in flash back into place.

Preventing the built-in flash from firing

Some automatic shooting modes give you the ability to turn off the flash if you don't want it. Look for details related to the shooting mode you've set in your camera's manual or shooting information display.

Some automatic modes don't let you disable the flash. If the camera thinks you need it but you don't want it, choose a shooting mode where you can disable the flash.

If necessary, choose your camera's Flash Off mode, shown in Figure 2-3, which is simply the Auto mode, but without the flash.

FIGURE 2-3: Flash Off mode is an automatic mode that disables the flash.

Customizing automatic flash settings

Many automatic shooting modes allow you to control whether the flash fires automatically, is forced to fire, or prevented from firing. Figure 2-4 shows how to change the automatic flash setting in the Portrait scene using a Canon dSLR. I've activated the setting in the left image and have chosen to turn off the built-in flash in the right image. The other two options are Auto Built-In Flash and Built-In Flash On.

Canon users can make changes through the Quick Control screen. Nikon users can use the Information display. You can leave the flash on Auto, set it to Auto plus Red-Eye Reduction, or turn it off. Sony users push the Function button to see shooting functions. Check your camera manual for specifics.

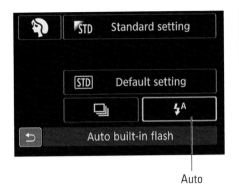

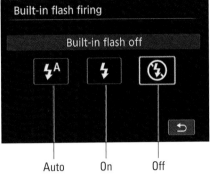

FIGURE 2-4:
Control the built-in flash in an automatic shooting mode.

Auto

Auto　On　Off

Manually Activating the Built-in Flash

When you're in an advanced shooting mode, it's up to you to pop the flash when you need it. This section gives you some pointers on knowing how, and when to do so.

Knowing how to use flash

Using your camera's pop-up flash is technically quite easy. Follow these steps:

1. **Choose a shooting mode that allows manual flash control.**

   Most often this includes programmed autoexposure, aperture-priority, shutter-priority, and manual shooting modes. Cameras tend to disable the flash button if you're in an automatic mode.

2. **Enable the flash.**

   Check your camera's menu to make sure flash is enabled (see Figure 2-5). If not, do so.

FIGURE 2-5:
The flash is enabled and ready.

3. Clear the flash.

Remove anything attached to the camera's hot shoe. Make sure there's enough space for the flash to pop up without hitting anything.

4. Press the flash button to raise it.

The flash button is on the left side of the built-in flash on most cameras (refer to Figure 2-1).

5. Press the shutter button halfway to meter and confirm flash is ready.

The camera may fire off a few pre-shot pulses to help set the exposure. This is part of *TTL (through the lens)* flash metering. Makers tend to call their latest version of TTL flash by different names. Canon uses E-TTL and E-TTL II. Nikon uses i-TTL. Sony uses ADI (Advanced Distance Integration). Pentax use P-TTL.

Wait for the sign that the flash is ready. Figure 2-6 shows one through a Canon viewfinder. Yours may be different. In this case a small flash symbol appears next to the battery status.

FIGURE 2-6: The viewfinder gives you information on the status of the flash.

Flash ready

6. Take and review your photos.

Your flash should fire and light up your subject or the scene.

7. If necessary, adjust the strength of the flash for follow-up shots using flash compensation, as explained later.

8. Lower the built-in flash when done.

This saves power and protects it from accidentally getting banged around.

Knowing when to use flash

If you don't know whether to pop the flash, consider these scenarios:

>> **You need more light.** Most of the time this happens indoors, where the lighting rarely compares to the natural light of the sun. Figure 2-7 shows a photo I took of my son Ben as he sat on the couch watching his sister open her presents. I was some distance away using a near-telephoto lens and flash. The flash performed perfectly, providing just the right amount of light.

FIGURE 2-7:
Interior photos often need flash.

>> **The subject is backlit.** Backlighting refers to the situation when your subject is standing in front of something bright. Strong light in the background fools the camera's sensor into thinking the exposure is fine, when it isn't. The camera wants to not overexpose the sky, which leaves your subject dark. To correct this problem, use the flash, as I did for the photo in Figure 2-8. Even a low-powered burst can light your subject and save the photo. (You could switch to spot metering, but that won't add any light to the scene.)

>> **The subject is in shadow.** Often, the lighting in the scene is decent, but from the wrong direction. I lit the scene in Figure 2-9 primarily from the window to the back right. Without the flash, the pie as well as the mug would have been too dark. This technique is called *fill flash*.

TIP

Try flash outdoors, even when your subject is not backlit. It seems strange, but fill flash brings faces out of shadow. Watch your exposure, though. You may have to use high-speed sync (covered in the next chapter) to limit the exposure.

FIGURE 2-8:
The flash helps
even lighting
differences
between the
background and
subject.

FIGURE 2-9:
Fill flash
brightens the
foreground and
makes the photo
look much better.

>> **You want better light.** The flash is a nice, clean, pure burst of light that can
look very good compared to some interior lighting. If you're in a room with
strong yellows or reds (see Figure 2-10), your photos may have strong color
casts if you don't use a flash. A flash can clear all that up. In this case, the
strong color of the wood paneling behind my wife threatens to overpower the
scene. Using the flash kept her from looking too warm.

FIGURE 2-10:
Use the flash to compensate for strong yellows and browns in the scene.

REMEMBER

You are only one part of the photographer–camera team. At times, the camera might suggest using flash when low light levels are sensed, as shown in Figure 2-11. Pay attention to the cues in your viewfinder or on the back of the camera. Depending on the model you're using, the shutter speed, aperture, or ISO may flash, indicating the camera is having trouble with the current exposure settings. Ultimately, you're in charge, but the camera may keep you out of trouble.

FIGURE 2-11:
This Nikon dSLR recommends flash when the lighting is poor.

Disabling the built-in flash

You can disable your camera's flash from the menu when in an advanced exposure mode. Look for your camera's built-in flash options and set it to Disable, as shown in Figure 2-12. While this might seem odd, you may want to pop the flash to help the camera focus using the AF-assist beam, but not want it to fire for the exposure. Disabling it will do that.

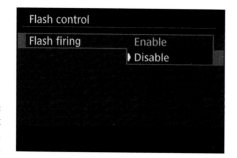

Tips on Using the Built-in Flash

Here's a list of things that will help make your flash photos better:

>> **Don't get too close.** Using a flash can mean harsh lighting and stark shadows if you're too close to your subject. Don't get right up into someone's business, like I did for the photo in Figure 2-13. Back off a bit.

FIGURE 2-13:
Sneaking up on a
sleeping kitty with
a blinding flash.

>> **Separate subjects from background.** A flash is a powerful burst of light. If your subject is standing too close to a wall (or a fancy photography background), he'll cast unflattering shadows. Figure 2-14 shows an example. To correct it, move your subjects away from the background, use a light diffuser (softens the light like a lampshade does; see Book 4, Chapter 3), or use an off-camera flash and angle it so that the shadow is hidden.

FIGURE 2-14: Notice the strong shadow cast on the background.

>> **Use slow sync to brighten a dark background.** When the flash lights some-one, often the camera thinks the overall exposure is bright. It compensates by underexposing the background, which leaves it dark. If you don't mind the effect, it can work — and even hide a messy or unappealing background. However, to reduce the effect, dial in negative flash compensation or use slow sync (an advanced option discussed later).

>> **Work with your subjects.** At a certain age, all my kids became experts at flash blocking. Whenever I approached them with my camera and flash, they would throw an arm over their eyes. Work with your subjects to try and prevent this.

>> **Avoid lens shadows.** Pop-up flashes aren't tall enough to shoot over large or long lenses and lens hoods. The lens casts an ugly shadow that ruins the photo. Know which lenses you can use with your pop-up flash, or which focal lengths are safe to use with your zoom lens.

>> **Use flash compensation.** This simple solution is effective for solving many flash problems.

>> **Consider an external (hot shoe) flash.** Buying an external flash unit (Canon calls them Speedlites and Nikon has Speedlights) that mounts in your cam-era's hot shoe is the next step into the larger world of flash photography and lighting. It opens a number of creative possibilities, such as off-camera and wireless flash. It's also easier to direct, diffuse, and bounce light from external

units. Most camera makers offer two or three external flash units in a range of prices and capabilities. External flash is covered in Book 4, Chapter 3.

>> **Practice.** Knowledge, combined with practical experience, is an unbeatable combination. Keep working with your flash to become an expert in using it.

REMEMBER

You don't have to become the end-all, be-all Master of Flash. You just have to know how to work your gear to create the photos you want. Start practicing in the situations you shoot most often.

Getting Fancy with the Flash

Using the built-in flash isn't that hard, but there are some techniques and settings that go beyond leaving everything on Auto. This section covers a few additional techniques and lists some more advanced options.

Enabling red-eye reduction

When using the flash, it's not uncommon to take photos of people who end up looking like they have red, glowing eyes. Red-eye is caused by the pupils in the eye not closing fast enough in response to the flash. This allows light to reflect off the back of the interior surface of the eye. It's a problem mostly among people with light-colored eyes.

The effect can be very distracting, and takes away from an otherwise good shot. Although you can try to remove red eyes in software, it is faster and easier to prevent it from happening.

Red-eye reduction causes the camera to emit a series of pulses from the built-in flash or Red-Eye Reduction Lamp, should it have one. This causes the pupil to contract before you take the photo. Enable red-eye reduction from the camera's menu system (see Book 1, Chapter 4) or in the camera's flash settings, as shown in Figure 2-15.

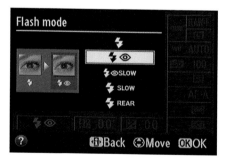

FIGURE 2-15:
Enable red-eye reduction when photographing people using the flash.

Canon dSLRs have a scale that appears in the viewfinder when the red-eye reduction feature is enabled, the flash is up, and you press the shutter button halfway to meter and focus. As you hold the shutter button halfway down, the scale shrinks and soon disappears. Red-eye reduction is most effective if you wait until this countdown process completes before taking the photo.

REMEMBER

There is one caveat (it's sort of a big one) I should mention before leaving red-eye reduction. The pre-flashes delay the whole process of taking the photo, sometimes by several seconds. Don't count on being able to capture fast-paced action or catching people in natural unposed shots when using this feature. If your subjects aren't aware of what's happening, they will often think that you've taken the photo when the pre-flashes fire, then start talking or blinking when you take the actual photo.

Using flash compensation

Flash compensation is a quick and easy way to adjust the strength of the flash without controlling it manually. In fact, it's the only way you can adjust the flash when your camera doesn't have a manual flash mode.

REMEMBER

Knowing how to manage flash compensation will help you take better flash photos reliably.

When you take a flash photo, review it before taking more shots. Note whether your subject is too dark or too bright. Compensate based on these factors:

>> **Dark subject:** Raise flash compensation or move closer.

>> **Bright subject:** Lower flash compensation or move farther away.

Check your camera manual for precise flash compensation details. You may be able to press a button or rotate a command dial to set it. Compensation is measured in stops of EV. With Canon cameras, you can also use the Quick Control screen. Press the Quick Control button and highlight Flash Exposure Compensation. After you press Set, the Flash Exposure Compensation screen appears, as shown in the left image in Figure 2-16. After you set it, you should see an indicator on your LCD monitor, as shown on the right in Figure 2-16, or in the viewfinder.

TIP

Always look for telltale signs like the indicator shown in Figure 2-16 to remind you that you've made exposure adjustments. When you move on to another subject or different lighting, reset it.

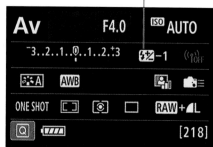

Flash exposure compensation

FIGURE 2-16:
Negative
numbers
reduce the
flash strength;
positive numbers
increase it.

Using FE Lock

Use Flash Exposure Lock (FE lock, sometimes called FV Lock) as you would Auto-exposure Lock (AE Lock). Meter the subject centered in the viewfinder, press the FE Lock button, and then recompose. The flash strength and overall exposure is locked until you release the button — even after taking multiple shots.

Controlling the flash strength manually

Setting the flash to manual mode lets you control the flash intensity yourself. Through the lens (TTL) metering (and variations thereof) that takes the flash into account is disabled. In other words, you've switched off the targeting computer and are relying exclusively on the Force. Here's a quick guide:

1. **Switch to flash mode.**

To set the flash strength yourself, you must switch the flash from its normal, *through-the-lens* mode of operation to manual using the camera's menu, as shown in Figure 2-17. Depending on the camera, look for this feature in the built-in flash settings or in the shooting menu.

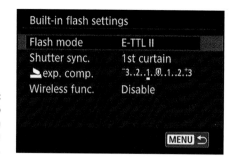

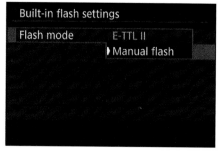

FIGURE 2-17:
Change to
manual flash
to set the flash
strength yourself.

2. **Set the flash strength.**

Flash strength works in reverse. Full power is considered normal (see the left image in Figure 2-18), and you *reduce it* to the level you desire (see the right image in Figure 2-18). Reduced flash strength is measured as a fraction of full power, and you reduce the power in steps.

Starts at full strength   Reducing output

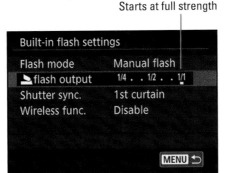
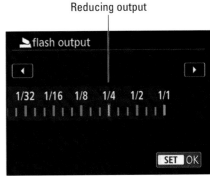

FIGURE 2-18: Setting flash strength manually reduces the power from full strength.

TIP

If you're not comfortable using the flash manually, stay in automated TTL flash metering mode and use distance and flash compensation to tweak the flash.

Unlocking more advanced features

Depending on your camera, the built-in flash may have many more features available to it. You may hardly ever need them, but here is a list of more advanced flash options worth knowing about:

>> **TTL Metering** meters through the lens. You may be able to change the TTL metering method. For example, Canon cameras have two settings: Evaluative and Average (see Figure 2-19). Evaluative tries to get the closest object exposure correct, even if that means the background is underexposed. Average accounts for the entire scene and generally fires a stronger flash.

>> **Flash sync in AV mode** is a feature on Canon dSLRs. It gives you some control over the flash sync speed when you have the camera set to aperture-priority mode. As shown in Figure 2-20, you can leave it on Auto, which is the default. This allows the camera to set any shutter speed. It can be really slow, or up to the flash sync speed of 1/250 second (which is the flash sync speed for this camera). The second option enables you to limit the shutter speed to moderate speeds, useful for keeping the blur out of handheld photographs. You can also fix the shutter speed when using the flash in aperture-priority mode to 1/250 second.

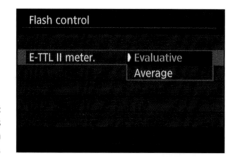

FIGURE 2-19:
Canon dSLRs offer two flash metering options.

FIGURE 2-20:
This Canon option gives you control over flash sync speed in Av mode.

>> **Slow-sync flash** (see Figure 2-21) slows the shutter speed so that the flash fires and ends the exposure. The result is a brighter background. Slow-sync flash works well indoors if you're shooting casual shots or portraits with still subjects. You can also take some great shots with movement in the background and a clear subject.

TIP

Try this tip for indoor photography: Pay attention to shutter speed and blur. If you don't want blur, try switching out of slow-sync flash or use a tripod.

FIGURE 2-21:
Enabling slow-sync flash on a Nikon dSLR.

TECHNICAL STUFF

>> **Rear-curtain sync (or second curtain)** flashes just before the exposure ends, as opposed to when it begins (normal, front curtain, or first curtain). You can shoot some creative scenes using rear-curtain flash and moving vehicles or people with lights. The lights move through the scene and the flash freezes things to finish the shot. I'm setting this option in Figure 2-22.

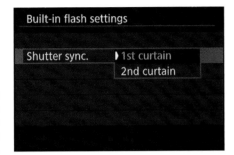

FIGURE 2-22: The difference between these options is when the flash fires.

>> **Wireless (or Commander)** lets you take flash photos with external flash units that don't have to be hard-wired to the camera (see Book 4, Chapter 3). The wireless setting uses infrared or radio signals to activate one or more external flashes. When acting as the *commander,* the camera's internal flash fires a low-powered pulse to set off one or more external flashes. Figure 2-23 shows several options available on a mid-range Canon camera that enable the built-in flash to control one or more external Speedlite flashes. Not all cameras can be a wireless master.

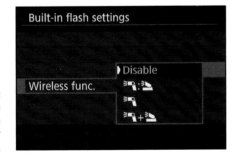

FIGURE 2-23: The built-in flash can often wirelessly trigger external units.

Chapter **3**

Using an External Flash and Accessories

s good as built-in pop-up flashes are (they're certainly better than nothing), they have some limitations. They're attached to your camera and shoot directly ahead at a constant angle. You can't tilt or swivel them. Not only that, long lenses sometimes get in the way and cast shadows. An *external flash* mounts to the top of your camera and solves these problems. In doing so, it opens a world of other creative lighting possibilities.

If you're interested in upping your game and being able to use an external flash creatively in situations than your camera's built-in flash, this chapter is for you. I show you what an external flash looks like, what the parts are, how to attach and remove it from your camera, discuss various accessories, and then finish with a number of different techniques that will make your flash photos better. If I hadn't written it, I would be reading it!

Getting to Know External Flash Units

External flashes come in two sizes: small and large. Within each category the flashes look and act very similar, and offer comparable features.

WHAT'S IN A NAME?

Different companies call external flashes by different names. I use the general term *external flash* or *flash* unless I'm referring to a specific flash name. You might run across some of these names:

- Canon: Speedlite
- Nikon: Speedlight
- Olympus: Flash
- Pentax: Electronic Flash Unit
- Sony: Flash, flash unit, external flash

Companies like Canon, Nikon, Sony, and others generally offer at least one small external flash that provides basic features in an inexpensive package. These models rarely offer bounce or tilt functionality, do not have many external controls, and do not have a display. They do, however, move the flash up and off the camera, and can be mounted on stands and used off-camera with longer flash cords that connect the hot shoe to the flash (see the later section, "Handling an External Flash").

The larger companies often have two or more styles of larger external flashes that have additional features than their smaller counterparts, come with external controls and displays, and tilt and swivel. Typically one model is a midrange unit listed at a moderate price (although still pretty expensive if you ask me). The other is the company's top-of-the-line external flash. It looks quite a bit like the midrange model, but has extra functions and features meant for professionals.

Although most external flashes are pretty similar, some flashes, such as ring flashes, look very different. A ring flash is a specialized type of flash unit designed to mount on your camera and shoot around the lens. These flashes are well suited to macro, close-up, and portrait photography.

Looking at the front

The front of the flash (see Figure 3-1) contains all the elements needed to light the scene. It may also contain different helpers.

>> **Flash head:** The part that holds the flash. All but the most basic models rotate up and swivel from side to side. Most lock in place; set them free with the release button. Some snap into place or move under resistance.

AF-assist illuminator Built-in wide panel Mounting foot

Wireless sensor Flash head Body

FIGURE 3-1:
Midrange flash
has power to tilt,
swivel, and more.

Not all flashes bounce or swivel. Some heads (entry-level models, normally) sit on top of the body and point straight ahead.

>> **Flash:** Here comes the light. Pay attention to where it's pointing. Small differences in positioning can make big differences in photos.

Snap or push Sto-Fen–type diffusers directly on the end of the flash. Other accessories, such as small soft boxes, also fit over the end of the head. Some accessories rely on hook-and-loop fasteners. Wrap the loop around the head and fix it securely to itself. The piece with the hook part attaches to it.

>> **Built-in wide panel:** A built-in wide panel is a handy aspect of many external flashes. The panel slides out and drops over the flash, directing the light from the flash to cover a wider area. Most flashes have these panels, but some aren't built in. If that's the case, the flash case should have a place to store the panel. Snap it on the flash head to use it. Pop it off when you're done.

Flip the wide panel down when you're using a wide-angle lens. When you pull the panel out, the flash should automatically set itself to that focal length. If not, set the proper zoom on the flash. When you finish, lift the adapter and slide it back in.

>> **Body:** Here are the guts — the controls, batteries, connections, and mounting foot.

>> **Mounting foot:** A metal or plastic plate that slides into the camera's hot shoe. The mounting foot is one of the more critical parts of an external flash. Make sure that the foot is clean and not bent. Most cameras use a standard *hot shoe,* a metal guide that sits on top of the camera. Sony has a different type of connection (the two types aren't compatible with each other) than the other manufacturers, but it serves the same purpose.

Beneath the foot are the electrical contacts that connect the camera to the flash.

- Don't try to place a flash unit on an incompatible camera. You can short out the flash or the camera.

- When mounting the flash on an external light stand with a shoe adapter (as opposed to using a mini stand that has built-in protection), protect the contacts from touching metal by covering them with a bit of electrical tape. When finished, make sure no residue from the tape is left on the contacts. If you're concerned about that, use a piece of paper or other slim, non-conductive barrier.

>> **AF-assist illuminator:** This feature helps the camera autofocus when the lighting is too dim for the camera's normal autofocus sensor to work. You can usually set boundaries for this feature in the camera's menu.

When the flash is mounted *off-camera* (it's wired to the camera, but not connected directly to the hot shoe), AF-assist doesn't work unless you're using a cord that supports the feature.

>> **Wireless sensor:** The sensor that detects signals from the camera that tell it what to do and when. Pay attention to the direction the sensor faces and be sure not to block it.

From the back and sides

You'll see a lot more of the flash sides and back. The back (shown in Figure 3-2) is where you control the unit.

LCD panel

Bounce angle index

Lock-release button

FIGURE 3-2:
The rear of the flash unit has important features and controls.

Controls   Lock lever   Battery cover

REMEMBER

>> **Lock-(bounce/swivel) release button:** Press this button to unlock the flash head and change the bounce or swivel angles. The button pops back out when you release it, locking the head in that position. Depending on the brand of flash you have, bounce may be called tilt and swivel may be called rotate.

If your unit has a locking button, *don't force the head* — you might break it.

>> **Bounce angle index:** Raised marks on the head show you the flash's bounce angle (the angle the flash is pointing at when not looking straight up; see ahead to "Bouncing and diffusing" in this chapter). Knowing the angle helps you duplicate setups.

>> **Swivel angle index:** A swivel index that shows how far from center you've swiveled the flash head. The index is hidden beneath the flash head in Figure 3-2.

TIP

When holding the camera vertically, swivel the flash to bounce light off the ceiling. If holding the camera horizontally, you may find it helpful to swivel the flash and bounce light off a reflector or neutral-colored wall.

>> **Battery cover:** A plastic piece covers the area where you insert batteries. To open the battery compartment, press the cover and slide it toward the bottom of the unit to release the catch. The cover (which can fit tightly) reveals the batteries. Be sure to slide down the cover completely and exert the force necessary to open it.

>> **Battery compartment:** Put your batteries here. Four AA batteries seem to be the standard for larger flash units. Smaller, entry-level models may need only two.

REMEMBER

Make sure you point your batteries the right way. Sometimes the orientation marks are inside the compartment instead of the door, which makes it tougher to see them. You should also remove the batteries from your flash when you're not going to use it for a while.

>> **Ready light:** Your flash may have a ready light on it. This tells you that it's ready to fire. The camera may blink the light or turn it a different color to relay more information about the status of the flash. Check your camera manual for details.

>> **Lock:** You may use a locking lever or ring to secure the flash on top of the hot shoe. Turn or slide the lever one way to lock the flash. Turn or slide it the other way to release the flash. A flash may also click into place.

>> **Controls:** Most flashes have several buttons and controls on the backs. Use them to control the flash.

>> **LCD panel:** Most midrange and above flashes have large LCD screens. They show you all the details of how your flash is set up and which mode you're in so you can glance at the flash and see what's going on.

>> **Other indicators:** The back of the flash always seems to have room for another light or indicator.

Accessorizing your external flash

Some flashes come with extras such as a diffuser and a couple of gels that you can use right out of the box. You can also find flash bundles that have many more helpful products as part of a large package.

Here are some accessories that you can use to modify your external flash:

>> **Diffusers:** A flash diffuser softens the light emitted by the flash, (ideally) getting rid of harsh shadows on your subjects. Diffusers come in a couple of varieties:

- *Hard plastic:* You can see mine in Figure 3-3. It's just a little plastic cover, but it works. If you buy it separately from your flash, make sure to buy one that's compatible with your flash unit. Push it onto the head so that it fits securely and doesn't fall off the first time you take a step.

  Check to see whether the brand you like comes in different colors. Sto-fen also has diffusers in green (for fluorescent lighting) and gold (to warm subjects).

TIP

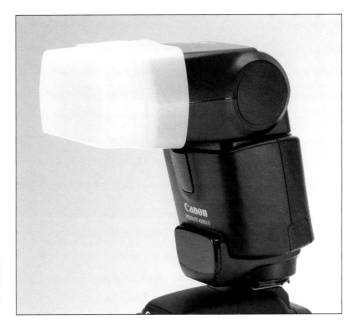

FIGURE 3-3:
You can't get any easier than this type of flash diffuser.

- *Soft box:* Fits on the flash head. Assembly is often required. The box slips over the end of the flash and extends some distance in front. I don't normally use it when the flash is mounted on the camera, because the box dips down a little. Mounted on a stand or sitting on a table, it's ideal.

- *Other creative diffusers*: The Interfit Strobies On-Camera Diffuser (`interfit photographic.com`) is a novel diffuser. It has an elastic opening that fits over your lens. The rest is a typical diffuser that extends up to diffuse light from the flash.

Using an External Flash and Accessories

CHAPTER 3 **Using an External Flash and Accessories** 385

>> **Bounce accessories:** Although you can find several types and brands of flash bouncers, LumiQuest (www.lumiquest.com) has a wide selection. It has products that will bounce, reflect, and diffuse light from your flash, all at the same time. They attach to the front of your flash with the help of a hook-and-loop strap, which you aim upward (your flash must be able to point up). Light from the flash hits the surface of the bouncer and is reflected toward the subject. In the process, it's softened. The downside to this type of setup is that you have to ensure enough headroom to use it, and there's the danger of coming across like a superflash freak.

>> **Mini stand:** Some flashes come with a mini stand (see Figure 3-4), also known as a *flash stand* or *Speedlight stand.* You can mount the flash on this small, plastic stand. If your flash doesn't come with one, you may be able to buy one.

REMEMBER

The stand is useful for taking the flash off-camera (if it can go wireless) and putting it on a table or the floor. Plus, its light stand socket underneath gives you an easy way to mount the flash on a larger light stand.

FIGURE 3-4:
Aside from being cute, mini stands are very useful.

>> **Wide-angle adapter:** Buy this adapter if your flash has no built-in adapter. It helps spread the light from the flash out to cover the additional angle of view that wide-angle lenses capture.

>> **Gel or filter:** Look for colored gel filters to add ambiance to a scene or use them for color correction.

>> **Adapter, bracket, cord, coupler:** The number of ways you can connect your flash to other gear is dizzying. Look for all these pieces of equipment

to get connected. Check the manual that came with your flash for additional guidance.

» **Case:** Flash cases are useful. They protect the flash and hold small accessories.

At some point you may want to look into studio-style lighting modifiers like umbrellas and soft boxes. By this time you may need a background and extra lights. As your setup gets more complicated, you will need to connect everything together (wirelessly or wired).

Handling an External Flash

This section details some of the camera-to-flash connections you can make with your flash. There's the tried-and-true hot shoe method, but also several other wired and wireless options for you to consider. Each has its own rationale.

Attaching it to your camera

Connecting an external flash to your camera is easy. If you're not used to it, practice a few times. Use a camera strap or tripod for additional support. Whatever you do, be careful.

WARNING

Don't force the flash onto a hot shoe if it seems to be sticking. You don't want to bend or break the flash foot or hot shoe on the camera. In addition, exercise care when threading items onto a stand or adapter. If the threads aren't aligned properly, you could strip the threads or get things stuck together.

These steps can help:

1. **Turn off the flash and your camera.**

   Don't rush. You don't want to short anything out.

2. **Hold the camera in one hand and the flash in another.**

   Experiment until you find the most comfortable method for you. I like to hold the camera with my right hand and work the flash with my left hand (discerning readers will notice that the pretty hands in Figure 3-5 are not mine; they are my wife's).

3. **Bring the flash in line with the hot shoe and slide it in.**

   Line up the mounting foot with the camera's hot shoe, as shown in Figure 3-5. This process takes place mostly by feel. When you slide the flash straight onto the shoe, you should hear a click.

4. **Lock down the flash, if you have a lock.**

   Don't forget this step or the flash could slide off the camera!

5. **Turn on the camera and flash.**

6. **Make any necessary settings or adjustments.**

   You're ready to rock.

Removing the flash

Removing the flash from your camera is the reverse of putting it on. Follow these steps:

1. **Turn off the camera and flash.**

2. **Grip the camera with one hand.**

3. **While supporting the flash, release it.**

   This step may involve turning a ring, moving a lever, or pushing a button.

   Keep one hand on the flash at this point so that it doesn't fall.

4. **Slide the flash out of the shoe.**

   Slide it straight back. Don't twist it! It will bind in the rails.

5. **Secure the flash without banging the camera on anything.**

   A camera swings around when it's attached to a strap. If you bend over to put away the flash, it swings away from you and bonks itself on whatever is in front of you.

Tilting and swiveling the flash head

If you have a flash that can be tilted and swiveled, get used to operating it. When it becomes second nature you'll be more likely to use this amazingly cool feature. Here's my technique:

1. **Secure the camera and flash.**

   If the flash is attached on the camera or a stand, hold and stabilize the camera or stand with your right hand.

2. **Push and hold the lock-release button with your left thumb.**

   You should grasp the flash head in the palm of your left hand, as shown in Figure 3-6, to provide the leverage you need to push the button. Use the same grip approach to position the flash head.

3. **Position the flash head.**

   Rotate the flash head upward to tilt, or turn the flash head left or right to swivel. Do not go beyond the limits of the flash or you'll crunch it. Remember, this stuff is typically plastic.

4. **Release the button.**

   You're primed and ready to bounce your flash.

FIGURE 3-6:
Make sure to hold the lock-release button as you tilt and swivel the head.

To tilt or swivel the flash when it's not mounted to anything, grip and hold the base of the flash with your left hand, then use your right hand to grasp the flash head. Your right thumb will be in perfect position to push the lock-release button and tilt or swivel the head.

Attaching a mini stand

To mount the flash on a mini stand, follow these steps:

1. **Make sure that the flash is turned off.**

2. **Connect the mini stand to the flash.**

- If the stand isn't attached to anything (such as a light stand), hold the flash body in your hand and slide the mini stand onto the mounting foot.

- If the mini stand is already mounted on a light stand, slide the flash onto the stand rather than sliding the mini stand onto the flash.

3. **Lock down the flash, if you can.**

To mount the mini stand to the light stand, screw it on.

Working the controls

This section briefly describes the common flash controls. Figure 3-7 shows the back side of a typical midrange Canon Speedlite.

Read your manual for detailed instructions for working your flash. Your flash has controls similar to these:

» **Power switch:** In this case, the flash combines a power switch with a locking mechanism that keeps you from accidentally jogging the dial and changing values.

» **Mode button:** Most flash units have several shooting modes. Use the Mode button to switch between them. Read your flash manual for details.

» **Function buttons:** Pressing these buttons either turns things on or off or cycles through various settings. The settings, in millimeters, should match the focal length of your lens (or come close if they're midway).

» **Wireless button:** Puts the flash in wireless mode. Very handy.

» **Test flash button and ready lamp:** On this model, the lamp that tells you the flash is ready and the button to test it is the same button.

» **Select/set button:** Press the Select/Set button to choose options.

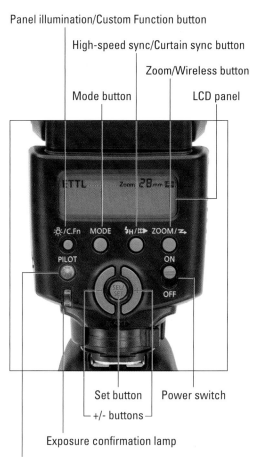

Panel illumination/Custom Function button

High-speed sync/Curtain sync button

Zoom/Wireless button

Mode button

LCD panel

Set button

+/- buttons

Power switch

Exposure confirmation lamp

Test button/ready lamp

FIGURE 3-7:
These controls are common to most external flash units.

>> **Increment/decrement button or dials:** Your flash may let you increase or decrease setting values (like focal lengths) or scroll through options. If so, use the increment/decrement buttons or dials to adjust the values.

>> **Other controls:** As mentioned in an earlier section, some flashes have other controls and indicators that aren't listed here. Some work for a single purpose and some work for multiple purposes.

>> **Two-button controls:** Some flashes require you to press and hold two buttons simultaneously in order to access certain settings and information.

>> **Navigating:** Your camera manual tells you how to get around the menu. Some buttons switch options; some buttons change the value of the option you're looking at.

Configuring Your External Flash

Because each flash is different, I can't show you specifics for every option. Turn to Book 4, Chapter 2 for general information on most flash modes, and read your flash manual.

I can make some general observations about two main parts: your settings and your standings.

Look for these options in your camera or flash menu:

>> **Flash Control menu:** Some cameras group built-in and external flash settings under a single flash menu. Select the flash menu (see the left image in Figure 3-8) to view flash settings (shown on the right in Figure 3-8). If your camera uses a separate menu for the external flash, select it instead.

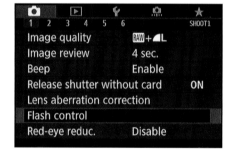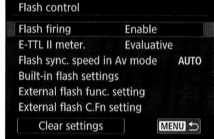

>> **Functions (shown on the left in Figure 3-9):** Spend a lot of time reading your camera and flash manual; standard external flash functions generally include changing the metering method, the focal length, high-speed sync, curtain synchronization, adding flash compensation, or controlling flash exposure bracketing.

>> **Custom functions (shown on the right in Figure 3-9):** Custom functions enable you to customize some features on your flash. Maybe you never could get conversions down and just have a general feeling of high-school dread when faced with the metric system; you may be able to change the distance display from meters to feet. Check into every nook and cranny for useful ways to work the way you want. You don't always have to leave things on their defaults.

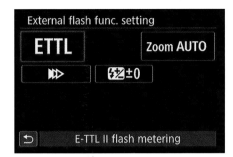

Flash functions

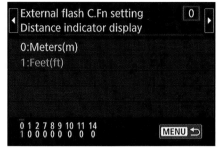

Custom functions

FIGURE 3-9: Investigating normal flash functions and custom functions.

Trying Different Techniques

An *external* flash (the flash unit that you can attach to your camera, not where you mount it) is useful and a lot of fun. Although built-in flashes are capable, an external flash

>> Offers more flexibility.

>> Has more power.

>> Gives you a greater range of freedom.

This section covers some of the techniques that are possible using *one* external flash. You can add more. The more you add, the more creative you can be.

Using high-speed sync

A flash is a useful device to have, even when you don't think you need one. Forcing the flash to fire, called *fill flash,* often makes your subjects look better and balance the brightness of the foreground and background. This is all well and good, but there are times when you run into exposure problems. If you need to use a faster shutter speed, enable your camera's high-speed sync feature (shown on the left in Figure 3-10), if available. As shown on the right in Figure 3-10, you'll be able to use faster shutter speeds and wider apertures.

High-speed sync (HSS) bypasses the camera's sync speed by pulsing the flash throughout the exposure. Figure 3-11 shows how effective this technique can be. I wanted to use a fill flash to keep my wife's face lit. Normally, that's not a problem. However, we were outside on a sunny day, and I also wanted to use a wide aperture. The exposure settings needed to capture the shot were far faster (1/2000 second) than the normal flash sync speed. I was able to successfully use the settings I wanted by enabling HSS.

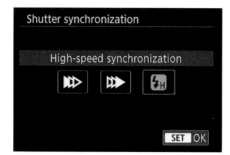

FIGURE 3-10:
Enabling HSS
opens faster
shutter speeds.

FIGURE 3-11:
HSS enabled
me to use fill
light *and* a wide
aperture on a
bright day.

REMEMBER

High-speed sync doesn't take you into some sort of super slow-mo, action-freezing mode. HSS lets you use fill flash outside on a bright day (or in a studio with bright lights) with a wide-open lens. This is an especially effective technique when shooting portraits.

Bouncing and diffusing

Bouncing (reflecting the flash off of a nearby surface) and *diffusing* (putting a translucent material between the flash and the subject) are two techniques you can employ to soften light from the flash. They both make shadows less prominent, reduce the chance of red-eye, and create a more natural shot.

Bouncing literally bounces light from the flash off a ceiling or other surface. Depending on how you're holding the camera, tilt or swivel the flash head so that it points at the ceiling or wall. The great thing about bouncing the flash is that you can do it even when you have no other gear with you. It's the ultimate fail-safe solution, provided you have an external flash unit with a tilt/swivel head.

Diffusing the flash requires extra equipment. Diffusers come in many shapes and sizes, including soft boxes, plastic diffusers, umbrellas, and more. Depending on what type you have, you mount it directly on the flash or between the flash and the subject. Many large diffusers require that you mount the flash off-camera and trigger it with a long cord or wirelessly. Diffusers have the same effect as lamp-shades. Light from the flash hits the diffuser, spreads out, and softens.

High ceilings make bouncing more difficult and may not provide enough light. If you're in this situation, switch to a diffuser and point the flash straight at the subject. You may want to consider picking up a small or large circular diffuser. I love my large diffuser (shown in Figure 3-12) and use it all the time, even when not using the flash. I can mount it on a stand, as shown in the figure, or have someone hold it between the bright sun and my subject. It's also very useful in the studio. I hold it between continuous lighting and very reflective subjects.

FIGURE 3-12:
This large diffuser is very practical.

Using an umbrella

Umbrellas are just what you'd expect, except they won't keep rain off your head. *Umbrellas* diffuse light from the flash even better than bouncing or using a diffuser. The catch is that you have to set up the umbrella on a stand with the flash, as shown in Figure 3-13. That limits how portable and spontaneous you can be. However, the results are almost always fantastic.

To control your flash on a light stand (which looks something like a tripod, but isn't meant to hold a camera) with an umbrella, you can make it wireless and use your camera's built-in flash for a trigger. You can also buy an off-camera cord that extends the range of your hot shoe or wirelessly trigger the flash. Vello (www.vellogear.com) makes a line of wireless flash triggers for different brands of flash.

FIGURE 3-13: Umbrellas are very effective tools to have when shooting portraits.

Focusing light with a snoot

Have you ever watched an old *Star Trek* episode where Captain Kirk sits in the captain's chair and his eyes are brightly lit but the rest of his face isn't? They created that effect with a *snoot,* a tube or rectangle on the end of the flash; it keeps the flash tightly focused on the subject. The longer the snoot, the more focused the lighting. The shorter the snoot, the more it expands. You can even make your own snoot out of things you have on hand (high-tech things like cereal boxes and tape).

I took the photo in Figure 3-14 with Gary Fong's Collapsible snoot with Power-Grid. I also moved the flash off-camera to the left of my son's face. The flash is much farther away than the camera. The result is a portrait that has a lot of close-up detail (impossible to capture with a straight shot using the flash), creative side lighting, interesting shadow, and a dark background.

Using a stand

Moving the flash off the camera and using a light stand has some advantages. You can position the flash in more locations than if it were attached to the camera, allowing you to come at the subject from different angles. You can light the subject and background, enhance or eliminate shadows, and do all sorts of other things — with one flash. A stand also enables you to move it closer or farther away from the subject. Aside from positioning, large stands enable you to use accessories like umbrellas, which attach to the stand.

FIGURE 3-14:
Snoots are
wonderful tools
to use.

TIP

Keep these points in mind when you shop for a light stand:

>> **Watch your weight.** Some stands are big and beefy. Some are flimsy. Make sure to buy a stand that's made for the weight you're going to put on it. While generally light, umbrellas can be large and extend out from the stand, affecting the center of gravity.

>> **Learn to adapt.** Your flash needs an adapter because its bottom has nowhere to attach to a tripod. A mini stand is the easiest adapter for mounting a flash to a light stand.

LIGHTSPHERE

Gary Fong's Lightsphere Collapsible Pro kit has a soft, collapsible diffuser that fits on the end of your external flash. It diffuses and softens your flash. You can customize the Lightsphere with different domes and gels. The kit also has a snoot with an optional grid (that divides the snoot into sections that further tighten the light beam).

Your mileage may vary, but I've been completely impressed with every aspect of this kit. A lot of ingenious people out there are devoted to making your flash photos the best they can be. If Gary Fong isn't for you, look at other products by other makers.

Elevating the flash with a bracket

I was skeptical at first about flash brackets. They make your dSLR look like an old-fashioned press camera with the flash on the side. I stuck with it and it started making sense. You can also use a setup like this to help prevent red-eye. Repositioning the flash so that it's not close to or directly above the lens prevents people from looking directly at the flash.

TIP

Photographers who mainly hold their cameras vertically know that when you attach an external flash to the camera's hot shoe, the flash sticks out to the side, not on top. Even if you can swivel the flash, it's no longer elevated. By putting the flash on a bracket, you can position the flash so that it works more like a traditional flash on the hot shoe. I think that's a great idea.

You need a short flash cord for this to work. Buy one that supports the features you need to work on your flash.

Cords galore

Not all of us can go wireless. For those photographers who are still physically connected:

>> **Sync cord:** One solution (it's getting rare) to connecting your camera to an external flash is to wire them together using *sync cords*. Not all flash units — nor all cameras — have sync cord sockets. Most often, you have to buy the most expensive unit a manufacturer makes to get one.

>> **Off-camera cord:** You can buy different types of cords that let you take your flash off the camera. Although technically they aren't sync cords, these cords serve the same purpose: Attach one end to the camera's hot shoe and the other end to the flash's mounting foot, as shown in Figure 3-15. Presto — they're connected. This type of cord is a workaround for not having a sync cord terminal on your flash and/or camera.

TIP

This setup is useful when I want to use fast shutter speeds with my external flash unit but want to position it off-camera. Wireless setups may not support the shutter speed you need.

Going wireless

When you move your external flash off-camera (whether wired with cords or connected wirelessly via infrared, optical, or radio signals), it's called a *remote flash* or *strobe*. Unless you're telekinetic, you're going to need a way to trigger your off-camera flash. Depending on your camera model and flash, you might be able to choose from one or more of these *remote triggering methods.* Make sure everything's compatible; not all cameras support all methods of off-camera flash and not all external flash units can be controlled in every way.

FIGURE 3-15:
Off-camera cords enable you to position the flash without going wireless.

REMEMBER

If your camera and flash are compatible, setting up a wireless shoot is *easy.* Set up the camera and flash to work wirelessly and make sure they're on the same group and channel. Within a few button presses, you'll be in business.

Wireless IR or optical pulse

Most midlevel and advanced flash units support one of two types of connectivity. Technically, they're different, but practically speaking, they act the same.

>> Wireless infrared (IR)

>> Optical pulse

REMEMBER

Check the manuals for your camera and external flash to make sure they use the same method. Wireless IR and pulse aren't compatible with each other.

Using either system is as easy as eating cake, and you don't have to buy anything extra to get it to work.

1. **Set up your flash on a light stand or a small flash stand.**

2. **Set up your camera and flash for wireless mode.**

    Both types of wireless units can only go so far (and bend at certain angles) from the camera.

3. **Make sure the flash and camera are on the same group and channel.**

Remember to consult your manual for specifics on how to check and change these settings. The group and channel assignment should be visible on the back of the flash unit. You'll have to find the camera's settings in the menu.

You can also buy a dedicated wireless transmitter, as shown in Figure 3-16. This unit replaces the built-in flash as the method of communication (with enhanced features), or provides the capability for cameras without a flash.

If you don't want your camera's built-in flash to affect the scene, but *do* want to use the built-in flash as a wireless trigger, consider buying an IR panel. These panels block the light from the internal flash but allow the infrared signal to pass and trigger the external unit.

FIGURE 3-16:
This is a dedicated wireless transmitter.

Wireless radio

You can try wireless radio remote flash triggers. In this case, transmitters send out radio signals that connect your camera with an external flash. Put the transmitter on your camera's hot shoe, and put the receiver on your flash unit. Third-party makers such as PocketWizard offer wireless radio. Camera manufacturers are following suit.

TIP

Radio systems can support multiple flash units as long as you have enough receivers, but wireless radios can get expensive the more flashes you have to control. Radio has a longer range and better placement options (it doesn't have to be in front of the transmitter) than wireless IR.

Wireless optical slave

This wireless option relies on a *slave unit* sensing the optical flash (in this case, you can see it; you can't see infrared or radio waves) from a *master* flash unit and then triggering the flash it's attached to. Figure 3-17 shows a strobe that can be triggered by another flash.

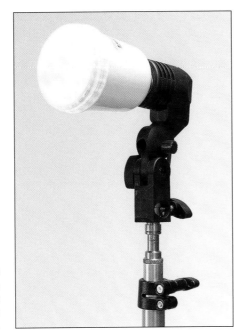

FIGURE 3-17: This slave strobe responds to a flash signal or a sync cord.

5

Managing and Processing Your Shots

Contents at a Glance

Chapter **1**

Transferring and Managing Photos

Photo management — yikes.

You probably bought a dSLR camera to *take* pictures, not to *manage* them. (I did.) I realized early on, though, that hundreds of photos quickly turn into thousands of photos and thousands multiply into tens of thousands. Photos are like rabbits, I tell ya!

At some point, you have to get serious and start laying down the law of photo management, which is the subject of this chapter. I show you which software to use, how to track your photos, and how to establish a big-picture workflow.

Getting a Workflow

Workflow is a hot topic in the digital SLR world because we can do much more with our creations than people who take photos with smartphones. We don't simply upload photos from our smartphones to Instagram. It begins with uploading photos from the camera to a computer, of course. Afterward, you can choose to organize, sort, rate, tag, process, edit, print, and archive photos.

A photography *workflow* has a couple of meanings. In a larger sense, it describes the process you follow as you work with your photos, beginning when you take them to when you're ready to archive them for long-term storage. *Workflow* also means the more limited process you follow to edit and publish your shots.

Workflow is a huge topic of debate, and the more detailed the workflow, the more people love debating it. Favorite topics include whether you should sharpen before you reduce noise or whether you should adjust brightness and contrast before you correct color. No universal workflow exists — all are based, in part, on opinion.

The following general workflow is a good one to start with:

1. **Set up the camera.** Your workflow starts with the decisions you make when setting up the camera to take photos. Your choices here affect later steps.

2. **Transfer (and import) photos.** Moving photos from your camera to the computer is to *transfer*. In many cases, this means simultaneously *importing* them into your photo management software. I like to immediately back up my photos after I transfer them to my computer.

3. **Manage.** Organize, sort, rate, geotag, filter, delete, and add keywords to your photos.

4. **Fast processing.** Quickly develop the photos that you think are worth keeping using a photo-processing application such as Adobe Lightroom. For example, you can make many photos look a lot better by tweaking brightness, contrast, and color, and making a few other basic adjustments. The idea is to spend a little time improving your photos and getting them printed or posted online. This step applies to Raw and JPEG images.

5. **Complex editing.** If you want to spend more time working on your photos, you can perform more complex work using a photo editor such as Adobe Photoshop. For example, you can make targeted adjustments with masks, mash up different versions of the same shot, exercise more control over removing dust and other distractions, and more. Some photos (especially HDR and panoramas) require special software.

6. **Publish.** The entire point of the workflow is to create materials worth publishing, such as a JPEG to place on your web page or Flickr photostream, or a high-quality TIFF file to print.

7. **Archive.** Back up the original photos. In addition, save any additional processing or editing you've done, either in the form of edited files or photo catalogs, in long-term storage.

REMEMBER

You can tailor this workflow example to suit your needs. In fact, you'll do a lot of tailoring, depending on several factors:

>> **Movies:** Do you need to change your workflow to work with movies that you've shot with your dSLR? That means more software and a substantially different editing and publishing process.

>> **Other people:** Do you have to fit into a process created by other people? Does someone else need to view or approve your work? Are you doing the approving?

>> **Time:** How much time do you have? Do you want to spend a lot of time or as little as possible per photo?

>> **Photos:** How many photos do you take? Must your workflow be able to handle tens of photos a week, or thousands?

>> **Hardware:** Do you have the camera and computer hardware to manage your workflow and run the software? Over time, of course, you will need to upgrade your system. Will you be working in an office/studio or on location? Weekend photo trips are fantastically fun. I like having a laptop with me to review photos and make backup copies. If you would rather travel light, take extra memory cards. You can preview photos on a TV, should you find yourself near one (in a hotel room, perhaps), so remember to take the correct cabling with you.

>> **Software:** What applications are you using? Are they current? Can they handle Raw files from your dSLR? Do you need anything else (panorama or HDR software, noise-removal plugins, other creative solutions)?

>> **Priorities:** In the end, deciding what to do (and what not to do) has a lot to do with your priorities. What's most important: speed, quality, compatibility, mobility, or something else?

The rest of this chapter walks you through each step.

Early Decisions

Your workflow begins with setting up your camera and taking photos. The most important decisions you have to make is what format, size, and quality you want the camera to record your photos in.

If you want more control over photo processing and editing, you should choose Raw or Raw+JPEG. Raw photos take the raw image data and store it so that you can use it later.

If you want a finished product right out of the camera, choose JPEG. JPEGs are created from the raw data, and then compressed to make them smaller. Unfortunately, the original data is lost in the process.

Think of it this way: Raw images are like negatives. You can develop them any way you like and print them later. JPEGs are like prints you get from the camera shop or kiosk. They're done. That's nice, but if you want to tweak the exposure or there's something about the color you don't like, it's much harder to correct. You won't get the same quality as if you were working with the original negative.

If you choose JPEG, you have a host of other decisions to make: the image size, quality, style, color, color space, orientation, aspect ratio, and so forth. You make these choices in-camera before you ever take the shot, and they are *final*.

Transferring Photos

Transferring (also known as *downloading* or *uploading*) photos and movies to your computer is a pretty simple process. You can transfer several different ways. Each has its pros and cons. Some methods require additional hardware, such as a card reader.

Connecting

Before you start transferring photos to your computer, you have to make a connection. This connection can be between your camera and a computer or, if you'd rather use a memory card reader, between the card reader and your computer.

Built-in Wi-Fi

Some digital SLRs have built-in Wi-Fi, which allows you to wirelessly upload photos to your computer or a smart device via a dedicated app. So cool, and about time. *Upsides*: No wires, no readers, no mess.

Downsides:

>> Not all cameras have built-in Wi-Fi.

>> Those that do may not support file transfer.

>> Wi-Fi can be difficult to set up, understand, and accomplish. I am pairing a Canon dSLR with my computer in Figure 1-1. This is just one of several involved steps required to get them to connect.

>> Wireless transfer uses battery power and may be slow, depending on your connection speed.

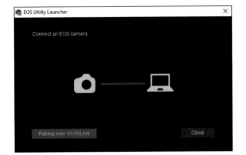

FIGURE 1-1:
Pairing enables the camera to connect to the Canon software.

Direct USB connection

Directly connecting your camera to your computer is the most straightforward, easy method. Connect your camera using the USB terminal, which is probably on the left side of your camera. *Upside:* The only thing you need, besides your camera, is the USB cable that came with the camera.

Downsides:

>> Your camera has to be on. If your battery is low and you have no backup, recharge the battery a bit so your camera won't die in the middle of a transfer. Should the camera power off, don't panic. The files on the camera should still be there. Simply recharge the camera battery and then restart the transfer. While the battery is charging, check the files that were transferred to make sure they are viewable. Delete anything on the computer that didn't transfer completely. If you were moving files, not simply copying them, you should check the file that was being moved for any damage by trying to view or edit it. The photos on either side of the power outage should be fine on both the camera and the computer.

WARNING

>> When you put your camera on a table and connect it to a computer (see Figure 1-2) with a cord that can be snagged, tripped on, pulled, or yanked (by you, your kids, your cats, or your dogs), you risk pulling the camera off the table. That will ruin your day.

Transferring and Managing Photos

FIGURE 1-2:
Secure your
camera when it's
connected to a
computer.

External USB card reader

External USB card readers take the camera out of the transfer equation. The card reader (see Figure 1-3) plugs into your computer. You feed the memory card into it and it handles the transfer. *Upsides:* You don't have to use your camera's battery and you don't have to worry about running out of juice in the middle of the transfer. You aren't endangering your camera. Also, if the card reader goes bad or gets broken, you can replace it quickly and cheaply.

Downsides:

» You have to either buy a card reader that handles multiple card types or buy a card reader for each type of memory card you have. (For example, the Sony A77 shown in Figure 1-3 can use either Memory Stick PRO Duo or SD cards, and other cameras may use different types.)

» External readers can litter your desktop. They also tend to fall off, forcing you to get on your hands and knees and look behind the computer to retrieve them.

» If you have multiple computers to transfer files to, you must either buy more card readers or move the one you have back and forth.

FIGURE 1-3:
Card readers that
can use different
card types are
very helpful.

Built-in card reader

Some computers and printers have built-in card readers. New iMac desktop computers, and MacBook Air and MacBook Pro laptops have built-in SD card slots. If you own a Windows computer, it might have come with an internal card reader. If not, you can install one. *Upsides:* Built-in models aren't as slippery as portable card readers, and can't fall off your desk.

Downside: Internal card readers aren't portable, unless you're using a portable computer.

Wireless file transfer adapters

For compatible cameras that don't have Wi-Fi, Canon's Wireless File Transmitter and Nikon's Wireless Mobile Adapter let you wirelessly transfer files from your camera to a computer or smart device (such as an iPhone). *Upside:* Get files off your camera when you want without tripping over cords.

Downsides:

» You have to buy more hardware.

» Wireless transfer sucks up lots of battery power.

Wireless memory card technology

An Eye-Fi card (www.eye.fi) transfers files from your camera to your computer. *Upsides:* It's portable, doesn't require additional hardware (beyond the memory card), is cool, and it gives you an unlimited amount of storage while you shoot.

Downsides:

>> Eye-Fi cards use your camera's battery to transfer, are slower than the other methods, and require a wireless network.

>> You have to install and set up software.

Downloading

After you've decided on a connection type, you choose a download method.

Automatic download

You can use a small computer program that automatically downloads the photos to the location you choose. Some are built into your computer's operating system. Others are extra software applications that come with your camera (such as Canon EOS Utility) or part of your image editor applications (such as Adobe Bridge or Lightroom). These programs often run in the background. They're ready to bounce into action the moment they sense a camera or card reader with a memory card has been connected. The programs normally have options for where photos are saved (plus folder names and whether to erase the photos from the card when you're done). I may be in the minority, but I can't stand these automated applications.

To choose a method, you must select the program you want to handle things when you insert a memory card into an external card reader or connect your camera to the computer, as shown in Figure 1-4.

The program you choose opens the next time you connect a memory card to your computer. As Figure 1-5 shows, my choice of Adobe Bridge opens the Bridge Photo Downloader.

Manual download

You can download photos yourself.

>> Drag the folder from the card reader to your drive and rename it.

>> Create folders for photos using your operating system and then select the photos and drag them to the appropriate folder.

I'm a hands-on kind of guy. I like to create folders and drag files myself, as shown in Figure 1-6. I organize my photos by camera and then by the date I downloaded them. I like being able to make a backup copy immediately.

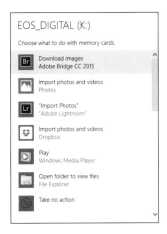

FIGURE 1-4:
Choose an auto import option from the operating system.

FIGURE 1-5:
Automatically download photos with Bridge.

FIGURE 1-6:
I like dragging and dropping files myself.

Transferring and Managing Photos

Getting a Grip on Your Pictures

Managing your photos involves finding the best way to name, store, edit, process, and keep track of the photo files on your computer. The more photos you have, the more you'll find it helpful to have a program assist you. I've split this section into several parts. One, which is quite short, discusses manual management. (Don't do it.) The next section is a software review. You should be aware of which software is available and know what each one can do. Although I can't describe single applications in depth, I can offer enough information to establish a general starting point as you decide where to spend your time and money. Knowing what you need and having a list of candidates is half the battle.

Manual management

If you like to start fires by rubbing two sticks together or you like to catch fish with your bare hands, this solution is right up your alley. File under R for ridiculous.

If you (or your spouse, significant other, special friend, or kids) feel the need to rename photos, tag and categorize them using a good organizer like Adobe Lightroom, I understand the need to make sense of things. It's hard to know what's what with a thousand photos named IMG_0641 through IMG_1641. If you must rename the files, make a copy of the photos to work on. Keep the originals somewhere safe and don't rename them.

Media management software

You have a lot of choices, ranging from pure media managers to applications that focus on Raw photo workflow and development. Plenty of basic photo editors have built-in basic management tools.

Adobe Bridge (see Figure 1-7) is one of the best (Adobe devotees would say *the only*) pure media managers. It's big, credible, versatile, well supported, and backed by a powerful company. Bridge is truly a bridge. It links your photos to your other applications in a way that lets you manage thousands of photos seamlessly. You can create and manage collections, rotate photos, apply different Camera Raw settings, and more from within Bridge, but you call on other applications to complete most development and editing tasks.

TIP

You don't buy Bridge by itself. Normally, it's included with a Creative Cloud subscription. You can download it for free using the Creative Cloud app.

FIGURE 1-7:
Bridge is a pro-
fessional media
manager that
has a great many
useful features.

Processing and managing software

This type of application focuses on photo processing and management. Photo enthusiasts can work with these applications, but they have features and capabilities that appeal to professionals, too.

Camera manufacturer software

Most camera manufacturers include free software that enables you to organize and process the photos you take with that camera. Canon calls its software Digital Photo Professional (see Figure 1-8). Nikon's free software is Capture NX-D. Sony's is Image Data Converter. Pentax ships Digital Camera Utility with its cameras.

I have dabbled with these applications in the past. They all have their strengths and weaknesses. Their main draw is that the same people who encode data into the camera's Raw file are the people who created the software that allows you to decode it. The camera manufacturer knows more about its files and proprietary settings than anyone else. If you are dedicated to a single brand and don't plan on changing, you should consider this approach.

FIGURE 1-8:
Digital Photo
Professional is
Canon's photo
management and
editing app.

Adobe Photoshop Lightroom

The most popular photo management and processing application is Adobe Photoshop Lightroom. It's moderately priced and available by monthly subscription. It's my tool of choice.

This Macintosh/Windows application is made for photographers. It has just about everything you need in order to import, manage, develop, and publish Raw and JPEG photos. Figure 1-9 shows the Library tab. (Look at all those cool photo-management tools.) From this tab, you organize, sort, tag, rate, select, and more.

In Lightroom, you can create a single massive, all-inclusive catalog or create different catalogs based on different cameras, projects, or years. When you import photos into an open catalog, they show up as thumbnails in the Library tab, where you manage them. You can view, sort, filter, rate, delete, search for, compare, create, and assign keywords, quickly develop photos, and edit metadata. You can also export photos in a number of different formats. I cover the Lightroom processing features (you can use them for JPEGs or TIFFs, if you want) in more depth in Book 5, Chapter 2.

TIP

To work with layers, masks, adjustment layers, artistic filters and effects, vector shapes, 3D support, text, frames, and other aspects unique to photo editors, you need to get a photo editor other than Lightroom.

FIGURE 1-9:
Adobe Photoshop
Lightroom is a
fantastic tool for
photographers.

Other applications

There are a host of other products available. This list is by no means all–inclusive:

» **Capture One:** Created by Phase One, Capture One isn't well known outside of professional circles, but it should be. Its bevy of management features are comparable to Lightroom. Import photos and then sort, rate, preview, organize, *tag* (add keywords to), develop, and publish them. Organize your photos in catalogs or work one-on-one with photos by using sessions. Capture One also has albums, which are virtual collections. I can't say enough good things about Capture One. It's fantastic, powerful, and professional, and it focuses on workflow and photo quality. Capture One Pro also has a very useful tethered shooting feature, which lets you control your camera from within the application and import the photos (and even apply processing to them) as you take them. It even supports Live View mode.

» **Google Photos:** Google's new photo organizer (with minimal editing tools) is called Google Photos. It replaces Picasa, which has been retired. All your photos are stored online and organized in albums. You have unlimited storage in the cloud for free.

» **Photos:** Apple has recently come out with its Photos app to replace iPhoto. It features photo editing and managing tools, and integrates seamlessly with the iCloud Photo Library. Import and organize photos, view, rate, tag, title, edit, and publish them. Photos is excellent for Macophile hobbyists.

Photo editors

This section lists three well-known photo editors.

Adobe Photoshop

Photoshop is the industry standard graphics editor. It has no photo management tools. Photoshop is available by subscription from Adobe, through Creative Cloud.

I used Photoshop for things that Lightroom can't do, or does poorly. I handle all basic image processing in Lightroom and, if necessary, export the photo to Photoshop to finish it. I can remove distractions from photos, create complicated layers to isolate adjustments to certain parts of the photo (the background, for example, or a person's face), apply creative filters, and more. Figure 1-10 shows that I've created several layers to handle different edits in this photo of a waterfall. Photoshop also opens and processes Raw photos with the help of Adobe Camera Raw.

Corel PaintShop Pro

PaintShop Pro (X9 is the latest version) is an all-in-one photo editor that feels a bit like a cross between Adobe Lightroom and Photoshop. You can manage, adjust, and edit photos using one application. PaintShop Pro supports Raw files from most cameras.

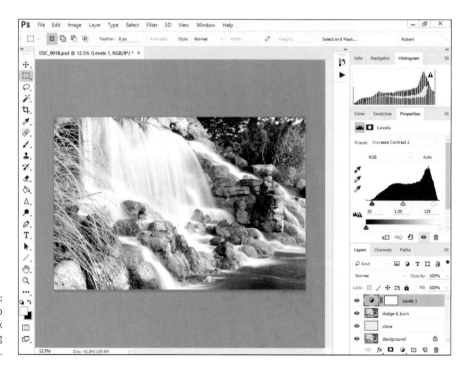

FIGURE 1-10:
Use Photoshop for more complex photo-editing tasks.

GIMP (GNU Image Manipulation Program)

GIMP is basically free Photoshop. Do you need more? Okay. The main drawback for photographers is the lack of built-in Raw support. If you need that, pass on GIMP. If you use JPEGs only and want to try out an advanced image editor with plenty of other features for free, give it a try.

Managing Photos

Get familiar with these management tasks as you try or invest in a particular piece of software. Think about how these tasks fit into your workflow:

» **Flagging** allows you to flag some photos as keepers, some as rejects, and leave the rest alone. I prefer to flag first, because it's faster and easier to tell if you want to work with a photo than it is to figure out if it's worth 4 or 5 stars. After you flag photos you may be able to hide photos in the interface by filtering non-flagged photos out.

» **Rating** allows you to rate your photos from one to five stars. Great if you need that level of discrimination. Once you rate photos, you can filter your collection by the number of stars a photo has.

» **Grouping** creates different structures to hold and organize your photos. It might be called a *library, catalog, project, album,* or *folder,* depending on the application. After it's created, you import photos into this structure, which keeps or separates one set of photos from another. That way, you don't have 10,000 pictures flopping around with no rhyme or reason.

» **Sorting** is when you identify a criterion, such as the date or time that you took a photo, or its filename, keyword, rating, or other EXIF data; the program sorts the photos or working files by that criterion.

- **Filtering** is similar to sorting, but weeds out photos based on the criteria you choose. You can make it so that you see only five-star photos, or those you took with a particular lens, or perhaps when the flash fired; all the rest are hidden.

- **Face Recognition** can be a great way to organize photos. If your photo management software supports this feature, you can use it to find photos of people, tag them with their names, and then use that information to search for or sort your collection.

- **Keywording or tagging** is a straightforward concept that's infuriating in practice. You tag every photo with descriptive keywords that help you organize, sort, find, and otherwise keep track of similar photos. The problem is coming up with a list of standard keywords and using them. For example, you might tag the same photo this way: 80D, landscape, f/8, sunset, Sigma, ultra wide-angle.

TIP

  Don't get too detailed when you're tagging.

- **Geotagging** identifies where a photo was taken. Most often, you identify where one or more photos were taken on a map and the coordinates are written to the photo file's *metadata* (helpful data, stored in the file, that isn't part of the photo itself; access it by looking at the photo's info with your operating system or photo program).

- **Stacking** different versions of the same photo on top of each other allows you to declutter the workspace.

Quickly Processing the Good Ones

Even casual photographers rarely have the time or need to process every single photo they shoot. Process good photos, not bad ones. Don't waste your time with them unless you have no other choice. You can find more details on how to quickly process your photos in Book 5, Chapter 2.

Advanced Editing When Desired

Many photos look fantastic when processed using applications like Lightroom. However, photo editors feature a different set of tools that open a world of advanced photo editing. These applications are optimized to work in layers, blend with opacity, use masks, and so forth.

Deciding whether you want to use a photo editor on some shots depends on finding the right balance for you. It takes extra effort, additional software, more time, and a certain amount of practice. However, you should know that many times it is very hard to perfect some photos without going this extra mile. I cover several advanced editing techniques in Book 5, Chapter 3.

Aside from the practical reasons, there are artistic benefits of using a photo editor in conjunction with your normal photo processor. I cover this aspect of using Photoshop in Book 5, Chapter 4.

Publishing

The process of exporting or saving your final files from your photo editor is called *publishing.* You might need to publish your work for any number of reasons: to print, upload to the Internet, send via email, or to use as a new desktop background. The sky is the limit.

General considerations

Read your software manual to find out the exact steps required to export or save your work. However, consider some general thoughts:

WARNING

>> **Preserve original material.** I can't stress this advice enough. *Never* save and overwrite original files. Always track names and versions so that when you select Save As, you aren't making a big mistake. JPEGs in particular suffer from *lossy* compression — they lose some quality every time you open, edit, and save them. If you're working with JPEGs, open, edit, and save as a *lossless* file type such as TIFF or a working format such as Adobe's PSD.

>> **Preserve working copies.** If you need to export your photo to an editor like Photoshop and create things like multiple layers, masks, and adjustment layers, do yourself a favor — save those working copies. If you *flatten* (compress all the layers into a single background layer) or delete them, you can't easily go back and change or update your work.

>> **Consider quality.** When saving and exporting, you'll have several file type and bit depth options. (You can read more about that in Book 5, Chapters 2 and 3.)

TIP

  • When emailing or uploading to the Internet, use JPEG.

  • When printing or archiving a high-quality copy, use TIFF.

» **Enter copyright and other descriptive information in metadata.** That's what metadata is for. If you publish your photos to the web, think about adding this hidden layer of protection to your photos.

» **Add a visible copyright or watermark.** This is another way to protect your photos. Whereas copyright and descriptive metadata are invisible, a watermark, mark, or copyright on a photo is visible for all to see. In Figure 1-11, I've created a copyright watermark in Lightroom that stamps my information in the lower-right corners of photos as I export them.

FIGURE 1-11: Adding a copyright watermark in Lightroom.

» **Strip metadata, if you want.** On the other hand, you may want to strip out any metadata to protect your secrets. Not all applications remove data, but you can save *copies* of final files to a format that doesn't have metadata and then open and save those versions to your final format.

» **Resize for the web.** Unless you want your full-size photos to be posted somewhere online, such as at Flickr or SmugMug, you should resize images to make them quite a bit smaller. On the web, 24 megapixels is serious overkill. (The *pixel count* is the total number of picture elements, or dots, in a photo; in this case, 24 megapixels stands for 24 million pixels.) Some sites may reduce the size of your photos anyway.

Resizing options

TIP

Pay attention to the resizing method you choose.

For example, Photoshop has these resizing options that appear on a drop-down menu in the Image Size dialog box (shown in Figure 1-12):

FIGURE 1-12:
Resize images to post on the web; no need for a 24 megapixel image on Facebook.

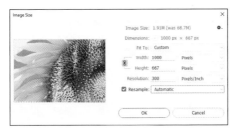

>> **Automatic:** Chooses the one Photoshop thinks will work best, based on the type of image you're resizing and whether you're enlarging or reducing it.

>> **Nearest Neighbor:** Preserves hard edges. Pay careful attention when you use this method. Examine the edges at 100 percent magnification to see whether the sharp edges cause jaggedness.

>> **Bilinear:** A good method in which colors are preserved and the image is smooth. You lose a bit of sharpness, however.

>> **Bicubic:** Works best for smooth *gradients,* such as a blue sky that transitions from dark to light; produces results similar to Bilinear, except a bit sharper.

>> **Bicubic Smoother:** Works best if you're enlarging an image. When you're reducing, this method looks almost indistinguishable from plain old Bicubic.

>> **Bicubic Sharper:** Works best if you're reducing an image. Distinctly sharper than all other methods, and much better than Nearest Neighbor. It produces sharpness without creating jagged edges. Still, pay attention to whether the level of sharpness suits your needs. If not, resize using Bicubic, and then come back and apply an Unsharp Mask and sharpen the image to the exact degree you want.

TIP

To display on the web, 800 to 1,000 pixels wide is a good start. That number is large enough to see detail yet doesn't produce a huge file size. Sites like Flickr accept the original photo sizes with no problem.

Saving and exporting

You often have plenty of detailed methods with which to publish photos. Choose the one that best fits your target media requirements. Table 1-1 summarizes several typical options.

TABLE 1-1   **Publishing Options**

Name	Description
Save As	Saves the file as a new type. Type a new name and choose other file options. Use instead of Save when you want to preserve a copy of your file or create a new type.
Save for Web	Saves a new file in a web-friendly format, such as GIF, JPEG, or PNG.
Export	Saves a copy of your file as a new file type. You can often change the image size, resolution, and attach color profiles when exporting. Some applications let you export data to other programs for further editing. If using a commercial printer, check to see if it prefers that you use this method, and what settings it suggests for your print.
Share	When set up with the proper username and password, this option saves your file online.
Print	Prints your photos on a printer connected to your computer or network.
Order Prints	Orders prints from a company. You will have to have an existing account or be ready to set one up and establish a payment method.

Figure 1-13 shows the Convert and Save dialog box from Canon's photo-editing application, Digital Photo Professional. Notice that you can change the image type, including the bit-depth, the resolution, resize it if you like, embed the color profile, and choose how much shooting information to leave in the file.

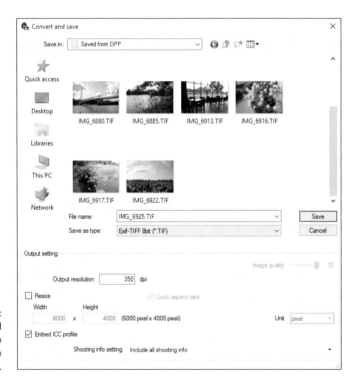

FIGURE 1-13: Converting and saving a photo in Digital Photo Professional.

TECHNICAL STUFF

On the other hand, you may be working in a professional environment where documents run through Adobe Bridge. You can publish PDF contact sheets or web galleries using the optional Adobe Output Module, which is installed separately from Bridge CC. If you use Lightroom or Photoshop, you'll likely print, export, or save archive copies from within those applications.

Archiving

Archiving preserves a copy of your photos (and working files) for long-term storage. Your digital photo collection is in some ways easier to safeguard than photo prints and negatives. The electronic files themselves are, for all intents and purposes, indestructible — as long as you ensure the safety of the media you store them in. You don't have to worry about prints getting bent or soaked with humidity, or about boxes of them occupying an entire room.

REMEMBER

Take time to plan your backup and archive process, and diligently carry out your plans. You can't throw a sleeve of negatives into a cardboard box and tuck them away in a closet.

Playing it safe

First, decide how you want to back up and archive your photos. You have to consider issues such as storage capacity, availability, and organization, in addition to the categories in this list:

WARNING

>> **Cost:** You want to pay as little as possible, but you have to strike a balance between being cost-effective and being simply foolish. Don't buy the cheapest (and possibly least reliable) equipment known to mankind to protect your valuable files.

>> **Capacity:** Digital photos and movies take up a lot of space. Choose a storage medium that fits your current and anticipated future workload. Table 1-2 lays out your options.

>> **Access:** Determine whether you can easily access your backups and whether an unforeseen circumstance (like a company going out of business and never updating its software) can prevent you from protecting your work.

>> **Security:** Assess your security situation to determine how safe (physically, and from a computer networking standpoint) the files are. Put the appropriate safeguards on your home or local network, such as Internet firewalls and password protection. In addition, files can be easily damaged if you store them at home and your house burns down. If that's your only backup copy, you've lost them.

>> **The future:** Consider how easy or hard it will be to transfer archived files from one storage device to another. For example, old hard drives may require a connection that will someday be obsolete unless you occasionally update your backup technology. In the very long term, provide *thumbnails* (small pictures) or a printed index or another form of inventory that, for example, your kids or their kids can easily figure out when you're long gone.

TABLE 1-2   **Archival Media Pros and Cons**

Media	Pros	Cons
CD-ROM/DVD-ROM	Data can't be erased; price per gigabyte isn't bad; no moving parts to the CD/DVD itself.	Limited capacity; most camera memory cards have more space; questionable media longevity.
Tape backup	Large capacity and longevity.	Cost for tapes, drive, and software; often uses file formats specific to one system; may require special software to back up and restore; can be "eaten" by disgruntled machines; data can be erased by strong magnetic fields. Feels like a 1980s solution.
Memory card or flash drive	Easy to use; doesn't occupy much space; no moving parts.	Cost per gigabyte makes for an impractical solution; would require 125 8GB digital camera memory cards to match the storage space of a single 1 terabyte drive.
Internal hard drive	Affordable; holds lots; fast; useful for temporary backups.	Moving parts; susceptible to crashing; difficult to swap in or out; data can be accidentally erased.
External hard drive	Affordable; holds lots; portability; can be stored off site; great for long-term storage.	Moving parts; not as accessible as an internal hard drive.
Solid State Drive (SSD)	Essentially a huge flash drive; no moving parts; exceptionally fast; can be internal or external.	Smaller capacity and higher price than normal hard drives, questionable longevity (yes, you read that right — SSD data degrades over time as you use the drive).
Network storage	Reliable, fast, networked RAID storage increases capacity, performance, and reliability.	Requires a network, must set up and administer, can be technically demanding, can crash, stored onsite.
Online/Cloud	The ultimate in off-site storage; no additional hardware needed; can be accessed from anywhere at any time.	Time and bandwidth required for initial backup; requires computer with Internet access; requires service subscription and an account in good standing; long-term viability depends on company health; vulnerable to unauthorized access, especially if you're famous.

Putting the plan into action

All the cool storage devices in the world are useless if you never use them. Have a plan for backing up and archiving your files. The key to making backups work is to develop a routine that matches the time and energy you're willing to invest. If the process becomes so laborious that you quit, it's worthless.

Follow these steps to walk through the type of plan I recommend, using a combination of extra *internal* (in your computer case; you'll have to install them yourself or find someone who knows how to do this) and *external* (sitting on your desktop in an enclosure of some sort) hard drives:

WARNING

1. **Complete an initial photo backup.**

   Back up new photos on internal or external (preferred) hard drives when you transfer photos and movies from camera to computer. You can't afford to lose the initial transfer. These files form the basis of your collection and can't be re-created.

   The mechanics of the initial backup are up to you. I simply copy and paste the photo folder to another location on an external drive. You may want to export photos from your photo-management software or use a backup program to copy a smaller bunch. This advice applies to each of the following steps.

2. **Perform a weekly internal (on your computer) backup of photo catalogs and working files.**

   Back up catalogs (which may contain the bulk of your adjustments) and any other working files to internal hard drives. If you can't afford to lose a single day's worth of productivity, consider daily backups. For a more relaxed timeline, back up catalogs, edited, and final files monthly.

3. **Perform an end-of-month external backup.**

   Back up everything to external hard drives, a file server, or a network. For a more relaxed timeline, back up quarterly or by project.

4. **Perform a biannual off-site backup.**

REMEMBER

   Create an off-site backup with all original photo files, catalogs, working, and final files. Put them in a storage barn on your property, rent a safety deposit box from a bank, or ask your grandparents to put them in their attic. Just make sure that they're physically separated from your computer and the building you're in. That way, if anything happens to your building, your photos and work files remain safe. For a more relaxed timeline, back up annually.

The plan I suggest may not work for everyone. One alternative, keyed toward a business environment, is to treat every job as a discrete unit and back up photos, catalogs and work files according to job number. When you transfer the initial photos, back them up. When you finish the job, back up everything and tuck things away on a hard drive devoted to that client. Depending on your workload and client list, you may have one hard drive for many clients or many hard drives for one client.

Chapter **2**

Quickly Sprucing Up Shots

N ot every photo that comes out of the camera looks as good as it can. Some aren't worth saving. Those that are can be made better with just a little effort. It's really not that hard to do, but it will improve your photography by a tremendous amount.

If you want to learn how to quickly spruce up your photos, this practical chapter is for you. I talk about how to decide what image quality settings to choose and how that decision will affect working with them in software, and then dive right in. I cover how to review and flag photos, how to get started developing them, then how to make brightness and contrast, clarity, color, and many other adjustments. The chapter concludes with a look at processing photos in the camera.

Software for Sprucing Up Photos

Whether you shoot and save Raw, JPEG, or both types of images, I recommend using an application like Adobe Photoshop Lightroom to manage and quickly spruce up your photos. Because Lightroom excels at making this part of the process painless and quick, I've chosen to feature it in this chapter. I use it as my main media manager and image processor, but I also shoot using many different makes and models of digital SLRs from several manufacturers. Having a standard application makes sense for me.

What Ligthroom *doesn't do,* which I lament at times, is give me access to certain camera functions that I can turn on or off in software. Canon's Digital Photo Professional, for example, allows you to change the strength of the Auto Lighting Optimizer setting, or disable it entirely. You can also change the Picture Style of Raw photos. You cannot perform these actions in Lightroom.

If you don't use Lightroom, don't panic. The processing principles that I outline in this chapter, as well as most of the details, are not wholly unique to Lightroom.

Feel free to experiment and try any software you like. Camera manufacturers support their cameras with software that helps you manage and edit your photos. Most are solid. There are also a number of other applications. You can find them by searching online.

Deciding on an Image Quality

The decisions you make when you set up your camera to shoot have an impact on the processing process. The main issue is whether to save your photos in JPEG, Raw, or both image formats.

If you plan to do more than tweak basic brightness and contrast, I encourage you to shoot in Raw. Raw image files have the best *raw photo data* that your camera can produce. Therefore, Raw images are considered the best *source material* with which to work.

When processing, JPEGs can't be pushed as hard as Raw photos before noise becomes troublesome. They simply have less information, which means you get to the noise sooner when turning things up. In addition, camera options like white balance, noise reduction, dynamic range limitations, color, and style are fixed in the JPEG and can't be edited or changed later.

REMEMBER

That fact doesn't mean that JPEGs are terrible. Absolutely not. You'd be very hard pressed to tell a JPEG produced from a Raw file versus one created by the camera, assuming the photo was well exposed and didn't need dramatic adjustments.

Benefits of Raw images

The advantages of shooting Raw images are numerous. Two of the most critical advantages follow:

» **Control:** When processing Raw images in software, you are in control of the process. Within certain bounds, *you,* not the camera, decide what goes into the JPEG or TIFF when you process a Raw file using software. When you change the white balance, exposure, color profile, and many other parameters during processing, you are simply interpreting the data differently. In the end, the JPEG file is a good end product, especially for web media. When taken right out of the camera, however, all the creative decisions that go into shaping the JPEG have already been made. By the time you look at it, the original data has been thrown out.

» **Flexibility:** When you process your camera's raw exposures into JPEG files, you still have the raw data to fall back on. You can reprocess them, if the mood strikes you, whether tomorrow, next week, or five years from now.

Challenges of working with Raw photos

Raw doesn't work for everything. There are costs associated with using the raw data files from your camera. If those costs outweigh the benefits for you, don't be afraid to move toward (or not change from) a JPEG workflow.

You may choose *not* to shoot Raw photos for these practical reasons:

» **Limited compatibility:** You can't throw up a Raw photo on Facebook or Instagram. Even if you can get them uploaded, people won't be able to look at them. You *have* to convert Raw photos to something like a JPEG to share them most places online. If you want to go from camera to the world in as few steps as possible, shoot JPEGs.

» **They take up space:** If your memory card is tight on space, you might not have the room to store Raw and JPEG files. Also consider how much hard drive space you're willing (and able) to use to store and work with photos. Raw files are much larger than even the highest quality JPEG your camera creates.

» **Slower shooting speed:** When you're shooting Raw, the camera simply has to move more data from the sensor through the processor to the memory card. You'll benefit from a faster *frame rate* (how many photos you can take per second) if you shoot and store JPEGs only.

TIP

» **Impact on processing time:** If you don't have the time to process Raw photos, JPEGs are your best solution. And remember, you can still edit JPEGs if you need to. Turn to the next chapter for more information.

If this is you, devote as much time as necessary in choosing between different JPEG processing options that your camera has. This is where you get to exercise limited creative control. You'll likely be able to adjust the photo's look by altering the Picture Control (Nikon), Picture Style (Canon), or Creative Style (Sony).

» **No need:** You may find that the JPEGs coming from your camera are just as good or better than what you can do yourself with Raw. If that's the case, use the JPEGs and don't worry about it.

Non-destructive editing

Raw workflow is more flexible than JPEG, because with Raw you don't make an adjustment, apply it, and move to another adjustment. Raw editors — and this includes import-to-final product photo managers and Raw processors like Lightroom — don't actually apply changes until you export the file.

For example, changes you make on the Develop panel are stored in the Lightroom database. The original files aren't affected, even if you crop the photo. You can press the Reset button at the bottom of the Develop panel to undo everything. You can also create virtual copies in Lightroom and compare alternative settings. Only when you export are the settings permanently applied to create the new file, and even then the original is left intact.

Getting Started

Your goal should be to take the photos you shoot and quickly make them look better using your photo software. I'm convinced that everyone can do this much. To get started, transfer the photo files to your computer (if you need help with this, turn back to Book 5, Chapter 1) and import them into your chosen application. As a reminder, I am using Lightroom to illustrate the general process.

Reviewing and flagging good photos

Whether you take 10, 100, or 1,000 photos a day, your first step toward sprucing them up is to realize something critically important: *You don't need to worry about them all.* That's right. Let the bad ones be bad and don't fuss over them. Spend your time making the good shots better. You'll be able to upload your prized shots to Facebook or tweet them far sooner if you work this way.

That means reviewing all the photos from a shoot, with the intended purpose of identifying the best shots. That may seem backward to you. I don't propose that you start at 350 and winnow out the bad ones so that you process what's left. That takes too much time and is, frankly, an unnecessary burden. Start your count at 0 and work your way up by flagging the best shots.

I'm reviewing photos in the Library tab of Lightroom in Figure 2-1. Except for the menu, which is off, I've got all the doodads and gizmos showing. You can show or hide each side panel, the Filmstrip on the bottom of the screen, and the Identity Plate/Module Picker at the top. If you use another application, it most likely has the same general elements that you see here.

FIGURE 2-1:
Reviewing photos in Lightroom's Library.

The first step I suggest you take is to rate photos with stars. That sounds great in theory, right? You have five levels to use. Rate your best shots with five stars, the next best with four, and so on. The problem with this is that haggling with yourself takes a tremendous amount of time and leaves you an emotional wreck. At this point, it's meaningless whether a particular photo is worth four or five stars. Heaven help the 1-star shots. All you really need to know is whether you want to post, print, or otherwise show it off. If the answer to that is yes, then it goes in the "good pile."

With Lightroom, use its Flag as Pick feature. Take a few seconds to look at each photo, and if the shot has "it," then flag it (see Figure 2-2). With this method, you're not rejecting photos; you're simply flagging the ones you want to work with. You may end up with four, seven, or more.

If you end up flagging the whole batch, reassess how you're choosing them. The only exception to this I can think of at the moment is if you want a ton of photos for a job or project and need volume. Otherwise, don't worry about limiting yourself.

FIGURE 2-2: Flag photos to identify the ones you want to work with.

After you flag the keepers, run through them again (see Figure 2-3) to make sure they qualify. If you've flagged photos that are close to identical, chances are you don't need both. If you don't have enough, go back to the collection and add more, if possible.

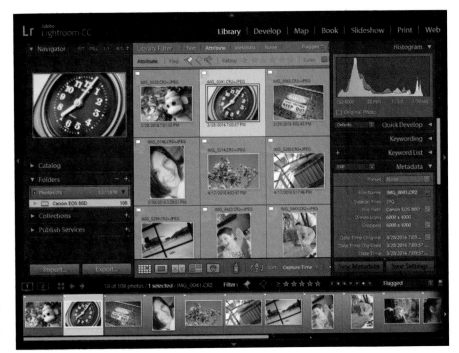

FIGURE 2-3:
Flagged photos
are identified by
a flag and can be
filtered.

I've got a secret. After you start, you'll realize that it doesn't take a whole lot of time to whip good shots into shape. Pass the bad ones over and don't worry about them.

Switching to the Develop panel

After you choose the photos you want to work on, switch to your application's Edit window. In Lightroom, this is the Develop panel, shown in Figure 2-4. The obvious visual difference between this and the Library panel is the appearance of controls on the right side of the screen. The navigation elements that were on the left have been replaced by panels suitable for image processing. I have turned off most of the additional panels and helpers that appear in the Develop panel for the rest of the chapter to focus on the photo at hand and the panel I want to describe.

While Lightroom suggests that you follow its panel order (Basic panel with white balance, tone, and "presence" first, followed by the other panels), you can work in any order you wish.

Quickly Sprucing Up Shots

FIGURE 2-4:
Developing
a photo in
Lightroom.

Setting the lens profile

The first thing I do is set the lens profile. This feature (see Figure 2-5) automatically corrects lens distortion and vignetting caused by the specific lens that took the photo. I've found that fixing this first always gives me a better photo to start with, and keeps me from having to make adjustments to fix distortion or exposure around the edges later. There are a couple catches: Lens correction data has to be available (which it is for most popular lenses) and you must be working with Raw photos (there is very little support for other formats). This feature is located on the Lens Corrections panel in Lightroom. Check Enable Profile Corrections, and identify the make of the lens, the model, and the profile.

Testing the waters

Next, I have a look in the Tone area of the Basic panel and click the Auto button. Lightroom evaluates the photo and makes the changes that it thinks will produce a photo with the best tonal range (from dark through bright) with as little highlight and shadow clipping as possible.

As shown in Figure 2-6, the results are sometimes great. I took this photo of a giraffe at our local zoo with a nice 300mm super telephoto lens and Nikon APS-C dSLR. It was a nice day, and the combination of the camera and lens created a great photo. In the end, it needed a bit more brightness and contrast, which Lightroom provided.

Of course, not every photo works as well as this one. Either way, I learn something. I may keep the settings and be done with it, or make a mental note of them to experiment with.

FIGURE 2-5:
Load the correct lens profile to automatically correct lens distortion and vignetting.

FIGURE 2-6:
Always check out the Auto button if your application has one.

Setting Brightness and Contrast

If you do nothing more to spruce up your photos, quickly tweak the brightness and contrast. It's simple and you don't have to have a degree in photography or photo manipulation to make your photos dramatically better. If you need a quick reminder about exposure and histograms, refer to Book 3, Chapter 1.

Adjusting the exposure

Lightroom's exposure control allows you to darken or brighten the photo. The numbers below it are f-stop equivalents, or EV. Negative numbers darken and positive numbers brighten.

Adjusting the exposure is sometimes a delicate dance. Raise or lower it until the photo looks right. Don't push exposure so hard either way that you blow out highlights or lose shadows. If you do, pull the control back. If you need to, rescue bright and dark areas of the photo with the highlights and shadow controls. Figure 2-7 shows a photo of my grandaunt Elouise and me taken a few years ago. I raised the exposure by 0.5 EV to brighten the photo.

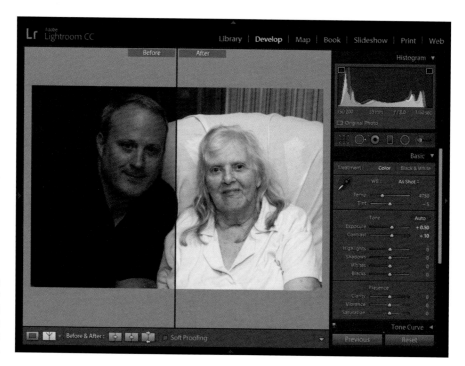

FIGURE 2-7: Brighten or darken photos using the Exposure control.

TIP

Carefully read the documentation that comes with your software. Some brightness controls compress highlights and shadows when they reach the edges of the histogram. This squeezes them together, limiting their range but preserving some detail. Others *clip* highlights to white and shadows to black when they reach the edge of the histogram, which essentially tosses data away.

See Book 3, Chapter 1 for more information on exposure and histograms.

Improving contrast

Overall, contrast is how far apart the middle-to-bright tones are from the middle-to-dark tones on the photo's histogram. Imagine two people standing near each other. That situation is comparable to a low contrast photo. There isn't that much difference between the tones. Imagine them standing farther apart. That situation is comparable to a photo having more contrast. There is a greater difference between the tones.

Experiment with the contrast control until the photo looks clear and well defined. Normally, photos with too little contrast appear to have a gray sheen on them. It dulls them, as shown in Figure 2-8. In this case, you can see the Before side is not as clear as when I increase the contrast. The cookies, plate, table, and bowl all look better.

FIGURE 2-8: This photo appears to have a gray sheen on it because it has too little contrast.

However, photos with too much contrast have shadows that are too dark and highlights that are too bright, with few mid-tones to connect them.

Protecting highlights and shadows

Normally, you want bright areas in photos, but you want to keep them from becoming so bright that they are a featureless sea of white. Likewise, you want dark areas in your photos, but you don't want them to be featureless black. I say featureless to emphasize the point. Uniform areas of white or black literally have no features, or details.

One way to protect them is to target them with highlights and shadows adjustments. This approach works best with Raw photos, because they have a greater dynamic range than JPEGs. This fact enables you to pull highlights back and bring shadows into a tonal range that fits into the histogram.

I've done just that with the photo in Figure 2-9. I chose this shot because it's a challenging scene and shows blown highlights caused by the setting sun and overly dark shadows in the trees in the original photo. Lightroom identifies these areas in red (highlights) and blue (shadows) to make it easier to tell when things are going wrong.

FIGURE 2-9:
It's important that you try to keep most highlights and shadows from clipping.

I made several adjustments to this photo to improve the exposure and color. In the end, I lowered the Highlights setting by a whopping 95 and increased the Shadows control by 40 to keep these areas from clipping. You'll find that many elements of exposure are connected, and that you may need to come back to these controls after making further adjustments.

TIP

You don't have to eliminate all bright or dark pixels. Bring them into balance so that the photo looks good.

Setting the black and white points

Lightroom has two more important tone controls that enable you to adjust brightness and contrast: Whites and Blacks. These are clipping controls. They adjust the white and black points in the image, which is to say, where clipping occurs. Highlights and Shadows adjust the brightness of the photo. The Whites and Blacks controls set the boundaries. In effect, you're saying "This is where white actually is" or "This is as dark as it gets" when you use the controls.

The effect of sliding them left and right is to darken or lighten the photo, but don't use them for that. Instead, drag them to expand or reduce the overall tonal range of the photo so that it fits nicely within the histogram. I did that on the foggy landscape scene in Figure 2-10. Note that I didn't change the brightness or the contrast of this photo, and yet it's brighter and has more contrast. Curious, isn't it? The result was caused by the fact that white tones are now whiter and the black tones are blacker.

Improving clarity and removing haze

Lightroom has two more controls that affect clarity and contrast of your photos: Clarity and Dehaze.

Clarity increases the local contrast of the photo by making edges stand out. I find that this makes photos look sharper and have greater detail (see Figure 2-11). Reducing it makes the photo look dreamy, softly focused, and misty. Be careful when increasing clarity on photos of people, as too much local contrast makes shadows on faces look very unattractive. Lightroom puts the Clarity control in the Presence section of the Basic panel, right above Vibrance and Saturation.

Lightroom has another interesting control called Dehaze. This feature enables you to add or subtract haze and fog from your photos. When it's used judiciously, I find it a great feature to use on outside shots that have plenty of blue skies and water, as shown in Figure 2-12. One minor point: The control works in reverse. Increasing Dehaze decreases 'de haze. Decreasing Dehaze increases 'de haze. Got that?

FIGURE 2-10:
Set white and
black points to
set the tonal
range of the
photo.

FIGURE 2-11:
Use Clarity to
emphasize
details with local
contrast.

FIGURE 2-12:
Use Dehaze to improve scenes with lots of blue sky and water.

Correcting and Improving Color

After making lens, brightness, contrast, highlights, shadows, clarity, and haze adjustments, I move on to color. I do things in this order because color is more subjective. Not every white balance or saturation adjustment is necessary, while getting the brightness correct seems fundamental. Therefore, I like nailing down exposure first.

Checking the white balance

Quite often, white balance is just fine. You only have to worry about it if you see something out of place. After you adjust the photo's brightness and contrast, you can better troubleshoot color.

Once again, Raw photos have the advantage over JPEGs. When you set the white balance in your camera, it appends your choice to the Raw data as a suggestion. The actual data is left alone. Software uses the setting to interpret the scene and display the photo. That means you can change the white balance setting to another preset in Lightroom, or decide on a specific color temperature yourself, using the original data.

If you shot only JPEGs, however, the camera used your white balance setting and processed the color accordingly when it saved the photo as a JPEG. While you can reinterpret it in software, you've lost the original data. I don't mean to sound overly dramatic. It's just that you have less wiggle room when adjusting the white balance of a JPEG.

Figure 2-13 shows the White Balance Selector over an area of a One Way sign that should be white. It's not. As you can see from the detail loupe, the RGB value is imbalanced. There is not enough red and too much blue. If this were white, they would be the same (or very close). Clicking this spot corrects the entire photo.

FIGURE 2-13: Adjust white balance by choosing a neutral spot in the photo.

Adjusting color vibrancy and saturation

These simple controls boost or cut color intensity. *Vibrancy* raises or lowers the saturation of weak colors, while *saturation* strengthens or weakens all colors. I've used a combination of both to enhance the color of a sunset in Figure 2-14.

FIGURE 2-14: Control color strength with vibrancy and saturation.

TIP

I like saturated photos. As I raise it, however, I'm careful to not make noise more visible or blow out highlights. Turning up *most things* while you edit or process runs these risks. When possible, I increase vibrancy first to see whether it does the trick. Vibrancy is more forgiving because you're not turning up all colors, just the muted ones.

Making Additional Improvements

After you get the basics under control, you should begin to look at more advanced photo editing. You may not need or want to apply every technique mentioned here.

>> **Sharpen:** Everybody likes sharp-looking photos. Factors such as the quality of your lens, focus, camera stability, shutter speed, and distance clearly have a large effect on how sharp a photo can be. Within those bounds, you can sharpen photos quite a bit. Figure 2-15 shows the Sharpening controls in the Detail panel of Lightroom.

Quickly Sprucing Up
Shots

TIP

If the photo has serious sharpness problems, try reshooting it with a better technique or leave it for editing, where you can use more sharpening techniques. Don't oversharpen photos. It makes the edges look artificial and makes noise more obvious. Oversharpening can also increase the appearance of noise in a photo.

» **Noise reduction:** Similarly, most raw converters have some form of noise reduction. Many let you reduce noise in the Luminance channel and/or the photo's color channels. Figure 2-15 also shows the Noise Reduction controls in Lightroom.

FIGURE 2-15:
Sharpen and reduce noise when necessary.

WARNING

Too much noise reduction removes a great deal of a photo's detail. If it's too much, try backing off. Third-party noise reduction *plug-ins* (small add-ons that provide new or better features to the software you're using) can give you more control over noise reduction and the ability to protect or sharpen details. You can also selectively reduce noise by using layers or masks in a photo editor.

» **Correcting perspective distortion:** Pointing the camera up makes vertical lines converge toward the top of the photo. This is called *vertical perspective distortion*, or vertical distortion. It happens most often when you photograph a building or something tall and you have to look up to get the whole structure in the shot. *Horizontal perspective distortion*, or horizontal distortion, happens when you angle the camera sideways as you take a shot. Horizontal lines run at an angle instead of being parallel to the frame or ground. Figure 2-16 shows the Transform panel in Lightroom where you can correct any distortion.

My point in this chapter is to give you the basics. Remember that many other features in most photo-editing applications enable you to perfect your photos. Aside from the basic controls I've mentioned, Lightroom has quite a few more features, controls, and options. While having them is great, don't think that you have to use them all.

FIGURE 2-16:
Correct perspective distortion using the controls in Lightroom's Transform panel.

Finishing Up

When everything else is finished, I straighten and crop the photo, if necessary, and then export it as a JPEG or TIFF.

Straightening and cropping

I prefer to straighten and crop photos last. That way I know I have all my other adjustments in the bank and can take my time deciding whether the photo needs anything else.

When I straighten and crop, I always keep in mind that my goal is to improve the final photo. Some photos don't need to be straightened or cropped. They look fine as they are. Don't think that you have to straighten every photo that is a half-degree out of perfect. You don't. However, if the alignment causes a distraction, you should try fixing it.

Figure 2-17 is a shot of my wife and daughter. We were playing Uno on the picnic table and I had my camera with me. I took this shot without thinking about the background too much. You can see an old computer case and shelf in the garage. While I can't get rid of everything, I can improve the photo by cropping those details out, and rotate them a bit so that they appear level.

FIGURE 2-17:
Rotating and cropping is about improving the final presentation of the photo.

Be aware that as you straighten photos, you lose the original corners. How much depends on how badly the shot is aligned in the first place.

Exporting images

REMEMBER

This isn't an editing task, but I do want to mention it: In Lightroom, you don't have to do anything to save or close files. After you're done developing a photo, you can select another one from the Library or another module. You can export a photo anytime.

Figure 2-18 shows the Export dialog box. I've created a preset called JPEG-1K Min with the settings I like to use to export a reduced-size JPEG. I save it to my desktop, resize it, strip all the metadata, apply a copyright, and use a watermark.

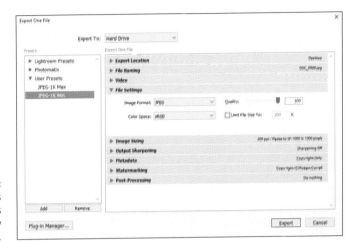

FIGURE 2-18: Export presets speed things up dramatically over time.

Processing Photos In-Camera

More and more dSLRs come with snazzy built-in raw processing tools that you can use at the spur of the moment and with a touch of a button. This development isn't limited to a particular price point, either. For example, the professional-level Pentax K-1 and the consumer-level Canon T6i both have impressive in-camera raw image processing (sometimes called *retouching*) options.

Canon cameras enable you to change brightness, white balance, picture style, and Auto Lighting Optimizer settings; turn on high ISO speed noise reduction; set the desired JPEG image quality and color space; and correct peripheral illumination, lens distortion, and chromatic aberrations! Not bad at all.

Nikon cameras have similar options: Change the image quality, size, white balance; adjust exposure compensation; change the Picture Control settings; turn on high ISO noise reduction; change the color space; and change the D-Lighting settings.

I'm going to use the Canon EOS 80D as an example. Here's how easy it is to process Raw photos and turn them into new JPEG images:

1. **Select RAW Image Processing from Playback menu 1, as shown on the left in Figure 2-19.**

2. **Choose a photo you want to process, as shown on the right in Figure 2-19.**

   Believe it or not, we heard a plane overhead just the other day. It seemed close, and wasn't going away. We decided to run out to see it, and discovered that it was skywriting. That's not something you see every day, and when you're writing a book on digital SLR photography, well, you run back into the house and grab your camera.

   After finishing (practicing, we think) some letters that seemed to make no sense to us, the pilot made a few smiley faces. So that's the story behind these figures.

3. **Select an adjustment you would like to make, as shown on the left in Figure 2-20.**

4. **Make the adjustment, as shown on the right in Figure 2-20.**

   In this case, I'm increasing the brightness by 1/3 of a stop.

5. **Save the photo, as shown in Figure 2-21.**

   The camera creates a new JPEG image from the raw data, gives it a new name, and stores it on the memory card.

Chapter **3**

Digging Deeper into Photo Editing

W hile this chapter is mostly optional, I encourage you to have a good look at it. I can't tell you how many times I've worked on photos in Photoshop *after* I processed them in Lightroom. In a perfect world, that wouldn't be necessary.

That's not to say this chapter is drudgery. I have a ton of fun using Photoshop. So much that I've thought about creating a YouTube channel that features me using the Clone Stamp tool for hours on end. It's creative, and yet it fills me with a down-to-earth sense of accomplishment that I thrive on.

So, have fun with this chapter. Don't approach it too seriously. I want to share some techniques that I use to make my good photos better. I don't load bad photos into Photoshop to try to rescue them. Those shots never make it past the initial flagging phase of my operation. Based on what you see here, come up with your own system.

Software for Editing Photos

As with the other chapters in this section, I must make an announcement about the software featured in this chapter before getting started. I'm using Photoshop CC to show tips and tricks on how to edit your photos in ways that are hard or impossible in applications like Lightroom.

It wasn't a hard choice, really. Photoshop is the premier photo editor and has been for many years. Although there are competitors, because Photoshop itself is available at a reasonable rate, there really is no reason to use another program. If you have Photoshop Elements, PaintShop Pro, or another app, you'll find most or all of the techniques I share translate with a minimum of fuss.

One final caveat: I assume you're using an app like Lightroom to perform most tasks required to get your photos into shape. Therefore, I don't cover issues like correcting exposure, contrast, and so forth in this chapter. If you want to investigate those issues, turn to Book 5, Chapter 2. There is always some crossover, of course, but I want to focus on things that are more suited to using an editor. By and large, use these techniques to make good photos better. Don't waste your time on bad stuff.

Dealing with the Mundane Stuff

I've written this section to address some of the housekeeping chores that support the features in Photoshop that I use in this chapter.

Creating a Photoshop file

Creating a Photoshop file begins, oddly enough, in Lightroom (or your photo processor of choice). Spruce up your best shots first. Ideally, you won't even need to mess with them in Photoshop. If that's the case, export them as JPEGs and put them up for people to see.

When you want to open a photo in Photoshop, you can take one of several different paths. I typically export a full-sized 8-bit TIFF with the AdobeRGB color space so that I have a file that I can see on my system. I then drag and drop the file onto Photoshop's workspace.

However, there are actually more efficient ways of doing this. Such as by choosing Photo➪Edit In➪Adobe Photoshop CC, as shown in Figure 3-1. If you've chosen a Raw file, it opens directly in Photoshop. If you have chosen a JPEG or other format, the Edit In menu has a few more options if you want to explore them.

Choose Edit➪Preferences and select the External Editing tab (see Figure 3-2) to view and change the settings Lightroom uses to send photos to Photoshop. It defaults to a compressed 16-bit TIFF at 300 dpi and with the ProPhoto RGB color space. That's a bit much. All you really need is 8- bits with the AdobeRGB color space. I prefer uncompressed TIFFs, but compressed TIFFs are smaller.

FIGURE 3-1:
Sending a photo to Photoshop to edit from within Lightroom.

You can also export your photos in Photoshop's PSD file format. I prefer TIFFs because I like seeing their thumbnails on my system, but you may not need that.

When you get the file open in Photoshop, save it by choosing File ⇨ Save As. Change the type to Photoshop (PSD). Choose a location and change the name if you like, and that's it.

Helpful Photoshop features

Photoshop has so many cool features that it would be impossible to even mention them all, much less tell you anything about them. However, you should be aware of a few key elements of the application that will help you edit photos. They are

>> **Panels:** The Photoshop interface is covered with panels. You can turn them on and off when needed, but you'll normally want the Tools, Properties, and Layers panels visible at all times.

FIGURE 3-2:
Lightroom
has several
preferences
that affect how
files are sent to
Photoshop.

>> **Tools:** Photoshop has a Tools panel on the left side of the interface. This is where you select tools like the Eraser and Marquee. Most have a keyboard shortcut. You won't need all the tools when you work with photos, but I typically need one or more of the selection tools, the Eraser, the Clone Stamp, and the Dodge and Burn tools.

After you select a tool, you can change parameters like brush size and hardness from the Options bar near the top of the screen. Then it's off to work.

>> **Keyboard shortcuts:** Photoshop is famous for its keyboard shortcuts. If you find yourself using a particular tool or feature all the time, learn the keyboard shortcut. It saves you a lot of time and hassle. My favorites are S for the Clone Stamp tool, M for Marquee, V for the Move tool, Spacebar to switch to the Hand, and Ctrl+Alt+Shift+E/⌘+Alt+Shift+E (Win/Mac) to merge visible layers to a new layer.

>> **Layers:** Layers make working with photos in Photoshop worth it. While most other features are available in Lightroom and other photo-processing applications, layers are the realm of photo editors. Layers allow you to stack changes on top of each other, blend them in different ways, and even organize and track your work.

>> **Adjustments:** Adjustments are the tools you use to alter brightness, contrast, color, and so forth. They come in two flavors: direct, which are applied

permanently to a normal layer, and adjustment layers, which are non-destructive and can be edited. I prefer the latter.

» **Masks:** Masks hide parts of layers and allow material beneath to show through. This feature makes many sophisticated editing techniques possible. You can sharpen the layer you're working on, for example, and mask out areas you don't want altered. The unsharpened photo beneath shows in the masked areas.

Coping with color management

Color management can be a tricky concept. Normal photo files have what's called a color profile. Color profiles help hardware like monitors and printers accurately reproduce the colors in the file to the best of their ability. That last part is key. Not every piece of hardware has the same abilities. As a result, a limited color profile was created that would work with just about anything. It's called sRGB and it has essentially gained default status.

The sRGB color profile works with everything you'll likely view, edit, or print your photos on. Although it has a smaller *gamut,* or total range of colors, it is essentially foolproof. I set my camera to save JPEGs in this profile. When I save photos for use on the web, I always select this profile for the final JPEG.

The AdobeRGB color profile defines a wider color space and is technically better than sRGB, but there's no guarantee it will work where you need it to. I work with my photos in Photoshop with this profile. I also send files to the printer in AdobeRGB. The last step in my process when saving a file as a JPEG is to convert the color profile from AdobeRGB to sRGB. It stinks, but it's necessary.

There are more color profiles available, but you don't really need to mess with them. Lightroom can use ProPhoto RGB, which has an even wider gamut than AdobeRGB.

One quirky thing to remember before moving on: Raw exposures don't pick up a profile until you convert and export them as a TIFF or JPEG.

Saving your final images

I prefer saving my working file in Photoshop (PSD) format for safekeeping. When you want a final image to print or post, convert the color profile and crop if necessary, and then flatten the image before saving as a JPEG or TIFF. I prefer naming my final versions with "-final" appended to the name. This keeps the versions straight.

Dodging and Burning

Dodging and burning are two (dangerous-sounding!) techniques that you can use to lighten *(dodge)* or darken *(burn)* areas with a brush. I use these tools to subtly elevate brightness in areas I want you to look at, to darken areas for drama, or to balance the photo.

TIP

When dodging and burning, I create a duplicate layer of the photo to dodge and burn on. It allows me to preserve the original photo and blend with opacity if I choose to.

After duplicating the layer, select the Dodge or Burn tool, choose a brush size and hardness, and then select a range. The Range option lets you target specific tones in the image: shadows, midtones, or highlights. All you do is brush it on, as shown in Figure 3-3.

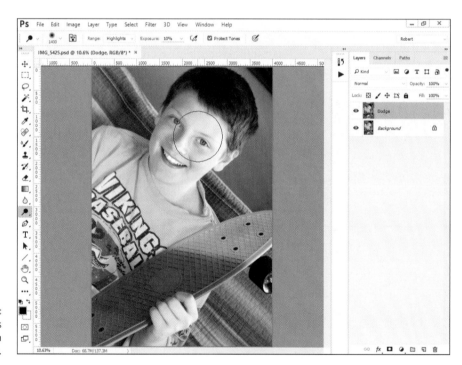

FIGURE 3-3: Dodge faces to brighten them a bit.

Dodging and burning work well to *emphasize* rather than correct. In other words, I dodge to brighten highlights in clouds, on water, or elsewhere to accentuate those elements. Quite often, I burn shadows (see Figure 3-4) or midtones for the opposite effect.

FIGURE 3-4:
Boost contrast
with a little
burning.

Using High Pass to Sharpen

While I generally prefer light sharpening in Lightroom, I sometimes forego it in favor of a technique known as High Pass Sharpen. Here's how to do it:

1. **Duplicate the layer you want to sharpen.**

2. **Choose Filters⇨Other⇨High Pass.**

    The High Pass dialog box opens, as shown in Figure 3-5.

3. **Select a radius, in pixels, and click OK.**

    You can think of this as a strength control. I generally choose something around 3 or 5 for light sharpening, or up to 10 for more, but it does depend somewhat on the size of the image. Photos from cameras with vastly different pixel counts behave differently. Experiment with your photos to see what you prefer.

    The layer will look odd. That's okay. Working as intended.

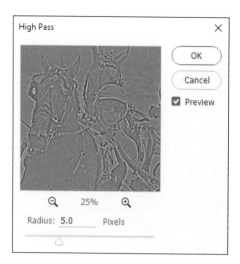

FIGURE 3-5:
Increase the
radius for a
stronger effect.

4. **Change the Blend mode of the sharpened layer to Overlay (see Figure 3-6).**

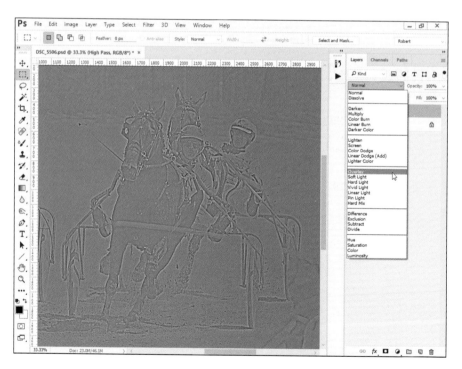

FIGURE 3-6:
Don't forget
to change the
blend mode.

5. **Adjust the strength further by lowering the opacity of the sharpened layer (see Figure 3-7).**

   You can also mask out different areas you don't want sharpened.

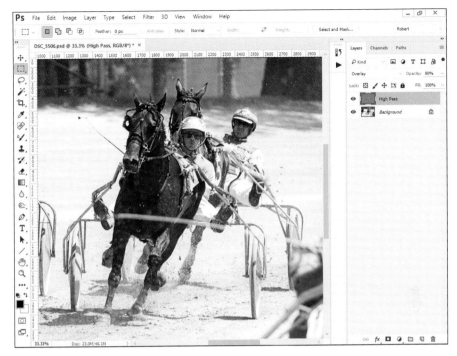

FIGURE 3-7:
I blended the
effect by slightly
reducing the
opacity of the
High Pass layer.

Making Minor Adjustments

Don't be afraid to make minor adjustments to brightness, contrast, and color. It's most effective if you use an adjustment layer to accomplish these tasks. When needed, I prefer these:

>> **Brightness/contrast:** If the photo looks like it needs a dab of brightness or contrast, toss a Brightness/Contrast adjustment layer on top. Tweak accordingly.

>> **Levels and curves:** These are more complicated adjustments but they are very effective at altering brightness and contrast (see Figure 3-8). Play around with the presets and experiment with the controls. They also can correct color imbalances by setting the white and black points of the photo.

>> **Vibrance:** Shabby or dingy colors make things look dull or prematurely aged. Give your photo a shot of color with the Vibrance/Saturation adjustment layer. Conversely, overly bright colors can be hard to look at. If that is the case, tone them down.

>> **Photo filters:** I like photo filters. They're the digital equivalent of physical filters that you put in front of your lens to filter certain types of light or ambiance. Book 3, Chapter 5 talks more about physical filters. The options in the Photo Filter dialog box are intuitive: Choose a filter type based on the description or a solid color, and then choose a density.

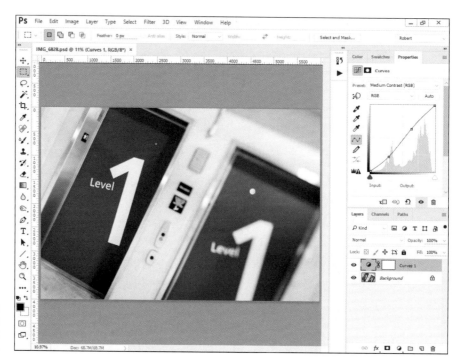

FIGURE 3-8:
Don't hesitate to tweak things a bit in Photoshop.

Applying Changes Selectively with Masks

If you don't need to sharpen an entire photo, don't. Likewise, if you only need to brighten the sky, keep your adjustments to that area and leave the rest alone. How? Masks.

Masks enable you to apply changes to selective areas of photos. I positively love using masks. They give you the freedom to repair, correct, or enhance specific areas of a photo without unnecessarily altering the entire thing.

I used two masks on the photo of my daughter in Figure 3-9. I darkened the background a bit with a Levels adjustment layer and increased contrast a small amount with the Curves adjustment layer. I used the mask on both layers to isolate the adjustments to completely different areas of the photo.

Adjustment layers are created with white masks, which have no effect. To mask out areas and prevent them from being affected by the adjustment layer, select the adjustment layer mask from the Layers panel and then paint black on the canvas over the areas you want to hide using the Brush tool (size it according to the area you want to paint). You'll see the mask update in the panel. Press the Backslash key to toggle the mask on or off as a rubylith overlay.

FIGURE 3-9:
Use masks to target adjustments to specific areas.

Mashing Up Versions of the Same Shot

I include this technique as a kind of last resort. I would not go to this trouble ordinarily. However, there are times when you just can't get a photo to shine the way you know it can by using a version developed as a whole. To wit: Create at least one virtual copy of the original photo in Lightroom. Process each one differently, according to the needs of different areas of the photo.

Quite often, this technique is helpful when working with a bright sky and a dark subject or foreground. Figure 3-10 shows a nice photo of a pasture in Oklahoma that I photographed near sunset. I could get the foreground to look good, or the sky, but not both. So I created a virtual copy and made two sets of adjustments. I exported them both and created a file in Photoshop to blend them together. Figure 3-10 shows the photo optimized for the green pasture and trees. The upper layer is turned off.

FIGURE 3-10: Load your photos into Photoshop and arrange them.

Figure 3-11 shows the upper layer turned on. The effect is dramatic. I used a mask to hide the foreground in the top photo, so the bottom layer shows through. Remember, this is the same photo. I didn't montage two shots together to create this effect.

FIGURE 3-11:
Mask out areas
on a photo that
you want to hide.

Stamping Out Imperfections and Distractions

It's not always possible to keep imperfections and distractions out of photos. While I don't necessarily encourage you to obsess over every aspect of every photo you take, covering up some imperfections or objects with nearby material is an effective way to improve your shots. The general process is called *cloning* because the tool you'll use most often in Photoshop is the Clone Stamp. The Spot Healing Brush and Healing Brush are two other useful cleaning tools. If you can handle the Clone Stamp, you can surely figure those out on your own.

Dusting and cleaning

Dust shows up as a big blob in your photo. It's most noticeable in the sky, but also appears in other light, evenly toned areas. To remove a dust spot or another small imperfection, follow these steps:

1. **Create a new layer above the photo background.**

   This is purely my preference. You can clone right on the photo layer if you want, but if you do, mistakes are far harder to correct.

2. Select the Clone Stamp Brush.

If cloning on a separate layer, make sure that the Sample is set to Current & Below. This enables you to select a sample from a layer beneath the one you are brushing on.

3. Configure the brush.

Specify a size large enough to cover the dust. In this case (see Figure 3-12), the brush is 220 pixels in size. I prefer using a hardness of 0% when cloning dust. The soft brush blends the new material very effectively. If you're cloning over textured areas and you can see your brush strokes, you may want to increase the Hardness.

4. Select a sample area.

Press Alt/Option (Win/Mac) and click an area with matching color, lightness, and texture. In this case, I selected a nearby area of the sky. Note that you may have to resample several times to get the tone just right.

FIGURE 3-12:
Matching the tone of the sample and destination is the hardest part.

5. **Paint over the dust spot.**

If you see that things aren't matching, undo and try again. If you've gotten a good match, you'll never know there was a dust spot there to begin with. Figure 3-13 shows the final version of my photo.

FIGURE 3-13:
The Clone Stamp is fantastic at removing dust and blemishes.

Removing other distractions

Dust isn't the only distraction you might want to remove from your photos. Other objects can divert attention from your subject or make the scene less than desirable. Figure 3-14 shows some unsightly light posts that take attention away from an otherwise gorgeous fountain. I am in the process of removing the left post in the figure.

TIP

Regularly select a new sample area to hide your work. Mix it up, but pay attention. If the texture and tones don't match, the replacement will be visible. You want it to be hidden, and you don't want features to repeat. Figure 3-15 shows the final result of this small section of the photo.

FIGURE 3-14:
Distractions like these light posts are fairly easy to remove.

FIGURE 3-15:
It's like they were never there.

Improving complexions

Another type of imperfection relates to complexion. I don't give my subjects total makeovers, but I routinely remove minor blemishes. The thing you have to be most careful of is matching the tone of the surrounding skin. The face is a wonderfully complex shape, full of curves. That makes it hard sometimes to remove zits without being obvious. I prefer to use the Clone Stamp, but the Spot Healing Brush is effective when the blemishes are not all packed together. Figure 3-16 shows an area with a handful of blemishes. I've created my separate layer and have the tool set up.

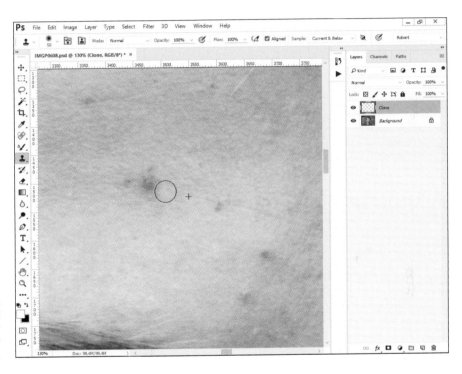

FIGURE 3-16:
People will thank you for improving their complexions.

Figure 3-17 shows the final result. While I tried to remove the most noticeable blemishes, I didn't try to smooth the skin and turn this into a glamour shot. I prefer to leave it as real as possible.

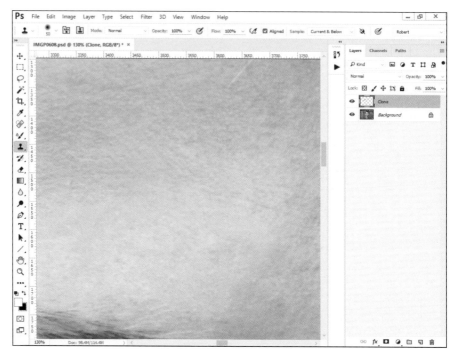

FIGURE 3-17:
The focus is
on the person
now instead
of their skin.

Adjusting Final Composition

I normally aim to finish the composition in Lightroom before editing in Photoshop. However, there are times when you realize after the fact that you want to recompose a bit. Here's how you can do it:

1. **Finish all the other work you want to accomplish.**

2. **Covert the background photo layer to a Smart Object.**

   Right-click it in the Layers panel and choose Convert to Smart Object.

3. **Click the Crop tool.**

4. **Mark the area of the photo you want to preserve.**

   Do this by drawing a crop area with the tool, as shown in Figure 3-18. You can also drag the corner and edge handles to change the crop boundaries. I prefer to set the tool to keep the original ratio.

5. **Uncheck Delete Cropped Pixels from the Options panel.**

   This makes sure the pixels you crop are preserved. It's vital that you don't forget this step.

FIGURE 3-18:
Mark the crop
area with the
crop tool.

6. **Double-click in the crop area to commit the crop.**

7. **If you need to recompose, click the Crop tool and click the photo in the workspace.**

You can also convert the bottom photo layer to a Smart Object before cropping.

Words of Caution and Encouragement

REMEMBER

You're much more likely to ruin a photo by heavy-handed editing than by leaving it alone. As you work with your photos in Photoshop, keep these thoughts in mind:

» **Fewer changes are better.** If you're trying to create a realistic interpretation of the photo, the less you mess with it, the better. A great-looking portrait is a perfect example. Resist the temptation to overdo something just because you can.

» **Go easy.** You run a greater risk of ruining the photo the harder you push things. A perfect example is trying to oversharpen.

>> **Accepting a photo.** The sensible solution is to find the spot where you can look at a photo and accept it for what it is. Not all photos are perfect. Some have noise; some have exposure problems; some have a bit of distortion. That's a reasonable life-lesson as well.

If you find yourself constantly struggling to make your photos look better in Lightroom or Photoshop, I would encourage you to take a look at your photography. Ask yourself what problems you face in editing and resolve to correct them when you take the photograph.

TIP

Here are some tips:

>> Take your shots at the lowest possible ISO so that you don't have to throw noise reduction at everything you shoot.

>> Support the camera so that it doesn't jiggle or jostle. That way, not every photo is blurry.

>> Frame well-designed shots so that you don't have to crop them later.

>> Try to keep distracting objects out of the background.

>> Hold the camera straight and level so you don't always have to straighten the photo.

>> Although no lens is perfect, use the best lenses you can.

REMEMBER

You *can* do it. Good, even great, photography isn't only for the most gifted with access to the best equipment shooting at the most stunningly beautiful locations. I'm convinced that everyone can be a good photographer by learning, practicing, observing, and identifying areas to improve in, and then correcting the things that are holding you back.

TIP

RANTING ABOUT NOISE

I'm convinced that most dSLR photographers worry too much about noise reduction. I used to, but have successfully gotten over most of it. I'm not saying that you should stand up and cheer over your noisy photos, but the truth is that unless you're blowing up a photo to ridiculous proportions, more noise than you may realize is acceptable.

Do yourself a favor. Go get an old photography book or look online for famous older photographs. Look at their flaws and realize that they are still magnificent. Being noise free isn't what makes them great. Go take those kinds of photos, and relax about the limitations of the technology.

Chapter **4**

Expressing Your Artistry

I think you'll find this a fun and rewarding chapter. It's amazing to see how your photos transform when you process them artistically. You can let your creativity loose as you convert them from color to black and white, colorize and tint photos, and apply artistic filters and effects. I also take a quick peek at creative styles and filters available in-camera.

Although you're using modern technology, don't think these pursuits are new. Photographers of all eras have manipulated, tweaked, and perfected their photos using whatever they could get their hands on.

Why Be Creative?

I write this section as a form of encouragement to those of you who want to get really creative with your photos. Don't be timid, and don't apologize. Not everyone is going to like your style, but that's the way the world works. Keep trying, learning, and improving. I've written down a few reasons for expressing your creativity that might help you overcome the doldrums:

» **For concealing:** Sometimes a color photo has something wrong that you can hide by converting it to black and white or colorizing. You may also be able to turn a "so-so" photo around by applying a creative filter. Don't let any photo go to waste. Turn the "Converting to Black and White" section and jump right in.

>> **For emphasis:** Often, you can use artistic techniques to emphasize certain elements. Details and geometry stand out and make a photo interesting when shown from a completely different point of view. The "Experimenting with Artistic Filters" section has a lot of great ideas that can help you emphasize aspects of your photos.

>> **For mood:** It's possible to create many different moods by converting a photo to black and white or using select color tints to colorize it. Different filters may have the same effect. Create whatever mood you're after. See the "Colorizing Your Photos" section for more information.

>> **For art:** No one says you have to have a solid reason to do anything artistic. It's your art. You decide. Some photographers have developed their own sense of style over the years regardless of what anyone else thought. Figure 4-1 is a stairwell that looks like MC Escher put it together. It's in the loading area of the building in Figure 4-16. The shot looks boring in color. As a black-and-white image, the lines, shapes, tones, and shadows leap out at you.

FIGURE 4-1:
Black-and-white photos have an artistry all their own.

Software for Your Artistic Endeavors

As with the other software chapters, I need to add a quick disclaimer before the action starts. I've chosen to feature Adobe Photoshop in this chapter because it represents the pinnacle of creative photo editing. It is more accessible than ever, and no longer costs an arm and a leg to get into (long-run costs are another story).

You can accomplish most of the tasks in this chapter using other applications, including software that comes with your camera. Specific features and capabilities will differ, however. If you're using something besides Photoshop, don't worry. The fundamentals of expressing your artistry are the same.

Converting to Black and White

Black-and-white (also known as B&W) prints evoke different feelings than do their color counterparts. In B&W, the focus is on tone, texture, and mood rather than on hue and saturation. They can be magical or somber or parts in between. This section shows you the easiest way to use Photoshop to change color photos to black and white. Conversion is different than shooting directly in black and white, which I cover near the end of the chapter. The advantage to conversion is that you have more control over how your photos are changed.

Using black-and-white adjustment layers

Not surprisingly, Photoshop has many powerful tools that change color images to black and white. Rather than try to show them all to you, I want to cut to the chase and feature the one I use the most: the Black & White adjustment layer. This technique gives you lots of control over how the final image looks and is relatively painless. For example, you can change blue skies into dark gray shades, green grass into lighter gray, and red features to medium gray.

I encourage you to make basic adjustments to your color photo in Adobe Lightroom. This includes lens corrections, overall exposure, protecting highlights and shadows, contrast, and so forth. Load the finished color photo into Photoshop. To convert color photos using Photoshop's Black & White adjustment tool, follow these steps:

1. **Click the New Adjustment Layer button and choose Black & White.**

    The button is at the bottom of the Layers panel. The Black & White option is in the middle of the second group from the bottom.

    Photoshop quickly creates the adjustment layer, as shown in Figure 4-2, and loads the default settings.

FIGURE 4-2:
The Black & White
adjustment layer
as it appears in
the Layers panel.

2. **Choose a different preset from the Properties panel, if desired.**

   Each preset is a predefined grayscale mix. Options include mixes like Darker, Infrared, Neutral Density, and Red filter. Scroll the list to find one that sounds interesting and select it. The effect on the photo is immediately updated. If you like, you can click the Auto button and see what Photoshop thinks.

3. **Manually adjust the effect using the color sliders, if desired.**

   Photoshop adjusts the gray tones in the image based on the position of each color slider (see Figure 4-3). Dragging a slider to the left darkens the gray tone for areas of the photo with that color. Dragging it right lightens the gray tone. The numerical values range from -200 (very dark) to 200 (very light).

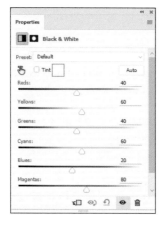

FIGURE 4-3:
Each color slider
affects the
tonality of the
black-and-white
image.

These controls make it easy to lighten or darken specific areas of the black-and-white image by changing the sliders for each color.

If you're more visually inclined, you can also click the On-image adjustment tool (the small hand with the index finger extended) and click a color in the photo you want to modify. *While you hold the mouse button down*, drag left and right

REMEMBER

on the photo to darken or lighten that area. The correct color slider automatically updates the photo.

You're not colorizing the image when you make changes to the color sliders. Instead, you're adjusting the *gray tone* of the specific color you choose. You can, for example, turn blues dark gray and reds light gray.

The final photo is shown in Figure 4-4. It represents a good example of how black and white can transform a photo. This large historical house looks great when converted to black and white.

FIGURE 4-4:
The finished conversion.

TIP

With practice, you can train yourself to see or think in black and white. You'll be able to more easily pick out potentially amazing tones, textures, and contrasts, and then bring them out as you take and process your shots.

When you've finished your black-and-white adjustments, you can continue to edit the photo like any other. If you need to make contrast, brightness, or other adjustments, you can use more adjustment layers if you like.

When you're finished making adjustments, I recommend importing your photo back into Lightroom or other photo-management program. After it's back in the fold, so to speak, you can continue to manage, edit, print, and archive the image, along with your other photos, using Lightroom.

Photo gallery

Okay, so you've seen that the process of converting your photos from color to black and white in Photoshop isn't that technically difficult. Time for a few examples.

Exploring cool presets

The presets contained in the Properties panel of the Black & White adjustment layer are good. That's one reason I like using Photoshop instead of Lightroom to mess around with black-and-white photos. Use them without modification or load one and use it as a starting point.

I used the Infrared preset on the photo in Figure 4-5. It's quite stunning how the leaves of the tree in the foreground and those on the far bank of the river appear to be brightly lit. That's the effect of the preset turning yellow and green colors into bright grayscale tones. The sky and water contrast nicely with the clouds.

FIGURE 4-5:
Explore presets like this one, which imitates infrared photography.

Muting colors with a black-and-white layer

Don't feel like you always have to turn a color photo fully into black and white. I like mixing things up by lowering the opacity of the Black & White adjustment layer and letting some color show through. Figure 4-6 shows the Layers panel of a photo. The adjustment layer is only 63% solid.

FIGURE 4-6:
Adjust the opacity of layers to blend color with black and white.

Figure 4-7 shows the final result. The colors have been muted and the image looks a little bit like an old, faded postcard. I was going to convert it entirely to black and white, but as I played around with the opacity of the adjustment layers, I found that I liked it with a little color. This technique is another way to integrate black and white into your creative repertoire.

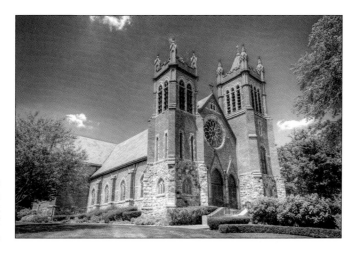

FIGURE 4-7:
Experimentation is an important aspect of creativity.

Using multiple black-and-white adjustments

Expressing your creativity artistry has a lot to do with thinking outside the box. One way of doing that is to create multiple Black & White adjustment layers and mask them in such a way that each one alters a specific part of the photo.

I did just that for this photo. Figure 4-8 shows the Layers panel. I have no less than four Black & White adjustment layers going on. Each one targets a different part of the photo. I have one for the sky, another for the trees and grass, another for the plane, and another for the tarmac.

Figure 4-9 shows the finished black-and-white image. I could not accomplish what I wanted creatively with a single black-and-white adjustment. It took four, each having different goals. I wanted the sky a little darker, so that the clouds were defined but not overdone. The trees needed to be brightened so they didn't appear to be in shadow. The plane had to be bright, but the colorful areas on the spinner and tail dark. Finally, the concrete looked best darkened. This is the only airworthy TP-51C in existence. It was converted from a P-51C to the dual-control variant in 2003.

FIGURE 4-8:
Use masks on different adjustment layers to target specific areas of the photo.

FIGURE 4-9:
A little extra effort pays off when the final photo is done.

Colorizing Your Photos

Colorizing (or *tinting* or *toning*) black-and-white images replaces black with one, two, or more colors, resulting in unique color effects that create different moods, tonalities, or apparent age. You can also colorize color photos. You can approach colorizing images in several ways. I'll run through a few that I use regularly.

Tinting the fast and easy way

Tinting your photos as you convert them to black and white is both convenient and easy. Here's how:

1. **Create a Black & White adjustment layer, as described in the "Using black-and-white adjustment layers" section.**

2. **Select the Tint option on the Properties panel, as shown in Figure 4-10.**

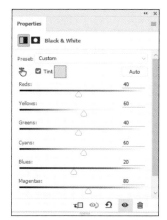

FIGURE 4-10:
Check the tint
box to colorize
using the
Black & White
adjustment layer.

3. **Click the color swatch to open the Color Picker.**

4. **Adjust the color to taste.**

   Click in the Color Picker to select a Tint Color or enter the numeric color values
   of your choice next to the appropriate radio buttons.

Figure 4-11 shows the finished image. (Yes, that's me. After a few days of not
shaving and posing hilariously for my wife. I rarely make it into my books. I'm the
one normally taking the photos.)

FIGURE 4-11:
Scruffy and
subtle tinting go
together.

Colorizing with Hue/Saturation

Another painless way to colorize photos is to use Photoshop's Hue/Saturation adjustment. It's a great method to quickly explore possibilities. You can use this technique for color or black-and-white photos. To give it a try, follow these steps:

TIP

1. **Create a Hue/Saturation adjustment layer.**

   You get more control over tonality by converting the photo to black and white first. To do so, create a Black & White adjustment layer, then a Hue/Saturation layer. If you forget, you can always create the Black & White adjustment layer second and drag it below the Hue/Saturation adjustment layer in the Layers panel.

2. **Select the small Colorize box beneath the sliders (see Figure 4-12).**

   It's a small box beneath the sliders. This removes the color from the photo and then applies the current *hue* (a fancy name for color) whose intensity is set with the Saturation control.

3. **Make Hue, Saturation, and Lightness adjustments.**

   To change the color, drag the Hue slider. Saturation affects the color intensity. Lightness controls the overall brightness of the photo.

FIGURE 4-12:
Colorize also applies a single hue to a photo.

Split toning using Color Balance

Split toning enables you to apply colors to a photo's shadows and highlights. This means you can selectively colorize black-and-white photos or create interesting special effects with color photos. The easiest way to split tone in Photoshop is to use a Color Balance adjustment layer.

Here's how:

1. **Create a Color Balance adjustment layer.**

2. **In the Properties panel, select Shadows from the Tone drop-down list.**

3. **Adjust the color sliders, as shown in Figure 4-13.**

   On the left side of this panel are three colors: Cyan, Magenta, and Yellow. The colors on the right represent the three color channels in an RGB image: Red, Green, and Blue. The sliders control the amount of the colors on the left in their corresponding color channels.

   For all intents and purposes, Color Balance works as if you have three color pairs: Cyan/Red, Magenta/Green, and Yellow/Blue. Drag the slider toward the color you want to increase.

   The side effect is reducing the opposite color. When you add cyan, you reduce red. When you add blue, you reduce yellow. You can't increase two opposing colors, magenta and green, for example, at the same time. It's an *either-or* proposition.

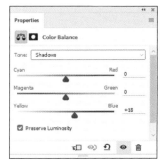

FIGURE 4-13:
Colorize by adjusting the color balance in each tonal region.

4. **Select Highlights from the Tone drop-down list.**

5. **Adjust the color sliders.**

   This time you're working in the highlight tonal range.

6. **Balance the effect by adjusting the opacity of the Color Balance adjustment layer.**

Figure 4-14 shows the effects of making the highlights in this shot of my wife magenta with yellow and the shadows a deep blue. It's quite fun to play with split toning.

Cross-processing with Curves

Cross-processing is a term that comes from the art of processing film with the wrong chemicals. Yes, it sounds wrong, but it's possible to create uniquely toned photos in the darkroom. Thankfully, cross-processing in Photoshop is easier than messing with smelly chemicals. To cross-process a photo (color or black and white) in Photoshop, follow these steps:

1. **Create a Curves adjustment layer.**

2. **Select the Cross Process (RGB) preset from the Preset drop-down list.**

Figure 4-15 shows the Curves panel with the Cross Process (RGB) preset loaded.

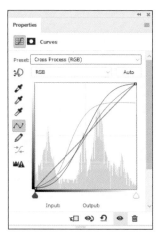

FIGURE 4-15:
The Cross
Process preset
in Photoshop.

3. **Alter the curve, if you want, by editing the RGB curve or selecting specific channels (R, G, or B) and altering those curves individually.**

You're free to continue editing or publishing your image. If you want to tone down the effect, try lowering the opacity of the adjustment layer. Figure 4-16 reveals the final, cross-processed photo. Notice the otherworldly tones and accentuated contrast applied to the image. That's the beauty of cross-processing.

FIGURE 4-16:
This large building looks great cross-processed.

TIP

It's possible to create a cross process look by using the Color Balance adjustment layer. Set the shadows to green and highlights to yellow. Other programs sometimes seem to ignore cross-processing. You can work around a lack of a cross-processing option by split toning.

Using color layers

Another approach to colorizing a photo is to use color layers. You can work with color or black-and-white photos. With this technique, you add layers filled with color (either a solid color or gradient) over the photo layer. You blend the color layer with the photo layer by lowering the color layer's opacity.

You should also experiment with blend modes. *Blending modes* affect whether (and how) layers on top allow other layers to show through. Normally, these layers don't allow other layers to show through because they're *opaque* (the opposite of transparent). You can change this behavior, which is what you're counting on to colorize the image.

You can use more than one color in more than one color layer and erase or blend them in creative ways. For example, you can create blue-tinted shadows and gold-tinted highlights. Some applications (Photoshop, but not Photoshop Elements) let you modify which portions of the color layer blend with the lower layer based on the tonality of either layer.

This technique is a bit more involved. It's not rocket science, but you'll have to do more work in Photoshop. To use color layers, follow these steps:

1. **Create a Black & White adjustment layer and adjust it to your liking; see the "Using black-and-white adjustment layers" section.**

2. **Click the New Adjustment Layer button and choose Solid Color.**

3. **Choose a color from the Color Picker; then click OK.**

4. **Change the blending mode on the Layers panel to Color.**

5. **Lower the color layer opacity to blend by using the Opacity slider on the Layers panel.**

   The Opacity slider controls the color intensity, as shown in Figure 4-17. The black-and-white image should show through even at 100 percent because you changed the blend mode to Color.

   If you have more than one color layer, all except the bottom one must have their opacity set to less than 100 percent. This allows the bottom color layers to show through. You'd think that changing the blend mode to Color mode would be enough, but it isn't.

REMEMBER

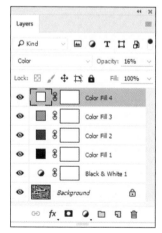

FIGURE 4-17:
Control color
strength by
lowering layer
opacity.

6. **Blend by masking areas on the color layer that you don't want to affect the photo.**

You can also control blending by using the Layer Style dialog box. Double-click by (not on) the layer name in the Layers panel to open it. Then change the Underlying Layer sliders to control what tones you want to accept the color.

7. **Add more color layers, if you want.**

It's possible to go all out and create duotones, tritons, quadtones, and more by adding more color layers. Have one or more colors tint the shadows, another for mid-tones, and another tint highlights.

Figure 4-18 shows the final result. I found this old, abandoned Pontiac Executive and quickly fell in love with it. They were in production from 1966 through 1970. Subjects like this are great to photograph. I like sleek and pretty as much as the next person (see the P-51 in Figure 4-9), but this car has a lot of grit.

FIGURE 4-18: Use multiple color layers for detailed color toning.

TIP

If your application doesn't support color blending but does use layers, blend with opacity.

Creating duotones

Duotones are a powerful, yet simple, Photoshop feature that automates the process of colorizing a photo with up to four colors, called *inks*. The process was created to expand the ability of printing presses to print more shades of gray. Using up to four colors to print the grayscale image resulted in much greater tonal range.

The greatest challenge you face is deciding what looks best to you, not implementing it.

REMEMBER

The drawback to creating duotones in Photoshop is that you have to convert the image to grayscale and then convert it to duotone. You can't stay in RGB, which is the standard color mode of most photos. But I have a way around that.

To apply a duotone, follow these steps:

1. **Create a Black & White adjustment layer and adjust it to your liking, as shown in the "Using black-and-white adjustment layers" section.**

   This converts the photo to black and white without destroying any information.

2. **Create a duplicate image with merged layers.**

   Do so by choosing Image⇨Duplicate. Check the Duplicate Merged Layers Only box in the Duplicate Image dialog box. Click OK.

   This gives you a copy of your photo, converted to black and white, that you'll use to create the duotone. It's a temporary working file that you'll use to convert the photo to the color format necessary to create duotones. When you've created the duotone, you'll reconvert it back to the original color format, then copy and paste it into your normal file. At that point, you can continue editing normally.

   You can close the original file for this part of the process as long as you save it in Photoshop format. You'll need it at the end.

3. **Convert the duplicate image to grayscale by choosing Image⇨Mode⇨Grayscale.**

   When asked, choose to discard the color information.

4. **Convert the duplicate image to Duotone by choosing Image⇨Mode⇨Duotone.**

   The Duotone Options dialog box shows a monotone initially, or the settings from your last application.

5. **In the Duotone Options dialog box, choose a duotone from the Preset drop-down menu.**

   I suggest first browsing through the extensive list of presets and applying those that you like. Figure 4-19 shows a preset loaded in the dialog box and the image visible onscreen. I selected the Bl 409 WmGray 407 Wm Gray option from the Preset menu.

   When you become familiar with duotones, load a preset that's close to what you want and use it as a starting point to create your own preset. You can apply a number of inks, create specific curves for each color, and choose the colors themselves (by using the Color Picker or browsing the extensive color libraries). Experiment with the settings in the dialog box.

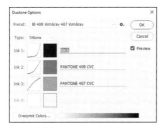

FIGURE 4-19:
Applying a duotone preset.

It's possible to save presets that you have changed. Choose the settings you like, and then select the small drop-down menu tucked between the Preset menu and the OK button — within this list are Save and Load Preset menus.

6. **Click OK.**

   You've created the duotone using the copied image. Now it's time to covert it back to RGB and put it back into your original file as a new layer.

7. **Convert the duplicate image to RGB by choosing Image⇨Mode⇨ RGB Color.**

8. **Select the layer in the duplicate image by pressing Ctrl+A/⌘+A (Win/Mac).**

9. **Copy the later in the duplicate image by pressing Ctrl+C/⌘+C (Win/Mac).**

10. **Switch to the original image file.**

    Reopen it if you have to.

11. **Paste the Duotone layer into the original file by pressing Ctrl+V/⌘+V (Win/Mac).**

12. **Close the copied duplicate image. There is no need to save this working file.**

    That's it. See Figure 4-20 for my final photo. I took this shot with the Canon TS-E 24mm f/3.5L II tilt-shift lens. While it looks okay in color, it's not really that memorable. When converted to black and white and given a little color, it's far more compelling.

TIP

If you're not working in Photoshop, create your own duotones using color layers. If using Lightroom, use the Split Toning feature.

Experimenting with Artistic Filters

I could play around with artistic filters all day. I really could. They are creative, inspiring, and easy to use. The challenge is finding the right photo to match up with the right filter, or combination of filters. The process involves a degree of trial and error.

Using the Filter Gallery

Your first stop should be the Filter Gallery, which is a special dialog box that allows you to preview and experiment with many different types of filters. To launch the Filter Gallery, follow these steps:

1. **Choose Filter ➪ Filter Gallery.**

   A large dialog box opens, as shown in Figure 4-21. A preview of the photo is shown on the left side. Click the magnification buttons at the lower-left corner to zoom in and out. You can press Ctrl+0/⌘+0 (Win/Mac) to view the entire photo.

   Individual filters are grouped by categories to the right of the preview window. Click the arrow by the category name to see the filter thumbnails associated with that category.

   Settings for the selected filter are shown on the right. The name of the currently selected filter appears in a drop-down list above the settings. If you prefer, you can select new filters using this list instead of the thumbnails.

   Additional controls are shown in the bottom of the dialog box. You can add or remove filters, turn them on or off, and rearrange them using the controls in this area.

FIGURE 4-21:
The Filter Gallery
dialog box is
full of creative
controls.

2. **Find and choose a filter that you want to apply.**

   Select filters from the thumbnails or the drop-down list. The thumbnails are arranged in these categories: Artistic, Brush Strokes, Distort, Sketch, Stylize, and Texture. The filters are alphabetized in the drop-down list.

3. **Experiment with the filter's settings.**

   I encourage you to experiment with different settings. Filters that may seem uninspiring may turn around if you tweak the slider controls a bit. If you're in a hurry, don't feel bad about having a quick look at the default settings and moving on if the result doesn't look promising.

4. **Click OK to apply or Cancel to quit the Filter Gallery without applying.**

I show a few examples of filters from the Filter gallery in an upcoming section called "Filter fun."

Applying other filters

If the Filter Gallery doesn't have want you're looking for, the Filters menu includes additional filters. Several are grouped with the Filter Gallery in the same area of the menu. There are numerous categories listed on the bottom half of the menu. To apply one of these filters, follow these steps:

1. **Select the Filters menu.**

2. **Choose the filter that you want to apply from the menu.**

   Most filters open a dialog box with one or more controls. Some, like Find Edges, don't.

3. **Modify the filter's settings, if possible.**

   Filters like Liquify open a complicated dialog box with many options and settings. Some, like Pointillize, are easy to understand and have very intuitive settings. Unfortunately, I don't have the room to go into all the interesting details. While I show a few examples in the section called "Filter fun," you should take advantage of the Photoshop Help menu and manual for more details about each filter.

Smart Filters

The process I've described thus far applies the filter you've chosen, whether from the Filter Gallery or not, to the layer you have selected. You can't change the filter once applied. You must Undo and then reapply the same filter or filters with new settings or use a different filter. If you want to edit filters, you should convert the photo layer to a Smart Object by choosing Filter⇨Convert for Smart Filters. Apply the filter as usual. To edit it afterward, double-click the filter name in the Layers panel (see Figure 4-22).

FIGURE 4-22:
The great thing about Smart Filters is that you can edit them.

Filter fun

Telling you about filters is one thing. Showing you is another. I've selected several of my photos and applied interesting filters for this section. I hope to give you an idea of the many artistic possibilities you have at your fingertips.

Extrude

Extrude is a funky filter. I love it. It's in the Stylize group of the Filters menu. When you select it, you get a few options. You can select the shape of the extrusion (blocks or pyramids), the size, depth, and make a few other choices. Aside from boosting the depth to 150, I left the settings alone for this photo in Figure 4-23. It's a macro of some resistors on the circuit board of my Marshall 9001 Stereo Valve Pre-amp.

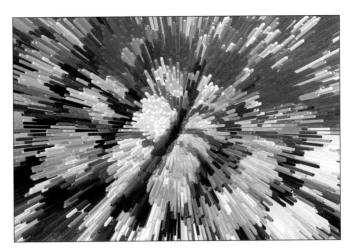

FIGURE 4-23:
Extrude is mind-blowing.

Stamp

Figure 4-24 is a photo of one of my electric guitars, after having applied the Stamp filter. Located in the Filter Gallery, the Stamp filter has an important requirement. Like some of the other filters in the Sketch group, the foreground and background colors determine the colors of the stamp. In this case, I chose black as the foreground and white as the background color. It turns the black guitar mostly white.

FIGURE 4-24:
Remember to set the colors before you apply the Stamp filter.

Cutout

The photo shown in Figure 4-25 is of horses racing past. I set up at this particular vantage point because I thought the sign was quite ironic. It's meant as a warning, but I found it funny. At any rate, I have applied the Cutout filter to the original photo. This filter is located in the Filter Gallery. It has simplified the color scheme dramatically and turned the photo into something you might make in art class with construction paper.

FIGURE 4-25:
The Cutout filter imitates the effect of a collage made from paper cutouts.

Poster edges

I took the photo in Figure 4-26 from inside the Gateway Arch in St. Louis. I'm at the very top looking due west. The downtown area is prominently featured in this photo, and the baseball stadium is visible to the left side.

This photo doesn't look like a photo anymore because I applied the Poster Edges filter to it. You can find it in the Filter Gallery.

FIGURE 4-26:
Downtown St. Louis as if it were hand drawn and colored.

Pointillize

Pointillize is a fun filter that I want to use on everything. It doesn't look good on everything though, so I have to hold back some. It has one option: the size of the dots. Pointillize is in the Pixelate group of filters.

Figure 4-27 shows the filter applied to a photo of my daughter on a swing right beside a lake. I didn't have to do much to prepare the photo for the filter. I exported a TIFF from Lightroom and loaded it into Photoshop, then applied the filter. Afterward, you can always import your work back into Lightroom to manage it.

FIGURE 4-27: Pointillize uses small circles of color to create the image.

Blurring with poster edges

Figure 4-28 is a photo of my son, Jacob, getting sprayed down with the garden hose in our backyard. I applied two filters to this shot. First, I duplicated the photo layer, then blurred it with a Radial Blur (that's with the Blur filters) set to zoom. I then masked his face, which means that I hid it. This allowed the unblurred version just around his face to be visible. I then merged a copy of all the visible layers to a new target layer (Ctrl+Shift+Alt+E for Windows, ⌘+Shift+Option+E for Mac) and applied the Poster Edges filter to that layer. I couldn't use a single Smart Filter because I wanted to mask the blur effect on his face but apply the Poster Edge filter to the entire photo.

With some persistence, patience, and experimentation, you can create really cool effects like this by stacking filters and being creative with different masks.

Using In-Camera Creative Styles and Filters

Don't think you have to wait until you get to your computer to turn on your creativity. Start before you shoot with camera styles and continue through playback with special filters.

Using in-camera styles

Creative styles (Nikon cameras call this feature *picture control*) are a type of in-camera processing option. I love them because they let me creatively push photos in different directions without having to be a photo-retouching expert.

The processing is applied to the raw data and saved as a JPEG. If you have the camera set to JPEGs only and then take photos with a particular style, such as black-and-white, what's done is done. You can't undo it or retrieve a color photo to start over from. If you've set the camera to store the raw data in the form of a raw image (or RAW+JPEG), the raw photo preserves the original color information.

Here are some of the standard creative styles you see on most cameras:

- » **Standard:** Your basic photo. Optimized for good all-round appearance.
- » **Neutral:** Toned down compared to Standard. Use if you plan to process it with software.
- » **Vivid:** Increases the saturation and contrast to add pop.
- » **Portrait:** Optimizes for people and skin tones. May be softer than normal.
- » **Landscape:** Optimizes for natural tones. May be more colorful and sharper.

>> **Black & White/Monochrome:** Choose this setting (see Figure 4-29) for a classic black-and-white photo (see Figure 4-30).

FIGURE 4-29:
You can shoot in black and white by selecting the correct style.

FIGURE 4-30:
In this case, the camera processed the black-and-white photo for me.

Some other options you may run across are:

>> **Sunset:** Use when you're shooting into or in the sunset. This style emphasizes the reddish-orange colors.

>> **Clear:** Captures transparent colors in bright areas. Good for lights.

>> **Deep:** Colorful and solid.

>> **Light:** Bright and airy.

>> **Night Scene:** Tones down contrast to make night scenes more realistic.

>> **Autumn Leaves:** Saturates reds and yellows.

>> **Sepia:** Applies an old-school tint to a black-and-white photo.

TIP

I strongly recommend saving RAW+JPEG if you want to experiment with different creative styles.

You may be able to customize the built-in styles on your camera by editing them. They most often have three or four tweakable parameters, such as contrast, saturation, and sharpness. You might even be able to download styles from the Internet and load them into your camera.

Applying in-camera filters

Many cameras have photo-editing and retouching features that allow you to process photos on your memory card instead of using a computer. Normally, you take the photo, and then apply the filter during using the camera's menu or during playback, as shown in Figure 4-31. Some dSLRs let you shoot in these modes.

FIGURE 4-31: In-camera filters and effects do not require a computer.

Figure 4-32 shows the image created by the camera using the Water Painting effect. As you can see, you can apply your creativity using your camera as well as a computer.

FIGURE 4-32: Experiment with different effects to find out what works best for a particular photo.

Chapter **5**

Creating Panoramas

Shooting panoramas is fun and relatively painless. Point the camera at something interesting. Take a picture. Pan the camera a bit (but not too far). Shoot again. Keep going until you've taken enough photos to create a panorama. After you get back to your computer, take each of the photos and load it into software that can stitch them together into a single image. This is panorama photography, in a nutshell.

Panoramas evoke oohs and aahs from everyone. It's rewarding to find a good scene that you want to capture in a format wider or taller than a standard photo and then make it happen. I show you how to take the photos and process them in this chapter.

Shooting Pan-tastic Panoramas

Shooting panoramas is an exercise in photography. The main point is to capture overlapping photos of a large scene that are fairly consistent in depth of field, exposure, and color.

REMEMBER

Technically you never actually photograph *the panorama.* You take shots of individual photos that, when merged or stitched together, create the final image that is the panorama. However, most people (including myself) aren't sticklers about it and simply refer to the process, in part or as a whole, as panorama photography.

Getting your camera ready

When shooting panoramas, there are two diametrically opposed approaches to setting up the camera. They both work. Choose the one that fits your personality. They are:

>> **Casual:** If you're interested in casually shooting panoramas, you can set up your camera however you want to. Even Auto mode works well.

I do recommend, however, that you use aperture-priority mode. Set the aperture to provide the depth of field that you want, and then let ISO and shutter speed vary. This keeps the depth of field consistent between shots.

If autofocus switches between subjects that are at vastly different distances, consider switching to manual focus. This keeps the focal distance consistent from shot to shot. I rarely remember to switch to manual focus and have yet to run into a problem.

>> **Controlling:** In this case, your goal is to set up the camera so that you can shoot consistent photos. For maximum control over your camera and the exposure settings, use manual mode and manual focus. You should also shoot Raw+JPEG so that you can control Raw processing yourself. Use the JPEGs for visualization. With them, you can quickly put a small panorama together to see whether you like it and want to work on the full version using the Raw photos.

Regardless of which type you are, you'll benefit by shooting Raw photos. This enables you to correct white balance issues in software easier than with JPEGs. It also alleviates the need to worry about the color space. If you save only JPEGs, set the white balance manually (so that it doesn't change) and if you want the highest quality shots, set the color space to AdobeRGB.

When I use a tripod, I use a remote to trigger the shutter. It's an important part of my un-bump, anti-jostle, and de-jiggle strategy. Set the drive mode to Remote, if necessary. Otherwise, leave the drive on Single, and leave the metering mode on multi-zone or pattern. You only need to change metering modes if there is a problem.

Shooting tripod-assisted panoramas

When you're ready to begin shooting frames, grab your camera and tripod and go find an interesting subject — the wider or taller, the better.

Then follow these steps to set up and shoot the photos:

1. **Mount and level your camera on a tripod.**

REMEMBER

   Normally, your camera should rotate on an axis that's as true to vertical as you can get it. Rotate your camera and make sure it stays level when you point it in a different direction. If you're like me, you use what you see through the viewfinder to ensure that the scene is level.

2. **Determine a framing strategy.**

   This step may sound overly complicated, but it may only take you a moment.

   - *Consider width/height:* Quickly (or for a really long time) consider how wide or tall you want your panorama to be and how many shots you think it'll take to capture it with your current lens. (That may just be the longest sentence in this book. A panoramic sentence.)

   - *Check landmarks:* Note key landmarks along the way that will help the software stitch the frames together. Try to put them in more than one shot.

   - *Center it:* Try to center the most important elements of the scene (especially the main subject) in a frame.

   In Figure 5-1, I imagined making a 4- to 5-frame panorama of one of my favorite bridges. Each separate photo has important parts of the scene, and overlaps details with the photos around it. I need them all to create the panorama.

FIGURE 5-1:
Picturing a
framing strategy.

REMEMBER

   Try to overlap each frame by about one-third. Overlap helps the panorama program *stitch* (assemble) the frames by providing good reference points. The more reference points, the greater the possibility of a successful stitch.

3. **Perform a dry run, if desired.**

   If you need to, visualize each shot by looking at it through your viewfinder or LCD monitor, pan, and look at the next one. Check out the landmarks that help you identify the boundaries of your photos and how much overlap will occur.

TIP

   If you have a tripod with a compass, you can make a note of the reading for the center point of each frame.

Take a few meter readings along the way to see whether exposure varies from one side of the panorama to the other. If you like, check your camera's histogram to make sure you're not blowing out any highlights. Decide on a final exposure if you're using manual mode.

4. **Pan to one side and shoot the first photo.**

   You can shoot from left to right, right to left, from top to bottom, or the reverse. It's all good.

5. **Pan and continue shooting photos to complete the panorama.**

   The photography part is finished when you shoot the last shot of the panorama. The rest of the work (and the subject of the rest of this chapter) happens in software. Figure 5-2 shows the final panorama.

FIGURE 5-2: The final panorama in black and white.

Shooting handheld panoramas

Shooting handheld panoramas is much more relaxed than using a tripod. You don't need the tripod, a remote shutter release, or any other equipment besides your digital SLR. I love shooting handheld panoramas. You can shoot them on the spur of the moment whether you're in the water, on the beach, or inside a famous landmark.

What you do need is a bit of hand-eye coordination and the ability to quickly, but steadily, pan the camera manually between shots.

You will likely need a higher shutter speed than when using a tripod, and ISO will probably be higher as well. Hold the camera as level as you can as you pan. Pause, focus, and take each photo, then rotate the camera to take the next. Pay attention to how much overlap you provide. Make sure it's a third of a photo or more. And practice.

Stitching Photos Together

Unless you have a camera that does it for you (I cover this later), panoramas don't merge themselves. Specialized software combines *(stitches)* the separate frames of the panorama into a single blended image.

Creating panoramas with Lightroom

Creating panoramas in Lightroom is delightfully easy. The feature is called Photo Merge, and you can activate it in the Library or Develop panels. Here's a quick rundown on how the process works:

1. **Select the photos you want to merge into a panorama (see Figure 5-3).**

They can be in JPEG or Raw image file format. I've created both, and while Lightroom complains that it can't access lens correction data for some JPEGs, the end result is not noticeably worse than using Raw images.

You can develop your photos prior to merging or wait until afterward. Not all settings are carried into the panorama. Frankly, I would wait until you've created the panorama to make adjustments on a single, consolidated image.

FIGURE 5-3: I've selected seven photos to create a panorama with.

2. **Choose Photo ⇨ Photo Merge ⇨ Panorama.**

You can also right-click and choose Photo Merge ⇨ Panorama, or press Ctrl+M/⌘+M (Win/Win).

The Panorama Merge Preview panel opens, as shown in Figure 5-4, with a few controls and a preview of the panorama. Lightroom automatically builds a preview of the selected projection and displays it. If it can't successfully build the panorama, it conks out on you.

FIGURE 5-4:
The Lightroom
Panorama Merge
Preview panel has
all the controls
you need.

3. **Select a projection type.**

Panorama projection types essentially correspond to different map projections you learned when studying maps and geography in Social Studies. The source photos partially cover the interior of a globe called the *panoramic sphere*. The challenge is how to present that three-dimensional information using only two dimensions. The answer is to project it onto a flat, two-dimensional plane. You can do that in different ways, which explains why Lightroom includes three projection types:

- *Spherical:* Photos from the panoramic sphere are assigned X and Y coordinates (just like latitude and longitude) and are mapped onto a flat surface. This option works well on wide-angle landscape shots because vertical lines and the horizon line, or equator, are straight. Vertical distances are stretched a bit compared to horizontal. This projection type is also called *equirectangular.*

- *Cylindrical:* The photos from the panoramic sphere are mapped as a cylinder and then unrolled. This option also works well with wide shots. Like the spherical type, vertical lines and the horizon remain straight. Vertical distances toward the top and bottom of the photo are stretched more than toward the center.

- *Perspective:* This type of projection, also known as *rectilinear* or *flat*, simply maps the pixels on the interior of the panoramic sphere directly onto a flat plane. This is close to how we see, but isn't always the best method to choose. The center of the panorama will look fine, but the outer areas can easily distort.

4. **Select Auto Crop and choose a Boundary Warp, if desired.**

   Auto Crop crops out all the white space surrounding the panorama to create a nice, clean border. Boundary Warp fills the white space with warped areas of the photo. If you max the Boundary Warp setting, you don't need to crop at all.

   A good compromise is to fill as much of the white space as you can using Boundary Warp, so long as it looks natural (you may have to try a few settings to see which one works best), then crop the rest using Auto Crop. I've done just that in Figure 5-5.

FIGURE 5-5:
I've used a combination of both border features in this case.

5. **Click Merge to create the panorama.**

   When Lightroom finishes, it creates a new, unlayered file using Adobe's Digital Negative Raw image file format (.dng) and places it in the same location as the source photos. It shows up in your Library accordingly.

6. **Edit your panorama normally, as shown in Figure 5-6.**

   Switch to the Develop panel and use the controls to improve your panorama.

7. **Export the final panorama (shown in Figure 5-7) when completed.**

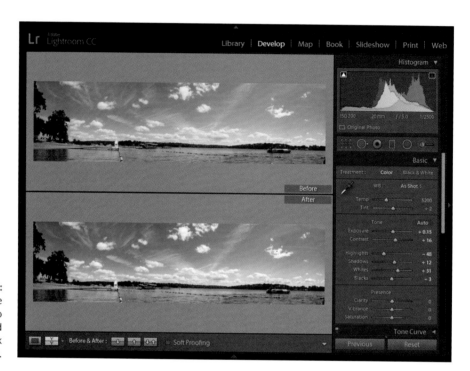

FIGURE 5-6:
Edit the panorama to spruce it up and make it look better.

FIGURE 5-7:
I shot the photos for this panorama in waist deep water.

Creating panoramas with Photoshop

Stitching together panoramas in Photoshop isn't difficult either. The main difference between using Photoshop and Lightroom is that Lightroom can immediately process Raw photos. Photoshop must open Raw images using Adobe Camera Raw. Select the photos in the Filmstrip, right-click, and choose Merge to Panorama. At that point, the process is identical to the Photo Merge feature in Lightroom.

Photoshop, however, has its own panorama feature, called Photomerge, which is slightly different. You have more projection types to choose from, and you can produce a layered file that enables you to correct blending problems. Here's how to use it:

1. **Open the photos you want to use for the panorama in Photoshop.**

You can use JPEGs, although 8-bits per channel TIFFs that you have already converted from Raw photos give you better results.

Alternatively, you can jump to Step 2 without opening any files. When you get to Step 3, click Browse to find the source files you want Photoshop to use to create the panorama.

2. **Choose File ⇨ Automate ⇨ Photomerge.**

The Photomerge dialog box opens (see Figure 5-8). Layout options are on the left. Source files and options are in the center. Most controls are fairly self-explanatory.

3. **Click the Add Open Files button.**

Photoshop adds their names to the list, as shown in Figure 5-8. If you need to add more, click Browse. If you want to remove one, select it from the central list and click Remove.

FIGURE 5-8:
I've added ten photos to create this panorama with.

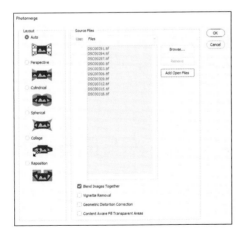

4. **Choose a layout:**

  - *Auto:* This option allows Photoshop to choose between Perspective and Cylindrical layouts.

  - *Perspective, Cylindrical, or Spherical:* These three options are identical to those from Adobe Lightroom. (See the "Creating panoramas with Lightroom" section.)

  - *Collage:* Throw everything together and align it like a collage. The software rotates and scales photos as required.

  - *Reposition:* This layout aligns each photo based on matching reference points but doesn't transform them in any way. This option can produce good-looking panoramas that don't suffer from undue amounts of distortion.

5. **Select other options.**

  You can choose from these four:

  - *Blend Images Together* automatically blends the photos together. Uncheck this to perform this task manually. I recommend leaving it checked.

  - *Vignette Removal* balances the exposure of the corners of each photo with the center.

  - *Geometric Distortion Correction* attempts to compensate for lens distortion.

  - *Content Aware Fill Transparent Areas* automatically fills gaps in the panorama, just like Boundary Warp does in Lightroom.

6. **Click OK to continue.**

  Photoshop creates the panorama and loads it into the interface as an unsaved file, as shown in Figure 5-9. Notice that each photo takes up its own layer and is masked to blend with the others. This is substantially different than Lightroom, and enables you to edit each layer separately. You see the entire panorama in the main window.

7. **Save the panorama as a Photoshop file.**

TIP

  Use the .psd as a multi-layered working file that you can use to tweak blending and make other adjustments. When finished, resize and crop, if desired, and then save a flattened copy as a TIFF or JPEG. Figure 5-10 shows the final panorama. I made a few minor adjustments to the brightness and contrast, removed my shadow, cropped the photo, and saved this flattened version.

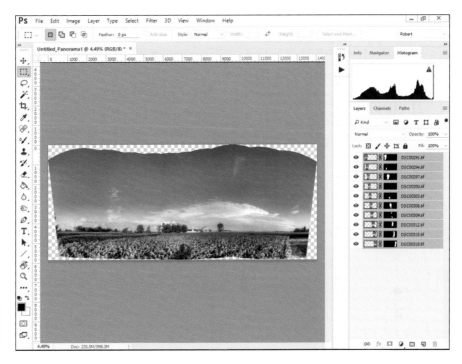

FIGURE 5-9:
Photoshop creates layered panoramas.

FIGURE 5-10:
Panoramas enable you to capture sweeping views with little distortion.

Stepping Up Your Game

There's nothing wrong with using what you have to shoot panoramas. Technically, you don't even need a tripod. It can be just you and your camera. However, some ingenious people have come up with tools that are designed specifically for making your panoramas easier and better.

Advanced blending in Photoshop

When working with panoramas in Photoshop, you can correct blending issues between different photos by editing the masks that Photoshop creates.

Zoom in to inspect the borders between each shot of the panorama. If things look unusual, you may be able to edit the mask of one or more layers to correct it. You can also soften mask edges to blend the photos better.

I had to do a lot of manual blending on the panorama of my wife, shown in Figure 5-11. I had a crazy panorama concept and convinced her to play along (we were renovating so please excuse the mess). I wanted to see what it would look like to photograph her several times and use the shots of her in a panorama. She changed outfits and moved positions between each shot. For this panorama, blending was important. As shown in Figure 5-11, the initial automatic panorama blended one of her poses completely out of the picture.

FIGURE 5-11: There should be three women in this photo.

Thankfully, I created this panorama in Photoshop, so I had access to the layered photos and masks. I had to work carefully with the masks and edit the one that covered her to put her back in. Figure 5-12 shows the final image (which is also a good example of cropping).

Using a panoramic tripod head

If you really want to get into panoramas, consider buying a dedicated panoramic tripod head. The only downside to using a dedicated panoramic head is effort.

Mount your camera and lens properly. Otherwise, there's no point in using it. You may have to take test shots to get it right. And, because each lens has different characteristics, this position changes depending on your lens.

TECHNICAL STUFF

When you rotate your camera on a tripod using a normal head, the camera rotates around the screw that connects them together. Although this is generally acceptable, it's not the ideal solution. Rather, you should be rotating the camera around the optical center of the lens, sometimes called the *no-parallax point,* the *entrance pupil,* or the *nodal point.* By changing the axis or rotation from the center of the camera to the nodal point (as always, there is some debate over this), your panorama photos line up much better because they won't suffer from as much parallax. *Parallax* is when nearby objects move between frames in relation to a far object.

Figure 5-13 shows a consumer-level Nikon dSLR mounted on the Nodal Ninja 4 panoramic head (www.nodalninja.com). The NN4 is a beefy, well-made series of locking brackets that hold your camera in position, whether you want to shoot horizontal or vertical panoramas. Getting the camera mounted takes a degree of precision, but once you set it up, you can quickly attach the same camera again without changing anything. One of the great things about the NN4 is that the unit rotates in incremental steps. You take a photo and then rotate the camera a set number of clicks to reach the next position.

Using specialized panorama software

The best current panorama package on the market works for both Windows and Macintosh; it's PTGui (www.ptgui.com). If you want to control just about every conceivable part of the panorama process and are considering displaying or selling your panoramas professionally, PTGui is for you.

FIGURE 5-13:
The Nodal Ninja 4 enables you to shoot precise panoramas.

This powerful all-in-one panorama application gives you customizable control points and significantly more projection types than most other programs. Two of the application's windows are shown in Figure 5-14. I loaded five images I shot of a lake into the program, and am in the process of stitching them together to form a panorama. I can set the horizon line as well as change many other parameters using the Panorama Editor window. If you're serious about creating HDR panoramas, download either PTGui or PTGui Pro and have a closer look for yourself. The Pro version even has its own HDR and tone mapping features.

Shooting HDR panoramas

High Dynamic Range photography (the subject of the next chapter) and panorama photography go well together. They both use special software to create a final image out of component photos. HDR photography uses exposure brackets to capture a greater range of light than normal in a single scene, while panorama photography uses the same settings to capture a physically larger scene in multiple photos.

To shoot a panorama in HDR, set up your camera to photograph exposure brackets. Shoot a bracketed sequence for each photo in the panorama, one of which is shown in Figure 5-15. Using HDR software, create a finished HDR image for each photo of the panorama, and then use Lightroom or other panorama-capable software to stitch together those HDR images to form the finished panorama. Figure 5-16 shows my finished panoroma.

You'll end up with at least three times the number of overall photos, and it takes more time to process everything and put the panorama together, but it's amazing what you can accomplish by combining these techniques together.

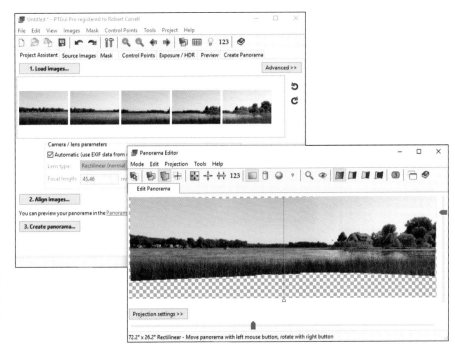

FIGURE 5-14:
PTGui Pro is a fantastic application dedicated to panoramas.

FIGURE 5-15:
These exposure brackets create a single photo in the panorama.

FIGURE 5-16:
HDR panoramas enable to you capture more details than usual.

Shooting Automatic Panoramas

Some cameras, mostly Sony dSLTs, shoot and process panoramas automatically. The camera handles all the complicated processing. Sony calls the feature Sweep Panorama (formerly Sweep Shooting). It's also available in 3D.

Panoramas are typically only saved as a single JPEG, which means that you do not have access to the individual shots that the camera used. No Raw images are saved either. You get the finished panorama only. Sony's 3D panoramas require two files. Figure 5-17 shows a panorama I shot using an inexpensive Sony dSLT and ultra wide-angle lens.

FIGURE 5-17:
The panorama
did not require
any software
to create.

TIP

Keep these things in mind when shooting automatic panoramas:

>> **Straight, level, and steady:** It can be hard to pan without tilting the camera. Pay attention to the indicators in the viewfinder, on the LCD, and in the scene. In addition, you have to pan at a steady speed. If you sweep too fast or too slow, the camera will get cranky and stop the shot.

>> **Stitching problems:** Automatic panoramas are awesome most of the time, but when the camera has trouble stitching the frames together, it may be messy.

>> **Keep at it:** It can be hard to center your subjects within the narrow side. For example, it took me three times to get a good panorama of my boys, because I kept cropping their heads or putting too much space above them.

>> **Zoom and inspect:** Zoom in and inspect your panoramas before moving on! It's impossible to see small errors in a huge panorama from a small thumbnail on the back of your camera. You can't possibly tell if there are stitching problems without zooming in and panning around.

IN THIS CHAPTER

» **Understanding what HDR is about**

» **Setting up your camera for HDR**

» **Photographing exposure brackets**

» **Creating and tone mapping HDR images**

» **Experimenting with alternate techniques**

Chapter **6**

Enjoying HDR Photography

High dynamic range (HDR) photography gets around your camera's limited ability to capture details in dark shadows and details in bright highlights in the same photo. It does this by using more than one photo to collect brightness information. Similar to shooting panoramas, HDR photography is a two-step process.

The first step is photography. Select a scene and take more than one shot with different exposure settings (see Book 3, Chapter 1 for more information about exposure). These are called exposure brackets. I explain what exposure brackets are and how to shoot them in the first part of this chapter.

The second step of HDR photography involves specialized software. You combine the exposure brackets into a single, high-dynamic range image, which you then tone map. Tone mapping is at the creative heart of the entire process. You use controls in the software that allow you to manipulate the HDR image and control how it looks. It's sort of like processing a Raw photo. You save the final result as a single, standard image file.

I walk you through each step in this chapter, and finish with a list of alternate techniques and ideas for you to try.

HDR Software

You probably knew this was coming. You'll need an application that can handle High Dynamic Range photography. As with the other chapters that rely on software to accomplish certain tasks, I've made the decision to focus on a single application.

Photomatix Pro, I choose you for this chapter! It's the leading HDR application out there. I like it. I use it. It even integrates with Adobe Lightroom as an export option. You can download a trial version at www.hdrsoft.com. The trial doesn't expire, which is nice, but it does add a watermark to the final image. I find that perfectly acceptable. It allows you to experiment with the full program for as long and as many times as you like before deciding whether to buy it.

Having said that, other applications are out there either devoted to or that dabble in HDR. If you prefer to shop around, by all means, do so!

Learning about HDR

High Dynamic Range (HDR) photography terminology can take a bit of getting used to, but the concept is remarkably simple: It's difficult to take a photograph of many scenes without losing details in the shadows, highlights, or in both areas. The solution is to artificially enhance your camera's dynamic range by using more than one photo.

The photos that capture the additional details are called *exposure brackets*. As shown in Figure 6-1, each records the same scene but uses a different exposure. Underexposed shots capture details in bright highlights. Overexposed shots capture details in dark shadowy areas.

FIGURE 6-1:
The exposure
brackets of this
scene capture
different details.

Special HDR software merges the bracketed photos into a single HDR image, which you *tone map* into a normal image. Tone mapping is interactive. You make many of the decisions that affect the final brightness, contrast, color, and overall look of the image. After tone mapping, the final image is converted into a JPEG or TIFF and saved, as shown in Figure 6-2.

FIGURE 6-2:
HDR can preserve
details in dark
and very bright
areas.

HDR photography can seem fickle at times. Don't hesitate to try it on every scene you can, but there are definitely certain situations where it works best. Look for scenes with high contrast and great lighting. HDR works exceedingly well in the morning and evening golden hours. The light is more magical and the results look fantastic. It can also work inside, as shown in Figure 6-3.

Enjoying HDR
Photography

FIGURE 6-3:
Look for colorful
scenes with a
high contrast
ratio and lots of
details.

Shooting Exposure Brackets for HDR

You'll have to change a few things from your normal routine to set up your camera to shoot exposure brackets using *automatic exposure bracketing* (AEB). It's not much, but it's important that you get it down. When ready, shooting the brackets with a tripod or even handheld is a breeze.

Configuring your camera

You only need to pay attention to a few settings to shoot good images for HDR. Here are my recommendations:

>> **Exposure controls:** Set your camera to aperture-priority autoexposure mode, as this ensures a constant depth of field across the different bracketed exposures.

Set the ISO manually. You do not want to leave Auto ISO on, as it can change between shots and mess with the brackets. If you're not using a tripod, or you're photographing moving clouds, you may need to raise the base ISO so you can get a faster shutter speed. When shooting outside with a tripod, I prefer ISO 100.

Shutter speed changes based on the exposure needed to shoot the brackets.

» **Image quality:** Set the image quality to include Raw photos. I use Raw+ JPEG so that I have the option of loading the JPEGs into Photomatix Pro to quickly see whether the scene was worth shooting or not.

» **Other settings:** Set the Drive/Release mode to Continuous so you don't have to keep pressing the shutter button.

If you will be using long shutter speeds, ensure that noise reduction is turned off. If you use JPEGs, you can (but don't have to) turn off any dynamic range tricks your camera uses to make JPEGs look better.

Turn off Image Stabilization if the camera is on a tripod or is otherwise solid. If you're shooting handheld, keep it on.

» **Total control:** If you're a real stickler, switch to manual focus and set the white balance manually. This ensures consistent photos across all the brackets.

» **AEB:** You need to turn on your camera's AEB feature and set it up. See the upcoming "Setting up automatic exposure bracketing (AEB)" section for details.

» **Tripod and remote:** I recommend using a tripod and a remote-shutter release when shooting HDR. It is possible to shoot handheld brackets, but you have to be steady and not move around.

I've made just about every mistake possible shooting HDR, including using shutter-priority mode (the aperture changed between shots), forgetting to save Raw photos, leaving on Image Stabilization when using a tripod, and more. To be honest, the differences were negligible.

Setting up automatic exposure bracketing (AEB)

Autoexposure bracketing (AEB) is a feature that enables the camera to automatically shoot exposure brackets of a scene. After you configure a few details, the camera handles changing the necessary exposure settings and shooting the right number of shots once you press the shutter button. It's a great timesaver, and a critical feature to have if you want to shoot handheld HDR.

Inexplicably, given the popularity of HDR, not all cameras have an autoexposure bracketing feature. If you can't find it anywhere in the menu system or hidden with the Drive/Release mode, you may not have one of them. The Nikon D3300 is an otherwise excellent camera, for example, but doesn't have AEB. If your camera is one of these, you'll have to shoot brackets manually (which I talk about in the "Manually bracketing exposures" section).

For those cameras that do have AEB, setting up it is pretty easy. You simply have to set the number of brackets you want to shoot and the exposure difference (in EV) between them.

How you turn AEB on differs from camera to camera; turn to your manual for the precise details. Some cameras set the number of brackets from a different menu, which takes some time. Other cameras make you choose the number of brackets and their distance apart each time you turn on the AEB feature. Still other cameras don't let you change the number of brackets. You can only modify the EV distance between them. I'm in the process of setting up the EV distance between brackets on a Canon in Figure 6-4.

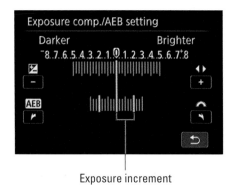

FIGURE 6-4:
Setting the EV difference between brackets.

Exposure increment

When starting out, I recommend shooting at least three brackets, each separated by 2.0 EV (see Figure 6-5). These settings capture a wide total dynamic range and don't flood you with a million-and-one files. I sometimes shoot five or seven brackets separated by 1.0 EV. You may choose to experiment; however, I've shot everything from three to nine brackets, separated by 0.3 EV to 1.0 EV. More files, separated by a smaller amount, capture a finer exposure gradient.

Exposure brackets

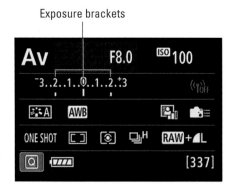

FIGURE 6-5:
The brackets show up as marks under the exposure index.

Double-check your camera's manual to see what shooting modes are compatible with AEB. Depending on your camera, you may need to be in an advanced autoexposure mode or your camera's manual mode. Manual mode requires you to set the starting exposure. The bracketing feature handles the rest.

Your camera may have more advanced AEB options. Look in your camera menu or manual for these features:

>> **Sequence:** Set the order the shots are taken. Most often (if you can change this setting), you can put the metered exposure first, in the middle, or last. (I prefer it first. That way I can spot it from the thumbnail in Lightroom faster than having to count exposures from the darkest or lightest.) The other exposures tend to be taken from dark to light.

>> **Auto cancel:** Most of the time, bracketing is canceled when you turn off the camera. Some cameras restart the bracketing sequence where you left off if you turn the camera off and back on. If you have a camera like this and don't like that behavior, you may be able to turn it off.

>> **Bracketing option:** Some cameras lump several different types of bracketing together. You may have to identify that you want *exposure bracketing* as opposed to white balance or another type of bracketing.

Many cameras indicate the bracket being shot in the viewfinder or on the camera back with a mark under the exposure meter.

Shooting the exposure brackets

After you configure your camera and enable AEB, shooting the brackets is ridiculously easy. Frame the scene, focus and meter normally, and then pull the trigger. If you have the Drive mode set to shoot continuously, simply hold the shutter button (or remote) down until the brackets are finished. If you have the Drive set to Single, press the shutter button as many times as you have brackets.

When returning to normal photography, make sure to turn off auto bracketing.

Tone Mapping in Photomatix Pro

The next steps are in software. Load or export photos into Photomatix Pro, generate the HDR image, and then tone map it. You'll end up with a final image; the one I shot and processed is shown in Figure 6-6, which is the front of a dramatic stone church with blue sky and clouds.

Enjoying HDR Photography

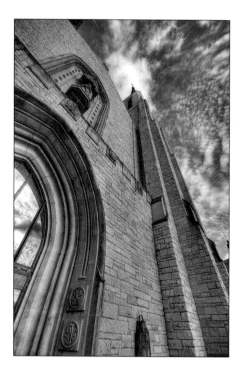

FIGURE 6-6:
The payoff for a
little extra effort
is an amazing
image.

TIP

When you *tone map* your HDR images (convert an HDR image into something more manageable), the software fun starts to happen. The problem is that tone mapping is sometimes so unpredictable that showing you how to do it well is difficult. Every HDR image is different. The key is to experiment with the controls and then practice, practice, practice.

Creating the HDR image

Before you get to tone mapping, you have to load the bracketed photos into Photomatix Pro and create an HDR image. It's very easy. Just follow these steps:

1. **Start Photomatix Pro.**

Download the free trial from www.hdrsoft.com. If you like what you see and buy it, you won't have to put up with watermarks.

When you launch Photomatix Pro, it starts out as an empty shell (see Figure 6-7). If you don't see the Workflow Shortcuts panel, choose View ⇨ Show Workflow Shortcuts.

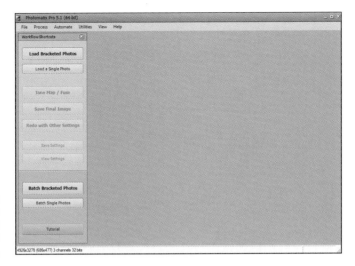

FIGURE 6-7:
The Photomatix
Pro interface is
pretty basic when
you start it.

2. **Select Load Bracketed Photos from the Workflow Shortcuts panel (refer to Figure 6-7).**

   The Loading Bracketed Photos dialog box opens, as shown in Figure 6-8. You can also drag and drop the brackets directly onto the program interface.

3. **Select your brackets (see Figure 6-8) and click OK.**

   You can also drag and drop the brackets into the dialog box.

TIP

A quick HDR preview using JPEGs can help you pare down things and decide whether to pursue bracketed sets. If you like what you see as you tone map the preview, process the file and save the settings. Use this as a concept file to refer to as you keep working. Then you can take the trouble to use your raw converter and aim for high quality knowing it will be worth the effort.

Check the Show 32-bit Unprocessed Image box (I call this the HDR image from this point on) if you want to see the actual HDR image. This enables you to save it later.

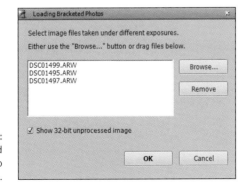

FIGURE 6-8:
Brackets loaded
and ready to
merge.

4. Set the Merge to HDR options.

Select from the following options that appear in the panel shown in Figure 6-9:

- *Align source images:* Adjusts for slight camera movement. There are four presets. You can include perspective corrections and increase or decrease the maximum shift if you show the alignment settings.

- *Crop aligned images*: This is pretty helpful when loading brackets shot without a tripod.

- *Show options to remove ghosts: Ghosts* are caused by moving objects that appear in one bracket and either move or disappear from the other brackets. You can identify problem areas yourself or have Photomatix Pro handle it automatically.

- *Reduce noise on:* Reduces noise in a variety of ways.

- *Reduce chromatic aberrations:* Reduces red/cyan/blue/yellow fringing.

The following options are visible only if you're using Raw photos to generate the HDR image:

- *White Balance:* The default setting As Shot is often adequate. Change if needed.

- *Color Primaries:* Choose between sRGB, AdobeRGB, and ProPhoto RGB. I prefer AdobeRGB unless I want to save a JPEG, in which case I set the option to sRGB.

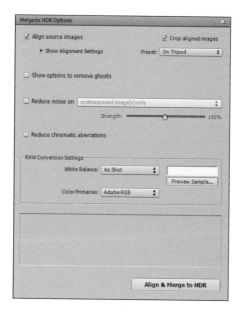

FIGURE 6-9: These options control how brackets are merged into a single HDR image.

5. Continue.

If you left the ghosting option unchecked, click the Align and Merge to HDR button.

If you checked it, click the Align & Show Deghosting button. After a bit of processing, you'll see the Deghosting Options dialog box. Choose your option (selective or automatic) and then follow the instructions. When finished, click OK.

6. Prepare to tone map.

If you checked the option to show the HDR image, it appears onscreen. As you can see from Figure 6-10, it's not usable like this. The reason is that your monitor is incapable of displaying photos with a wide dynamic range. You have to tone map the HDR image to make something useful out of it.

FIGURE 6-10:
The HDR image waiting to be tone mapped.

At this point, you're ready to start tone mapping. Save the HDR image (File⇨Save As) if you can't immediately start. Then you can reload it at your leisure.

If you left the option to see the HDR image unchecked, you'll immediately enter the tone mapping mode.

TIP

If you know that you want to use all the same HDR settings, try *batch processing*. You'll set up rules for Photomatix Pro to follow as it creates HDR images out of any number of bracketed sets. This is very nice.

Tone mapping the HDR image

I wanted to give this section a title like "Tone mapping your HDR image in Photomatix Pro the quick and easy way (without all the fuss)," but it was too long.

Enjoying HDR Photography

My goal is to help you narrow down some of the features and options so that it's possible for you to get started without being overwhelmed. Figure 6-11 shows the options you need. Here goes:

1. **Select a process and method.**

   Tone mapping is the standard HDR process that I cover. Use it to create anything from classic HDR images to more realistic interpretations. Exposure Fusion has several different methods and can lead to more natural-looking photos.

   Details Enhancer is the method I use for most of my images. You have a lot of creative options and can create anything from highly contrasted HDR to more traditional photos. You can also choose the Contrast Optimizer or Tone Compressor. Each of these approaches has fewer options to deal with.

FIGURE 6-11:
Tone mapping an HDR image in Photomatix Pro.

2. **Make adjustments.**

   This is where you have to play with the program. I can't tell you a single setting that can make every image look good. You can start out by investigating different presets that come with the program. They are located in the Presets window.

You can also just wing it. For each control, move it through its entire range to see what it does when at the minimum and maximum. Continue through each one until you reach the bottom. The Details Enhancer controls that have the greatest effect of the look of your photo, and need a bit of explanation, are:

- *Strength:* Controls the overall amount of contrast and detail enhancement applied to the image. Although it isn't technically the strength of the overall tone mapping effect, it acts like it. For a dramatic effect, raise Strength toward 100. Conversely, to create a more realistic effect, reduce strength to 50 or lower.

- *Tone Compression:* Controls how hard to squeeze the dynamic range of the image. Move the slider to the right to increase the compression, which reduces the dynamic range. Shadows are brightened and highlights darkened more to get everything to fit. Move it to the left to ease up on the compression, which increases the dynamic range. Shadows and highlights are affected less.

- *Detail Contrast:* Accentuates local contrast. The default is 0. Higher settings amplify local contrast and darken the image. Can boost drama. Lower settings reduce local contrast and lighten the image.

- *Lighting Adjustments:* Controls the level at which contrast enhancements are smoothed out. This setting plays a large role in determining how the final tone mapped image looks. It's also responsible for much of the debate over the "HDR look," both good and bad. Smoothing comes in two modes. You control smoothing in one with a free-ranging slider. Higher values produce more smoothing, and lower values result in less. If you check the Lighting Effects Mode box, you see discrete buttons to control the smoothing strength.

There are additional controls at the bottom of the Adjustments dialog box that enable you to reset the settings to their defaults, redo and undo actions, and load or save presets.

3. **Click Apply.**

   Photomatix Pro cogitates, calculates, and burns some electricity as it renders your image. It appears in a Finishing Touches panel, as shown in Figure 6-12.

4. **Add finishing touches, if desired, and press Done.**

   Adjust contrast, color, and sharpening to one degree or another. If you plan to edit the photo in Lightroom or another application later, you can dispense with this. However, it's nice to have these features so that you can quickly spruce up your image and be done.

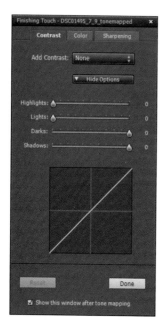

FIGURE 6-12:
You have the option of sprucing up the image up before saving.

5. **Save your image by choosing File ➪ Save As.**

   Select a location and enter a new name, if desired. Change the type and check the additional options if you like. I prefer to save my tone mapped images as 8-bit TIFFs. I also save the tone mapping settings, as shown in Figure 6-13.

   You can also select Save Image. In that case, Photomatix Pro applies the settings you have previously selected.

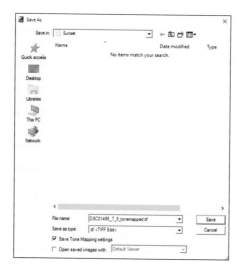

FIGURE 6-13:
I like saving the settings with the image.

6. **Finalize your photos.**

   Tone mapped images don't always look perfect when they leave Photomatix Pro. Load them into Lightroom or use Photoshop to lessen noise, sharpen, improve tone, and any other tasks you think will perfect them. Figure 6-14 shows my completed image of this scene.

FIGURE 6-14: High-contrast sunsets are perfect for HDR.

Trying Alternate Techniques

In the earlier sections, I slimmed the process to the bare minimum. HDR photography is an immense field with many different options and possibilities, however. A number of different techniques might work for you. Try them to see whether you're interested.

Using your camera's HDR modes

Your camera may have a built-in HDR feature. It handles shooting the brackets, creating the HDR image, and tone mapping it, all in one go. You can see some Canon options in the menu in Figure 6-15. They're a good sample of what options you can expect now and in the future from in-camera HDR:

>> **Adjust Dynamic Range:** Set to Disable HDR by default. To turn on HDR, set to Auto or choose from one of the discrete EV ranges (from +/-1 EV to +/-3 EV).

» **Effect:** Select an effect. Options are Natural, Art Standard, Art Vivid, Art Bold, or Art Embossed.

» **Continuous HDR:** This is a neat option. Select 1 Shot only if you want to shoot one HDR sequence and return to normal shooting. Set to Every Shot if you want to keep shooting HDR.

» **Auto Image Align:** Set to Enable (best when shooting handheld) or Disable (best when using a tripod).

» **Save Source Images:** This option may not be available on all cameras. Select All Images if you want to save all the source images, including JPEGs and RAW. I highly recommend this setting because you can use software to create your own HDR images using the source photos later, in case you don't like the camera's result. Only choose HDR Image if you want the take-it-or-leave-it solution.

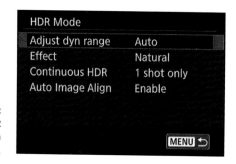

FIGURE 6-15:
Setting up HDR
mode on a Canon
EOS 80D.

Preparing your images differently

You can choose one of several ways to load images into an application like Photomatix Pro to create and tone map an HDR image. The path you take depends on what files you use:

» **Raw images directly from the camera:** You can throw your Raw photos into most HDR applications and they'll dutifully convert them into an internal data format to use in creating the HDR image. You'll hardly notice a thing. That's good if you're in a hurry and don't mind letting the HDR software handle it.

» **JPEGs directly from the camera:** You can load JPEG brackets into HDR applications. None of them complain a bit, even Photoshop. JPEGs need no conversion or processing. The caveat here is quality. It may be hard to notice unless the scene has a lot of wide gradients, but JPEGs don't produce the same quality as Raw exposures or TIFFs converted from Raw exposures.

>> **Converted Raw photos:** If you want the best quality and the most control over the HDR process, convert your Raw photos to TIFF files before processing them into HDR images. You can convert them to JPEGs if you like, but then you should just use the JPEGs from your camera if that's the case.

If you use Adobe Lightroom, you can buy the Photomatix Pro export plug-in. It streamlines your workflow by letting you select single exposures or brackets and sending them over to Photomatix to process into HDR. You even have the option to automatically import the result into Lightroom. You don't have to convert the Raw exposures yourself with this method. Lightroom applies your development settings to the exposures as it converts them to TIFFs and sends them to Photomatix.

Trying single-exposure HDR

Many HDR applications let you tone map a single Raw photo. Although not technically HDR, I refer to the practice as *single-exposure HDR*. You can also think of it as an alternate Raw processing technique.

By tone mapping a single Raw exposure, you access and manipulate the total dynamic range that's already in the shot (but often hidden) in ways that traditional Raw processing software doesn't. The result can seem as though the shot has more dynamic range than it really does. Figure 6-16 is the final result of processing a single Raw exposure in Photomatix Pro. I tone mapped it and then did some minor editing in Photoshop. Voilà.

FIGURE 6-16:
Use single-exposure HDR as an alternate processing tool.

Creating your own brackets from a single shot

This section is for total nerds. I will keep it short and to the point. You can create your own exposure brackets from a single Raw photo. I've done this many times. It's possible to unlock quite a bit of dynamic range from a single Raw photo and use that when tone mapping.

Use Lightroom or Adobe Camera Raw to create three partially processed versions of the same Raw photo. Separate their exposures by 2.0 EV so that you have an underexposed, a properly exposed, and an overexposed photo. Don't worry about other processing settings: Focus on the exposure differences. However, you can apply the same lens correction and transformations, including rotating and cropping, as long as you use identical settings on all three versions of the photo (although it would be interesting to experiment with wildly different settings). Export the three images as 8-bit TIFFs and load them into Photomatix Pro. Create an HDR image and tone map.

Manually bracketing exposures

Most cameras now have AEB features that make shooting exposure brackets a snap. It wasn't too long ago that some cameras did not. In that case, you were required to shoot the exposure brackets manually.

Frankly, manual exposure bracketing is a pain. It slows you down and makes shooting handheld HDR almost impossible. I remember having to go to the trouble of manually bracketing with my Sony Alpha 300. I suppose it was a rite of passage.

While I would choose auto over manual brackets in most situations, knowing how to bracket manually can be a useful skill. For example, you may want to set up a shot with a number of brackets and EV difference that your camera won't shoot automatically. In those rare instances, you should resort to manual bracketing.

Now, it's not rocket science. It's just slow and irritating. Enter your camera's manual shooting mode, choose an aperture and ISO, and then meter the scene. Based on that reading, adjust the shutter speed to shoot the brackets. Unlike my preference when using AEB, I prefer to start with underexposed photos and move progressively brighter when shooting manual brackets. I find this approach quicker to execute and less prone to error because I do not have to jump back and forth along the exposure scale.

Over time, you should be able to knock out a bracket of three to five exposures fairly quickly, assuming that the shutter speeds are reasonably fast.

Using other applications for HDR

Photomatix Pro isn't the only HDR application on the market. Other standalone HDR applications are available, and some photo editors have HDR modules. Adobe Photoshop as well as Lightroom have HDR features built into them. While I don't have room to show you everything, you can load exposure brackets into their HDR workflows just like you would panorama photos.

To create and tone map an HDR image in Photoshop, load your images, then choose Automate ⇨ Merge to HDR Pro. Tone map the merged image using the controls in the Merge to HDR Pro dialog box. I suggest choosing a preset to see what sort of effects are possible and then tweaking individual parameters.

In Lightroom, select the brackets and press Ctrl+H/⌘+H (Win/Mac) to launch the HDR Merge Preview dialog box. There are only a few options, as shown in Figure 6-17. You can choose Auto Align, Auto Tone, and decide how much to deghost the images.

FIGURE 6-17:
Applications like Lightroom feature basic HDR processing.

6

Showcasing Different Scenes

Contents at a Glance

Chapter **1**

Portraits

I love photographing people. I specialize in spontaneous shots of people in everyday life. It's very rewarding.

When you take photos of people, you normally want to open the aperture (see Book 3, Chapter 2) to create a shallow *depth of field* (area of focus). This separates subjects from the blurred background and looks really nice.

When people are moving, make sure to dial in a fast enough shutter speed (see Book 3, Chapter 3) so they don't blur. ISO (see Book 3, Chapter 4) often has to rise to pick up the exposure slack. Don't be afraid of a higher ISO. It's better to have a noisy photo that you can work with than nothing at all. If necessary, get additional lighting or use a flash.

Capturing Birthday Moments

I took the photo shown in Figure 1-1 on my son Jacob's birthday. He had just opened the skateboard he wanted and was beaming with joy. Digital SLRs make great birthday party cameras. We have four kids, so I get a lot of practice.

Interior shots with inexpensive lenses (even when mounted on a mid-range Canon APS-C dSLR like this) tend to be frustrating because there isn't a lot of light inside. Inexpensive lenses don't normally have large maximum apertures, especially when zoomed in. I don't like using a flash in these situations, so I'm under even more pressure to get a good exposure.

In these cases, keep two things in mind: Shutter speed is important, and shooting with a moderately high ISO may be necessary. If necessary, switch to shutter-priority mode. This shot was taken using aperture-priority mode at 46mm, f/5.6, 1/80 second, and ISO 1600.

Keys to this photo:

>> Use image stabilization to keep the camera steady.

>> Don't let the shutter speed drop past 1/60 second.

>> Expect high ISOs.

>> Open windows and turn on lights.

FIGURE 1-1:
Open windows
to let light in and
expect ISO to rise.

Using a High-Quality Primes Lens

Figure 1-2 is a portrait of my wife I took early one summer evening. Although it looks like a bright afternoon, it's past 7:30. The light is amazing. I took this shot with a professional 50mm prime lens mounted on an entry-level consumer dSLR from Nikon.

When shooting portraits, try to open the aperture as wide as practical so that the background blurs pleasingly. The blur differentiates the background from the subject, which makes them stand out more.

The combination of crop factor and focal length makes this a near telephoto portrait. I was able to open up the aperture nice and wide. That helped the camera set an acceptable shutter speed and ISO. This shot was taken using aperture-priority mode at 50mm, f/2.8, 1/80 second, and ISO 280.

Keys to this photo:

>> Framed off-center to include background (cropping optional).

>> Fast, professional near-telephoto prime lenses perform magnificently.

>> Smooth, aesthetic tone caused by natural light from windows.

>> Aperture not so wide that the depth of field shrinks to nothing.

FIGURE 1-2:
Quality lenses help you capture fantastic shots.

Snapping Casual Portraits

I was literally heading out the door with my Pentax K-1 full-frame dSLR when I looked over and saw my son Sam playing on the computer. I told him to smile and took this casual snapshot shown in Figure 1-3.

If you have your camera with you, always be ready for action. Casual portraits that you take at a moment's notice often capture a person's natural beauty and personality better than posed shots.

The professional-level camera and lens make a difference in this shot. The light from the window, although gorgeous, is not like being outside. I opened the aperture and was able to use a fast shutter speed and very reasonable ISO. This shot was taken using aperture-priority mode at 68mm, f/4.5, 1/100 second, and ISO 400.

Keys to this photo:

>> Quick, casual shots often produce the most natural-looking portraits.

>> It's hard to beat a 36.4 MP full-frame camera and quality lens.

>> When inside, take advantage of natural light from windows.

FIGURE 1-3:
Be ready to take photos at a moment's notice.

Posting Group Photos

Figure 1-4 shows a group shot of my wife and three generations of women from a family we're good friends with. It's a classic group photo that I took one afternoon at a baseball game for the kids.

I love this shot. It was bright and beautiful outside, but late enough that the sun was not directly overhead. The colors pop, and everyone is happy and smiling. I had the two on the top row lean in so that everyone would be on or close to the same focal plane. It's very hard to get everyone in focus if the group is spread out from front to back.

I shot this with a top-end consumer-level Canon dSLR and standard zoom lens. This shot was taken using aperture-priority mode at 27mm, f/4, 1/1000 second, and ISO 100.

Keys to this photo:

>> I had them look down at me to keep them from squinting.

>> Frame using the Rule of Thirds.

>> Take two or three shots in situations like this and choose the best one.

>> Line people up at the same distance so they are all in focus.

FIGURE 1-4: Try to get everyone lined up.

Using a Telephoto Lens

I don't normally use a 300mm lens to take portraits, but I had been using the lens earlier to take photos of harness racing. We were on our way home and stopped to eat, then decided to take some "tourist" shots. The photo of my son, Ben, in Figure 1-5 turned out really nice. This was a posed shot —nothing spontaneous about it. He is sharply focused and well lit. The natural late-afternoon light is not casting any harsh shadows. The background is very nicely blurred. I stood well back from him and used a monopod to support the camera and heavy lens. It's a keeper.

I used a mid-range Nikon dSLR with a nice 300mm telephoto lens. This shot was taken using shutter-priority mode at 300mm, f/4, 1/1000 second, and ISO 200.

Keys to this photo:

>> Posed and framed using portrait orientation.

>> Relaxed composition that features plenty of background.

>> Natural late afternoon light.

>> Great lens produced awesome bokeh.

FIGURE 1-5:
Telephoto lenses create amazing bokeh.

IN THIS CHAPTER

» **Capturing a scene's breadth and depth**

» **Shooting landscapes up close**

» **Working in the city**

» **Taking advantage of the weather**

» **Timing your shots for dramatic effect**

Chapter **2**

Landscapes

When photographing landscapes, you have to go where the scenery is. That makes it fun and rewarding in a different way than other subjects. You'll also have to deal with weather, sunlight, and other environmental factors that you have no control over. Despite sounding like a raw deal, it's actually a great feeling when you are at the right place at the right time to capture a magnificent scene with your digital SLR.

My advice is to routinely take trips to all sorts of places, near and far. Shoot at different times, but especially during the golden hour (the hour after sunrise and before sunset when the light is very appealing). Mix things up. The photos I've chosen for this chapter do precisely that: I took them at different times of the year, at different hours of the day, in different weather, and with different cameras. Each one is unique, but they are all landscapes.

Using an Ultra Wide-Angle Lens

On the surface, there's not much to the photo in Figure 2-1. However, I can't take my eyes off it. My family and I were visiting Detroit on a photo excursion and had made it to the Grosse Pointe area. It was a hot and sunny afternoon. Having discovered the beauty of Lake St. Claire, I got the camera and tripod out and took some shots. This photo has got most of the ingredients for a classic landscape: tripod, remote, aperture at f/8.

My lens choice was critical for this scene. With so much to see, composing and framing landscapes is a critical skill to develop. The Rule of Thirds is important. While this is ostensibly a shot of the lake, rather than make it all about the lake, I included the tree on the left. It provides contrast to the blue expanse of water and sky.

I took this photo with a Sony APS-C dSLT in aperture-priority mode at 10mm, f/8, 1/320 second, and ISO 100.

Keys to this photo:

>> The 10-20mm ultra wide-angle lens makes this shot expansive.

>> I framed the scene using the Rule of Thirds.

>> Shot using a tripod and remote.

>> Classic f/8 landscape aperture delivers infinite depth of field.

FIGURE 2-1:
Most landscapes maximize depth of field.

Getting Up Early

The bridge shown in Figure 2-2 is about a half mile from where I live. I drive past it constantly, and for some time I struggled with how best to photograph it. At one point, I had planned to get out on a sunny morning and capture the sun reflecting off the water, which turns the bridge a nice gold color. The morning I took this photo, however, was foggy. Recognizing an opportunity, I grabbed the camera and went to the bridge to see what I could photograph.

While still a landscape, this shot has a completely different impact than the last shot. It's almost the opposite: nearby instead of far away, creatively using the foreground, shrouded in mystery instead of well-lit, morning light instead of mid-day, almost normal focal length instead of ultra-wide, f/4 instead of f/8, and handheld instead of tripod. Yet it works!

I took this shot with a Nikon APS-C dSLR in aperture-priority mode at 24mm, f/4, 1/40 second, and ISO 110.

Keys to this photo:

>> Intervening branches add complexity while fog removes details.

>> Diffuse early morning light very different than during the day.

>> Composed with the bridge at an angle.

>> Focal length close to normal makes this an unusual shot.

FIGURE 2-2:
Don't be afraid to shoot intimate landscapes.

Going Different Places

It's possible to shoot "landscapes" in the city too. On the same trip to Detroit, we went downtown several times to see the sights. One afternoon we visited Greektown. The scene in Figure 2-3 is filled with the hustle and bustle of a district devoted to entertainment. As I looked at the scene through the viewfinder, I saw a woman walking toward me. The rest of the frame was so busy and yet anonymous. I knew that she would add something personal. I had to wait until she got close enough and then take the photo.

I took this shot with a Sony APS-C dSLT in aperture-priority mode at 22mm, f/8, 1/250 second, and ISO 100.

Keys to this photo:

>> Timing and opportunity to photograph the woman walking toward me.

>> Framed the street using the Rule of Thirds.

>> Aperture provides great depth of field while shutter speed prevents blur.

>> Wide angle makes the scene feel large.

FIGURE 2-3:
Cities are man-made landscapes.

Getting Out in the Weather

Figure 2-4 shows a winter scene that I photographed in late November on the shore of another lake. The day was cold and decidedly wintery. It snowed several inches and the wind was blowing forcefully. In a word: Perfect! I had not been up to this lake outside of the summer, so this was a perfect opportunity for fun and photography.

This looks like another classic wide-angle moment, but the fact is I zoomed in and used a normal focal length to make the circle of benches more prominent; more than they looked at 18mm.

I took this shot with a Canon APS-C dSLR in aperture-priority mode at 37mm, f/5, 1/200 second, and ISO 100.

Keys to this photo:

>> Making the effort to be out in the cold and snow.

>> Rule of Thirds divides the scene nicely into fore, mid, and background.

>> Normal angle gives the benches greater importance.

>> A study in low-contrast, virtually monochrome beauty.

FIGURE 2-4: Good composition and framing are vital when shooting landscapes.

Waiting for Sunset

Sunsets are another classic landscape ingredient. The challenge is being at the right location when they happen, and then having the patience to finish what you start. Don't get caught up thinking the moment is over as the sun dips out of view. Sunsets are constantly changing. Take shots before, during, and after. You never know which photo will strike you as "the one."

In the case of Figure 2-5, I was taking a 3-photo exposure bracket that I thought would make a good HDR image. The dark shot brought out the beauty of the sky and reflections on the water best. While the camera thought the scene needed more light, it was the perfect exposure for this photo.

I took this shot with a Canon full-frame dSLR in aperture-priority mode at 28mm, f/4, 1/2500 second, and ISO 100.

Keys to this photo:

>> Creative decision to use a dark shot.

>> Colorful sky combined with reflection on river contrasted with dark foreground and riverbanks.

>> Full-frame quality with great lens at low ISO delivers details and smooth color gradients.

>> Classic wide-angle focal length captures breadth of the river.

FIGURE 2-5: Sunsets make gorgeous subjects.

Chapter **3**

Action

I f you want to take action shots, you must make shutter speed your top priority. All else is secondary. Use the largest aperture you can and raise the ISO as much as you need to. A blurry action shot isn't worth printing and framing. I know. Believe me!

The other part to keep in mind is how transitory things are: People, planes, horses — whatever you're after is in motion. Put your camera in a continuous focus mode so that it keeps focusing as long as you have the shutter pressed half-way. Use a single AF point, unless it's something whose motion is so random you can't track it; in that case, you can try a zone or other more advanced AF mode if you have it.

Tracking the Action

You can't get much more action-oriented than the photo I took of the Lockheed Martin F-22 Raptor performing a demonstration flight at an airshow in Figure 3-1. It literally screamed by overhead. To capture this sort of action, you need a fast shutter speed and the reflexes to frame a moving target, focus, and take the photo before you lose the shot. I also used a monopod to support the camera and large lens I was using. I took this shot with a Nikon APS-C dSLR in shutter-priority mode at 300mm, f/4.5, 1/1000 second, and ISO 125.

TIP

When photographing a quick subject, don't point the camera at one spot and expect to get a good photo as they move through the frame. Instead, pan and track them as best you can, using continuous focus to lock on. This takes practice, so hone your skills on squirrels, birds, or whatever you can find at home.

Keys to this photo:

>> Very fast shutter speed needed to photograph the fast jet.

>> Super telephoto lens to capture action at a distance.

>> Monopod required to support heavy camera and lens.

>> Fast tracking, panning, framing, and focusing skills.

FIGURE 3-1:
This was an awesome fly-by.

Using an External Flash

Although I don't normally use a flash when shooting action, it's possible to take advantage of high-speed sync when using an external flash. This offers faster shutter speeds than you can normally shoot with the camera's built-in flash.

I did just that for the photo in Figure 3-2. I was at an outdoor mall with my wife and the kids taking fun shots with my Nikon APS-C dSLR and AF-S NIKKOR 24-70mm F2.8G ED zoom lens. I wanted to use a fill flash to light their faces a bit better but because I was shooting action I needed a fast shutter speed. I took this shot in aperture-priority mode (oddly enough, but considering the bright sunlight, flash and aperture, I knew I would have a fast shutter speed) at 70mm, f/3.5, 1/1600 second, and ISO 100.

Keys to this photo:

» External flash made high-speed sync possible; automatically enabled using Nikon's Auto FP High–Speed Sync mode.

» Very quick shutter speed freezes the action perfectly.

» Fantastic lens renders the scene beautifully.

» Near-telephoto focal length let me stand back.

FIGURE 3-2:
Using high-speed sync for action fill flash.

Finding the Right Spot

If you're going to photograph action that is somewhat repetitive and predictable, choosing the right location is paramount. For example, the photo I took in Figure 3-3 captured horse and driver as they push toward the finish line at a harness race. While the specific action at that moment was unpredictable, they made the same turn and came down the front straightway the same way every single time. Knowing this, I was able to set myself up at a few different locations that day with an excellent sense of what I was going to see each time they came past.

In the moment, I had to quickly sense the best shot and press the shutter button at just the right time. This isn't like a portrait where you can line people up and tell them to hold still. Although it might seem like hit or miss, your sense of timing is very important. The great thing about action like this, though, is that I got a lot of practice.

As with other action shots with lots of motion, this required a fast shutter speed. I used a Nikon APS-C dSLR and 300mm super telephoto lens set to f/4 for this shot. The shutter speed was 1/1000 and the ISO was 500.

Keys to this photo:

>> Location, location, location.

>> A sense of timing to capture the right moment.

>> Fact action requires fast shutter speeds.

>> ISO can rise unexpectedly.

FIGURE 3-3:
Finding the right location makes capturing the right moment easier.

Great Light Is Great

My goal has been to include a wide range of shots in this book. Not everyone can go to an NBA game and photograph superstars shooting 3-pointers or driving the lane. For many people, backyard fun with their families is where the action is.

I took the photo shown in Figure 3-4 one day near the end of November. We were horsing around in the yard. The kids were pretending to score touchdowns and then leaping up on a piece of play equipment we have. Sam (to the right) looks like he's guarding Jacob, but he's actually celebrating his *Lambeau Leap*.

The thing that strikes me about this shot is how beautiful it is. The light enabled me to capture it with a fast shutter speed. I took this shot with a Sony APS-C dSLT in shutter-priority mode at 35mm, f/4.5, 1/250 second, and ISO 125.

Keys to this photo:

>> Great light makes capturing action easier (and prettier).

>> Not everything has to be 1/1000 second. Sometimes 1/250 is fine.

>> You don't always have to use a super telephoto lens. I shot this with a standard zoom lens on a Sony APS-C dSLR at 35mm.

>> Action is action, whether it's in the backyard or at the Olympics.

FIGURE 3-4:
Consumer-level cameras can capture beautiful photos in many conditions.

Pushing to the Limits

When you're photographing people in action, especially indoors, you often have to push the camera to its limits. I took the photo shown in Figure 3-5 during a practice session of our church band. The lighting was gorgeous, but not overly strong. The bokeh is fantastic. It's soft enough that the subject is distinct and separate from the background.

While I could talk about this photo more, the takeaway is this: I had to push a professional camera and lens to their limits to get this shot. You can't get much better combination than the full-frame Canon 5D Mark III and EF 70-200mm f/4L IS USM telephoto zoom lens, and they were barely able to capture this moment. I had to raise the ISO on the 5D Mark III to a staggering 12800 to take this shot at 1/250 second. I took this in shutter-priority mode with the lens set to 135mm. The camera set the aperture to f/4.

Keys to this photo:

>> Some conditions require the best equipment, and even they can struggle.

>> Professional cameras shoot much better photos at high ISOs.

>> Interior lighting may look fine to your eye but not be strong enough to support really fast shutter speeds.

>> Use shutter-priority mode when photographing performers on stage.

FIGURE 3-5:
A superior camera and lens can shoot at high ISOs with little to no noise.

IN THIS CHAPTER

» **Composing effective close-ups**

» **Increasing shutter speed for crisp shots**

» **Magnifying the scene with diopters**

» **Using a reversing ring for an extreme close-up**

» **Setting up a studio shot**

Chapter **4**

Close-ups

I love zooming in and capturing close-ups. So much so that I'm virtually always on the lookout to capture unique details from a different perspective. Although you don't have to have anything besides a dSLR and a typical zoom lens (see Book 2, Chapter 1), you can invest in lenses with better close-up potential, and look at a host of other gear that can help you capture close-ups and macros very effectively.

Photographing close-ups is a really fun way to express yourself as a photographer. You're compelled to focus on smaller details than usual, which encourages you to grow creatively. Over time, you really do start to see things in a different light, whether the photo is of a flower, a bracelet, ice on a door, or a penny.

Join me in this chapter as I discuss five of my favorite close-ups. I walk you through what I did and how it worked.

Zoom In

Not every close-up has to be a microscopic examination. As shown in Figure 4-1, they can often be relatively relaxed. My wife was preparing food outside and the early evening light was incredible. It was spring, and we were itching to be outside. Instead of cleaning off the table, I used her tools as props for the background. You can see a knife and a colander of radishes as well as a paper napkin strategically placed around the African violet.

I used a professional Canon full-frame dSLR and lens for this photo. Certainly overkill, but I'm not complaining. I zoomed in to 73mm, which is in the near/medium telephoto range. Other than that, this was very close to a normal handheld shot. The aperture was f/4, shutter speed 1/800, and ISO was only 100.

Keys to this photo:

>> Great late-afternoon light is warm and inviting.

>> I composed this shot purposefully, choosing my props and positioning them around the central subject to create the scene.

>> Near telephoto focal length on a full-frame camera gave me a nice, loose close-up that included more than just the flower.

>> No extra gear or effort required; I used what I had immediately available.

FIGURE 4-1:
Quite often, shooting close-ups is just a matter of zooming in.

Notice Your Surroundings

Along those same lines (working with what you have), I shot the scene in Figure 4-2 without any special equipment. However, in this case I was using a consumer-level Nikon dSLR and 50mm prime lens. You can't zoom in or out with a prime lens. I had to step closer to my subject to make my subject appear larger. Which I did, and am very happy with the result.

I took this shot in the morning on December 24. It was brutally cold, and ice had formed on one of our storm doors. It wasn't hard to notice, but you have to take advantage of moments like this and grab a camera. Bracing myself, I got close and angled the camera. I had taken shots with the image sensor of the camera parallel to the ice. They were nice, but I wanted something unique. I used a Nikon APS-C dSLR and 50mm prime lens set to f/3.5 for this shot. The shutter speed was 1/2500 and the ISO was 100.

Keys to this photo:

>> Unique depth of field perspective captured by getting close, opening the lens, and angling the camera.

>> No special gear or other equipment.

>> Handheld with fast shutter speed ensures crisp shot with a lot of sharp details.

>> I had to be willing to get a camera and quickly take a shot.

FIGURE 4-2: Always be on the lookout to photograph unique scenes closely.

Close-ups

Look for Unique Perspectives

Now it's time to unleash some extra equipment on you. I captured the close-up of a sunflower shown in Figure 4-3 using a diopter attached to the lens of a consumer-level Canon dSLR. The lens wasn't anything fancy, just your standard 18-55mm inexpensive kit lens. Diopters magnify things, just like corrective eyeglasses do for people (see Book 2, Chapter 3 for more information on diopters). I love using diopters. They are easy to carry, relatively inexpensive, and if you use a large set with step-down rings, you can use them on many different lenses.

And I love this shot. I shot it late in the day (time always matters) when the light struck it from the side. I zoomed in to 55mm and, with a +10 diopter attached, was able to capture a totally unique perspective of this amazingly colorful plant using a standard zoom lens. The aperture was set to f/6.3 and the ISO rose to 640. Even at f/6.3, the depth of field is very narrow. In a twist of irony, the shutter speed was 1/640 second. I must have had the camera in 640/640/6.3 mode.

Keys to this photo:

>> Diopters mounted on a standard zoom lens increased the magnification to make this close-up possible.

>> Early evening sunlight illuminates this detailed scene wonderfully.

>> Always pay attention to shutter speed when shooting handheld close-ups.

>> ISO rose to compensate for smaller aperture and fast shutter speed.

FIGURE 4-3:
Diopters are an inexpensive but effective way to magnify subjects.

Whatever Works, Works

You're going to laugh at this one. I was experimenting with a few reversing rings. They enable you to mount lenses on your camera backward, which turns normal lenses into close-up/macro lenses. I realize they aren't everyone's cuppa tea. You have to manually focus, aperture control can be a problem, and it's just odd. However, I have some old NIKKOR manual focus lenses that work perfectly with the rings. I can control the aperture on the lens, and even mount them on Canon dSLRs, like I did here.

The funny part is that I was looking for interesting subjects to photograph when I grabbed this turquoise bracelet I bought my wife one year in Texas (that's another story). She followed me outside to help. We went around the back of the garage and she held the bracelet up against the black trash bin that we have. It worked fantastically as a backdrop and she was able to steady her arm on it. That helped me focus and shoot a crisp photo; see Figure 4-4. I used a Canon APS-C dSLR with 50mm NIKKOR manual focus lens set to f/2. The shutter speed was 1/250 second and the ISO was 200.

Keys to this photo:

» Reversing rings are totally cool but require some effort to use.

» Use what you have to help capture the shot: an old lens, bracelet, and trash bin. As long as it works it doesn't matter.

» Wide aperture and bright light enabled me to set shutter speed to 1/250 to ensure a sharp photo.

FIGURE 4-4: Use what you have to make every photo better.

Focus on Small Details

Finally, I present you with President Abraham Lincoln (see Figure 4-5). On a penny, of course. But wow, what a penny. This one has been through some rough times. It's getting up in years and has a lot of gouges on the surface. I thought it made the perfect subject.

I shot this in my studio using a consumer-level Nikon APS-C dSLR and digital Holga lens. To increase the magnification, I used the 60mm macro attachment that pops onto the main Holga lens. I mounted the camera on a tripod and moved the penny (placed on a piece of wood) back and forth in order to focus. I used Live View to compose the shot, and needed to raise the ISO to 3200 to brighten the scene.

Even though the Holga lens has a small aperture, the depth of field of this shot is very narrow. I focused on the word Liberty and the date so that they would be the sharpest items on the surface of the penny. I could have shot the penny straight on, which would have meant the entire surface would be in focus, but that was a more boring photo. I chose this approach instead.

Keys to this photo:

>> Taken with a digital Holga lens with macro attachment.

>> Shot in my studio using Live View and a tripod.

>> Even with bright lighting, the ISO rose dramatically because of the aperture and nearness of the camera.

>> I chose a damaged penny as a more interesting subject.

FIGURE 4-5:
The small details on this penny are what make the shot interesting.

IN THIS CHAPTER

» **Exploring different approaches with a favorite location**

» **Looking for unique vantage points**

» **Photographing bits and pieces of your life**

» **Experimenting with different processing ideas**

» **Pushing yourself to expand your boundaries**

Chapter **5**

Odds and Ends

s this really the final chapter? Well, then, I want to leave you with five memorable photos to enjoy. Unlike the other subject-related chapters in this book, these shots aren't related in terms of their nature or the specific techniques I used. If I could choose a few general points to emphasize, they would be these:

Do not limit yourself or your creativity. What's the point of limiting yourself? I don't know. Don't, and don't let others tell you what your style should be or how to go about it. Measure your effectiveness by the end result. If it moves people, possibly just yourself, you've succeeded.

Always be on the lookout to photograph every type of subject, whether traditional things like people, landscapes, and action, or a statue, fountain, or pie.

Finally, processing plays a vital role in modern digital photography. Of course, it always has. People just forget how much effort Ansel Adams went to. He mastered a unique style of photography in his day and continues to inspire photographers of all ages. His style was not one-dimensional. It included his composition skills, how he set up and shot each scene, and very importantly, the effort he expended developing his shots and making prints.

Lion's Head

The photo in Figure 5-1 is of a fountain at a nearby park. I am captivated by it to such a degree that I routinely photograph it with whatever new camera I have. It's the head of a lion, cast in copper, and basin. Both have a nice patina on them. The surrounding concrete is fairly bland and featureless, however.

I took this shot early one October morning, before the water was turned off for the winter. I set my Nikon APS-C dSLR on a tripod and framed this very specifically so that the head was not in the center. I have photographed this scene so many other ways I was after a very particular look. I used a very small aperture, f/16, to get the entire head in focus. I used a fast shutter speed of 1/250 second to partially stop the water, but had to raise the ISO to 400 to get the right exposure. I processed the photo to emphasize contrast in the shadows.

Keys to this photo:

>> A subject I was very familiar with.

>> Uniquely framed.

>> Small aperture to ensure adequate depth of field (I have numerous photos where just the nose is in focus).

>> Elevated ISO to counter small aperture and fast shutter speed.

FIGURE 5-1:
Return to your favorite scenes and continue to photograph them.

General Wayne and His Horse

Figure 5-2 is of our local namesake, General Anthony Wayne, atop his unnamed horse. The horse has one hoof raised and is looking down. I got very close to take this shot, positioning my tripod right under the horse's head. I wanted a different type of shot than you normally see. I chose to focus on the horse, and let the General be a background element.

I processed the shot in black and white. It seemed to fit the subject better. Rather than focus on the blue sky and green trees, your eyes are pulled into the details of the horse and General Wayne behind. This is one of my prized shots. I adore it.

I used a Nikon APS-C dSLR with a professional 24-70mm zoom lens set to 38mm. The aperture was f/2.8, the shutter speed was 1/320 second, and the ISO was 100.

Keys to this photo:

>> Unique vantage point.

>> Wide aperture to limit depth of field.

>> Normal focal length ensured that I was able to capture the horse and rider.

>> Processed in black and white.

FIGURE 5-2: Do not always focus on the obvious thing.

Home Cooking

And now for something completely different. The photo shown in Figure 5-3 is of a delicious, home-baked pie my wife made late one February afternoon to cheer us all up and chase the winter doldrums away. It's just a pie, right? Oh, but it's more than that, which makes it perfect for this chapter.

I shot this very casually. I walked into the kitchen, positioned the pie so that the natural light from the window illuminated it, and took a few shots. I realized that our goofy pig salt and pepper shakers would add to the scene, so I put them in the corner of the frame. I left the drip in the front alone.

In the end, it's a great food shot. Not something you might see in a book where everything is pristine and nothing is out of place. However, this shot has an appealing homespun character that I love. I used a Nikon APS-C dSLR and 50mm prime lens set to f/5.6 for this shot. I didn't want a wider aperture, because I wanted as much of the pie to be in focus as possible. The shutter speed was 1/80, and the ISO rose to 1800.

Keys to this photo:

>> Handheld, spur-of-the-moment shot of everyday life.

>> Natural light illuminated the scene nicely, but wasn't very strong.

>> Limited aperture to try to maximize the depth of field.

>> ISO rises quite often when shooting inside.

FIGURE 5-3:
Use natural light whenever possible.

Dramatic Fountain

I took the shot in Figure 5-4 of the James Scott Memorial Fountain at Belle Isle Park, near Detroit, late one August afternoon. The sun was bright and the sky was blue, but rather featureless. The wind was blowing the water from the fountain around, which makes for a more interesting photo.

What I want to highlight about this photo are the processing decisions I made. I didn't want a standard shot. I wanted something dramatic and bold. I tried over-saturating the photo, but didn't like that approach. So I went the other direction and experimented with black and white. I realized at some point that I didn't want to convert it to pure black and white. Therefore, I processed the foreground and background with different settings, and made them partially transparent. That gave the photo an interesting color tint.

I used a Sony APS-C dSLT with standard zoom lens set to 18mm. Unusually, I had the camera set to Auto mode. The aperture was f/11, shutter speed 1/200 second, and ISO was 100.

Keys to this photo:

>> Unique processing to create a dramatic photo.

>> Used masks to make targeted changes to different areas of the photo.

>> Vertical orientation limits the view horizontally and keeps your attention on the fountain and water.

>> Shows that even Auto modes can produce exceptional photos.

FIGURE 5-4: Experiment with settings in software to see what you like and what works.

Art Deco in Bronze

Finally, I want to share the interesting photo I took inside a local bank, shown in Figure 5-5. The bank (originally named Lincoln National Bank and Trust) was built in 1929-1930 and is well-known for its art-deco style. I spent a few hours inside the lobby one day shooting exposure brackets for HDR from numerous angles. Before I left, I went up to the second level, which overlooks the lobby below, and discovered this amazing bronze work of art.

I set up my tripod and shot seven exposure brackets, each separated by 1.0 EV. I merged them into an HDR file when I got home and tone mapped it to achieve this relatively natural-looking result. I used a Nikon APS-C dSLR and ultra wide-angle lens set to 20mm. The wide-angle focal length let me get close to the artwork. I set the aperture to f/5.6 and used an ISO of 100. The 0.0 EV bracket had a shutter speed of 1/2 second.

Keys to this photo:

>> HDR photography enabled me to capture a full range of light and dark details in this interior scene.

>> I used a tripod to stabilize the camera and remote shutter release to keep it from shaking as I took the photos.

>> The ultra wide-angle lens enabled me to get very close to the subject and yet still have a wide angle of view.

>> The subject is a great example of the art-deco style.

FIGURE 5-5: HDR photography enables you to capture many scenes that would otherwise be impossible.

Index

H

Handheld Night mode, 134

handheld panoramas, shooting, 502

handheld shooting, with a flash, 186–187

hard plastic diffusers, 385

haze
about, 357–358
reducing, 325
removing, 441–443

Haze filter, 357

HD movies, 21

HDMI terminal, 43

HDR (Nikon), 260

HDR images
creating, 522–525
tone mapping, 525–529

HDR modes (Canon), 260, 529–530

HDR (high dynamic range) photography
about, 259, 515–516
configuring camera, 518–519
converted Raw images, 531
creating brackets from single shot, 532
HDR modes, 529–530
JPEG images, 530
learning about, 516–518
manually bracketing exposures, 532
Raw images, 530
setting up automatic exposure bracketing (AEB), 519–521
shooting exposure brackets for, 518–521
shooting panoramas, 512–513
single-exposure HDR, 531
software for, 516
tone mapping in Photomatix Pro, 521–529

HDR/Dynamic Range mode, 135

heat, dealing with, 63–64

height, emphasizing, 181–182

high contrast scenes, shooting, 358

high dynamic range (HDR) photography
about, 259, 515–516
configuring camera, 518–519
converted Raw images, 531
creating brackets from single shot, 532
HDR modes, 529–530
JPEG images, 530
learning about, 516–518

manually bracketing exposures, 532
Raw images, 530
setting up automatic exposure bracketing (AEB), 519–521
shooting exposure brackets for, 518–521
shooting panoramas, 512–513
single-exposure HDR, 531
software for, 516
tone mapping in Photomatix Pro, 521–529

high ISO levels, 317–319

High ISO Speed Noise Reduction, 313

High Pass Sharpen, 459–461

Highlight Tone Priority (Canon), 260

highlights, 109, 440–441

high-speed film, 304

high-speed sync, 20, 393–394

histograms
about, 112, 247–248
brightness, 248
color, 249
interpreting, 247–253
reading, 249–253

Holga cameras, 82

Holga lenses, 193–194, 222–225

hood mount, 83

horizon, for cityscapes, 174

horizontal perspective distortion, 447

hot shoe (external) flash
about, 40, 371–372, 379
accessories for, 384–387
for action photography, 551
attaching, 387–388
attaching mini stand, 390
back, 383–384
bouncing, 394–395
bracket, 398
buying, 31
categories of, 379–380
configuring, 392–393
controls for, 390–391
cords, 398
diffusing, 394–395
front, 380–382
high-speed sync, 393–394
for in-studio shooting, 190
removing, 388–389
sides, 383–384

About the Author

Robert Correll is a creative and passionate photographer who is an enthusiastic author. He's written all three editions of *Digital SLR Photography All-in-One For Dummies,* and written or co-authored numerous other *For Dummies* guides to popular dSLR models, including the Canon EOS 5D Mark III, the 80D, 60D, Rebel T6i, T5i, T5, and T3, the Sony A77, A65, A55, and A35. His other titles include *High Dynamic Range Photography For Dummies* and two editions of *HDR Photography Photo Workshop.* He's written books on other subjects that range from restoring old or damaged photos using Photoshop to photography with Digital Holga lenses, photographing rivers, lakes, and moving water, audio engineering, music production, and more. When not writing and taking photos, Robert enjoys family life, playing the guitar, bass, and ukulele, and recording music. He graduated from the United States Air Force Academy.

Dedication

To my family.

Author's Acknowledgments

I'm grateful to have worked with so many talented people. Their time, skills, devotion, and attention to detail have helped me reach the high goals I set for this edition of the book.

In particular, I am deeply thankful to the wonderful publishing team at John Wiley & Sons. Rebecca Senninger and Steve Hayes are part of the talented team of editors who helped create this book. I am also thankful to technical editor Theano Nikitas, whose insights and expertise helped keep the content of the book as accurate as possible.

I have many thanks to give to the individuals and companies who have been so helpful over the lifespan of this book. Special thanks go to: Christine Castaldi and her dad, Tom, Byron Hooley, Bill Bailey of Nodal Ninja, Robert Gantt of Gary Fong Inc., Keri Friedman of LensBaby, Stephanie Murano of Lomography USA, Joost Nieuwenhuijse of New House Internet Services B.V. (developers of PTGui and PTGui Pro), and Roger Cicala of LensRentals.com. Many thanks also to Canon, Nikon, Pentax, Sony, Sigma, Opteka, Adorama, B&H Photo, Fotodiox, Norman Camera, Sunny Schick Camera, Holga Direct, Adobe Systems, HDRSoft, and many, many other manufacturers and retailers for their fine products and service. I would also like to thank the sales and delivery staff who have helped me over the years. As you can see from this list, I've spent quite a lot of time and effort checking out as many cameras, lenses, and other products as possible as I have prepared for this edition of the book.

Many thanks to my agent, David Fugate of Launchbooks.com.

I have a warm place in my heart toward all the locations I've shot at over the years. That includes trips to Michigan, Oklahoma, Indiana, Ohio, Illinois, Missouri, and all the camps, parks, towns, zoos, national monuments, churches, cities, rivers, races, airshows, and other locales in between.

As always, thanks to my wife and children for encouraging, supporting, loving, and sustaining me.

Thank you for reading this. You're the reason we all worked so hard putting it together!

Publisher's Acknowledgments

Executive Editor: Steven Hayes

Project Editor: Rebecca Senninger

Technical Editor: Theano Nikitas

Editorial Assistant: Serena Novosel

Sr. Editorial Assistant: Cherie Case

Production Editor: Siddique Shaik

Front Cover Image: Courtesy of Robert Correll